METAPHOR
AND ORGANIZATIONS

edited by

David Grant and Cliff Oswick

SAGE Publications
London ● Thousand Oaks ● New Delhi

Contents

Acknowledgements   vii

Notes on Contributors   viii

List of Tables   xiii

List of Figures   xiv

Introduction: Getting the Measure of Metaphors   1
David Grant and Cliff Oswick

Part I   Metaphors of Organization: Scope and Application

1   Some Consequences of Taking Gareth Morgan Seriously   21
    Iain L. Mangham

2   Metaphor in the Development of Organization Theory   37
    Geoffrey MacKechnie and Gemma Donnelly-Cox

3   The Triune-Brain Metaphor: The Evolution of the Living
    Organization   53
    Gerrit Broekstra

4   Metaphors in Organizational Research: Of Embedded
    Embryos, Paradigms and Powerful People   74
    Stewart R. Clegg and John T. Gray

Part II   Metaphors of Organizing: Language and Discourse

5   Metaphors in Popular Management Discourse: The Case of
    Corporate Restructuring   95
    Richard Dunford and Ian Palmer

6   Metaphor in Organization Theory: Following in the Footsteps
    of the Poet?   110
    Dawn E. Inns and Philip J. Jones

7   Metaphors and Metaphorization in Organizational Analysis:
    Thinking Beyond the Thinkable   127
    Robert Chia

Part III Metaphors in Organizational Settings: Impact and Outcomes

8 Metaphors, Metaphoric Fields and Organizational Change 147
   Robert J. Marshak

9 Telling Tales: Management Consultancy as the Art of
   Story Telling 166
   Timothy Clark and Graeme Salaman

10 In the Image of Man: Organizational Action, Competence and
    Learning 185
    Erik Døving

11 Can You Resist a Dream? Evangelical Metaphors and the
    Appropriation of Emotion 200
    Heather Höpfl and Julie Maddrell

Part IV Metaphor and Organizations: Issues and Directions

12 The Organization of Metaphors and the Metaphors of
    Organization: Where Are We and Where Do We Go
    From Here? 213
    Cliff Oswick and David Grant

13 An Afterword: Is There Anything More to be Said About
    Metaphor? 227
    Gareth Morgan

Index 241

Acknowledgements

Our thanks go to Sue Jones, Rosemary Nixon, Hans Lock and their colleagues at Sage Publications for their helpful advice and encouragement. We would also like to thank Cherry Combes and John Montgomery for their enthusiasm and administrative support as this project progressed.

Notes on Contributors

Gerrit Broekstra is Professor of Management and Systems Sciences at the Netherlands Business School, Nijenrode University, the Netherlands. For some years he held the same position at Erasmus University, Rotterdam, where he was also, in 1985–6, co-founder and Dean of the Rotterdam School of Management. He holds a Ph.D. in physics, was President of the Dutch Systems Society for seven years and President of the International Federation for Systems Research, Vienna from 1988 to 1992. He also taught as a visiting Professor of Organization Behavior at the Kellogg Graduate School of Management, Northwestern University, Chicago. His research interests include linking cybernetics and systems thinking, and its most recent branch of chaos and complexity theory, to the problems of organizational change.

Robert Chia is Senior Lecturer in the Department of Accounting, Finance and Management, University of Essex. He has over 16 years industrial/commercial experience in manufacturing management and human resource management. Prior to taking up an academic career he was Group Human Resource Manager of a large multinational manufacturing corporation based in the Asia-Pacific Region. His research interests cover a wide range of academic disciplines including the logic of language, different philosophical systems of thought and their implications for management thinking, critical studies of culture and the links between imagination and complexity theories. He is currently undertaking a systematic examination of the implications of Bergson and Whitehead's 'process' philosophy for management studies.

Timothy Clark is Research Fellow in International Management in the Open University Business School. He has published widely on different aspects of the management consultancy industry and is the author of *Managing Consultants* (1995). He is currently undertaking, with Graeme Salaman, a wide-ranging study of managers' use of management consultants. In addition, he is the UK member of a cross-national research group called the International Organization Observatory. This group is working towards a regular series of comparable Europe-wide surveys using a panel of large business firms.

Stewart R. Clegg is Foundation Professor of Management at University of Western Sydney Macarthur, Australia, and is Head of the Department of Management and Marketing. He was a founder of APROS (Asian and

Pacific Researchers in Organization Studies) in the early 1980s, and has been the Co-editor of the *Australian and New Zealand Journal of Sociology*, as well as being Editor of *Organization Studies*. He also serves on the editorial boards of several other leading journals. Among the 15 books he has published are *Power, Rule and Domination* (1975), *Organization, Class and Control* (1980 with David Dunkerley), *Organization Theory and Class Analysis* (1989), *Modern Organizations: Organization Studies in the Post-modern World* (1990) and *Capitalism in Contrasting Cultures* (1990). He has published widely in journals, including *Administrative Science Quarterly, Organization Studies, Organization Science, Sociological Review, Theory and Society* and the *British Journal of Management*. He was a consultant to the National Taskforce of Inquiry into Australia's Leadership and Management Needs into the 21st Century, which reported in 1995.

Gemma Donnelly-Cox is a Lecturer in Business Studies (Organization Theory) in the School of Business Studies, Trinity College, Dublin. Her research interests include institutional approaches to organizational change and innovation. She is currently involved in collecting and analysing Irish data for the GLOBE Leadership Programme, an international study of leadership behaviour co-ordinated by Bob House at the Wharton School.

Erik Døving is a Research Associate and Ph.D. candidate in the Department of Organization Sciences at the Norwegian School of Economics and Business Administration, Bergen. He is also a Lecturer in Organization Theory and Behaviour at the Norwegian School of Management. His doctoral research centres on the concept of organizational learning and how it occurs in large corporate structures.

Richard Dunford is Professor of Management in the Management Group, Victoria University of Wellington, New Zealand. His research and teaching interests range across organization theory, organizational behaviour and corporate strategy. He has published in a range of journals that includes *Administrative Science Quarterly, Labour and Industry, Journal of Management Education, Organization Studies* and *Academy of Management Review*, and is author of *Organizational Behaviour: An Organizational Analysis Perspective* (1992). His current research centres on the management of the aftermath of organizational restructuring. Most of the time he struggles valiantly to cope with the competing demands of research, teaching, administration and the desire to have a vaguely normal home life.

David Grant is a Lecturer in Human Resource Management and Industrial Relations at the Management Centre, King's College, University of London. His current research interests include Japanization, UK industrial relations legislation and analysis of the language, ideology and beliefs surrounding human resource management. He has published in all of these areas and is co-editor (with Cliff Oswick) of *Organization Development: Metaphorical Explorations* (1996).

John T. Gray lectures in Management and is Director of the MBA Program at the University of Western Sydney Macarthur, Australia. He has held senior executive positions in adult education and health care and has also enjoyed a successful career in consultancy, having founded the Management Skills Company in 1976. He retains a directorship of this firm, through which he has consulted for public and private sector organizations, principally in the areas of the management of change and innovation. His current research examines the links between interpretative schemes and innovation in professional services.

Heather Höpfl is Professor of Organizational Psychology and Research Director at Bolton Business School. Her Ph.D. was on the subjective experience of time. She has worked as an industrial researcher, as a teacher, and as a tour manager for a theatre company. Her research interests are primarily concerned with dramaturgy and social theory. She is Chair of SCOS, the Standing Conference on Organizational Symbolism (1995–1998). She has published largely on organizational culture and interpretative approaches to organizations. She is Adjunct Professor at the University of South Australia.

Dawn E. Inns is Senior Lecturer in Organizational Behaviour at the University of Westminster. She obtained an MA in Organizational Analysis and Behaviour (International Variant) from Lancaster University. This included five months at the Université Catholique de Louvain in Belgium. Previous to this she worked at INSEAD in France, organizing management education seminars. Her current and recent research interests include: metaphor and organizational language; effects of computer and tele-communication networks on organizations; and cross-cultural comparisons (France/England). She is a doctoral candidate at the Centre for Social Theory and Technology, Keele University. Her Ph.D. is on the topic of 'identity'.

Philip J. Jones is Senior Lecturer in Organizational Behaviour at the University of Westminster and visiting Lecturer at King's College, University of London, where he is currently completing a Ph.D. He has been involved in extensive consultancy work with international manufacturing companies and is a member of the Institute of Personnel Development. He has research publications concerning the evaluation of management training (thesis area), team development, empowerment, leadership and metaphor and organizational language.

Julie Maddrell is International Development Officer, University College Salford – a post which combines her experience in both education and marketing. She began her career in 1976 as a teacher of Religious Education and went on to hold posts as Head of Sixth Form, Head of Expressive Arts and Head of Year. An interest in business management and the desire to run her own business influenced her decision to leave teaching in 1988 and join an international direct marketing company. As Group Director she became responsible for a large sales team based in the UK and USA. In 1991 she returned to education to complete her Ph.D., which is an investigation into the barriers to women managers' career development.

Geoffrey MacKechnie is Senior Lecturer in Organizational Behaviour in the School of Business Studies, Trinity College, Dublin. He is currently Head of Department and Director of the School's Senior Executive M.Sc. programmes. His primary research interest is organization design and his recent publications include work on organizational networks, public sector management and managing professionals in complex organizations.

Iain L. Mangham is Professor of Management Development in the School of Management at the University of Bath. His publications have been largely concerned with dramaturgical perspectives on social and organizational life, and with power performance and organizational change. His focus in addressing these issues continues to be the activities of senior managers, particularly where they claim to be operating as teams. He is currently reading, researching and writing about the same issues with the same focus, but has recently developed an interest in morality, ideology and character, which may lead him in quite another direction.

Robert J. Marshak is President of Marshak Associates. He has been an organizational consultant for over twenty years, specializing in strategic organizational change, managing conflict and differences, and the develop-ment of executives and change agents. In addition to his consultancy practice, he is Professor-in-residence at the School of Public Affairs, the American University, Washington DC and a visiting senior research fellow at the Management Centre, King's College, University of London. He has worked extensively in Korea (where he is on the Board of Directors for the Training and Development Consulting Institute, Seoul) and has authored several articles about East Asian culturally based models of change. He has published in a range of journals, including *Journal of Applied Behavioral Science*, *Organizational Dynamics*, *Organization Development Practitioner*, *The Annual Handbook on Developing Human Resources* and *Training and Development Journal*.

Gareth Morgan is Distinguished Research Professor at York University in Toronto, and author of seven books, including *Sociological Paradigms and Organizational Analysis* (1979, with Gibson Burrell), *Beyond Method* (1983), *Images of Organization* (1986), *Riding the Waves of Change* (1988) and *Imaginization: The Art of Creative Management* (1993). His current research focuses on the use of metaphor in creating organic, self-organizing approaches to the theory and practice of management that embrace paradox and contradiction as defining features of all knowledge and action.

Cliff Oswick is Senior Lecturer in Organization Theory and Development at the Management Centre, King's College, University of London. His current research interests relate to metaphor, rhetoric and other aspects of organizational discourse. He admits to adopting a 'scatter gun' approach to organizational research and has published in a range of diverse journals. This includes recent contributions to *Journal of Psychological Type*, *Modern Management*, *Journal of Higher and Further Education*, *Journal of European Industrial Training*, *Personnel Review* and *Accounting Education: An International Journal*. He is also co-editor (with David Grant) of *Organization Development: Metaphorical Explorations* (1996).

Ian Palmer is an Associate Professor in the School of Management at the University of Technology, Sydney, where he currently teaches subjects on organizational analysis and arts management. He has published in a range of national and international journals, including *Sociology*, *Journal of Industrial Relations*, *Asia Pacific Journal of Human Resources*, *Labour and Industry* and *Journal of Management Education*. His most recent research is in three areas: reframing and metaphors, arts management and strategic human resource management.

Graeme Salaman is Reader in Sociology in the Social Science faculty, the Open University. His current research projects include an ESRC-funded study (No. R000234869) of competence-based architectures in organizations entitled 'Making up Managers' (with Paul du Gay); and an investigation of managers' use of management consultants (with Timothy Clark). He has published extensively over many years in the sociology of work and organizations, and human resource strategies. His most recent books include *Managing* (1995) and *Strategic Human Resource Management* (1995, with Chris Mabey).

List of Tables

3.1	The force, fit and fluctuation paradigms of change	58
5.1	Metaphors for external conditions and strategic responses	100
5.2	Metaphors for internal conditions of pre-downsized organizations	100
5.3	Metaphors for how organizations downsize	102
5.4	Counter-metaphors	104
8.1	Examples of thematic coherence in the metaphoric field	154

List of Figures

4.1 Paradigms, metaphors and puzzle solving: Three concepts for understanding the nature of organization science   77

4.2 Paradigms, metaphors and related schools of organizational analysis   78

4.3 The embryonic industry complex and a focal firm   86

Introduction: Getting the Measure of Metaphors

David Grant and Cliff Oswick

They are here, there and everywhere. They run right through our language. They are used to make sense of the situations we find ourselves in. They shape our perceptions and can influence our attitudes and behaviour. Metaphors are, to quote Morgan, '*a way of thinking* and *a way of seeing*' (1986: 12).

No one could deny the pervasiveness of metaphors, but that does not mean that we should not question and analyse their value, particularly in relation to organization science. Accordingly, this book does not represent an attempt to legitimize or glorify metaphor's role in the study of organizations; it does not seek to "sell" metaphor to the reader. Instead, it aims to provide a major contribution to our understanding of metaphor by extending existing debates and by generating new concepts and theories. In effect (and metaphorically speaking), the book represents an attempt to get the measure of metaphors – no less this opening chapter, which seeks to contribute to the process by providing an understanding of their significance and of the main issues surrounding them. In it, we commence with an explanation of how metaphor works. Subsequent sections then go on to familiarize the reader with two key areas of debate and discussion concerning metaphor's usage in organizational analysis. They are issues that will surface in various guises throughout this book. One concerns the status accorded to metaphor. The other relates to attempts to place different kinds of metaphor into hierarchical and non-hierarchical typologies. Finally we present a synopsis of the book's structure and a discussion of each chapter.

The inevitability of metaphor

Seen as allegories or as figures of speech, metaphors may appear to be no more than simple literary or linguistic tools, yet there is far more to them than that. They are the outcome of a cognitive process that is in constant use – a process in which the literal meaning to a phrase or word is applied to a new context in a figurative sense. But what is it about this process that is so important? Why do we resort to using it so frequently? Why is metaphor an inevitable feature of our everyday lives?

The answer to these questions is linked to our attempts to make sense of the environment around us. In order to achieve this we often draw on pre-existing knowledge, and this is exactly what metaphors do. They enable the transfer of information about a relatively familiar subject (often referred to as the source or base domain) to a new and relatively unknown subject (often referred to as the target domain) (Lakoff and Johnson, 1980; 112; Ortony, 1993: 1; Sackmann, 1989: 465; Tsoukas, 1991: 568). In short, we assert that 'subject A is, or is like B, the processes of comparison, substitution, and interaction between the images of A and B acting as generators of new meaning' (Morgan 1980: 610). Metaphors therefore have what Schön (1993) has termed a 'generative' quality (see also Barrett and Cooperrider, 1990; Morgan, 1986; Tsoukas 1993). They operate as 'a process by which new perspectives on the world come into existence' (Schön, 1993: 137). More specifically, and in the context of this volume, their generative quality can be used to bring new perspectives on *organizations* into existence.

There is nothing new in the application of metaphors to the study of organizations. In fact, there is a long historical association between the two. Morgan, for example, finds evidence of Herbert Spencer's application of a biological metaphor to the term 'organization' as early as 1873, so that 'the state of being organized in a biological sense was the basis of the metaphor for arranging or co-ordinating in a general sense' and was also used as a metaphor for 'a body, system or society in a general sense' (1983: 610). He goes on to explain how two particular metaphors have dominated theories of management and organization since this time. The first concerns the metaphor of the organization as a machine (Fayol, 1949; Taylor 1911; Weber, 1946) and includes theories that portray the organization as "rational" or "goal"-oriented (Etzioni, 1960; Georgiou, 1973; Gouldner, 1973; Thompson, 1967). The second metaphor portrays the organization as an organism. Morgan notes how ascribing "organismic" status to organizations can be seen not only in Spencer's (1873) work, but in subsequent schools of thought about organizations as well. Examples given include the Hawthorne Studies (Roethlisberger and Dickson, 1939), socio-technical theories (Trist and Bamforth, 1951), contingency theory (Lawrence and Lorsch, 1967) and structural functionalism (Parsons, 1951, 1956). These two metaphors have also been set up as a continuum so that, for example, Burns and Stalker's contingency theory (1961) contrasts mechanistic and organistic organizations (Morgan, 1983: 601–607).

Organization science and the status of metaphor

There can be little dispute about the inevitability of metaphor. Nor about its having a generative quality. However, the legitimacy and value of metaphor in the social sciences, especially in relation to organization science, has been the subject of considerable debate and is something that will be discussed on a number of occasions in this volume. This debate centres on the relevance and appropriateness of what a metaphor generates and whether it is anything that actually increases our knowledge and understanding of the phenomenon under consideration. In short, and as both Tsoukas (1993) and Morgan (1980, 1983) have noted, it is not so much the existence of metaphors in organization science that is called into question by the literature, rather it is whether metaphors should be accorded a positive or negative 'status'.

Positive status

The suggestion that metaphors ought to be assigned a positive status in relation to organization science is based on the belief that metaphors are – in line with their generative capacity – "liberating" in orientation. In practice, they entail using a combination of both language and thought to construct a non-literal meaning and apply it to reality in order to shape and enhance our appreciation of that reality. Couched in these terms, metaphors can be seen as important to the advancement of knowledge and understanding. Thus, to Ortony they should be seen as powerful educational devices. To him, metaphors are 'necessary and not just nice' because they are a process that 'correlates highly with learnability' and creates 'insightful personal under-standing' (1975: 51). Seen in this light, it is perhaps not surprising that metaphors have been described as essential to the continuing process of re-evaluation and change that occurs both within the wider social world (Black, 1962; Manning, 1979; Morgan, 1980, 1983) and more specifically in the context of organizations (Barrett and Cooperrider, 1990; Morgan, 1981, 1983, 1986, 1989, 1993; Morgan and Ramirez, 1984; Sackmann, 1989; Srivastva and Barrett, 1988; Tsoukas, 1991; 1993). It is a constructivist-oriented view, influenced by and shared with a number philosophers, cognitive psychologists and linguists who have discussed the role of metaphor in society (see, for example, Johnson, 1981; Lakoff, 1987; Lakoff and Johnson, 1980; Lakoff and Turner, 1989; Ortony, 1993).

The liberating orientation of metaphors has been described in a number of ways. Three, in particular, merit attention. The first is that metaphors are an 'invitation to see the world anew' (Barrett and Cooperrider, 1990: 222). The argument here is that our existing pre-conceptions about a particular phenomenon may be completely altered by the application of a metaphor. We may suddenly see a familiar situation in a completely new and highly informative light (Lakoff and Johnson, 1980: 132). It is this that led Tsoukas to note how metaphors 'encourage different ways of thinking, which enable social scientists and lay people alike to focus upon, explain, and influence different aspects of complex organizational phenomena' (1991: 566). Taking such a view suggests we ought not to accept that what we perceive as social reality is incontrovertible. To do so is to fall into the trap of believing that the social system which surrounds us is not the outcome of human actions and emotions but is instead inevitable, rigid and unchanging (Berger and Luckmann, 1967; Weick 1979). In essence, then, metaphors offer a way out of this trap. They can be used to 'generate alternative social realities' (Tsoukas, 1993: 324).

A second interpretation of the liberating role of metaphors is one that focuses on the value of metaphor where it 'facilitates the learning of new knowledge' (Barrett and Cooperrider, 1990). The emphasis here is not about metaphor's role in the reinterpretation of already known phenomena, but on its value where we encounter something that is a completely new experience (Petrie and Oshlag,1993). As an example, Barrett and Cooperrider discuss the case of a science student unable to grasp the structure of the atom. Getting the student to use the metaphor 'the atom is a solar system' portrays the neutrons and electrons revolving around the gravitational centre and allows new understanding to emerge (1990: 223).

The third way in which metaphors have been described as liberating follows on from the first two interpretations. Its proponents emphasize that the application of metaphor to either new or existing phenomena is in itself a process of experimentation. In keeping with this line of argument metaphor can therefore be used deliberately as an investigative tool (Barrett and Cooperrider, 1990). Such an approach is highly apparent in organization science. There is a considerable literature which takes metaphors and uses them to unlock the complexities of organizational theory and behaviour (Brink, 1993; Brown, 1977; Manning, 1979; Morgan 1981, 1986; Morgan and Ramirez, 1984; Weick, 1979). More specifically, there is a tranche of Organization Development (OD) literature which uses metaphor to diagnose organizational problems and to then construct solutions to these problems that can be to the benefit of the organization's performance (Barrett and Cooperrider, 1990; Marshak 1993; Oswick and Grant, 1996; Sackmann, 1989; Srivastva and Barrett, 1988; Warner-Burke, 1992).

Negative status

The positive status assigned to metaphors is not one that is universally shared. Two main criticisms are apparent and both suggest that, far from being liberating, metaphors can actually constrain knowledge. The first of these criticisms is that if science is about exactitude, then it follows that something that is applied in a figurative sense cannot be of any use to scientific investigation (Beer, 1981; Boulding, 1987; Bourgeois and Pinder, 1983; Bunge, 1973; Pinder and Bourgeois, 1982). In keeping with Popper's (1958) proposition, science is founded on falsifiable hypotheses that permit us to establish truths. Metaphors cannot offer this since they 'are stated in terms that do not have enough clear content to be falsifiable' (Pinder and Bourgeois, 1982: 643). Moreover, the danger of metaphors is that if they are not based on such hypotheses, yet are couched in seductive figurative language, it becomes hard to get rid of them. By way of example, take the title of this chapter: It incorporates a metaphor conveying the idea that we wish to increase our knowledge about metaphor itself. But getting the measure of metaphors in a literal sense is in fact impossible. One cannot measure them using a mathematically based value or weighting. The exercise the metaphor describes is qualitative in nature not quantitative. So, yes, the metaphor works, at the figurative level, but what is the value of that?

Such an argument has important implications where it is asserted that the study of social phenomena and more specifically organizations should be treated as a science. Taking it to its logical conclusion would mean that if metaphors are of no scientific value then the apparent reliance on metaphor in the organizational literature means that the term 'organization *science*' is a misnomer.

The idea that metaphors are simply figurative devices that need to be purged from scientific language is in line with the non-constructivist view of the world (and metaphors) described by Ortony (1993). It is a view which sees empirically based science as the only route to understanding the reality which we live in. Thus, when it comes to metaphors, the non-constructivist position treats them as

> rather unimportant, deviant and parasitic on 'normal usage'. If metaphors need explaining at all, their explanations will be in terms of violations of linguistic rules. Metaphors characterise rhetoric, not scientific discourse. They are vague, inessential frills, appropriate for the purposes of politicians and poets, but not for those of scientists because the goal of science is to furnish an accurate (i.e. literal) description of physical reality. (Ortony, 1993: 2)

As Tsoukas (1993) points out, metaphor's scientific credentials and therefore their liberating value have been challenged in three further ways. All three suggest that metaphor can be 'misleading' (1993: 326) in the pursuit of scientific knowledge. First, they do not create a theoretical definition of whatever it is that is being studied. Consequently, they are criticized as being 'imprecise' since one cannot tell whether a metaphor endows the phenomenon under scrutiny with theoretically relevant or irrelevant characteristics. Second, there is no way of measuring the 'goodness of fit' of a metaphor. To work, it relies on us recognizing how and why the source domain of the metaphor is useful when applied to the target domain. But quantifying the extent of its success in achieving this is difficult, if not impossible. We are talking about something that is in fact a personalized cognitive process, so that even where a metaphor is explained to us, it may be that it works well for one person but does not work so well, if at all, for another. Third, and as discussed by Døving in Chapter 10, there is the possibility that a metaphor can be 'pushed too far'. This tends to occur where scientists take concepts from one scientific field and apply them to another in a metaphorical form. The borrowing of a scientific concept needs to be 'informed', but it is argued that most scientists have insufficient knowledge of other disciplines for this to be a realistic proposition. Metaphors are thus put to use, with scant regard for their limitations and relevance and in such situations serve no useful scientific purpose (Tsoukas, 1993: 326).

The second main criticism of metaphors is less concerned with their scientific value than with their propensity to reify and act as ideological distortions. One advocate of this belief is Tinker (1986). To him, a metaphor that describes a social phenomenon would only be of value where it explains and 'recognises social inequality and domination and points to political opportunities for liberation and emancipation' (1986: 378). All too often, says Tinker, this is not the case. He takes a number of metaphors used in organizational analysis and demonstrates how their generative qualities can be 'socially partisan' in that they play down structural conflicts and fail to identify inequalities of power (1986: 363). For instance, representation of organizations as biological, organismic or mechanical entities means that we expect them to behave automatically in ways that are in keeping with such entities and accept such behaviour without question. Such acceptance means that organizations are perceived as 'immutable, unchangeable, and uncontrollable' (1986: 375) when in reality they are subject to the actions of management and the owners of capital. In short, metaphors create a 'false consciousness', one that shields organizations from any critical social analysis (1986: 378).

Types of metaphor

A second debate surrounding metaphor, and one that also pervades this book, concerns types of metaphor. Those involved in the debate believe metaphors can be liberating and assign them a positive status, but they also believe that the extent to which they achieve this is influenced by type. A number of typologies are apparent. In essence they can be broken down into two groups – hierarchical and non-hierarchical.

Hierarchical typologies

Hierarchical typologies of metaphors start with those which most influence our ways of thinking and seeing the world and work down to those which are of minor or peripheral significance. At one level this is an extremely useful way in which to examine the liberating features of each type. However, this view has its limitations and needs to be qualified. A hierarchy could imply that it is possible to measure the impact of one type of metaphor against another. This is an impossible task because, as we have already seen elsewhere in this chapter, the cognitive nature of metaphors combined with their reliance on figurative language means that their effects are unquantifiable and unmeasurable.

Schön's (1993) work provides a good example of a hierarchical typology. His argument is that it is important to distinguish between 'surface' and 'deep' metaphors. A deep metaphor is a metaphor which determines 'centrally important features' of the idea or object being examined (1993: 149; see also Sternberg et al., 1993). It forms the basis on which subsequent surface-level metaphors are formed. An example of a deep metaphor might be the metaphor of the organization as a human entity. As Døving's work (Chapter 10 in this volume) shows, the subsequent development of surface metaphors such as organizational action, competence and learning are all based on this deeper metaphor, but in discussing them we do not use the word 'human'. Hierarchical distinctions between metaphors similar to that made by Schön are apparent elsewhere and in relation to the study of organizations. Alvesson (1993) talks of 'first'- and 'second'-level meanings attached to metaphors (also discussed by Inns and Jones in Chapter 6 of this volume). Others have examined the characteristics and organizational implications of 'surface' and 'root' metaphors (Dunn, 1990; Grant, 1996; Mangham, 1994; Srivastva and Barrett, 1988).

An alternative, hierarchical typology of metaphors is given by Black (1993), who sees metaphors as either 'strong' or 'weak'. A strong metaphor incorporates two key features. The first is 'emphasis', whereby the words used to apply the metaphor are so effective that they provide what Ortony has described as a 'compact', 'vivid' image of something 'inexpressible' (1975: 53). In short, the words do their job so well that it is difficult to substitute or vary them. The second feature is 'resonance'. This means that once the metaphor is understood it lends itself to further elaboration and proves 'relatively rich in background implications' (Black, 1993: 26). In contrast, a weak metaphor is neither emphatic nor resonant and 'might be compared to an unfunny joke, or an unilluminating philosophical epigram' (Black, 1993: 26).

A more extensive hierarchy of metaphor is put forward by Tsoukas (1993). He proposes that a model of analogy advanced by Gentner (1983, 1989) be extended and applied to the way in which metaphors work. His argument is that metaphors attempt to construct similarities between two different phenomena (the source and target domains). Depending on which one of the five types of 'domain similarities' that they fall under, some are more successful than others at achieving this. Their success is determined by the extent to which the transfer of information between the two domains reveals that they are both based on similar 'attributes' and 'relationships'. The five domain similarities along with the examples given by Tsoukas (1993: 337–338) are:

- *Abstractions* – where the source domain is based on a set of relationships that are similar to those in the target domain. However, this relational structure does not have any clear-cut attributes that can be transferred to the target domain and the ensuing comparison is therefore based on relationship similarities only. Tsoukas uses the example of 'the organization as a control system'. From this we might go on to deduce that the organization control system is based on a network of sensors that detect change and alter the organization's behaviour. Thus, we have transferred information to the target domain which concerns the human nervous system, yet we never actually consider that we are using the source domain to achieve this.

- *Analogies* – which involve the transfer of a clearly identifiable structure or set of characteristics from the target to the source domain. Analogies take relationships within the source domain and apply them to the target domain (e.g. 'Orchard Road is to Singapore what Oxford Street is to London'). The source and base domains share few attributes.
- *Literal similarities* – which transfer both relationships and attributes from the source to the target domain (e.g. 'milk is like water').
- *Mere appearances* – where specific attributes are transferred between the source and target domains but there are no relationship similarities (e.g. 'the surface of the lake was calm and clear like a mirror').
- *Anomalies* – where the two domains share few relationships or attributes (e.g. 'a computer is like coffee').

Tsoukas' analysis of these five types suggests that, in terms of their value, they should be placed in the descending order given above, that is, from abstractions down through to anomalies. His argument is that the most effective metaphors for generating scientific knowledge about organizational phenomena are those that lead to the formulation of abstractions (1993: 342). For him, abstractions are important to the process of 'theory building . . . because they operate at a high level of generality, reveal the generic properties of a variety of phenomena and can thus be used to explain phenomena across widely different domains' (1993: 338).

The final hierarchical typology worth considering is that which relates tropes to metaphors. It is a typology that concentrates on what have been described as the four 'master' tropes – metaphor, metonymy, synecdoche and irony (Manning, 1979; Morgan 1983; White; 1978). In each case the trope is seen as a particular form of metaphor. The trope of metaphor is defined as the medium through which two separate conceptual domains are compared and one is understood in terms of the other. The trope of metonymy can be understood using an example given by Gibbs:

> Metonymy involves only one conceptual domain in that the mapping or connec-
> tion between two things is done within the same domain. Traditional rhetoric
> defines metonymy as a figure of speech wherein the name of one entity is used to
> refer to another entity that is contiguous to it. . . . Thus, referring to a baseball
> player as a glove, as in 'we need a new glove at second base,' uses a salient
> characteristic of one domain (the glove part of the baseball player) to represent the
> entire domain (the player). (1993: 258-259)

Gibbs goes on to explain that the third trope, synecdoche, is an opposite of metonymy. It occurs: 'When the two things being compared form a part–whole relationship (that is, when glove is part of the whole baseball player)' (1993: 259). The fourth trope is irony. It involves the use of the in-appropriate in order to describe something in a paradoxical and contra-dictory way. An example given by Morgan is that of anarchy as a good form of organization (1983: 602).

It should be pointed out that not everyone believes that the four master tropes can be placed in any order of ascendancy. For example, Manning's discussion of their usage in organization science leads him to conclude that

'I do not believe that any one of them is "higher", more abstract, or illuminating than the others' (1979: 663). However, those such as White (1978) have argued that degrees of trope sophistication do indeed exist. They consider metaphor to be the most basic trope, followed by metonymy, synecdoche and irony, with each increasing in explanatory value. Others have adopted a somewhat different stance. They believe metaphor 'makes meaning in a primal way', in other words it is the *source* of comparison between two different objects or situations. Metonymy, synecdoche and irony are therefore portrayed as 'secondary forms within the domain or context forged through metaphor' (Morgan, 1983: 602). To illustrate how this works, and in the context of organizational analysis, take, for example, a whole metaphor and its associated terminology discussed by Marshak (Chapter 8) in this volume – the organization as a machine. Its relationship with the secondary forms of metonymy and synecdoche is forged in the following ways: Metonymy is employed where, having considered the whole metaphor, we think of the organization's leader as an "engineer", talk about enhancing its "output", "repairing" it, and so on. Synecdoche, as the reverse of this process, takes one part of the whole metaphor and uses it to reveal the whole. To stick with the machine metaphor, this would be revealed where, having identified a particular course of action that needed to be taken at their organization, people talked in terms of "setting the wheels in motion".

Non-hierarchical typologies

Non-hierarchical typologies of metaphor do not seek to assign relative values to the different types of metaphor they identify. Instead, they focus on understanding how each type of metaphor works and when and where each type is used. Two typologies merit attention. The first is the distinction drawn between dead, live and dormant metaphors (Brown, 1927; Fraser, 1993; Lakoff and Johnson, 1980; Tsoukas, 1991).

Dead metaphors are described as having 'become so familiar and so habitual that we have ceased to become aware of their metaphorical nature and use them as literal terms' (Tsoukas, 1991: 568). Day-to-day examples of such metaphors include "chair leg" and the "teeth" of a saw. They also pervade organization science, indeed, organization is in itself a dead metaphor (taken from the Greek word *organon*, meaning tool).

A key feature of dead metaphors is that, alone, they are unable to provide any useful contribution to the study of the particular characteristics of the phenomenon they describe. Thus, the dead metaphor of organization offers us few insights into understanding organization phenomena such as training, development, leadership and motivation. For this to occur we may need to use live metaphors (Tsoukas, 1991: 569).

Live metaphors are those which 'require both a context and a certain creativity to interpret adequately' (Fraser, 1993: 330). Their appeal is that 'they particularly lend themselves to further conceptual development' (Tsou-kas, 1991: 568) and thus they appear throughout this book. Morgan's (1986) *Images of Organization* contains a number of live metaphors, including organizations as 'brains', 'psychic prisons', 'machines' and 'organisms'.

Dormant metaphors are used as literal terms but are distinguishable from dead metaphors because they are in fact semi-literal. This is because although the metaphorical bases of the words and phrases they use are not automatically apparent, they can quickly be identified. As such, they play a positive role in organization science – examples include organization behaviour, or organizational structure. Dormant metaphors can develop into either dead or live metaphors.

A second non-hierarchical typology of metaphors is discussed by Palmer and Dunford (1996). This concerns the 'deductive' versus 'inductive' approach to their application. The deductive approach involves taking a metaphor, imposing it on a particular organizational phenomenon and then seeing if it offers something of value. Examples of deductive metaphors in this volume are Clark and Salaman's (Chapter 9) analysis of the client–consultant relationship in management consultancy in terms of 'the art of story telling' and Broekstra's (Chapter 3) application of 'the triune-brain metaphor' to organizations (see also Barrett and Cooperrider, 1990; Inns, 1996; Morgan, 1981; Morgan and Ramirez 1984; Oswick 1996). In contrast, the inductive approach seeks to discover those underlying metaphors that are already in use and which influence our ways of thinking and seeing. Examples of the approach in this volume include Døving's (Chapter 10) discussion of the metaphors of organizational action, competence and learning and Dunford and Palmer's (Chapter 5) examination of metaphors that dominate the language surrounding corporate restructuring (see also Brink, 1993; Broussine and Vince, 1996; Morgan 1986; Srivastva and Barrett, 1988).

Metaphor and organizations: The structure of the book

The above sections have highlighted key debates concerning the status of metaphor and the typologies that surround it. As they move through this book, readers will find that it extends these debates while also generating new concepts and theories. The book is divided into four thematic parts and it is to these and their associated chapters that we now turn.

There is a considerable literature concerning the application of metaphor to organization theory. Accordingly, Part I of the book provides a set of critical essays that consider the use of metaphors to create new theories of organization and reinterpret existing theories. However, debate about metaphor's relevance and use in the study of organizations has not been confined to the theoretical context. Parts II and III of the book reflect this by focusing on two further important issues. Part II examines the pervasiveness of metaphors in organizational discourse and language. It analyses the construction of these metaphors and assesses what it is about this construction process that makes some metaphors powerful tools with which to manage the organization. Part III investigates the relevance of various metaphors to a number of organizational situations and whether they actually impact on attitudes and behaviour within the organization. Finally, Part IV of the book provides an agenda for the use of metaphors in organization research. In so doing it suggests some new directions that this research might take.

Part I: Metaphors of organization: Scope and application

It is now ten years since Gareth Morgan's (1986) work *Images of Organization* was first published. It was greeted with great acclaim, one eminent reviewer suggesting that it 'rewrites the history of recent organization theory' (Schön, 1993). It remains a highly influential piece doing exactly what it sets out to achieve – encouraging new ways of thinking and seeing organizations.

In Chapter 1, Iain Mangham sounds a note of caution about the way in which work such as *Images of Organization* encourages us to apply metaphors while believing that they have a virtually unlimited use. Mangham's argument is that two types of metaphor exist: a primal, basic metaphor that is 'cognitively well entrenched'; and conceptual metaphors that are apparent in our everyday language. This amounts to a hierarchical typology of metaphor, one in which the basic metaphors (of which there are very few) should be seen as leading on to the formulation of other ordinary conceptual metaphors. His concern is that Morgan's work plays up the use of everyday conceptual metaphors but fails to draw attention to the basic metaphors on which they are based. Moreover, Morgan's suggestion that there is a limitless supply of meaningful everyday conceptual metaphors is unfounded. Only basic metaphors offer unlimited applications to organization science; the type of everyday conceptual metaphors that Morgan focuses on are limited in their scope and application and their over-use may therefore constrain our ability to question and re-conceptualize the social world around us.

At the heart of Mangham's chapter is his concern about the appropriateness of certain metaphors to organization theory – a concern shared by Geoffrey MacKechnie and Gemma Donnelly-Cox (Chapter 2). These authors evaluate the historical contribution of metaphor to the development of organization theory. They note how the work of prominent organization theorists has used a rich array of metaphorical terminology in order to identify their field of study. However, the work of most theorists can be seen to stem from one of two categories of metaphor: 'the study of a rare skill', which was the focus of many early studies and helped to explain the division of labour that was occurring at this time; or 'the anthropological study of organizations, which appears more frequently in later works' and was conceived by sociologists who tended to focus on the development of the organization and how it survived in its environment. MacKechnie and

Donnelly-Cox suggest that anthropological metaphors dominate current organization literature. However, because the division of labour remains a crucial issue, the rare skill metaphor provides a sounder basis for contemporary organizational theorizing than the anthropological metaphor. Somewhat in line with Tinker's (1986) argument (see above), MacKechnie and Donnelly-Cox go as far as to suggest that the anthropological metaphor is misleading because it hides what is an important social issue from any real critical analysis.

Chapters 3 and 4 represent specific examples of how metaphors can be used in the development of organization theory. In Chapter 3 Gerrit Broekstra presents the 'triune-brain evolution of the living organization'. He regards this metaphor as a valuable tool with which to explain and understand the evolution of organizations over the last 150 years. His argument is that, broadly speaking, three stages of organizational evolution can be discerned and that these are linked to the business cycle. These are the emergence of the functional, divisional and network organization. Until recently, organizations had moved through the mechanistic and organismic paradigms of organizing and organizational change, but the advent of network organizations suggests movement to a new 'evolutionary' paradigm, one where organizations have to learn to cope with uncertainty and rapid change. Broekstra acknowledges the contribution of other brain metaphors (Beer, 1981; Morgan, 1986) to organization theory, but proposes that the metaphor of the triune brain is far more apt. This is because each of the three parts of the brain that it describes corresponds to the triune evolution of organizations and their associated forms of organizational structure. The power of this metaphor is that it articulates both what has happened in the past and what is happening now. Furthermore, suggests Broekstra, it helps us to understand the actions and behaviour of modern network organizations. In so doing, it opens our eyes to the fact that as well as having physical properties, these organizations genuinely exude a 'corporate consciousness'.

In Chapter 4 Stewart Clegg and John Gray apply a particular metaphor to a specific type of organization. Their choice of metaphor is not, however, their own. Asked by the Australian Government to research new industrial sectors and the innovative firms within them, these authors duly found that all they were given in order to identify what and where these sectors were was the metaphor of 'embryonic industry'. In fact, this proved to be an asset rather than a liability. Clegg and Gray used the metaphor as the focus of their research and discovered its liberating properties, finding that where participants focused on the metaphor it enhanced the quality of the data that they provided. Their chapter shows how, as the research progressed, the metaphor developed to the extent that the language and symbols surrounding it became constituent elements of the final report.

The value of Clegg and Gray's chapter is that, while supportive of the role metaphors can play in organization theory and associated research, they also point out the limitations and dangers of applying metaphors in such circumstances. Their work finds that a metaphor such as embryonic industry can be 'embedded' in a particular paradigm and that this needs to be recognized in order that we do not become "locked in" to only one way of thinking about the issue. It also suggests that to control for spurious and inaccurate use of the metaphor it is useful to have researchers, participants and third parties monitor its development as the research proceeds.

Part II: Metaphors of organizing: Language and discourse

The use of metaphorical language in management language and discourse has received scant attention. In Chapter 5 Richard Dunford and Ian Palmer start to redress this deficiency by analysing the metaphors used in the popular management literature to describe corporate restructuring through downsizing. The authors argue that the metaphorically based language applied to downsizing situations plays an important part in the way in which such situations are interpreted and courses of action identified. This can be seen in the two types of corporate restructuring metaphors that their research identifies. These are (1) core downsizing metaphors and (2) counter-metaphors. The metaphorical language surrounding the first views the process as one where firm, violent and drastic action is needed in order to improve the performance of the organization. These metaphors suggest that without such changes the organization will simply expire. Therefore the changes are a necessary evil – one where there will be no gain without pain. The metaphorical language surrounding the second provides more critical pessimistic portrayals of downsizing, exposing the need for sensitive hand-ling of the issue by management and its impact on those who survive it.

Dunford and Palmer conclude with an important discussion on whether the metaphors found in the popular management literature represent either the views and interpretations of those writing about downsizing or the observations and accounts of those who action and experience it. This raises questions about the extent to which any form of metaphorical language described in the organizational literature is actually used in organizations themselves. It also begs the question of cause and effect: If such meta-phorical language is put into action, we ought to ascertain whether it is the product of managers having read the literature or whether it is a language of their own choosing (which may in itself go on to influence the literature).

In Chapter 6 Dawn Inns and Philip Jones suggest that the study of language and discourse will become a major area of interest within organiz-ational analysis. To them, metaphor as a 'cornerstone' of language, will therefore attain an even higher status in organization theory and research. 'Following in the footsteps of the poet', they seek to identify any tools and concepts associated with the use of metaphor in poetry that would be useful when applying metaphor to the study of organizations. In taking this approach, their chapter has some relevance to the debate about the positive versus negative status of metaphor in the study of organizations discussed earlier.

Inns and Jones argue that metaphor in poetry encourages creativity and imagination and that it can also be used to provide vivid images in relation to the emotions and perceptions the poet is trying to convey. These are attributes that surface where metaphors are applied to organizational phenomena. However, comparison of metaphor's use in poetry and organization theory and research finds differences as well as similarities. It suggests that organizational scientists have very different expectations of metaphor in comparison to poets. They desire metaphor to go beyond the demands made on it by poetry by providing an empirically sound analytical framework with which to study organizational phenomena. In effect, organizational scientists demand that where metaphorical discourse and language is applied to their field of study it takes on a genuinely scientific mantle. Those who believe that it achieves, or at least goes some way to achieving, this could be said to accord metaphor a positive status; those who do not could be said to accord it negative status.

Robert Chia's work (Chapter 7) suggests that where metaphors achieve a positive status this should not be perceived in terms of their value as scientific tools. On the contrary, to him, the increasing interest and use of metaphors in organizational analysis derives from a growing appreciation that, on their own, the workings of an organization are not easily translatable into the hitherto literal and 'rigorous' language of scientific discourse. By definition, metaphors do not seek to provide this type of language and therefore offer attractive 'handles' through which organizational realities can be analytically grasped and meaningfully explored.

Chia goes on to point out that there is none the less a danger in using metaphors; that there is a tendency to forget that they are merely figures of speech which serve as short-hand 'explanatory principles' in our scheme of things. If mishandled, they have a tendency to ossify into the literal through frequent unreflective use so that their ability to evoke our sensibilities and illuminate tenuous relationships becomes severely curtailed. Chia advocates that the purpose of metaphors should be not so much about whether organizations can be understood as say machines or cultures, but about relaxing the boundaries of thought through a process of 'metaphorization'. To him this process is essentially a paradigm-shifting activity designed to cultivate the imagination. Organizational analysis in this revised sense becomes one of cultivating mental agility through thought experiments with metaphors and multiple paradigms of understanding. It is not a process to be used simply for knowledge generation, theory building or knowledge dissemination of what is already known. This only serves to perpetuate the status quo. Instead, it ought to force us to re-evaluate, re-conceptualize and reinterpret what is going on around us. If Chia is correct, his work has important implications for the management of organizations. It suggests that where management can be encouraged to see the value of metaphorization they will be better equipped to deal with the increasingly unpredictable and volatile business world in which they and their organizations must operate.

Part III: Metaphors in organizational settings: Impact and outcomes

It was noted earlier that the application of metaphor to organizational settings has been the focus of a considerable amount of OD-related literature. The first two chapters in this part of the book both assign a role to metaphors in OD, but do so in very different ways.

In Chapter 8 Robert Marshak proposes a meta-theory of organizational change that highlights the symbolic meaning system running through an organization. A key feature of this system is metaphor. For Marshak, the symbolic meaning systems of organizations invariably display key metaphors that operate as if in a 'field'. The idea of a field conveys the pervasiveness of the key metaphor. Such is its power that it will act to define the reality and determine the behaviour of the organization and its members. As such, the 'metaphoric field' that an organization operates in will impact on its ability to innovate and change.

Marshak argues that the problem with metaphoric fields is that they can be very rigid. They not so much prevent an organization from changing, as stop it adopting changes best suited to the situation it finds itself facing. Innovation and change that is inconsistent with the themes and values of the metaphoric field is unacceptable and rejected by the organization. Innovation and change that fits with the field is readily accepted. Using a series of case studies he demonstrates that only when the significance of an organization's symbolic meaning system along with its associated metaphoric field is understood and identified is it possible to implement any innovation or change. This does not necessarily mean that the organization's symbolic meaning system needs to be 'replaced'. It may for instance only require that it is 'recognized' or 'reframed'.

Timothy Clark and Graeme Salaman (Chapter 9) take metaphor into the realms of OD in order to critically assess the relationship between clients and management consultants. An intriguing picture is presented, one where clients have difficulty in determining the quality of consultancy services prior to purchasing them and where consultants must find a way by which to convince clients of their worth. In short, a relationship emerges which, say the authors, is best explained by using the metaphor of the consultant being highly accomplished in 'the art of story telling'! While the metaphor has its humorous side, it also serves to reveal a number of important features underpinning the client–consultant relationship.

If we are to believe Clark and Salaman's assessment, one may ask how are consultants able to set up a relationship which primarily and so obviously suits them as the service provider, rather than the client as the customer? The answer, according to the authors, rests on the ability of consultants to tell 'strong' stories. Such stories have two important attributes. First, they enable the consultant to manage meaning and therefore the reality of what they are doing for the client. Second, they invariably highlight the importance of management work and show it as a heroic and valuable profession – an image that naturally appeals to the management audience at which it is directed.

In Chapter 10 Erik Døving suggests that although organizational "action", "competence" and "learning" have become popular elements of organization theory, they do not transfer to the organizational setting as readily as we might like to believe. Each is a metaphor that projects essentially human properties or abilities onto a non-human entity called "organization". Accordingly, they are what Døving terms 'anthropomorphic' metaphors. He does not deny the influence of these three metaphors, nor that they can be of considerable use in organization science. His concern is that during their application to the organizational setting the metaphors may force irrelevant information upon it, that they may be inappropriate or that they may be redundant. In particular, these problems may result in a situation where, because organizations are inhabited by real humans, anthropomorphic metaphors are easily confused with literal descriptions. Thus, even where such metaphors seem appropriate, we should, according to Døving, by linking the individual and organizational level, give an account of why and how they apply. Moreover, we should develop a way of measuring such constructs. He goes on to propose a theoretical framework that does this in relation to the three anthropomorphic metaphors under discussion. In effect, it is a framework that simultaneously justifies and limits their use.

Chapter 11 serves as a warning about the manipulative way in which metaphors can be used by certain organizations. Heather Höpfl and Julie Maddrell's exploration of evangelical metaphors and their use in organizational settings leads them to argue that they offer a medium through which to inspire 'visions', arouse 'emotions' and transform the behaviour of organizational members. In particular, they examine the performance of organizational leaders whose use of evangelical metaphors enables them to instil commitment among their subordinates. The authors' use of an ethnographic research methodology brings together accounts of individual behaviour and reflections, recollections and observation of the manifest behaviour of the organization under scrutiny. It leads them to suggest that evangelical metaphors are used to foster 'illusions' that appropriate the emotions of organizational members. Ultimately, such appropriation serves the interests of the organization not the individuals concerned.

Part IV: Metaphor and organizations: Issues and directions

In Chapter 12 we use the notion of a journey to explore *where we are now* in terms of research on metaphor and to consider *where we should be going*. It is suggested that much of the past work falls into two distinct categories (or *tracks*), namely the 'organization of metaphors' and the 'metaphors of organization'. We contend that the future value of metaphor will be determined by the extent to which research concentrates upon exploring three main *routes*. First, we highlight the need for well-focused empirical work which uncovers the metaphors-in-use within organizations. Second, the merits of using metaphor as a means of undertaking research, rather than being an end product of research, is evaluated. Finally, we evaluate the research utility of metaphor where it relates to the master tropes (metaphor, metonymy, synecdoche and irony).

As was noted earlier, it is ten years since Gareth Morgan's influential work *Images of Organization* (1986) was first published. It is therefore fitting that he writes the closing chapter to this volume (Chapter 13). His chapter serves two purposes. First, as an afterword, it allows Morgan the chance to review, develop and critique some of the themes and issues raised by the other contributors to the book. Second, it allows him the opportunity to expand the debate about the role and process of metaphor and to suggest those areas where future advances in metaphor-related research will occur. He believes that, in a world where we are placing more and more emphasis on electronic modes of communication and knowledge generation, the influence of metaphor is likely to increase in importance.

Morgan's discussion of these issues sees him presenting a personalized view of the ontological and epistemological status of metaphor and showing that it is in fact highly influential in shaping the terms of inquiry in traditional as well as social science. This creates a challenge which needs to be recognized and embraced by researchers in both fields since it has profound implications for the way in which they go about their present and future work.

To return to our opening lines: Metaphor is here, there and everywhere. It shapes the way we think and the way we see. As such, and as a number of the contributors to this book argue, for the foreseeable future it will play a highly influential role in the shaping of organization theory and analysis. It is therefore vital that we understand exactly how metaphor works and that we appreciate its strengths and weaknesses. Without this knowledge we cannot feel certain of its value as an empirical tool in organization science, nor can we can ever feel confident of knowing when it is appropriate to dispense with its services.

References

Alvesson, M. (1993) 'The play of metaphors', in J. Hassard and M. Parker (eds) (1993) *Postmodernism and Organizations*. London: Sage Publications, pp. 114–131.

Barrett, F.J. and Cooperrider, D.L. (1990) 'Generative metaphor intervention: A new behavioral approach for working with systems divided by conflict and caught in defensive perception', *Journal of Applied Behavioral Science*, 26 (2), 219–239.

Beer, S. (1981) *Brain of the Firm*. Chichester: John Wiley and Sons.

Berger P.L. and Luckmann, T. (1967) *The Social Construction of Reality: A Treatise in the Sociology of Knowledge*. Garden City, NY: Anchor.

Black, M. (1962) *Models and Metaphors*. Ithaca, NY: Cornell University Press.

Black, M. (1993) 'More about metaphors', in A. Ortony (ed.), *Metaphor and Thought* (2nd edn). Chicago: University of Chicago Press, pp. 19–41.

Boulding, K.E. (1987) 'The epistemology of complex systems', *European Journal of Operational Research*, 30, 110–116.

Bourgeois, V.W. and Pinder, C.C. (1983) 'Contrasting philosophical perspectives in administrative science: A reply to Morgan', *Administrative Science Quarterly*, 28 (4) 608–613.

Brink, T.L. (1993) 'Metaphor as data in the study of organizations', *Journal of Management Inquiry*, 2, 366–371.

Broussine, M. and Vince, R. (1996) 'Working with metaphor towards organizational change', in C. Oswick and D. Grant (eds), *Organization Development: Metaphorical Explorations*. London: Pitman Publishing, pp. 557–572.

Brown, R.H. (1977) *A Poetic for Sociology: Toward a Logic of Discovery for the Human Sciences*. Cambridge: Cambridge University Press.

Brown, S.J. (1927) *The World of Imagery*. London: Kegan Paul, Trench, Trubner.

Bunge, M. (1973) *Method, Model and Matter*. Dordrecht: Reidel.

Burns, T. and Stalker, G.M. (1961) *The Management of Innovation*. London: Tavistock.

Dunn, S. (1990) 'Root metaphor in the old and new industrial relations', *British Journal of Industrial Relations*, 28, 1–31.

Etzioni, A. (1960) 'Two approaches to organizational analysis: A critique and suggestion', *Administrative Science Quarterly*, 5 (1), 257–278.

Fayol, H. (1949) *General and Industrial Management*. London: Pitman Publishing.

Fraser, B. (1993) 'The interpretation of novel metaphors', in A. Ortony (ed.), *Metaphor and Thought* (2nd edn). Chicago: University of Chicago Press, pp. 329–341.

Gentner, D. (1983) 'Structure mapping: A theoretical framework for analogy', *Cognitive Science*, 7, 155–170.

Gentner, D. (1989) 'The mechanisms of analogical learning', in S. Vasniadou and A. Ortony (eds), *Similarity and Analogical Reasoning*. New York: Cambridge University Press, pp. 199–241.

Georgiou, P. (1973) 'The goal paradigm and notes towards a counter paradigm', *Administrative Science Quarterly*, 18 (2), 291–303.

Gibbs, R.W. Jr (1993) 'Process and products in making sense of tropes', in A. Ortony (ed.), *Metaphor and Thought* (2nd edn). Chicago: University of Chicago Press, pp. 252–276.

Gouldner, A.W. (1973) 'Reciprocity and autonomy in functional theory', in A.W. Gouldner (ed.), *For Sociology*. Harmondsworth: Penguin, pp. 190–225.

Grant, D. (1996) 'Metaphors, human resource management and control', in C. Oswick and D. Grant (eds), *Organization Development: Metaphorical Explorations*. London: Pitman Publishing, pp. 193–208.

Inns, D. (1996) 'Organization development as a journey', in C. Oswick and D. Grant (eds), *Organization Development: Metaphorical Explorations*. London: Pitman Publishing, pp. 20–34.

Johnson, M. (1981) *Philosophical Perspectives on Metaphor*. Minneapolis, MN: University of Minnesota Press.

Lakoff, G. (1987) *Women, Fire and Dangerous Things: What Categories Reveal about the Mind*. Chicago: University of Chicago Press.

Lakoff, G. and Johnson, M. (1980) *Metaphors We Live By*. Chicago: University of Chicago Press.

Lakoff, G. and Turner, M. (1989) *More than Cool Reason: A Field Guide to Poetic Metaphor*. Chicago: University of Chicago Press.

Lawrence, P.R. and Lorsch, J.W. (1967) *Organization and Environment: Managing Differentiation and Integration*. Boston: Harvard University Press.

Mangham, I.L. (1994) 'Management, metaphors and reality'. Plenary Address to conference titled 'Metaphors in Organizational Theory and Behaviour', held at the Management Centre, King's College, University of London, 28–30 July.

Manning, P. (1979) 'Metaphors of the field: Varieties of organizational discourse', *Administrative Science Quarterly*, 24, 660–671.

Marshak, R.J. (1993) 'Managing the metaphors of change', *Organizational Dynamics*, 22 (1), 44–56.

Morgan, G. (1980) 'Paradigms, metaphors, and puzzle solving in organization theory', *Administrative Science Quarterly*, 25 (4), 605–622.

Morgan, G. (1981) 'The schismatic metaphor and its implications for organizational analysis', *Organization Studies*, 2 (1), 23–44.

Morgan, G. (1983) 'More on metaphor: Why we cannot control tropes in administrative science', *Administrative Science Quarterly*, 28 (4), 601–607.

Morgan, G. (1986) *Images of Organization*. Beverly Hills, CA: Sage Publications.

Morgan, G. (1989) *Creative Organization Theory*. Newbury Park, CA: Sage Publications.

Morgan , G. (1993) *Imaginization: The Art of Creative Management*. London: Sage Publications.

Morgan, G. and Ramirez, R. (1984) 'Action learning: A holographic metaphor for guiding social change', *Human Relations*, 37: 1–28.

Ortony, A. (1975) 'Why metaphors are necessary and not just nice', *Educational Theory*, 25, 45–53.

Ortony, A. (1993) *Metaphor and Thought* (2nd edn). Cambridge: Cambridge University Press.

Oswick, C. (1996) 'Insights into diagnosis: An exploration using visual metaphors', in C. Oswick and D. Grant (eds), *Organization Development: Metaphorical Explorations*. London: Pitman Publishing, pp. 136–153.

Oswick, C. and Grant, D. (eds) (1996) *Organization Development: Metaphorical Explorations*. London: Pitman Publishing.

Palmer, I. and Dunford, R. (1996) 'Understanding organizations through metaphor', in C. Oswick and D. Grant (eds), *Organization Development: Metaphorical Explorations*. London: Pitman Publishing, pp. 7–19.

Parsons, T. (1951) *The Social System*. Glencoe, IL: Free Press.

Parsons, T. (1956) 'Suggestions for a sociological approach to the theory of organizations', *Administrative Science Quarterly*, Part 1: 63–85, Part 2: 225–239.

Petrie, H.G. and Oshlag, R.S. (1993) 'Metaphor and learning', in A. Ortony (ed.), *Metaphor and Thought* (2nd edn). Chicago: University of Chicago Press, pp. 610–620.

Pinder, C.C. and Bourgeois, V.W. (1982) 'Controlling tropes in administrative science', *Administrative Science Quarterly*, 27 (4), 641–652.

Popper, K. (1958) *The Logic of Scientific Inquiry*. London: Hutchinson.

Roethlisberger, F.J. and Dickson, W.J. (1939) *Management and the Worker*. Cambridge, MA: Harvard University Press.

Sackmann, S. (1989) 'The role of metaphors in organization transformation', *Human Relations* 42 (6), 463–485.

Schön, D. (1993) 'Generative metaphor: A perspective on problem setting in social policy', in A. Ortony (ed.), *Metaphor and Thought* (2nd edn). Cambridge: Cambridge University Press, pp. 135–161.

Spencer, H. (1873) *The Study of Sociology*. London: Kegan Paul and Tench.

Srivastva, S. and Barrett, F. (1988) 'The transforming nature of metaphors in group development: A study in group theory', *Human Relations* 41 (1), 31–64.

Sternberg, R.J., Tourangeau, R. and Nigro, G. (1993) 'Metaphor, induction and social policy: The convergence of macroscopic and microscopic views', in A. Ortony (ed.), *Metaphor and Thought* (2nd edn). Chicago: University of Chicago Press, pp. 277–305.

Taylor F.W. (1911) *The Principles of Scientific Management*. New York: Harper.

Thompson, J.D. (1967) *Organizations in Action*. New York: McGraw-Hill.

Tinker, T. (1986) 'Metaphor or reification: Are radical humanists really libertarian anarchists?', *Journal of Management Studies*, 23, 363–384.

Trist, E.L. and Bamforth, K.W. (1951) 'Some social and psychological consequences of the longwall method of coal getting', *Human Relations*, 4, 3–38.

Tsoukas, H. (1991) 'The missing link: A transformational view of metaphors in organizational science', *Academy of Management Review*, 16 (3), 566–585.

Tsoukas, H. (1993) 'Analogical reasoning and knowledge generation in organization theory', *Organization Studies*, 14 (3), 323–346.

Warner-Burke, W. (1992) 'Metaphors to consult by', *Group and Organization Management*, 17 (3), 255–259.

Weber, M. (1946) *From Max Weber: Essays in Sociology* (ed. by H. Gerth and C.W. Mills). New York: Oxford University Press.
Weick, K.E. (1979) *The Social Psychology of Organizing* (2nd edn). Reading, MA: Addison-Wesley.
White, H. (1978) *The Tropics of Discourse*. Baltimore: Johns Hopkins University Press.

PART I

METAPHORS OF ORGANIZATION: SCOPE AND APPLICATION

1

Some Consequences of Taking Gareth Morgan Seriously

Iain L. Mangham

Metaphor is an aspect of our lives so ordinary that we use it every day automatically and unconsciously and with so little effort that we rarely find occasion to remark upon it. Whatever our pedigree or education, our waking thoughts and, possibly, our sleeping ones are shaped by metaphor. As we grow up in our families and communities, we acquire a command of basic, everyday metaphor which we deploy throughout the rest of our lives. It is not – most decidedly not – merely a matter of words. Aristotle had it wrong when he claimed that metaphor was a matter of having 'an eye for resemblances'. Some thousands of years later, the *Oxford English Dictionary* has it wrong when it claims that metaphor is: 'The figure of speech in which a name or descriptive term is transferred to some object different from, but analogous to, that to which it is properly applicable.' Metaphor, far from being simply a poetic device or merely a matter of names and descriptive terms, is, above all else, a mode of thought.

This aspect of metaphor was clearly recognized in Gareth Morgan's influential text *Images of Organization*, which was published in 1986. In it, he notes that: 'Metaphor is often just regarded as a device for embellishing discourse, but its significance is much greater than this. For the use of metaphor implies *a way of thinking* and *a way of seeing* that pervade how we understand our world generally' (1986: 12). Recently, he repeated his comments: 'metaphor is not just a literary or linguistic device for embellishing or decorating discourse. It's a primal means through which we forge our relationships with the world' (Morgan, 1993: 227). Unfortunately, Morgan has not taken his own assertions as seriously as he might have done. His comments upon metaphor as a mode of thought are sparse and have been largely restricted to passages in which he urges the coining of 'fresh metaphors'. At times he appears to believe that there are no limits to the creation and deployment of metaphors (1993: 283), but elsewhere he appears to recognize that some do not 'resonate', 'hit a chord' or 'ring true' (1993: 290). He does not explore how the creation of metaphors is or is not linked to ways of thinking. He has done a great deal to bring the attention of students and practitioners to the kind of figurative language that they have become accustomed to in describing and working in organizations, but he has done little to explore the *primal* means by which we forge our relationships with the world.

This chapter seeks to boldly go where Morgan has not trod, or has, at best, trod somewhat gingerly. I will seek to show that there are a limited number of basic metaphors that structure our thought. I will indicate what one or two of these are; discuss their properties; illustrate them by reference to Morgan's own work; show by reference to his work and the work of people such as Peter Vaill and Karl Weick how they are extended, elaborated, questioned and formed into composite metaphors; comment upon idiosyncratic metaphors; and, finally, indicate why Morgan's claim that there are no limits to metaphor needs to be qualified.

Recently, I passed some comments upon the nature of scholarship in organization studies (Mangham, 1994). My contention was that many of us writing in this area display little more than the most nodding of acquaintances with the disciplines from which we derive many of our ideas. It is important, therefore, that I declare the nature of my own nodding acquaintance with the research and scholarship that has focused upon metaphor in the last twenty or so years. I have followed much of it since my initial interest was aroused in writing one of my earlier books where I introduced the notion of organizations as texts and the idea of managers learning to 'read' them (Mangham, 1978). About ten years ago, Michael Overington and I wrote extensively about the use of a particular metaphor – organizations as theatre – in another book and a number of articles (Mangham and Overington, 1983a, 1983b, 1987). Some five years ago, together with Annie Pye, I completed another book, which among other things took up once more the theme of managers 'reading' and 'wrighting' (as in play*wright*, ship*wright* – one who shapes) their enterprises (Mangham and Pye, 1991). The present chapter is informed by discussions that I have enjoyed with my colleagues over the years, by some of the articles which have discussed metaphors over the past few years (Barrett and Cooperrider, 1990; Clancy, 1989; Deetz and Mumby, 1985; Sackmann, 1989; Sapienza, 1987; Srivastva and Barrett, 1988), but, more particularly, by the writings of cognitive philosophers, cognitive linguists and cognitive semanticists. My primary source for this chapter is the work of George Lakoff and Mark Johnson.

Somewhat unusually, their pioneering and stimulating text *Metaphors We Live By* (Lakoff and Johnson, 1980), written some fifteen or so years ago, proved to be as good as its blurb promised: 'An arresting book [that] will make you think in a whole new way, about the language we use.' More recently, this text has been followed up by a number of others (Johnson, 1981, 1987, 1993; Lakoff, 1987, 1993; Lakoff and Turner, 1989). It is this body of work to which I wish to draw attention in what I have to say here. I have nothing original to say about the nature of metaphor; such originality as there is in this chapter lies in the application of the ideas of cognitive philosophers, semanticists and linguists to the area of organizations and organization theory.

My starting point is Lakoff's article on the contemporary theory of metaphor, in which he dismisses the so-called classical theory whereby metaphor is defined as a novel or poetic linguistic expression and proposes that the locus of metaphor is not in language at all, but 'in the way we conceptualize one mental domain in terms of another' (1993: 203). In effect, he turns research into metaphor on its head; instead of starting with the notion of literary or poetic metaphor, he argues that what he terms 'cross-domain mapping' is central to ordinary language out of which literary metaphor emerges. Everyday metaphor, he argues, is *basic* and is characterized by 'a huge system of thousands of cross-domain mappings, and this system is made use of in novel metaphor' (1993: 203). Lakoff repeatedly notes that the big difference between contemporary theory of metaphor and the views of metaphor that were identified some years ago is that 'a huge system of everyday, conventional, conceptual metaphors has been discovered. It is a system of metaphor that structures our everyday conceptual system, including most abstract concepts, and that lies behind much of everyday language' (1993: 204). As common as novel metaphor is, its occurrence is rare by comparison with conventional metaphor, which is present in many of the sentences that we utter when we talk about organization.

Morgan and metaphors

As I indicated earlier, I propose to illustrate the points I wish to make by reference to Gareth Morgan's writings. In what follows, I will begin by identifying some of the linguistic expressions that Morgan uses when he is not writing specifically about metaphor, and will then focus upon what I take to be his unconscious and automatic use of a couple of basic, everyday, conventional, conceptual metaphors. My examples are derived largely from *Riding the Waves of Change: Developing Managerial Competencies for a Turbulent World* (Morgan, 1988), which appeared a couple of years after his pioneering text on the nature of metaphor in organization theory. *Riding the Waves* is a text bursting with metaphorical expressions. In the first ten pages or so, Morgan offers the notion of *forces* shaping the world economy, of managing through the *rear-view mirror*, he talks of *eras making demands*, of environmental *turbulence*, of *sleeping giants*, of change and uncertainty *calling* for new abilities, of competence going *hand in hand* with abilities, of managers dealing with a wide range of forces *within and outside* their organizations, of management *challenges*, of new *waves* coming, of managers learning to *ride* or moderate these waves, of *fracture-lines*, of *synthesizing insights*, of the managerial turbulence *that lies ahead*, of managers *launching* initiatives, of *helicoptering*, of managing through the *umbilical cord*, of *refining* products, of *flatter* organization *structures*, of *stakeholders*, of *actors* and *performance*, of problems being *rooted* in socio-economic contexts, of *levels* of *growth*, of industrial relations *climates*, of *bridge building*, of *reframing*, of *blending* abilities, of *building* mindsets, of *generating* capacity, of *step by step* guidance, of *flux*, of *revolutions*, of a *wealth* of insight, of *polarization*, of *cutting edges* and managers *sharpening* their influence, of *attack* and *defence*, of *antennae* and *good noses*, of *drives towards* the future, of *new avenues* for development, of *navigation*, of *tensions*, *games* and *positions*, of *trials* and *balance*, of taking things *on board*, of *reaping* rewards, of *life-cycles*, of *evolution*, of big *pictures*, of *impacts*, of *recipes*, *umbrellas*, *interests*, *networks*, of *backfires*, of *going with the flow* . . .

Even though *Riding the Waves* does not explicitly discuss figures of speech or modes of thought, it is reasonable to assume that Gareth Morgan knows his metaphor from his elbow. For the most part, he does. When he is aware of a metaphor he often signals it to us by placing it in self-conscious quotation marks: "bridge building", "adding value", "good nose", "fractures", "helicoptering", "managing through the umbilical cord". In other instances, although he neglects the quotation marks, he probably knows that he is deploying metaphorical expressions: stakeholders, waves, cutting edges, framing and reframing. In a handful of cases, however, it is possible that he is utilizing conceptual metaphors in an automatic and unreflecting manner. When he wrote of growth and development and of life-cycles, he probably did not stop to reflect that in so doing he was considering organizations as forms of life. It may be that when he set down the words and phrases referring to drives, to avenues, to roadblocks, to directions and ends, he did not stop to consider that these were expressions of a basic, everyday, conventional, conceptual metaphor: purposes are destinations, which, in turn, is clearly related to the equally basic, everyday, conventional, conceptual metaphor that maps the movement of organizations and individuals on to the notion of life as a journey. When he noted that managers must cope with events within and outside their organizations, he may not have been aware that he was relying upon another basic, everyday, conventional, conceptual metaphor: that in which categories are taken to be containers. Equally, when he wrote of wealth, of interests and rewards, he may have simply assumed the familiarity that we all have with the basic, everyday, conventional, conceptual metaphor that causation is a commercial transaction, whereby we see our physical and social interactions in terms of exchange, debt, credit, profit, and so on.

Everyday experience, everyday phrases, everyday metaphors

Cognitive linguists claim that the terms and concepts that we use acquire their meaning relative to the larger frames or schemata that we develop to understand the kinds of situations that we encounter (Fillmore, 1985). Linguists and psychologists claim that our conceptual system is, for the most part, structured by systematic metaphorical mappings (Gibbs, 1990). In general, the argument is that we understand more abstract and less well-structured domains (such as action in complex organizations) via mappings from more concrete and highly structured domains of experience (such as our bodily experience of vision, movement, the manipulation of objects, and so on). The latter domains are not normally understood metaphorically at all. Things that we think of as being straightforwardly physical – machines, organisms, bodies, the ground, the stars, the moon, and so on – fall into this category, as do things like journeys, departures, destinations, burdens, obstacles, plays, games, and so on. Lakoff and Turner argue that we conventionally understand these by virtue of 'their grounding in what we take to be our forms of life, our habitual and routine bodily and social experiences' (1989: 59). Concepts that apply to these *basic* levels of experience are, the argument runs, those which are most likely to achieve priority in the way we organize and structure our conceptual system (Johnson, 1987: 22). A closer look at *Riding the Waves* will provide an illustration of the operation of a basic metaphor:

> There is an old adage that if you don't know where you are going, any old path will get you there. An innovation can be wonderful. But it can have absolutely nothing to do with where my firm is going. (1988: 47)

> The world is such a changeable place that you need to have a well-articulated long term sense of where you are going, which gives you the base, the confidence, to take on whatever adaptability issues come along without losing your sense of direction. (1988: 46)

Morgan offers these quotes from managers in a chapter called 'Sharing the Vision', and reinforces them in his own words: 'Sustaining this overarching sense of corporate direction was seen as one of the most important tasks'; 'Yet to develop in a coherent and ordered way, they need a clear sense of where they are going . . .'; 'When people have a good sense of what their organization stands for and where it is going, they can determine the course and appropriateness of their behaviour.' Phrases such as 'they can arrive at a situation', 'it is important that the leader . . . move his or her followers toward . . .', 'methods must be found to nudge the organization in the right direction . . .', 'participants often hit major roadblocks that can easily overwhelm . . . the group', recur throughout the book, confirming the reliance upon the life is a journey metaphor. In Morgan's case we can see that organization is personified and thus imbued with life and, since life is often thought of in terms of movement and direction, organization comes to be thought of as a matter of having life and direction (1988: 47–50, 189).

It is a basic, everyday, conventional, conceptual metaphor which relies upon a number of correspondences between the two conceptual domains of life and journeys. The person leading a life is a traveller. His/her purposes are destinations. The means for achieving purposes are routes, avenues, paths. The choices in life are cross-roads. Progress is the distance travelled. Difficulties in life are obstacles to travel (Lakoff and Turner, 1989: 4). Morgan relies upon it when, by implication, he personifies the organization and/or its members as travellers seeking direction and moving forward together.

He also calls upon a related metaphor: purposes are destinations. 'It is absolutely crucial to have a good understanding ... of why you are in business and what you are doing' and 'You need a sense of corporate purpose' (1988: 46) are two illustrations of recourse to this metaphor. There are several more. Again a commonplace metaphor, one which we tend to use automatically and without reflection. It is, of course, very closely related to the life is a journey metaphor. When we think of life as purposeful we think of it as having destinations and paths towards these destinations, which makes life a journey; a kind of pilgrim's progress. We talk of ourselves and others as having had "a good start to life"; we speak of successful people as "having a good sense of where they are going" and of the less successful "having little sense of direction", as "having taken the wrong turning" and, occasionally, as having "reached a dead end".

Sticking with the notion of the organization metaphorically involved in a journey, we need to understand Lakoff's point that such a metaphor involves understanding one domain of experience – life in organizations/the organization as a living entity – in terms of a very different domain of experience – journeys. Technically, 'the metaphor can be understood as a mapping (in the mathematical sense) from a source domain (in this case, journeys) to a target domain' (in this case organizations). The mapping is tightly structured. Lakoff argues that there are ontological correspondences, according to which, in this case, elements of the domain of organization (e.g. the organization, its purposes, the difficulties in realizing them, etc.) correspond systematically to entities in the domain of a journey (the travellers, destinations, obstacles, etc.). These correspondences permit us to reason about organizations using the knowledge we use to reason about journeys (Lakoff, 1993: 206).

Basic, everyday, conventional, conceptual metaphor depends upon conventional knowledge. In order to understand, say, organizational purposes in terms of destinations, we must have appropriate knowledge of journeys and journeying. Lakoff and Turner remind us that one of the reasons that the notion of life (or in our case organization) as a journey is powerful is that it makes use of common and general knowledge of journeys (1989: 61). When someone talks of journeys we assume starting points and finishing points, diversions and side-tracks, the need, on occasion, to retrace our steps, and so on. It is important to recognize that basic metaphors such as this have a skeletal structure rich enough to distinguish them from other kinds of activities, but not so rich as to rule out variety. Accordingly, Lakoff and Turner argue that to the extent that we view life as purposeful, those purposes are viewed as destinations, and we act accordingly by setting out to reach them, deciding which road to take, surmounting obstacles or going round them, taking advice from the natives or from other travellers, and so on. The metaphor is derived from everyday experience (1989: 60). Lakoff notes that to achieve most of our everyday purposes 'we either have to move to some destination or acquire some object. . . . The correspondence between achieving purposes and either reaching destinations or acquiring objects is so utterly common in our everyday existence that the resulting metaphor is completely natural' (1993: 240). Every day we regularly achieve our purposes by going to a certain location, we regularly experience the source and the target domains together.

Basic metaphors may not only be grounded in recurrent direct experience, they may also be communicated to us by our culture. The notion of life as a play, for example, may be widely used despite the fact that many of those making use of it have never attended a theatrical performance. It is a very productive everyday, conventional, conceptual metaphor which includes actors, scenes, settings, props, scripts, cues, costume, playwrights, prompts, casting, roles, parts, rehearsals, and so on. We all make use of it when we talk about playing our roles, about making a scene, dressing for the part, playing to the gallery, turning in a good performance, or whatever. Similarly when we talk of organizations in terms of machinery or life forms, the expressions we use are partly the product of our direct experience and partly the product of our culture.

It is important to bear in mind that metaphor is not simply a matter of what is said. What constitutes the organization as a journey metaphor is not any particular word or expression, although words and expressions allow us to infer its presence. It is a prerequisite to any discussion of metaphor that we make a distinction between basic conceptual metaphors which are cognitive and particular linguistic expressions of these basic, everyday, conventional, conceptual metaphors. Lakoff reminds us that if metaphors were merely linguistic expressions, we would expect different linguistic expressions to be different metaphors (1993: 209). Thus, "hitting major roadblocks" would constitute one metaphor and "nudging the organization in the right direction" would constitute another. But we have already identified one overarching metaphor – where the organization personified is conceived as being on a journey. Morgan's reference to driving by looking through the windshield rather than by looking through the rear-view mirror, idiosyncratic though it may be, can also be seen to be part of this journeying metaphor (1988: 158). It is this unified way of conceptualizing organization that is realized in several different linguistic expressions. Lakoff argues that it is the ontological mapping across conceptual domains that is key. A metaphor, he claims, is not 'just a matter of language, but of thought and reason' (1993: 208). Indeed, he asserts that the language is secondary. The mapping sanctions the use of source domain language and inference patterns

for target domain concepts. In effect the source domain creates structure in
the target domain. For example, the development of organization need not be
viewed as a journey. There is no reason why organizations should be viewed
as having a destination, as following paths or routes, experiencing obstacles
or roadblocks. That particular structuring of our understanding of them
comes from the structure of our knowledge of and experience of journeys.
When we reason about organizations in terms of direction, destinations,
cross-roads, diversions, and so on, we are importing a pattern of inference
from the domain of journeys to the domain of organizations. For example,
when Morgan writes of the organization hitting major roadblocks we can
infer, because of our experience of journeys, that unless it finds a way
around the obstacle it will not reach its destination. As Lakoff and Turner
put it: 'much of our reasoning . . . involves inferences of this sort' (1989:
62). The power to reason about so abstract a notion as organization, for
example, comes largely through metaphor.

Once we have learned the skeletal form of a basic, everyday, conventional, conceptual metaphor, we do not have to learn it again each time that
we use it. As the adjectives insist, it is *conventionalized* and *everyday*
and, as such, it is used automatically and effortlessly. And that, Lakoff and
Turner argue, is part of the power of such metaphors: that they are alive
and are used constantly and unconsciously. 'Anything that we rely on
constantly, unconsciously, and automatically is so much part of us that it
cannot be easily resisted, in large measure because it is barely even noticed'
(1989: 63). To stick with the idea of organizations being purposeful and
being involved in journeys, many of us use it ourselves. In so doing we
accept its validity. When someone like Morgan uses it, therefore, we are not
inclined to notice it, leave alone question it.

Basic, everyday, conventionalized, conceptual metaphors can therefore be
seen to have persuasive power over us. Their power derives from a number
of sources. One is the power of being there: The existence and avail-
ability of a basic, everyday, conventionalized, conceptual metaphor makes it
difficult to question it even if we notice it. The idea that an organization is
something imbued with life and has purposes as an individual has purposes
is another metaphor that is rarely questioned. A further source of power is
the power of evaluation: We not only import structure from the source
domain, we also import the way we evaluate. For example, when one of
Morgan's executives argues that 'You have to be ready to move very
quickly . . . If you can get to the point where you are ahead . . .', he is clearly
against standing still, he is viewing lack of speed as a lack of sufficient
progress rather than, for instance, keeping in mind the story of the tortoise
and the hare. Finally, there is the power that basic metaphors have to
structure: if, for example, organizations are reified and conceived of as
machines, then those who work in them can be seen as mechanisms, as parts
in need of repair, refurbishment or replacement. If they are conceived of as
having life, as organisms, then it becomes natural to think of life-cycles, of

maturity, of organizational death, and so on. If they are seen as being engaged upon a journey, then it is natural to talk of routes, paths, difficult terrain, fresh water, friendly natives, or whatever.

The parameters of metaphor

Lakoff and Turner remind us that it is important to avoid crude dichotomies when we talk about metaphor, but then go on to offer three parameters along which metaphors differ. I have indicated one of them above: the distinction between conceptual metaphors and linguistic expression. The second parameter is conventionalization, which applies at both the conceptual and the linguistic levels. At the conceptual level, a metaphor such as an organization is going somewhere, is engaged or needs to have purpose/destination is conventional to the extent that it is automatic, effortless and generally "established among members of a linguistic community". Such a metaphor is likely to be deeply conventionalized by many of us writing about and working within organizations. Similarly the metaphor that organizations are forms of life, with its related entailments of evolution and adaptation, is likely to be deeply conventionalized for most of us. The metaphor which holds that organization is a psychic prison, on the other hand, may be deeply conventionalized for a particular sub-community of us, but, as is noted by Døving in Chapter 10, it is certainly not conventionalized across the community of those of us engaged in organization studies and is probably rarely referred to in the everyday conversations of those of us working within organizations.

The third parameter along which metaphors may differ is what Lakoff and Turner refer to as basicness: 'The basicness of a metaphor is its conceptual indispensability' (1989: 56). Basic, everyday, conventional, conceptual metaphors differ in their degree of cognitive indispensability. Of the range that Gareth Morgan offers – wittingly and unwittingly – we cannot really dispense with the idea that organizations have purposes and that purposes are destinations. Imagine purging all organization and management texts of reference to goals that we aim for and struggle to reach, of directions, of missions, of cross-roads and junctions, of obstacles and blockages that we have to get round. Likewise, it would be difficult to dispense with the notion that organizations are adaptive organisms or are mechanisms. The thoughts that organizations are games, are political, are plays, similarly appear to be indispensable parts of our ways of seeing and being in the world; dispensing with them could alter our ways of construing events and our behaviour. Organizations that are psychic prisons or are brains, on the other hand, may not yet have achieved the status of cognitive indispensability. Metaphors, therefore, range from those that it is virtually unthinkable for anyone to dispense with to those where the majority of lives would not differ a jot if we did not happen to have this metaphor.

Ringing true, hitting chords and resonating

Any discussion of metaphor must take place on two levels: the conceptual level and the linguistic level. Let me offer another passage from Morgan to ground the discussion:

> Managers and organizations are confronting wave upon wave of change in the form of new technologies, markets, forms of competition, social relations, forms of organization and management, ideas and beliefs, and so on. Wherever one looks, one sees a new wave coming. And it is vitally important that managers accept this as a fundamental aspect of their reality, rise to the challenge, and learn to ride or moderate these waves with accomplishment. (1988: xii)

Ignoring the competing metaphorical expressions and the issue of whether or not one can moderate a natural phenomenon such as a wave, we can see in this passage the notion that the manager should take advantage of the wave to travel in the appropriate direction. There is nothing idiosyncratic about the conceptual metaphor; purposes are destinations and organizational life is a journey, but, arguably, Morgan is offering a somewhat novel or idiosyncratic expression of it. In a similar manner, as I have indicated, where he talks about driving by looking through a rear-view mirror, he is also offering an idiosyncratic expression of the same basic, everyday, conventional, conceptual metaphor.

In Morgan's other books, particularly in *Images of Organization* and *Imaginization*, he attempts to create not only new expressions of a particular metaphor, but 'new ways of thinking about organizations'. A novel conceptual metaphor cannot by its very nature be deeply conventionalized in our thought and its expression will, therefore, be necessarily idiosyncratic. Thus when Morgan writes of organizations as psychic prisons, his thoughts are necessarily as idiosyncratic as his expressions. I will return to this particular metaphor shortly; for the moment it is important to remember that idiosyncrasy of linguistic expression may or may not express idiosyncrasy of thought, 'but idiosyncratic thought always requires idiosyncratic language' (Lakoff and Turner, 1989: 50).

There can be no doubt that new ways of thinking and talking about organizations can be created. At both the conceptual level and the expressive one, resources exist to construct a variety of metaphorical concepts and ways of expressing such concepts in language. As Morgan seeks to demonstrate in *Imaginization*, given a well-structured concept, an inventive person or group can find a way to understand another concept – such as organization – by using it. For example, the managers cited in Morgan's text find ways of making sense of organization as a yogurt and organization as a spider plant. That is, they understand the concept of organization in terms of what they know about yogurts and spider plants. There are important differences, however, between such idiosyncratic conceptualizations and the basic metaphors that I have been discussing here which, for example, Morgan uses automatically and unwittingly in discussing spider plants and yogurts. In his discussion of the metaphor of the spider plant, he comments: 'With a shared understanding of the vision and *direction* in which the overall system is trying to *move*, the various parties can self-organize their activities autonomously, yet in an integrated way. They know when they are working within agreed upon parameters. They know when they are *stepping outside'* (Morgan, 1993: 77; my italics). In his discussion of organization as a yogurt, he and his managers are soon into talking in terms of *culture* (in the sense that organisms are cultures), into notions such as *maturity*, triggering notions of life-cycles, into ideas such as *adaptability*. It is true that basic, everyday, conventionalized, conceptual metaphors, such as that italicized above, are part of the common conceptual appreciation shared by members of a culture. However, notions of organizations as yogurts or spider plants are not. Lakoff and Turner remind us that there is a fixed correspondence between the structure of the domain to be understood (in this case organization) and the structure in the domain in terms of which we are understanding it (journeys). Basic, everyday, conceptual metaphors operate automatically, are understood in terms of common experiences and are widely conventionalized in our language; there are a 'great number of words and idiomatic expressions in our language whose interpretations depend upon those conceptual metaphors' (Lakoff, 1993: 230). There are, on the other hand, no words or idiomatic expressions in our language whose meanings depend upon a conceptual connection between organizations and spider plants or between organizations and yogurt. Such metaphors do not ring true, do not hit chords, nor do they resonate, since they are not widely conventionalized in everyday expression. Indeed, as I have indicated, they rely on other metaphors for their elaboration and development.

The titles of Morgan's books give a clue to what he is about: *Images* of Organization and *Imag*inization. The layout of the latter, with its jokey titles and childlike sketches and drawings, confirms that Morgan is not mapping concepts on to other concepts. What he is dealing with are more fleeting metaphors which involve the mapping of images. The pages concerned with designing our organization as a spider plant literally map pictures of spider plants on to pictures of organizations and talk about managers being in pots, about stems leading, linking them to projects, about offshoots and cutting them off. Here the relevant domains are a matter of mental images. Morgan superimposes the image of a spider plant onto the image of a decentralized organization (he writes the words in, lest we miss the point). This is so graphic and so specific that one can see immediately that it is not a case of a basic, everyday, conventional, conceptual metaphor being used. It will not be used unconsciously and automatically over and over again in reasoning about lives, even, I suspect, about the lives of the managers who invent it. It is a "one-shot" image.

Where Morgan goes beyond images and seeks to develop novel metaphors, he runs into difficulty. When he writes of organizations as machines or organisms, he is drawing attention to metaphors which we normally utilize in an automatic and unconscious manner; metaphors that are, to a large extent, basic and conventionalized. When, however, he writes of organizations as psychic prisons, he fails to strike a chord because our experience of the domain of psychic prisons is limited (Morgan, 1986: 15). To be sure, one can appreciate the connection when it is pointed out, but both the expression of the metaphor and the basis of it are idiosyncratic. As a consequence, metaphors such as this are presently used in a deliberate and very self-conscious manner. Whatever insights and new perspectives they develop will only structure the way we think with our express permission; they are not automatic or conventionalized. Unlike his recourse to the spider plant or the yogurt, they may, of course, become so. The idea of organization as a psychic prison manifests a richness of knowledge and inference that allows for considerable development. Even though it may presently fail to resonate with the everyday experience of a large number of people, it may still enter our vocabulary through our culture. To the extent that we readily talk about repression, denial, rationalization, sublimation, and the like, the process may be well underway.

Extending, elaborating, questioning and combining

Lakoff's position is that though there are a large number of potential conceptual metaphors, only a very few of these ever achieve the status of basic metaphors. This is similar to Morgan's argument that 'many of our conventional ideas about organization and management build on a small number of taken-for-granted images, especially mechanical and biological ones' (1986: 12). Both writers seem to accept that a relatively small number of basic, everyday, conventional, conceptual metaphors can be combined and expressed in a wide variety of linguistic expressions. Lakoff et al., however, appear to believe that new metaphors arise from old ones, whereas Morgan appears to hold that we can conjure them out of the air.

One mode of building upon a basic metaphor is to extend it. Morgan does this when he takes the organization to be a traveller on a journey and offers the idea that the journey is undertaken on a wave. This allows him to talk of turbulence and provides the image of a somewhat hazardous journey. He could have extended the metaphor further by talking of rocks and wrecks, currents, undercurrents, eddies and tides. Peter Vaill picks up a related theme when he talks of 'the metaphor of permanent white water'. He likes the metaphor because it has strong visual appeal. It 'vividly conveys a sense of energy and movement. Things are only very partially under control, yet the effective navigator of the rapids is not behaving randomly or aimlessly' (1989: 2). In both cases the authors manage to tap into the basic conceptual metaphor of journeying whilst signalling that journeys have become much more hazardous than they used to be.

Both authors indicate by their idiosyncratic expression of the basic, everyday, conventional, conceptual metaphor that it may be in need of considerable extension and elaboration. Morgan talks a great deal of the turbulence produced by wave upon wave of change and about the need to be able to ride it: 'To ride the waves of change impacting one's organization one must do more than react. One must anticipate change and position oneself to deal with opportunities and challenges so that one can ride at the crest of new developments' (1988: 28). He struggles with the notion of direction, however, with the image of the manager riding the waves, but 'knowing where their organization is going', and is concerned that having too clear a sense of direction can prejudice the journey (1988: 48). Peter Vaill is clearer about the problem: 'some of our more cherished ideas are not good maps for the courses of action that executives are trying to follow. . . . We have to question some of the maps that we have' (1989: 4). Both of the authors, by their use of linguistic expressions, raise interesting issues about the nature of journeys that contemporary organizations are undertaking, but both tap into that basic metaphor in their talk of direction, obstacles, maps, destinations, and the like. Even those who would deny the idea of purpose and destination recognize its basicness in the need to deny it. Both Vaill and Morgan extend it by their talk of turbulence, forces, being out of control, and so on. The images they promote appear to indicate that, whatever its desirability, navigation may well be impossible in the conditions presently faced by organizations. 'In the world of permanent white water, inspiration is battered and negated by the turbulence and change' (Vaill, 1989: 27). Given their interest in the education or guidance of managers (their role as ocean pilots, as it were), they are both reluctant to conclude that the possibilities of steering a course in any specific direction in conditions of turbulence are somewhat slight. Their linguistic extension and elaboration of the basic, everyday, conventional, conceptual metaphor, however, clearly invites such thoughts and reflections and may, eventually, become part of its conventional language.

Morgan and Vaill appear reluctant to question the boundaries of our everyday metaphorical understandings of important concepts. Karl Weick, whose work is characterized by a poet's skill in the deployment of metaphor, is less circumspect, more willing to entertain the implications of the expressions that he chooses to use. In 'Managing change among loosely coupled systems' (Weick, 1982), Weick taps into a basic, everyday, conventional, conceptual metaphor of organization whereby it is characterized by a cycle of input, throughput, output and feedback. He follows the so-called open systems theorists in questioning and elaborating it. His objective is to extend the boundaries by questioning them. 'Our understanding of change against a backdrop of loose ties is underdeveloped because most models used to think about change rely heavily on connections, networks, support systems, diffusion, imitation, and social comparison, none of which are plentiful in loosely coupled systems' (1982: 378). Here Weick is both using the organization as a system metaphor and pointing out the breakdown of the metaphor when people find they cannot predict much of what happens in organizations – when, to go back to the metaphor used by Vaill and Morgan, managers hit permanent white water. 'The image', Weick asserts, 'is that of a sequence of events that unfolds unevenly, discontinuously, sporadically, or unpredictably, if it unfolds at all' (1982: 381). He argues that the concept of a loosely coupled system is 'an attempt to reintroduce some indeterminacy into conventional portraits of systems' (1982:381).

Throughout this piece, which is brilliantly sustained, the major point being made by Weick is the inadequacy of the conventional systems metaphor. He explicitly challenges every element of the nature of relationships implied by conventional systems thinking. Loose coupling exists, he claims, if A affects B suddenly rather than continuously, occasionally rather than constantly, negligibly rather than significantly, indirectly rather than directly and eventually rather than immediately. In sustaining the challenge, he goes well beyond the normal use of the metaphor without totally abandoning it. His novel metaphoric expression 'a loosely coupled system' resonates with us because of what we automatically assume about ordinary, everyday, tightly coupled systems.

I will use Weick in turning to what is arguably the most powerful of ways that basic, everyday, conventional, conceptual metaphors are developed. A further quote from the same chapter:

> Furthermore, loosely coupled systems may store innovations that are not presently useful. Change diffuses slowly, if at all, through such systems, which means that components either invent their own solutions – which may be inefficient compared with other solutions available in the system – or they die. To construct a loosely coupled system is to design a system that updates itself and may never need the formal change interventions that sometimes are necessary to alter the hard-wired routines in tightly coupled systems. (Weick, 1982: 390–391)

One of the things that characterizes good writing is the simultaneous use of several metaphors in the same passage; the ability, that is, to produce passages that ring true, hit chords and resonate. Here Weick lightly produces echoes of basic, conventional metaphors such as organizations as containers (storing innovations), as mechanistic or machine-like (components and hard-wired routines), as purposeful (inventing, seeking solutions and efficiencies), as manifesting life and, possibly, death, and as a system that is self-sustaining (adapting and updating itself). Importantly, these metaphors cohere. The work here, as Lakoff and Turner put it in another context, is conceptual, 'a matter of putting complex metaphorical concepts together rather than merely putting words together' (1989: 71). Each of the metaphors that Weick taps into has a strong experiential grounding. They are basic and they are general rather than highly specific. Together they form a composite which is an elaborated version of an organization as both human and machine; a sensitive android. Weick's crafting of this passage produces a richer and more complex set of metaphorical connections than the utilization of a single metaphor would do alone. And it does it because being largely unconscious of the basic metaphors underlying this passage, we apprehend rather than work at making the connections.

Conclusions

This chapter has been an attempt to bring the ideas of Lakoff and his colleagues to the attention of those who read and write organization theory. I have chosen to make use of the work of Gareth Morgan in highlighting and illustrating some of the points because his texts on metaphor and the stimulation of new ways of thinking about organization have promoted a great deal of discussion.

As Morgan and others have argued and the work of Lakoff et al. confirms, metaphor is anything but peripheral to the life of the mind. It is central to our understanding of ourselves and our relations with the world. I have attempted to show how metaphor deals with fundamental aspects of our conceptual systems. Cognitively well-entrenched metaphors are difficult to change. The more basic a conceptual metaphor is, the more it will be systematically connected to other metaphors and the more implications it will have for the way that we think. It is highly unlikely that we can change (or, for that matter, would wish to change) those metaphors that we regard as indispensable. Drawing heavily upon the work of Lakoff and his colleagues, I have attempted to show that good writers, far from inventing new metaphors, illuminate our minds and our practices by extending, elaborating, questioning and compositing basic, everyday, conventional, conceptual metaphors. I believe that I have shown that while there may indeed be no (or few) limits to one-shot, image metaphors, there are likely to be limits to the invention of basic, everyday, conventional, conceptual metaphors. Not only may it take a long time for novel metaphors to enter our everyday language, the fact that good writers and managers can utilize the ordinary metaphors we live by in order to take us beyond them may sometimes, perhaps often, blind us to the need (if need there is) to fundamentally reconceive our world.

References

Barrett, F.J. and Cooperrider, D.L. (1990) 'Generative metaphor intervention: A new behavioral approach for working with systems divided by conflict and caught in defensive perception', *Journal of Applied Behavioral Science*, 23 (4), 219–244.

Clancy, J.J. (1989) *The Invisible Powers: The Language of Business*. New York: Free Press.

Deetz, S. and Mumby, D. (1985) 'Metaphors, information and power', *Information and Behaviour*, 1, 369–386.

Fillmore, C. (1985) 'Frames and the semantics of understanding', *Quaderna di Semantica*, 6 (2), 222–253.

Gibbs, R.W., Jr (1990) 'Psycholinguistic studies on the conceptual basis of idiomaticity', *Creative Linguistics*, 1 (4), 1443–1541.

Johnson, M. (1981) *Philosophical Perspectives on Metaphor*. Minneapolis, MN: University of Minnesota Press.

Johnson, M. (1987) *The Body in the Mind: The Bodily Basis of Meaning, Reasoning and Imagination*. Chicago: University of Chicago Press.

Johnson, M. (1993) *Moral Imagination: Implications of Cognitive Science for Ethics*. Chicago: University of Chicago Press.

Lakoff, G. (1987) *Women, Fire and Dangerous Things: What Categories Reveal about the Mind*. Chicago: University of Chicago Press.

Lakoff, G. (1993) 'The contemporary theory of metaphor', in A. Ortony (ed.), *Metaphor and Thought* (2nd edn). Cambridge: Cambridge University Press, pp. 202–252.

Lakoff, G. and Johnson, M. (1980) *Metaphors We Live By*. Chicago: University of Chicago Press.

Lakoff, G. and Turner, M. (1989) *More than Cool Reason: A Field Guide to Poetic Metaphor*. Chicago: University of Chicago Press.

Mangham, I.L. (1978) *Interactions and Interventions in Organizations*. New York: John Wiley and Sons.

Mangham, I.L. (1994) 'Speaking in tongues', *Organization*, 1 (1), 35–38.

Mangham, I.L. and Overington, M.A. (1983a) 'Performance and rehearsal: Social order and organizational life', *Symbolic Interaction*, 5 (2), 205–222.

Mangham, I.L. and Overington, M.A. (1983b) 'The theatrical perspective in organizational analysis: An introduction', *Symbolic Interaction*, 5 (2), 173–185.

Mangham, I.L. and Overington, M.A. (1987) *Organizations as Theatre: A Social Psychology of Dramatic Appearances*. Chichester: John Wiley and Sons.

Mangham, I.L. and Pye, A.J. (1991) *The Doing of Managing*. Oxford: Blackwell.

Morgan, G. (1986) *Images of Organization*. Beverly Hills, CA: Sage Publications.

Morgan, G. (1988) *Riding the Waves of Change: Developing Managerial Competencies for a Turbulent World*. San Francisco: Jossey-Bass.

Morgan, G. (1993) *Imaginization: The Art of Creative Management*. London: Sage Publications.

Sackmann, S. (1989) 'The role of metaphors in organization transformation', *Human Relations*, 42 (6), 463–485.

Sapienza, A.M. (1987) 'Imagery and strategy', *Journal of Management*, 13 (3), 543–555.

Srivastva, S. and Barrett, F. (1988) 'The transforming nature of metaphors in group development: A study in group theory', *Human Relations*, 41 (1), 31–64.

Vaill, P. (1989) *Managing as a Performing Art*. San Francisco: Jossey-Bass.

Weick, K. (1982) 'Managing change among loosely coupled systems', in P. Goodman and Associates, *Change in Organizations*. San Francisco: Jossey-Bass, pp. 375–408.

2

Metaphor in the Development of Organization Theory

Geoffrey MacKechnie and Gemma Donnelly-Cox

What is organization theory a theory of? This is not a straightforward question. There is a rich array of terminology and definitions lying at the centre of the subject but these are not easy to reconcile with each other. While some organization theorists have declared their field of study to be simply organizations, others have tried to be more specific and have focused on organization (or organization*al* or organiz*ing*) systems, structures, configurations, modes, forms, processes or governance systems. Is the diversity a sign of vigour and inventiveness – or does it indicate conceptual confusion and weakness? The latter view is trenchantly argued by Sandelands and Drazin:

> The words commonly used to describe the process of organization (or 'organizing') do not and *could* not have the existential warrant supposed for them. These words do not explain how organizations came about, but instead mystify the process in a welter of misbegotten abstractions and unauthentic processes. By calling attention to these words, better theories of organization can be made. (1989: 458)

They go on to argue that a number of important propositions in organization theory rest on words which have dubious predicates and suggest that organization theory should make more of a place for critical linguistic analysis: 'Words are all we have to communicate understanding; getting them straight is what theory-making is all about'. (1989: 459)

It is difficult to deny that close attention should be given to the meaning of the words used in organization theory. In particular, it is hard to find an unambiguous and generally agreed definition of the essence of the subject of study. Morgan (1983) recognizes this and suggests that, at an early stage of development, a science can best develop through the creative use of metaphor.[1] He argues that metaphor provides a prefiguring image of the phenomena to be studied which, although inevitably false and misleading to some degree, will permit the development of hypotheses.

Following this line of argument, we shall examine the analogies and metaphors used by selected prominent theorists to identify their field of study. We shall adopt a historical approach, commencing our discussion with the early theorists and moving forward through the twentieth century.

We shall then consider how these "prefigurations" can be used to clarify what organization theory is a theory of.

Early theorists: The study of a rare skill

The first explicit attempts to offer an explanation of organization came at the end of the nineteenth century with the appearance of the large-scale organizations characteristic of modern society.[2] Early practitioner-theorists generally considered themselves to be writing about *management* – take, for example, Fayol's industrial management or Taylor's scientific or shop management – or about *administration* – such as Metcalfe & Urwick's dynamic administration. These words denote an activity[3] and these writers regarded management or administration as a new and difficult activity requiring rare and elusive skills. They had a fairly straightforward agenda – to discover principles to be followed, precepts to be respected and examples to be guided by.

Chester Barnard was probably the practitioner who played the most important part in the transition to conscious theory building. He acknowledged that the existing literature had been successful in describing and analysing the superficial characteristics of organizations, but considered that it was 'like descriptive geography with the physics, chemistry, geology, and biology missing' (1938: viii). His aim was to sketch a portion of a theory of organization and his theoretical object was 'formal' organizations:

> For the present, formal organizations may be described rather than defined. The most important of them are associations of co-operative efforts to which it is possible and customary to give definite names, that have officers or recognized leaders, that have reasons for existence that may be approximately stated – such as governments, government departments, churches, universities, labour units, industrial corporations, symphony orchestras, football teams. Formal organization is that kind of co-operation among men that is conscious, deliberate, purposeful. (1938: 4)

This was clearly a tentative first attempt and later he was to offer a broader conceptualization: 'When the acts of two or more individuals are co-operative, that is, systematically co-ordinated, the acts by my definition constitute an organization' (1948: 113).

Barnard seemed to be struggling with two slightly different concepts. The easier, given the label 'formal' organization, is the proliferation of corporate bodies that can be noted by casual observation in modern society, but which are difficult to capture in a precise definition. His second definition appears to recognize that these are no more than clear examples of a pervasive phenomenon – systematically co-ordinated acts. He did not really manage to explain the relationship between 'formal' organizations and organizations in general.

Barnard alludes to a further theoretical difficulty in reaching a clear conceptualization of an organization. He deals with this through the metaphor of a whirlpool:

This is a realistic thing to one who gets into it, and it seems real enough to anyone who watches it. When you use the name nearly everyone knows what you mean, and there is no other name commonly covering the same thing. (1948: 14)

The problem is that there are comparatively stable uniformities between the streams of molecules of water, but the actual molecules are continuously replaced. The uniformities come from abstract forces rather than the actual constituent parts. By analogy, the uniformities in an organization cannot be explained merely by reference to the choices and behaviours of the individuals involved at any particular time – the organization demonstrates certain patterns independently of the individuals who come and go just as the whirlpool demonstrates patterns independently of particular molecules of water.

Although Barnard went well beyond his contemporaries in seeking to find a sounder theoretical base for the study of organization, he did not depart from the tradition of treating the management of them as intrinsically difficult:

But in fact, successful co-operation in or by formal organizations is the abnormal, not the normal condition. What are observed from day to day are the successful survivors among innumerable failures. The organizations commanding sustained attention, almost all of which are short-lived at best, are the exceptions, not the rule. It may be said correctly that modern civilization is one characterized by the large residue of organizations that are in existence at any one time; but this does not imply that the particular organizations of that time have been or will continue to be in existence long. Similarly, it is recognized that the existence of a population does not necessarily imply longevity, but merely the balancing of constantly recurring deaths by births. Thus most co-operation fails in the attempt, or dies in infancy, or is short-lived. (1948: 4)

It is appropriate to move on to Herbert Simon, who derived many of his ideas from Barnard. His benchmark book with James March follows Barnard in making 'formal organizations' the principal theoretical object, and adopts a similar means of dealing with the problem of definition:

This book is about formal organizations. It is easier, and probably more useful, to give examples of formal organizations than to define the term. The United States Steel Corporation is a formal organization; so is the Red Cross, the corner grocery store, the New York State Highway Department. The latter organization is, of course, part of a larger one – the New York State government. But for present purposes we need not trouble ourselves about the precise boundaries to be drawn around an organization or the exact distinction between an "organization" and a "nonorganization." (March and Simon, 1958: 1)

In spite of this manifesto, March and Simon were not principally concerned with organizations, formal or otherwise. Their analysis was concerned more with the nature of the administrative processes within organizations – principally the way decisions are made and the way the individuals involved influence each other – which in his first book Simon announced as 'the art of getting things done' (1947: 1).

To summarize: the early theorists started from a conception of management or administration as a set of skilled practices, and later moved to a more analytic consideration of organizational processes, with the "formal organization" being construed as the major theoretical object. However, a satisfactory definition of the formal organization proved elusive.

Organizational sociologists: The anthropological metaphor

In the early 1960s and 1970s, contingency theory took centre stage. Since the theory relied upon formal comparisons, explicit attention to the theoretical object was required in order to give a reasonably clear basis of comparison.

Among the first contingency theorists, "management" and "administration" remained popular: for example, Burns and Stalker (1961) described their mechanistic and organic ideal types as *management* systems; Stinchcombe (1965) distinguished between craft and bureaucratic *administration*; Woodward (1958) first published her findings under the title *Management and Technology*.

Management and administration, as theoretical constructs, both denote *activities* aimed at coping with the exigencies that arise from the operations being engaged in. The contingency theorists were seeking to identify better and worse administrative ways of performing these activities, so they shared the general orientation of the early theorists, albeit in a more carefully reasoned and discriminating way. They were less concerned with "the organization". For example, Burns and Stalker drew their data from parts of large firms as well as from independent firms – they were interested in the patterns of relationships between managers rather than the organizations as entire entities.

However, as contingency theory developed, the phraseology began to change. For example, Lawrence and Lorsch aimed to study 'the organization as a system' (1967: 6) and to understand large organizations as a whole. There is a change of emphasis, from a focus on effective management or administrative activities to a focus on the attributes of "an organization".

Nevertheless, there was little attempt by contingency theorists to define what they meant by "an organization", other than to describe it as a system (implying a set of phenomena linked by cause–effect relations) or as a structure (implying a stable set of relations between phenomena). Structural characteristics became the favoured basis of comparison, probably reflecting the dominance of sociologists in the structural-functional tradition, and the theory is now commonly referred to as 'structural contingency theory' (Grandori, 1987).

Therefore, as contingency theory developed it became a theory of certain attributes, predominantly structural characteristics, of an ill-defined entity. The weakness at the heart of the theory is reflected in the confused use of the qualifying adjectives "organization" and "organizational" as applied to structure, system, analysis, and the like. For example, "organization analysis" and "organizational analysis" were frequently used interchangeably.

When examined carefully, it is apparent that "organization analysis" has the connotation of the analysis of an entity; while "organizational analysis"

has the connotation of the analysis appertaining to a more general phenomenon of organization. This has echoes of Barnard's dilemma: How should
organization be defined? Either as entities such as business firms, churches,
and so forth, or as the systematically co-ordinated acts of individuals which
are commonly, but not exclusively, performed within these entities? This
"problem of level" is discussed at greater length by Døving in Chapter
10.

The failure to resolve this issue contributed to the decline of contingency
theory. First, the ill-defined theory which became the centrepiece attracts
the charge of reification: 'the attribution of concrete reality, particularly the
power of thought and action, to social constructs' (Silverman, 1970: 9).
Silverman notes that contingency theorists tend to treat organizations as
being similar to biological organisms. He raises a number of questions: Can
organizations be attributed with needs and goals? Is it useful to conceive of
social forms in terms of health and pathology? If contingency theorists are
treating organizations as similar to organisms, should they be studying the
way they are rather than the way they ought to be (1970: 119–121)?

Contingency theory was vulnerable to these criticisms. It posited a
connection between an organization and its environment in which the
organization definitely adapted to environmental conditions through "powers
of thought" – indeed, the theorists went well beyond a biological metaphor
to what is more accurately an anthropological metaphor. However, they
were accused of failing to specify the nature of these cogitations and falling
into the error of determinism – that the environment in some way "causes"
the organization to be the way it is.

Further, since "an organization" cannot have aspirations or goals, the
notion of effectiveness at the centre of contingency theory became suspect.
Effective for whom? If the adaptations recommended by contingency theory
were effective, they must be effective for specific people – such as the
management, or perhaps a dominant coalition within management, whose
interests could not be assumed to be identical with the membership of the
organization as a whole.

Organizational sociologists became increasingly troubled by these criticisms. In a major review of organization theory, Pfeffer (1982) dismissed
contingency theory in a few pages, accusing it of lacking definition. The
leading sociologists instead turned their attention to a more macro level of
analysis. Pfeffer himself, in collaboration with Gerald Salancik, developed
what became known as the resource dependency theory, focused on the
external rather than the internal dependency of organizations. However,
the anthropological metaphor[4] (which we consider to be the primary source
of the difficulties) was retained:

> This book discusses how organizations manage to survive. . . . Survival comes
> when the organization adjusts to, and copes with, its environment, not only when
> it makes efficient adjustments. (Pfeffer and Salancik, 1978: 2, 19)

The efficient adjustments of contingency theory have been moved from the centre of the stage, but the notion of the organization 'coping' preserves the anthropological metaphor intact.

The major alternative development in organizational sociology, population ecology, could be said to rely on the anthropological metaphor in trumps. Hannan and Freeman (1977), probably the most influential proponents of this theoretical initiative, declared themselves dissatisfied with the near universal focus on *the* organization and *its* environment. They argued for a parallel development at what they described as the 'population' (and ultimately, the 'community') level:

> Populations of organizations must be alike in some respect, that is, they must have some unit character. ... We can identify classes of organization which are relatively homogeneous in terms of environmental vulnerability. (1977: 934)

Without denying that organizations engage in rational (anthropological) efforts to adjust to environmental conditions, Hannan and Freeman go on to argue that a more important element in organizational adjustment is played by Darwinian environmental forces. On this line of argument, environmental change impacts on organizations by eliminating those which are poorly suited to the new conditions, and favouring those which turn out to be well suited – an argument reminiscent of Barnard's observations on the transitory nature of formal organizations.

For an explanation of how adaptation to the 'blind forces of the environment' occurs, Hannan and Freeman point to biology:

> We must identify an analogue to the biologist's notion of species. Various species are defined ultimately in terms of genetic structure. As Monod (1971) indicates, it is useful to think of the genetic content of any species as a blueprint. The blueprint contains the rules for transforming energy into structure. Consequently all of the adaptive capacity of a species is summarized in the blueprint. If we are to identify a species analogue for organizations, we must search for such blueprints. These will consist of rules or procedures for obtaining and acting upon inputs in order to produce an organizational product or response. (1977: 934–935)

The biological and anthropological metaphors, therefore, lead to a further metaphor, a blueprint. This blueprint, which comprises an equivalent of DNA, is the key to an understanding of the processes by which organizations adjust. The Darwinian analogy, therefore, runs as follows: Organizations can be divided into species which share a common vulnerability to changing environmental conditions; within each species there is a blueprint which differs in detail; as environmental conditions change, the environment 'selects'[5] for survival those organizations with the appropriate blueprint.

Not surprisingly, population ecology is more commonly referred to as a perspective rather than a theory. As Døving discusses in Chapter 10, the ideas of species and so forth are far from operational (and indeed have not been operationalized very successfully in subsequent research). Nevertheless, the ecologists can be credited with pursuing the anthropological metaphor to its roots and arriving at the underlying notion of a blueprint.

Another prominent sociological theory of organization which has a definite anthropological flavour is generally labelled the institutional approach. Unlike resource dependency or population ecology, its content is disparate and assumptions differ between utilizers. However, theorists who subscribe to 'the new institutionalism in organizational analysis' (Powell and DiMaggio, 1991) take as their focus the *institutionalized organization* and the process by which it becomes institutionalized. Pressure from "out there" in the environment, from "institutions", be they social, societal or some collective of bodies with which the organization interacts (often described as an *institutional field*), affect the way they structure and behave.

Like resource dependency and population ecology, the institutional approach attempts to shift from a focus on the organization to a more macro perspective – perhaps in an attempt to escape from the limitations of the anthropological metaphor. Unlike resource dependency theorists, who link attainment of financial and other resources with survival, and population ecologists, who rely on rather vague environmental selection processes, institutional theorists suggest that organizations seek to conform to societal norms. For them, organizations which alter their structure to conform achieve legitimacy, and legitimacy facilitates survival (Scott, 1992).

Although institutional theorists focus on external explanations, the theoretical object of their attention remains the organization and its structure. This has led to accusations that this *macro* approach in fact leaves the organization as something of a *black box* (Zucker, 1991). More specifically, the institutional approach is criticized on the grounds that it says very little about the process of achieving a legitimated structure:

> We risk treating institutionalization as a black box at the organizational level, focusing on content at the exclusion of developing a systematic explanatory theory of process, conflating institutionalization with resource dependency, and neglecting institutional variation and persistence. (Zucker, 1991: 12)

In summary, the sociological theories of organization we have reviewed have moved from a focus on the internal characteristics of organizations towards a closer attention to the nature of the external influences on organizations. However, they are all built round a view of organizations as entities with anthropological features – adapting, coping, seeking legitimacy, and the ilk.

Non-sociological theories: The practice of organizing

While organizational sociologists retained a focus on "the organization" and the anthropological metaphor, a rather different line of development was initiated by Karl Weick (1979, 1st edn 1969). In his book *The Social Psychology of Organizing* (rather than *of Organization*), he saw organizing as an activity rather than an entity, defining it as 'a consensually validated grammar for reducing equivocality by means of sensible interlocked behaviors' (1979: 3).

This is not the place to examine this rather impenetrable definition in detail, but we can note that the noun in the centre of it is a 'grammar'. Weick goes on to explain what he means by a grammar:

> The grammar consists of recipes for getting things done when one person can't do them, and recipes for interpreting what has been done. (1979: 4)

As well as explaining the grammar metaphor by a further metaphor of recipe, Weick clearly sees organizing as something that happens whenever two or more people act in collaboration – very similar to Barnard's definition of an organization occurring whenever two or more persons engage in systematically co-ordinated acts. For Weick, the process of organizing applies equally to trivial and transitory activities and to the activities which take place in IBM. In all cases:

> There is a shared sense of appropriate procedures and appropriate interpretations, an assemblage of behaviors distributed among two or more people, and a puzzle to be worked on. The conjunction of these procedures, interpretations, behaviors and puzzles describes what organizing does and what an organization is. (1979: 4)

Here, Weick is trying to specify the content of organizing – procedures, interpretations, behaviours and a puzzle. He does not explicitly relate these to his 'grammar' and 'recipe' metaphors. Perhaps these are the ingredients blended by the recipe, with grammar signifying the "shared sense" by which the individuals concerned achieve a common understanding of the ingredients and what might be done with them, in the same way as grammar gives a common understanding of how to choose and arrange words to make sense.

Weick side-steps the issue of "organizations", anthropological or otherwise, by denying the distinction between what organizing does and what an organization is. In other words, if individuals are interlocking their behaviours to follow procedures and work on puzzles, then they are an organization. General Motors or IBM are no more than arenas in which this type of behaviour typically occurs. As with the early management theorists, organization is construed as an activity.

Weick's choice of 'organizing', rather than "organizations" as the centre of his analysis was followed by Jay R. Galbraith,[6] a contingency theorist who departed considerably from the sociological tradition. While most contingency theorists offered a typology of structural arrangements, Galbraith (1973, 1977) framed his analysis round the use of different *design strategies* to create what he called an *'organizing mode'*. An 'organizing mode' is a more dynamic concept than structure, and has the connotation of a method or a way of doing something. Following Weick, the centrepiece is the process of organizing rather than the organization. Galbraith adds the requirement to choose among a set of modes in order to ensure that the organizing is performed effectively, implying that the choice and implementation of organizing modes is not obvious or straightforward.

A mode of doing something denotes a means to an end, which is consistent with the idea of a tool – a metaphor favoured by Charles Perrow:

'Basically, an organization is a tool that masters use to generate valued outputs that they can then appropriate' (1986: 260).

The use of the word 'tool' gives Perrow's work a very different flavour to Galbraith's. There is no sense of any great difficulty in 'generating valued outputs' and a tool suggests a more concrete, unambiguous process than Galbraith's modes. Nevertheless, both 'mode' and 'tool' have the same connotation of a facilitator in getting something done.

A construct from economics: The market as organizational form

The primary metaphor applied to organization by economics raises a number of questions in relation to the development of organization theory. It is a metaphor which can be attributed to economists having traditionally concerned themselves with the logics of wealth creation through markets. What can be seen as a basic "structure–conduct–performance" paradigm starts with different market structures; analyses the rational conduct within each structure; and then derives the outcome which is evaluated as the performance of the system as a whole in terms of allocatory efficiency. Firms and households are deemed to be the inhabitants – the basic source of supply and demand respectively – but are strictly speaking abstract postulates which are deemed to be maximizing their utilities.[7]

In the theory of the firm, it is recognized that in practice firms will frequently engage in irrational conduct of one sort or another, but the long-term patterns of behaviour are deemed to be shaped by the rational conduct predictable through economic analysis. For this reason, economists have been concerned to discover "tendencies" and outcomes that can be predicted "in principle". The detailed activities in real life firms are inevitably contaminated by idiosyncrasies and errors; these may be of interest for some purposes but actually obscure rather than add to true economic analysis. This means that the metaphor traditionally applied to the firm in economics is a variant of the anthropological metaphor – a person stripped of all attributes other than acquisitiveness and rationality.

This somewhat dismissive treatment of organizations has little to contribute to organization theory. However, a critique of the conventional view has been developed in recent years under the heading of institutional economics. In this analysis, the hierarchical firm is regarded as an alternative to the market structure as a way of conducting economic transactions. The question to be investigated becomes that of determining when and why hierarchical organization is more efficient than market organization for conducting transactions.

This is not the place to examine the substantive issues covered by institutional economics. However, we can look at the way two prominent economists, Oliver Williamson and Douglass North, construe organization and organizations.

Williamson (1975) described both markets and hierarchies as organizational forms, a term that has been widely followed. This is decisively
incompatible with the anthropological metaphor in any of its guises. A
market, a set of autonomous agents engaging in economic exchanges, cannot
by any stretch of the imagination be construed as analogous to a person.
Indeed the chief merit of the phrase 'organizational forms' is its vagueness
– "forms" is the weakest possible imagery. It is perhaps in recognition of
this fact that Williamson becomes later more specific and substitutes the
phrase 'governance system' for organizational form. Governance implies the
imposition of an order by a common authority by allocating legal or quasi-
legal entitlements and obligations. Organization becomes an underpinning
that permits economic transactions to be conducted successfully.

A different perspective on the practice of organizing is offered by
Douglass North (1991), a neo-classical economist, in a game-playing
metaphor. He uses the terms 'institutions' and 'organizations', but, unlike
the sociological theorists, does not consider organizations to be legitimacy-
seeking actors. If institutions are the rules of the game (his game is
American football), organizations are the teams.[8] Both institutions and
organizations are structures for human interaction, but they differ:

> A crucial distinction is made between institutions and organizations. Like institu-
> tions, organizations provide a structure to human interaction. . . . Conceptually,
> what must be clearly differentiated are the rules from the players. The purpose of
> the rules is to define the way the game is played . . . but the objective of the team
> within that set of rules is to win the game – by a combination of skills, strategy
> and co-ordination; by fair means and sometimes by foul means. Modelling the
> strategies and skills of a team as it develops is a separate process from modelling
> the creation, evolution, and consequences of the rules. (North, 1991: 4–5)

These economists have sought to elaborate the abstracted and truncated
anthropological metaphor of the theory of the firm. They have proposed
rules or governance systems as the essential underpinning of organized
action and the central object of study. The conventional emphasis on
organizations as entities (anthropological or otherwise) is largely discarded –
though it lingers rather uneasily at the edges of North's conceptualization.

What do the metaphors tell us?

We have assembled an array of expressions which have been used by a
range of prominent theorists to specify the theoretical object of organization
theory. The somewhat bewildering nature of the phraseology appears to
confirm the contention of Sandelands and Drazin (1989) that the words of
the subject merit closer attention. According to Northrop Frye, the use of
metaphor and similar figures of speech 'is a mode of analogical thinking and
writing in which the verbal expression is "put for" something which by
definition transcends adequate verbal expression' (1983: 15).

This echoes Morgan's (1983) argument, mentioned at the beginning of
this chapter, that metaphor is necessary at the early stage of a science when

the phenomena to be studied are unclear. In his 1986 book, Morgan himself offers no fewer than eight metaphors which have been applied to different aspects of organizations: machine, organism, brain, culture, political system, psychic prison, flux and transformation, instruments of domination. He sees these as offering a variety of systematic ways of thinking on how we can or should act; and in particular allowing us to escape from organizational problems which rest with our (limited) ways of thinking.

Morgan distinguishes between the aspects captured by one or other of the metaphors, and the thing itself that they are aspects of. He uses the simile of the blind men each examining a part of an elephant as they attempt to describe the entire animal:

> However, the problem of understanding organization is more difficult (than the elephant) in that we do not really know what organizations are, in the sense of having a single authoritative position from which they can be viewed. While many writers on organization attempt to offer such a position – for example, by defining organizations as groups of people who come together in pursuit of common goals – the reality is that to an extent we are all blind men and women groping to understand the nature of the beast. ... We can try to decompose organization into sets of related variables: structural, technical, political, cultural, human, and so forth: but we must remember that this does not really do justice to the nature of the phenomenon. ... The division between the different dimensions is in our own minds rather than in the phenomenon. (1986: 341)

It is not clear how he reaches the conclusion that the division between the dimensions is 'in our own minds', but for present purposes the main point is that for Morgan the essence of organizations (or *organization* – he slips between one and the other without explanation) remains beyond the reach of metaphor.

Does our review help us to find the master-metaphor that Morgan fails to reach? Perhaps not, but we can try to make some sort of a classification of the different candidates. We can start by noting that the orthodox view is to treat *organizations* as the object of study. These theorists, predominantly sociologists, approach organizations as entities which need to be observed, analysed and eventually understood. They normally construe organizations as organisms through a biological, or more precisely an anthropological, metaphor. The organisms are deemed to exist in an environment and seek to thrive, or at least survive, in that environment. This leads to a research strategy of observing organizations, in case studies or through comparative analysis, in order to understand the entity better.

This view can be contrasted with an earlier tradition which construed organization as *activities* requiring skills which are difficult to accomplish and sustain successfully. This broad conceptualization was sustained by later theorists who treated the subject of study as that of *organizing* – an activity rather than an entity – for which the appropriate research strategy becomes that of identifying the difficulties inherent in organization and ways of coping with them.

What are the merits of these distinct conceptualizations? The anthropological metaphor has a common-sense appeal: After all, "formal" organizations are a pervasive feature of modern society which clearly requires
investigation. Further, they appear to be something more than the activities
of the individuals who happen to be members at any particular time. Scott
makes this point more precisely:

> We will fail to perceive the importance of organizations for our lives if we view
> them only as contexts – as arrangements influencing the activities of individual
> actors. Organizations must also be viewed as actors in their own right, as
> *corporate persons*, to use Coleman's phrase (1974). They can take actions, utilize
> resources, enter into contracts, and own property. Coleman describes how these
> rights have gradually developed since the Middle Ages to the point where it is
> now accurate to speak of two kinds of persons – *natural* persons (such as you and
> me) and corporate or *juristic* persons (such as the Red Cross and General Motors).
> (1992: 7)

Scott may well be right that the legal status of organizations is an important
contributing factor to the common-sense view, but does not make a very
convincing argument. The invention of juristic persons is a fiction which
was adopted essentially as a matter of legal convenience. It is hardly a
sufficient justification for construing organizations as actors in their own
right. That said, it is true that they appear to be something more than the
activities of the individuals who happen to be members at any particular
time.

Whatever the legal status of organizations, there are still weaknesses in
the anthropological metaphor which must be taken seriously. Most obvious
is the attribution of emotions, rationalizations, and so forth, to the whole
rather than to the individuals making up the parts (examined in detail by
Døving in Chapter 10). This clearly short-circuits the subtleties of actual
causation. It also allows for spurious causations to be unobtrusively attributed to life-cycles, maturation effects, survival instincts and other "natural"
processes without specifying what takes the place of a genetic code.

A second weakness is the irresolvable problem of determining the
boundaries of "an organization". For example, Barnard and Weick both
recognized that organization or organizing can be traced back to the simplest
case of two or more people engaging in an activity which one person could
not perform alone. When does organizing become "an organization"? This
issue is left to one side. There are many other difficulties in reaching
unambiguous definitions of the boundaries of an organization in terms of
membership, assets, and the like. All this means is that the "anthropological
organization" is a nebulous and ultimately arbitrarily defined object of
study.

A deeper weakness is the influence of the anthropological metaphor on
research strategy. We have noted that it leads researchers to treat organizations as comprising an entity to be observed systematically in order to
understand it better. Research is considered to gain in quality the greater the
range of organizations studied and the more that measures are chosen which

are equally meaningful to all organizations. The resulting data are carefully analysed to find the common features – the real nature of the beast.

This whole line of approach is criticized by Starbuck:

> North American and English research has been paying too much attention to averages. The study of averages has become so prevalent that social scientists do not even have to explain why they think averages are the appropriate variables to study. Other social scientists often accuse the deviants who fail to study averages of doing valueless work, as if averages were the only information of value. (1992: 889)

In his research on knowledge intensive industries which stimulated this comment, Starbuck found that the exceptionally successful law firm, from which he could draw important conclusions, was far from average; indeed, it was the outlying firm on most of his measures. The average firm told him very little of interest. He concludes: 'Fixation on averages makes social science blind to individuality, excellence, complexity, interaction, and subcultures' (1992: 889).

This argument is in line with the "organizing as a rare skill" position. The essence of a rare skill is to be found in those with unusual prowess. For example, if one wished to study an athletic skill, say high-jumping, the sensible starting point would be to study the very best high jumpers, with the objective of discovering the particular juxtapositioning of muscle, body weight, and so forth, which facilitates upward thrust. It would be bizarre to attempt to cover the greatest number of schools, clubs and other locations in which it is practised in order to get a full understanding of high-jumping. This research strategy would probably yield some mildly interesting data on the generally poor standard of performance in the population at large, but very little on the art of high-jumping. It is wrong to presume that every time that someone jumps this in itself generates data which can contribute to our understanding of jumping.

By contrast, every observation of a biological species, say a lion, makes a valid contribution to our understanding of the nature of lions – lions are a naturally occurring phenomenon and every lion tells us something about lionhood. However, organizing (as the tool and mode metaphors emphasize) is a human contrivance and yields its secrets in a different way. The research strategy which follows from biological and anthropological metaphors is therefore misplaced.

The skilled practices conceptualization of organization avoids this hazard, but has weaknesses of its own. There appears to be a persistent recognition that organization is more than the transient practices of those engaged in organizing. As well as the legal powers referred to by Scott, organizations are generally acknowledged to acquire some existence independent of the members who might come and go – hence the attraction of the anthropological metaphor.

A number of the non-anthropological metaphors can be seen as attempts to capture this element. 'Grammar', 'recipe', 'governance system', 'rules of the game', all hint at a continuity which underpins sustained exercises of organizing. If we wish to follow Sandelands and Drazin's injunction to pay more attention to the words of organization theory, referred to at the beginning of this chapter, these are words to concentrate on. They are metaphors which are directed at the gap between *'organization'* and *'organizations'* which has lain at the centre of organization theory since the time of Barnard.

Conclusions: A theory of what?

After considering the phraseology and metaphors of some prominent theorists, are we any further in determining what organization theory is a theory of? No unequivocal answer has been found, though some common themes have been identified. However, it would be churlish not to offer a personal view on how some sense can be made of the attempts to define the central theoretical object.

A reasonable starting point is to accept that *organization* occurs whenever more than one person addresses a task that cannot be accomplished by one person acting alone; in other words, to study organization is to study the exploitation of the division of labour.

We can then move on to accept that division of labour is not easy. We can presume that the early development of very elementary forms of division of labour – by hunter-gatherers and the like – involved considerable inventiveness and learning; each time more elaborate forms of division of labour were attempted, further innovations became necessary.

This view is consistent with the "tool" and "mode" metaphors, which portray organization as a means to achieving certain outcomes. It is also consistent with the "rare skills" premise of the early management theorists, who were keenly aware of the difficulties involved in the major elaboration of division of labour of their time.

Some of the metaphors we have encountered illustrate the nature of these difficulties. Thus *grammar* suggests that successful exercises of division of labour are rooted in the articulation of mutual understandings (implying a shared culture). The *game* metaphor suggests the existence of rivalry culminating in winners and losers, with *rules* designed to ensure that the rivalry does not undermine the dramatic tension of the game. From this we can infer that organization creates a similar need to deal with winners and losers (shares in the output) without permitting rivalry to undermine the viability of the division of labour. The rules need not be equitable and will be open to abuse and challenge, as demonstrated by the political and domination metaphors.

Other difficulties can be discovered by examining the aspects of organization suggested by Weick's four content elements of organizing and Morgan's images. If *procedures* are intrinsic to successful division of labour, this implies intelligent use of cause–effect relations, hence the machine metaphor. *Puzzles* are cognitive by nature and therefore evoke the brain metaphor. *Interpretations* are meanings which therefore must be understood through both the culture metaphor (shared meanings) and the organism/flux and transformation metaphors (implying the need to generate new meanings). The requirement for *interlocked behaviours* may well generate events that are describable by both political and psychic prison metaphors, but also companionship, support and affection suggested by the team/game metaphors (which both Morgan and Weick neglect).

We see these metaphors, therefore, as elements of *organizing* as an activity, reflecting the very real difficulties that must be overcome if division of labour is to be accomplished successfully (in this we are disagreeing with Morgan's contention that they are distinctions which merely reside in our minds). We do not deny that successful organizing activities commonly become established over time, and acquire a momentum which has some independence of the immediate thoughts and aspirations of the individuals concerned. Nor do we deny that sustained and elaborate exercises of division of labour have required legal entitlements and obligations to be attached to the collective as well as to the individuals concerned. To this extent, "the organization" becomes something more than a set of organizing activities. However, we do not agree that it is helpful to apply biological or anthropological metaphors to "the organization" in order to create a convenient theoretical object for organization theory. On the contrary, we consider that the appearance of this metaphor has proved profoundly misleading.

Notes

1. In this chapter we shall not distinguish between analogy, metaphor and associated figures of speech such as metonymy and synecdoche and irony.
2. Pollard (1968) suggests that while many texts on agricultural estate management were published in the eighteenth century, the methods of management of factories in the early industrial revolution were kept a close secret because of the intense competition.
3. Hedlund (1993) tells us that the verb 'to manage' derives from the activity of breaking in and training horses. The word *manège* refers to the arena in which horses are trained on long leading ropes which only allow them to go round and round.
4. We use the term 'anthropological metaphor' purposefully. We do not believe that these theorists are intentionally anthropomorphic. We return to a discussion of the implications of this approach at the conclusion of the chapter.
5. Although the notion of the environment having powers of selection is clearly to be treated as a shorthand, we can note that the anthropological metaphor casts a long shadow.
6. Galbraith came to organization theory from engineering.
7. Indeed, a fundamental theoretical problem for economics was to explain the existence of firms; in principle, there was no reason why all economic activity should not be carried out by individuals engaging in market transactions.
8. The game-players metaphor has long been applied to interactions inside organizations as easily as to interactions between organizations, most notably by Michel Crozier (1964).

References

Barnard, C. (1938) *The Functions of the Executive*. Cambridge, MA: Harvard University Press.

Barnard, C. (1948) *Organization and Management*. Cambridge, MA: Harvard University Press.

Burns, T. and Stalker, G.M. (1961) *The Management of Innovation*. London: Tavistock.

Coleman, H. (1974) *Power and the Structure of Society*. New York: W.W. Norton and Co.

Crozier, M. (1964) *The Bureaucratic Phenomenon*. London: Tavistock.

Frye, N. (1983) *The Great Code: The Bible and Literature*. London: Ark.

Galbraith, J.R. (1973) *Designing Complex Organizations*. Reading, MA: Addison-Wesley.

Galbraith, J.R. (1977) *Organization Design*. Reading, MA: Addison-Wesley.

Grandori, A. (1987) *Perspectives on Organization Theory*. Cambridge, MA: Ballinger.

Hannan, M.T. and Freeman, J. (1977) 'The population ecology of organizations', *American Journal of Sociology*, 82 (5), 929–964.

Hedlund, G. (1993) 'Assumptions of hierarchy and heterarchy, with applications to the management of the multinational corporation', in S. Ghoshal and D.E. Westney (eds), *Organization Theory and the Multinational Corporation*. London: St Martin's Press, pp. 211–236.

Lawrence, P.R. and Lorsch, J.W. (1967) *Organization and Environment: Managing Differentiation and Integration*. Boston: Harvard University Press.

March, J.G. and Simon, H.A. (1958) *Organizations*. New York: John Wiley and Sons.

Monod, J. (1971) *Chance and Necessity*. New York: Vintage.

Morgan, G. (1983) 'More on metaphor: Why we cannot control tropes in administrative science', *Administrative Science Quarterly*, 27 (4), 601–607.

Morgan, G. (1986) *Images of Organization*. London: Sage Publications.

North, D. (1991) *Institutions, Institutional Change and Economic Performance*. Cambridge: Cambridge University Press.

Perrow, C. (1986) *Complex Organizations: A Critical Essay* (3rd edn). New York: Random House.

Pfeffer, J. (1982) *Organizations and Organization Theory*. Marshfield, MA: Pitman Publishing.

Pfeffer, J. and Salancik, G.R. (1978) *The External Control of Organizations: The Resource Dependence Perspective*. New York: Harper and Row.

Pollard, S. (1968) *The Genesis of Modern Management*. Harmondsworth: Penguin.

Powell, W.W. and DiMaggio, P.J. (eds) (1991) *The New Institutionalism in Organizational Analysis*. London: University of Chicago Press.

Sandelands, L. and Drazin, R. (1989) 'On the language of organization theory', *Organization Studies*, 10 (4), 457–478.

Scott, W.R. (1992) *Organizations: Rational, Natural and Open Systems*. Hemel Hempstead: Prentice Hall.

Silverman, D. (1970) *The Theory of Organizations*. London: Heinemann.

Simon, H. (1947) *Administrative Behavior*. New York: Macmillan.

Starbuck, W.H. (1992) 'Learning by knowledge-intensive firms', *Journal of Management Studies*, 29, 882–898.

Stinchcombe, A.L. (1965) 'Social structure and organizations', in J.G. March (ed.), *Handbook of Organizations*. Chicago: Rand McNally, pp. 212–231.

Weick, K.E. (1979) *The Social Psychology of Organizing* (2nd edn). Reading, MA: Addison-Wesley.

Williamson, O.E. (1975) *Markets and Hierarchies*. New York: Free Press.

Woodward, J. (1958) *Management and Technology*. London: HMSO.

Zucker, L.G. (1991) 'Organizations as institutions', in S.B. Bacharach (ed.), *Research in the Sociology of Organizations*. Greenwich, CT: JAI Press, pp. 1–47.

3

The Triune-Brain Metaphor: The Evolution of the Living Organization

Gerrit Broekstra

In the global game of corporate renewal there have been disappointingly few winners. This is a fact that has gradually started to dawn on many executives who have once (or quite possibly more than once) committed themselves to improving their companies' competitiveness by adopting some alleged panacea.

This chapter suggests that the flurry of new techniques and ideas about organizing and managing may be relatively insignificant if viewed in isolation, but when perceived as parts of a total phenomenon they have a far deeper meaning. The explosion of techniques primarily signals an experimental period of more wrenching transition towards a fundamentally new paradigm: the evolutionary paradigm. This paradigm is associated with the intriguing metaphor of the brain, particularly with that of the triune brain as conceptualized by MacLean (1990). As such it provides an articulation of the emerging more intelligent network forms of the living organization. Put simply, the argument presented here is that, at a time when continual organizational self-renewal is a necessary condition for survival, organizations once thought of as machines controlled by managers are now better thought of as brains. It is argued that the brain metaphor is particularly appropriate to the modern organization, which is in effect a complex dynamic system poised at the edge of order and chaos, and largely, as Kelly (1994) maintains, out of control.

Never before has the Western business world witnessed the kind of explosion of "business fads" as the one that occurred in the 1980s. A plethora of highly trumpeted change philosophies, methods and techniques, ranging from quality circles to core competencies, and from culture change to empowerment, were eagerly adopted by thousands of managers and corporations. However, in many cases, they were hastily dropped again with little or no positive effect, usually in an atmosphere of blaming everything and everyone, and particularly blaming that never resting phantom in the organization called "resistance to change". As a result of these failed attempts to change the entrenched assumptions and ingrained ways of doing things, frustration and even cynicism prevail in many firms. They suffer from the failed-change syndrome.

Despite the obvious failures the merry-go-round continues. Pascale et al. (1993) caustically remind us that the definition of insanity is quite appropriate here: doing the same thing over and over again, like banging your head against the wall, but expecting different results each time. There appears, then, to be a certain mindlessness in all this. Most organizations still seem to be relatively unintelligent things when it comes to changing their ways of providing value to society. As cybernetician Stafford Beer (1979) would have it, organizations are inclined to be pathologically autopoietic, that is, they tend towards the closing of the organizational mind indulging primarily in self-serving and self-maintaining behaviour.

The fallacy of modern Taylorism

Peddling buzzwords, the new gurus of the 1980s were propelled into the highly profitable status of emperors of the business world – without any serious questions being raised about their clothes. One exception was *Business Week*, which in 1986 alerted its readers to the sheer volatility of the proliferation of management gimmicks and quick fixes by publishing a sarcastic cover story on 'What's in – what's out'. The magazine pointed out 'how faddishness has come to dominate management thinking', and warned of the general tendency among companies to 'evade the basic challenges they face'.

In the first half of the 1990s, this early counter-voice started to gain in strength. For example, in 1990, Michael Beer et al., on the basis of their pioneering research on the revitalization attempts of a diverse range of companies, warned against the 'fallacy of programmatic change', and emphasized the widespread lack of understanding of what it takes to really bring about fundamental change. In 1992, Eccles and Nohria took a swing at the 'obsession with newness', and in advocating a deeper understanding of the essence of management they suggested there was indeed life beyond the hype.

In 1993, Pascale et al. referred to the managerial propensity to indiscriminately adopt business fads as the 'doing trap'. Being confronted with transformational change rather than incremental change, they suggested that managers meditate on the deeper levels or the 'hidden dimension' of a company's being. In the same vein, Drucker (1994) challenged corporate change efforts by claiming that all these allegedly new business techniques were basically 'how to do' tools, whereas the central corporate focus should be on 'what to do'. Drucker argued that the 'theory of the business' of most companies today no longer fits reality.

It may be self-evident that most new business techniques are solutions in search of a problem, but it is worse when the change attempts are directing precious energy towards "doing things right", rather than "doing the right thing". And here we come to the heart of the matter: the prevailing managerial ideology. Managers are primarily efficiency- rather than effectiveness-oriented. The result is, as Janov (1994) contends, a means–end confusion. Faced with a problem of effectiveness (a "what to do" or "being" issue), while pursuing more efficient business processes and organizational practices, managers tend to aggravate all sorts of simmering dilemmas, conflicts and paradoxes.

Related to this perennial efficiency–effectiveness dilemma, is the parts–whole distinction as observed in systems thinking. Without exception business fads constitute partial approaches to improving the business. Some are directed at changing attitudes of people (e.g. empowerment), others at changing the task (e.g. Business Process Re-engineering), and so on, to the virtual exclusion of all other aspects. None takes into account the effects on the whole. Furthermore, "doing" is local and therefore partial. It has its effect locally in a manager's interaction network and is immediately visible. By contrast, "being" is an emerging, holistic phenomenon which is more complex and hence arises more slowly into one's awareness.

Change initiatives which go beyond incremental improvements arising from a predominantly efficiency orientation require an entirely different change logic that we have barely begun to explore. Transforming or remaking a company requires a systemic logic which is much more far-reaching than anything that is offered by the present hype – hype which bears a remarkable similarity to Taylor's efficiency orientation prevailing during the first part of this century.

The complexity perspective

A more benevolent way of looking at the phenomenon of the rise and fall of business fads is obtained in expanding our view and placing the present episode of "explosive development" in a more encompassing frame of organizational evolution. We clearly live in a time of transition in which the global social-economic system is undergoing large-scale transformations. The buzzwords are well known, but they are widely recognized as symbols of deep shifts on a world-wide scale announcing the demise of the Industrial Era and its associated institutions. Globalization of competition, newly emerging economies, information technology, mass customization, knowledge society, postmodernism and fundamentalism come to mind.

Viewed from an evolutionary perspective, business organizations as well as public institutions are interacting players in this world-wide transforming organizational ecosystem. They are experiencing the resultant pressures and struggle to respond individually by experimenting with new forms and functions. Such a period of transition may indeed be characterized by frantic evolutionary experimentation with novel ways of coping with the new complexities. Moreover, it can be regarded as a sign of deep self-organizing forces at work.

The new sciences of chaos and complexity, which have also recently gained such enormous popularity, may shed some light on this phenomenon

(Waldrop, 1992). The Santa Fe Institute's interpretation of the science of complexity suggests that new structure and order may spontaneously arise as a consequence of newly emergent behaviour in non-linear, complex, dynamic systems. This has been described as a transitional phase where 'unrestrained evolutionary experimentation' may lead to an initial proliferation of new types of social organization (Lewin, 1992). An anthology of all the newly promoted organizational forms proves the point: the hollow, virtual, horizontal, intelligent, network, knowledge-creating, inventive, spider-web, cluster, learning organization, and so on.

A complex non-linear system may essentially exhibit three classes of behaviour: (1) relatively frozen and (2) entirely chaotic separated by (3) a small 'edge of chaos' (Lewin, 1992: 53). The latter narrow transition region between order and chaos is the more interesting as it constitutes the 'no-man's land, where chaos and stability pull in opposite directions' (Lewin, 1992: 51). This edge of chaos appears to be analogous to a phase transition and also appears to be the locus of maximum creativity for the system. Even more striking, if unrestrained, systems appear to have a tendency to self-adapt to this edge of chaos where the maximum capacity for innovation is exhibited (Kauffman, 1993).

Poised at this critical state on the edge of chaos, a system may exhibit self-organized criticality, a characteristic discovered by Bak and Chen (1991). This phenomenon may shed some light on the explosive development of new business tools and organizational forms. When sand is piled on a table, a critical point of saturation will be reached where each additional grain of sand may cause avalanches of differing size. Poised at this critical state, the distribution of avalanches appears to obey an inverse power law such that many small avalanches and relatively few big ones occur, with intermediate ones falling in between.

This sand-heap metaphor appears to be strikingly appropriate when applied to the phenomenon of business fads. The size of the avalanches compares to the scope of influence that the various business fads exert. Most business fads have a short and somewhat uninfluential lifetime, such as Theory Z and the One-Minute Manager. Relatively few have a far greater impact. Total Quality Management and Business Process Re-engineering perhaps belong to this category. Others take an intermediate position, for example the learning organization. In short, the explosive burst of business fads has 'the signature of a system that has got itself to the critical state. Got itself, perhaps, to the edge of chaos' (Lewin, 1992: 61).

The science of complexity teaches us that complex dynamic systems, whether physical, biological or societal, have the same underlying internal dynamics and exhibit common emerging patterns. Poised at the edge of chaos, a long period of stability may be punctuated by a relatively rapid period of tremendous instability and a transition between different levels of organization, perhaps, though unpredictable, towards increasing levels of complexity. The flurry of collective activity that accompanies such transitions may also be a sign of impending collapse, or at least some form of mini-collapse (Lewin, 1992).

Under the present turbulent conditions it becomes relevant to ask the question whether the tacit basic assumptions underlying our fundamental view of organizational reality, that is, the dominant paradigm, are still valid. We are currently experiencing a major paradigm shift which runs deeper than any of the surface turbulence which organizations are experiencing may indicate. The new science of complexity has revolutionary insights to offer here that may help to articulate the new paradigm.

Paradigms of change

Oversimplifying somewhat for clarity, it is possible to distinguish between three different paradigms in the short history of conceptualizations of organizing and the management of change (Broekstra, 1992). The distinction presented has been inspired particularly by the work on self-organizing systems by the systems thinkers Jantsch (1973, 1980) and Nicolis and Prigogine (1989). Jantsch (1973) foresaw the tremendous implications of the new second-order cybernetics and related developments in physical chemistry and biology, which he subsumed under the banner of the paradigm of self-organization. He briefly indicated a description of three types of systems:

1   mechanistic systems do not change their internal organization;
2   adaptive (or organismic) systems adapt to changes in the environment through changes in their internal organization by using pre-programmed information;
3   inventive (or human action) systems change their internal organization in accordance with their intentions to change the environment by inventing (internally generating) information.

These three descriptions show a remarkable insight in the evolution of the paradigms that also govern our present state of thinking about organizations. Table 3.1 shows the three paradigms of organizing and organizational change: mechanistic, organismic and evolutionary. They will be discussed further, together with the associated main organizational forms: the functional, divisional and network organization.

The corresponding metaphors are the machine, the organism and the brain. These three main metaphors were popularized in Morgan's (1986) seminal book *Images of Organization*. Inspiration for the paradigms presented in Table 3.1 has also been derived from the work of Miles and Snow (1984, 1994), who published extensively on the evolution of organizational forms or configurations. Recently, others have come up with similar three-pronged distinctions of organizational forms, such as Janov's (1994) gestaltist interpretation of fixed, adaptive and inventive organizations. Nonaka and Takeuchi's (1995) pioneering work on the knowledge-creating company

Table 3.1   *The force, fit and fluctuation paradigms of change*

Paradigm	System thinking	Metaphor	Order through	Organization form
Mechanistic	Closed	Machine	Force	Functional
Organismic (Equilibrium)	Open	Organism (Information-processing)	Fit	Divisional and Business Unit
Evolutionary (Non-equil. self-organ.)	Complex (Knowledge-creating)	Brain	Fluctuation	Network

and processes of self-renewal in Japanese companies has also helped to sharpen the formulation of the third paradigm.

It is worth noting that the three organizational forms (Table 3.1) are not seen as mutually exclusive, but rather as progressively encompassing, representing increasingly higher levels of complexity. Each higher level encompasses, though in a considerably modified form, the previous lower levels. This will become much clearer during the subsequent discussion contained in this chapter.

The mechanistic paradigm

The oldest paradigm is the mechanistic one, where the organization is basically viewed as a special-purpose clockwork machine. Rooted in the nineteenth-century materialist/reductionist world view, this was the dominant paradigm which started with the inception and rapid rise of large hierarchical business organizations after the Great Depression of the 1870s. The environment, including customers, was a non-issue, hence closed-system thinking focused managerial attention inward on the efficient running of the internal organization. The "business fads" of those days were the management techniques developed under the banner of Scientific Management, of which the American engineer Frederick Taylor was the most well-known proponent.

According to the nineteenth-century mechanistic outlook and fuelled by the division-of-labour specialization philosophy, humans were supposed to behave like the efficient parts of a machine. The alienating effects of these scientific management practices and the classical bureaucracy principles of organizing were later seemingly softened up by the Human Relations movement.

The principles of impersonalized bureaucracy led to an emphasis on centralized hierarchy, position, power distance, uniformity of rules and practices, conformity, routinization and an obsession with vertical control. Still quite visible in the machine-like way many of today's organizations operate, these mechanical principles ensure that 'organizational life is often routinized with the precision demanded of clockwork', thus on the flip side, as the German sociologist Max Weber already argued, 'eroding the human spirit and capacity for spontaneous action' (Morgan, 1986: 24-25). Consequently, the ordering principle became known as the command-and-control imperative, which by virtue of its basically coercive character, may well be referred to as "order through force".

The emergence of the functional organization　The rise during the nineteenth century of the big modern industrial enterprise with its tall hierarchies of salaried managers and functional departmentalization makes for both a fascinating and a dramatic story. Furthermore, when it is viewed through the lenses of the science of complexity, it appears to be full of lessons for understanding today's transitional period.

The story commences in the decades preceding the economic depression of the 1870s. The civil engineers of the railroad companies in the US pioneered a new organizational form, naturally acting from the same mechanistic philosophy underlying the construction of their company's physical machinery and infrastructure. From an evolutionary viewpoint, this story is quite relevant.

Briefly, in the post-depression period of the 1840s, when the railroad (and telegraph communication) infrastructures expanded rapidly, the centralized administrative hierarchy gradually emerged as the dominant form among the railroad companies. However, this did not happen without having been contested by the remarkably more effective decentralized divisional form of the Pennsylvania Railroad Company (Chandler, 1977). This is another salient instance of the systemic phenomenon of "lock-in", the evolutionary caprice proposed by scientists at the Santa Fe Institute. Lock-in occurs when one system, often an inferior one succeeds, while a superior one fails. An overt illustration being the way in which the market locked into the technologically inferior VHS videotape format in preference to Betamax (Waldrop, 1992). It comes therefore as no surprise that some people who take a keen interest in the history and future of organizational forms tend to view the dominance of the bureaucratic hierarchy in the last century as a historical aberration (Hock, 1995).

At the start of the Great Depression of the 1870s, the large vertically integrated, multifunctional industrial organization was virtually non-existent. However, as the American business historian Alfred Chandler (1977) has pointed out, this had changed by the turn of the century. To assure the high-volume flow of goods, major American industries adopted a multifunctional bureaucratic form by integrating mass production and mass distribution processes. These efficient 'special-purpose machines' were designed to produce and distribute a limited line of goods and services in large volume and at low cost, governed by the principle of centrally co-ordinated specialization (Miles and Snow, 1994).

From a macroscopic point of view, the sudden emergence of a new form of social organization, and the tremendous evolutionary experimentation associated with it, appears to constitute an authentic example of a big-change phase transition in a spontaneously self-organizing ecology of organizations driven to the edge of chaos. The interesting pattern we may discern during this transition runs somewhat as follows. First, we saw the development of new technologies and infrastructures (railroads and telegraph) during a period of relative economic expansion. Then, those enterprises involved in these developments pioneered a new organizational form to deal with the arising complexities of their own creation. Next, after a severe economic recession, the new form acted as a precursor. Not until it was adopted on a large scale by other organizations, thus enabling them to harness the new technologies, did the economies start to greatly expand again. A similar pattern occurred around the emergence of the divisional form, and appears to be occurring now around the evolving network form of organization (Broekstra, 1993).

The emergence of the divisional organization   The story of the development of the multidivisional organization is extensively dealt with in Chandler's (1962) study of the expansion and subsequent decentralization of some of the largest US enterprises. It began with a sharp economic downturn in the early 1920s that almost toppled General Motors (GM). At this time GM was a mere conglomerate of companies without much central direction, making cars, trucks, refrigerators, parts and accessories brought together by the empire-builder William Durant.

Related diversification of products and market segmentation had become the name of the organizational logic governing the new competitive game. Toffler (1985: 41) called it 'destandardization of output in response to rising consumer demands for variety,' which in turn was fuelled by a 'push toward individualization'. In view of the consequent destabilization of the markets and production processes, the weakness of the commonplace centralized, functionally departmentalized structure, where 'a very few men were still entrusted with a great number of complex decisions' (Chandler, 1962: 41), soon became apparent. The functional form was a good fit for the mass markets and standardized products required prior to the First World War, but gradually became a misfit in a world of increasing variety and diversity.

In the early 1920s, Alfred Sloan at GM pioneered the multidivisional organization headed by a general office. At first it was merely a new way to administer more effectively its sprawling aggregate of companies and to boost corporate financial synergy (Sloan, 1963). Soon the advantages of this more decentralized structure became apparent, inasmuch as each product division focused on a distinct market to meet the demands of product diversification – a car for every pocket. What Miles and Snow (1984) called an 'early fit' of strategy and structure helped GM grasp the largest share of the automobile market in the US and, for decades, maintain its position as the leading car manufacturer in the world.

Not until after the Great Depression of the 1930s and subsequently the Second World War, when the economies started to boom again, was the divisional form copied by most large corporations. With occasional "ups-

and-downs", the decentralization tendency has endured, although it is now frequently seen under the banner of the autonomous business unit. It should be noted, however, that a business unit itself is usually organized according to the functional form. A business unit is largely a self-sufficient entrepreneurial form comprised of all those functions needed to effectively add value to a particular product–market–technology combination or geographical area. It operates of course within the context of an overall strategic direction and, hence, is subject to centrally controlled performance evaluation. In short, the divisional organization as a portfolio of 'special-purpose machines, each independently operated to serve a particular market and centrally evaluated on the basis of economic performance for possible expansion, contraction, or redirection', provided the multidivisional corporation with a great capacity for adaptation (Miles and Snow, 1994: 39).

The organismic paradigm

Shortly after the Second World War, when the organizational logic of divisionalization gained wide popularity, a new paradigm was born which, while encompassing the mechanistic one as a special case, transcended way beyond it. This new way of thinking about organizations constituted a perfect conceptual underpinning of the divisionalization philosophy according to which each unit of organization has to adapt to its own environmental circumstances, and therefore needs to be largely self-sufficient and autonomous. The organismic image is that of a biological organism which by adapting to its external environment has a better chance of survival. Some organizational units faced with a more stable and predictable environment would therefore flourish with a more mechanistic form and operating logic, others in a more turbulent and unpredictable environment would be better off with a more organic form. Strategic choice became an option, thus allowing for different 'species' of organization (Morgan, 1986).

It is possible to put a more or less precise date to the inception of the new paradigm. In 1950, one of the founding fathers of the systems movement, the Austrian biologist and philosopher Ludwig von Bertalanffy, published a seminal article on open systems in physics and biology in *Science*. His organismic approach exerted a major influence on the development of the sociotechnical systems approach to organizations pioneered by the famous Tavistock Institute in London. Based on Bertalanffy's systems ideas, they conceived an organization as a system that is embedded in, and open to, a changing environment to which it needs to adapt in order to survive. This system, then, consists of a collection of aspects, technical, social, and so on, which interact in a balanced way to form an integral whole, thus imposing the need for external and internal fit on the system. The Tavistock notion of a sociotechnical system has been elaborated by a number of scientists to become the standard view in organizational analysis and understanding in the second half of this century.

Lawrence and Lorsch (1967) and Miles and Snow (1978) were among the most influential scholars in establishing this organismic paradigm characterized by open-systems thinking. Using a closely related line of argument Galbraith (1973) advocated the concept of an organization as an information-processing system. His insights into the intricacies of organization design are intimately matched by the traditional first-order cybernetics notions of control, such as those represented by Ashby's Law of Requisite Variety. Despite all the hype, even today's trendy ideas around the learning organization still fall largely into this realm of traditional cognitive, information-processing, open-systems thinking (Nonaka and Takeuchi, 1995).

Many conceptual working frameworks were developed to express the order-through-fit principle. Inspired by Miles and Snow's (1978) 'adaptive cycle', the Consistency Model, which synthesizes a number of approaches, was formulated (Broekstra, 1986). This systemic model connects a number of key organizational processes such as entrepreneurial, technological, administrative and human resource processes with the systems of culture, politics and dominant coalition, each related to an environmental counterpart, through mutual consistency relationships. In order to be effective, over time this pattern of relationships needs to converge towards a coherent whole or organizational configuration (Broekstra, 1991).

Clearly, the organismic paradigm was less efficiency-oriented and more effectiveness-oriented than the mechanistic paradigm. However, the environment was regarded as more or less a given concrete entity to which the organization had to adapt, and not as a complex system of processes that co-evolved with those of the organization. Furthermore, the rationality of the consistency and configuration approach was basically dominated by a belief in an equilibrium perspective. Tavistock researchers Eric Trist et al.'s original observation about the nature of the relationships between the key variables in a system succinctly clarifies this point: 'if they [the variables] are not consistent, interference will occur, leading to a state of disequilibrium, so that achievement of the overall goal will to some degree be endangered and in the limit made impossible' (1963: 7).

Thus the organismic paradigm became the epitome of near-Darwinian gradualism emphasizing linear, incremental change in groping towards an ever better fit of the organizational unit with its environmental niche, interpreted as an equilibrium state. The term "equilibrium" is, however, somewhat of a misnomer. Equilibrium would mean death. "Temporary stability" would be a more accurate expression. From Prigogine's work we know that complex systems, like business organizations, which belong to the class of dissipative structures, exhibit order as a kind of temporary stability only in far-from-equilibrium conditions.

Temporary stability may hold true during a period of convergence towards a particular consistency configuration (Tushman and Romanelli, 1985). Yet, at a time when wholesale organizational renewal is at stake, fluctuations such as inconsistencies, paradoxes, conflicts and misfits become more important. As Miles and Snow (1994) noted, fit is a dynamic process, and yesterday's fit may become today's failure. This is precisely the situation that many organizations are facing today. Thus, a more encompassing perspective is needed, and is indeed gradually taking shape.

The emergence of the network organization   Sensing an 'organizational revolution' in the making, Miles and Snow (1984, 1986) were among the first to forecast the emergence of more flexible network forms of organizations, which started to pop up in more significant numbers mainly after the recession of the early 1980s. They made a distinction between various forms, such as stable, internal and dynamic external networks (Miles and Snow, 1992, 1994), and contrasted them with the older functional and divisional forms. The latter were perceived as less well suited to the demands of the new environments of global competition and rapid technological changes.

Although the network form has not yet reached a definitive mature form, and its complete system of underlying organizing principles is not yet well crystallized, some features stand out more clearly than others. For example, the complexity of, and, in particular, the innovation rate demanded by the new environments forced companies to focus their units on their respective distinctive competencies, and out-source non-distinctive activities. Thus networks of loosely coupled and collaborating dependencies are gradually created among basically autonomous units, both internally and externally.

Badaracco (1991) has argued that this focusing, and vertical disaggregation combined with loose coupling, cause a 'blurring of boundaries' between and within companies. Limerick and Cunnington noted that another distinguishing feature of these networks is the renewed search for synergies, but that 'synergies are sought and achieved by the parts themselves, and not superimposed on them by various structures or staff' (1993: 60). Miles and Snow (1992) added that networks rely more on contractual market mechanisms than administrative processes to co-operatively manage resource flows.

Limerick and Cunnington (1993) contended that the central idea of the new paradigm underlying the network of relationships is the twin concepts of autonomy and collaboration. They invented the paradoxical term 'collaborative individualism' for this phenomenon. Bartlett and Ghoshal (1989) perceived a similar trend among large multinational corporations in search of a 'transnational solution': the integrated network. They noticed the tendency among large corporations to disperse, yet specialize their assets and capabilities through the use of strong interdependencies. This pattern of interdependency was achieved by self-enforced co-operation among otherwise autonomous units.

The most conspicuous feature of the network organization is its capacity for self-renewal. In viewing an organization as multiple relationships in action, Janov (1994) contrasted the newly emerging vision-driven inventive organizations with the older goal-driven fixed and mission-driven adaptive organizations. Emphasizing innovation and renewal, she urged managers to go beyond adaptation, and 'provide the unexpected'.

Likewise, recognizing innovation as the key competitive issue today, the Japanese management scholar Nonaka (1988) urges us to think about innovation and renewal in a whole new way. He has written extensively about organizational self-renewal, most recently with Takeuchi (1995). Central to their insights is that knowledge creation is the driving force behind innovation and self-renewal. Japanese companies tend to distinguish between the explicit, which typically characterizes the Western orientation, and tacit aspects of knowledge creation, which is more typical for the oriental approach. Badaracco (1991) used the terms 'migratory' versus 'embedded' knowledge to describe these differing approaches. This distinction allows for a more holistic, dynamic and multilevel approach to innovation. Tacit knowledge includes subjective insights, intuition, experience, emotions and the use of metaphors. This type of knowledge can be thought of as that which is embedded in the deep structure of an organization (Broekstra, 1995).

In this context, Nonaka and Takeuchi's 1995 seminal book also proposed a new type of organizational form, which includes a middle–up–down management process and the hypertext structure. The latter structure is particularly interesting because the underlying idea makes sense from an evolutionary point of view, and builds on previous insights about parallel or collateral structures (Broekstra, 1986; Kanter, 1980; Zand, 1981). Briefly, Nonaka and Takeuchi proposed that bureaucracy and task force structures are complementary, so that their type of inventive organization has a non-hierarchical, self-organizing structure that co-exists with its formalized hierarchical structure. The hierarchical structure handles the routine work. The parallel structure constitutes a network of horizontal, across-units and project teams pursuing creativity and innovation. This is not to be confused with the matrix structure, because at any one point in time, in the hypertext organization organizational members belong and report to only one structure.

It would be a mistake to assume that the network organization has minimal, if any, formal authority or order-giving hierarchies. Hierarchy-bashing may be fashionable, but is pure nonsense. Certainly, the evolution of organizations has shown a punctuated process of dehierarchization since the swift emergence of the steep hierarchical pyramid over a century ago. The progressive 'complexification' of the world at large and the associated increasing rate of innovation appear to be the main driving forces behind the process of dehierarchization of organizations. As the pyramid flattens, self-steering emerges through increasingly smaller self-sufficient units. Thus, there also appears to be a concomitant process of miniaturization: from bureaucracy, through divisions, to business units, and finally to self-organizing teams.

The network organization of the future may contain elements, though considerably modified, of all previous organizational forms. As a result of this evolutionary development, the network organization of the future may consist of three overlapping layers: the hierarchy, autonomous units and the "cerebral cortex" of an intelligent network of relationships, greatly facilitated by the emerging electronic infrastructures. A good example of such a development has been proposed by Hock (1995), founder and retired chief executive of the VISA organization, a non-stock, for-profit, membership corporation. Contemplating its original radical organizational principles – equitable ownership, maximally distributed power and governance, etc. – and to express his idea that this organization was profitably balancing on the edge between chaos and order, he dubbed the innovative term the 'chaordic organization' for this type of network. Another radical example is the 'Internet organization', where 'no part knows the whole, the whole does not know all the parts and none has any need to' (Hock, 1995: 14). This may almost sound like blasphemy to today's modern managers. But, beware, the chaords of the future are already among us, quietly preparing to totally alter the competitive landscape.

The evolutionary paradigm

A few remarks have already been made about the new science of complexity that may become an important pillar for the new evolutionary paradigm. A few additional remarks are in order. Complex dynamic systems, while getting "better" at their games of interaction as time passes, tend to generate order of increasing complexity which emerges spontaneously. Of particular importance for organization theory and change are previous developments in complexity science such as Prigogine's dissipative structures (Nicolis and Prigogine, 1989) and Maturana and Varela's notion of autopoiesis (Varela, 1979). These have led to a re-conceptualization of organizations as having a deep structure that is organizationally closed (Broekstra, 1991). Recognizing an organization as a living system (the third paradigm) and not as a machine for information-processing (the second paradigm), Nonaka and Takeuchi (1995) also concede that a knowledge-creating organization is basically an autopoietic system.

Limerick and Cunnington (1993) contend that the primary motivation behind the design and use of network organizations is to provide the stimulation necessary for innovation. Of particular importance is their insight that loose coupling is the central notion of the network concept. They refer to Orton and Weick, who point out that loose coupling implies 'a situation in which elements are responsive, but retain separateness and identity' (1990: 203). Loose coupling is to be distinguished from tight coupling and decoupling. The science of complexity would suggest that decoupling refers to the frozen regime, whereas tight coupling entails that any disturbance would rapidly diffuse throughout the entire system, causing chaos. For example, too little communication could stifle an organization into a frozen status quo, whereas an overload of communication could cause confusion and chaos. The small edge between frozen order and chaos is the region of loose coupling.

This makes a lot of sense because, as noted, the edge of chaos is also the region of the highest creativity and innovation. Kauffman (1993) has performed fascinating experiments on random Boolean networks, the results of which appear to support this point of view. Transferring his findings from the realm of artificial life to the world of organizations, we are lured into hypothesizing that, naturally poised on the edge between order and chaos, organizations start to abandon the evolutionary "accident" of machine behaviour and become living organizations. After millions of years of research and development, the brain, as the most highly developed form of a living organization, then becomes a natural candidate for a metaphor which may help explicate the most salient features of the new organizational network form.

The triune-brain metaphor

Through the science of complexity, and the related alternative orientation in cognitive science called connectionism, 'the brain has once more become the main source of metaphors and ideas' (Varela et al., 1991: 87). Self-organization and the emergence of global coherence, from local rules in neural-like nets, have received considerable attention in the last few years. Particularly, the debate about the origin of mind and consciousness as emerging distributed phenomena of the intrinsic operation of the brain itself has gained best-selling status.

There are a number of intriguing similarities between the evolution of the triune brain and the evolution of the three organizational forms discussed above. With the emergence of the network organization, interest in the 'intelligent organization' has been increasing (Broekstra, 1992). Likewise, with the advent of the artificial life movement, the level of interest in the 'living organization' is on the rise. In this context, the triune brain is a rich metaphor for understanding organizational functioning and change, and that deserves further metaphoric, or "as if", exploration.

MacLean (1990) distinguished in the human forebrain three basic evolutionary formations that reflect an ancestral relationship to reptiles, early mammals and recent mammals. Thus, the architecture of the brain comprises three-brains-in-one – in effect, three relatively autonomous, but loosely coupled systems.

Briefly, the oldest "reptilian brain" located at the base of the forebrain regulates the primary vital functions such as breathing, eating, sexual behaviour, territoriality, intimidation of the opponent and 'formation of social hierarchies' (Jantsch, 1980: 166). In the reptilian brain, the daily master routines and subroutines are embedded, manifesting other basic behaviours such as the struggle for power, adherence to routine, imitation, obeisance to precedent, and deception (MacLean, 1990). It is this kind of reflex behaviour that is hard to change; it has only a very limited learning capability and therefore is not equipped for coping with new situations. The reptilian formation can be compared with the functional form of organization, as it is characterized by efficient routine behaviour in performing the primary functions of the corporation in a basically hierarchical context, usually governed by deeply ingrained rules and values.

During the second phase of evolutionary development came the "paleo-mammalian formation" or limbic system, in itself a totally integrated system. Receiving information from both the inner and outer world of the organism, it 'processes information in such a way that it becomes experienced as feelings and emotions become guiding forces for behavior' (Jantsch, 1980: 167). It is primarily geared towards self-preservation. It seeks to maintain equilibrium through homeostasis and can be changed through operant learning, meaning the immediate application of reward and punishment (the so-called Skinnerian behaviour shaped by its consequences). It is basically short term in orientation and contributes significantly to the formation of a personal identity (Jantsch, 1980).

The behaviour of the limbic system appears to compare most closely to that of the business unit structure. Here middle management is involved in short-term "homeostasis" for sustaining a fit with the unit's local environment, and, in the process, sustaining a distinct identity in the marketplace. Business unit management is also subjected to a kind of operant learning in attempting to attain its target budgets. The emotional and non-verbal aspects of the limbic system are mirrored in Nonaka and Takeuchi's (1995) observation that emotions are a part of tacit knowledge. Also the "middle management" role of the limbic system is reflected in the importance they attributed to the role of middle management in the knowledge-creating process.

Finally, encompassing the two older brain systems, like a 'judge's wig' (Beer, 1972), sits the more recently developed "neomammalian formation", chiefly the neocortex: seat of verbal communication, intelligent learning, problem solving, creativity, and so on. Its orientation is primarily towards the external world and is more long-termist than the limbic system. The "thoughts" of the neocortex and the "emotions" of the limbic system are to some extent independent phenomena and are often not in agreement. The famous example is smoking: you know you have to quit (cortex); you get mad when someone tells you so (the old mammal); and, subsequently, you don't change your habit (the reptile). It is suggested here that, though by comparison only to a modest extent, the cerebral mechanisms of the neocortex compare with that part of the internal network organization which is the parallel network of relationships within clusters of "neurones" focusing on longer-term innovation and renewal.

Like the triune brain, the architecture of the internal network organization comprises three layers in one: the functional layer, the layer of units, and the parallel circuitry of teams, task forces and other "horizontal" institutionalized relationships, overlaying the evolutionary older systems. They constitute three different modes of organizational intelligence, functional, unit and network intelligence, which need to be clearly distinguished both conceptually and structurally.

An example of this is provided by a successful Dutch co-operative bank, consisting of hundreds of local co-operative banks and a central organization, once, a century ago, itself an innovative concept to provide credit to farmers. Now, in this bank functional intelligence relates to providing standard products, such as checking and saving. Unit intelligence refers not so much to the autonomy of the local banks, though important, as to the bank's institutionalized product/market segmentation, providing more advanced mass-customized products and services. Both are heavily supported by information technology and are basically more or less centralized. The essence and strength of the co-operative system, however, is revealed in its hard-to-copy network intelligence. Through decentralized, and intimate, local interactions with their members, the local co-operative banks have a unique opportunity to greatly enhance innovation with long-term effects (this is comparable to Hock's chaordic membership organization discussed earlier).

A final remark should be made about the position of top management. Although senior managers and executives should be largely involved in corporate renewal, the organizational "neocortex" is not thought to be located at the apex of the traditional pyramid. On the contrary, the creative intelligence is thought to be distributed like a neural network across the entire organization. However, top management, guided by a vision of appropriate organizing principles, has an important role as the architect of this network and as a catalyst to promote self-organizing processes in it, keeping the organization poised on the edge between the Scylla and Charybdis of frozen order and complete chaos.

Does an organization have a mind?

Most organizations, public and private, come across as pretty mind-less. But there is some hope. If the brain is the seat of the mind, and organizations are developing the kind of network connectedness that is apparently needed to attain some minimal complexity for mind-like phenomena to emerge, the above question becomes quite pertinent, if not gripping. Inevitably, the next question would then be about consciousness.

Gustavsson (1992), in his treatise on consciousness in organizations, noted that culture may be better viewed as a manifestation of an underlying collective (un)consciousness. Allen and Kraft (1982) played on that idea in calling culture the 'organizational unconscious', a term reminiscent of Jung's collective unconscious.

Arguably, it is time that we start to take the concept of corporate consciousness seriously. This does not just mean "conscious-of-ness". Organizations already employ terms like cost consciousness, quality consciousness, and so on, meaning to be aware of costs and quality. The consideration of corporate consciousness should not preclude the analysis of characteristics such as its holographic nature (Cardamone, 1986; see also Morgan, 1986), its architecture and its transcendental nature, as a collective, subjective experience with a sense of self. This is not as far-fetched as it may sound and brings us back to what was said at the beginning of this chapter where Pascale et al. (1993) referred to the hidden dimension of a company's *being*. With all the centrifugal forces acting internally on a company nowadays, the need for a sense of shared selfhood is frequently expressed by, for example, the need to identify a corporate identity through shared values.

Under the two previous paradigms organizations were basically subject to forces of fragmentation. Fragmented consciousness can only be the source of limited, local intelligence, and hence the cause of undesirable side effects upon "the whole". With the advent of the more holistic network organization, the development of coherence in corporate consciousness holds the promise of increased creative intelligence and synergy in its inventive parts, such as self-managing task forces geared towards product and process innovation.

Gregory Bateson (1979) has formulated a set of criteria that, if satisfied by any system, will lead us to recognize that the system is a mind. He added that if one wants to understand such a system, one will 'need sorts of explanation different from those which would suffice to explain the characteristics of its smaller parts' (1979: 67). Among these criteria of mind he listed the following:

1   A mind is an aggregate of interacting parts (equivalent to the notion of the loosely coupled network).
2   Interaction between the parts of mind is triggered by difference (corresponding to the present emphasis on order-through-fluctuation, contention and paradox).
3   The mind requires collateral energy (which reminds us of the Gestalt approach's emphasis on raising awareness to mobilize energy in change processes [Nevis, 1987], but also Prigogine's (1989) conception of the brain as a dissipative structure).
4   The mind requires circular chains of determination (compare the concepts of organizational closure [Broekstra, 1991] and catalytic closure [Kauffman, 1993], both necessary, according to the artificial life movement, for the emergence of coherent order in living systems).

This can only be an impressionist sketch of where the new metaphor of corporate mind and corporate consciousness may lead us. It goes beyond the scope of this chapter to provide an answer to the opening question of this section. Clearly, as the saying goes, further research is necessary. But, at first sight, contemplating the strong applicability of Bateson's criteria to the conceptualization of an organization under the evolutionary paradigm, it may be that we are asking the wrong question. The question may have to be rephrased: *Is* an organization a mind (of sorts)?

Some speculative conclusions

The implications of the new evolutionary paradigm and the triune-brain
metaphor run far deeper, particularly for business organizations, than the
above cursory excursion into corporate consciousness may have revealed.
Pondering on the quantum revolution in technology and economics, Gilder
(1989: 17) opened his influential book with the assertion that: 'The central
event of the twentieth century is the overthrow of matter', that is, by
information. In an equally profound book on the bio-logic of the new
machines, Kelly (1994: 126) paraphrased by asserting that: 'The central
event of the twenty-first century will be the overthrow of information.'
There he referred to the emergence of self and self-consciousness from the
'out-of-control' circularities in network systems, the same strangely attract-
ing self-referential things the science of complexity, including second-order
cybernetics, and the artificial life movement have been coming up with.

We now see that the evolutionary drift appears to manifest a beautiful
sequence of, first, matter being replaced by information as the dominant
paradigm and, next, while we are virtually drowning in information overload, information being replaced by consciousness. Clearly, in our scheme,
matter, information and consciousness also figure as the fundamental con-
secutive notions behind the organization as a machine, an organism and a
brain, respectively.

To be sure, a new metaphor such as that of the triune brain is not just an
"as if" game. *Homo ludens* tends to take its games seriously. A new
metaphor may accelerate the development of a new way of organizing and
managing by articulating and synthesizing its fundamental underlying
assumptions about the world. That said, the concept of consciousness-as-
emergence advocated by Artificial Life research is certainly progressive with
respect to the more simplistic concept of consciousness-as-information
processing held by Artificial Intelligence. However, the emergence of
consciousness from the inner workings of complex dynamic systems still
carries a materialistic undertone.

The final, admittedly bolder, step has been taken by business scholars like
Harman (1988) and Ray and Rinzler (1993). Following 1981 Nobel Prize
winner Roger Sperry, they gave full recognition to the primacy of consciousness as a causal reality. Having abandoned Descartes' metaphysics of
dualism of mind and matter as separate entities, we may now perceive
wholesale replacement of today's "materialistic monism" by a new metaphysics. Materialism entails that matter/energy is thought to be the 'basic
stuff of the universe', and that matter gives rise to mind. By contrast, and in
keeping with the "perennial wisdom" of the world, the third metaphysics
holds that consciousness is the 'ultimate stuff of the universe' so that it is
'mind giving rise to matter' (Harman, 1988).

As Einstein rightly said: 'Scientists are tamed metaphysicists.' It may
sound like a pipe dream to think that managers, one day, will talk in terms
of "anchoring our organization in a coherent corporate consciousness". But

let us not forget what happened to Copernicus and Galileo. Moreover, the world is moving much faster today. If we agree that 'knowledge is the new competitive resource' (Nonaka and Takeuchi, 1995: 7), and we follow the ancient Vedic wisdom that 'knowledge is structured in consciousness', logic would require that consciousness is the new competitive resource. After all, the world is as we see it.

References

Allen, R.F. and Kraft, C. (1982) *The Organizational Unconscious*. Englewood Cliffs, NJ: Prentice Hall.

Badaracco, J.L. (1991) *The Knowledge Link: How Firms Compete through Strategic Alliances*. Boston: Harvard Business School Press.

Bak, P. and Chen, K. (1991) 'Self-Organized Criticality', *Scientific American*, 264 (1), 46–53.

Bartlett, C.A. and Ghoshal, S. (1989) *Managing across Borders: The Transnational Solution*. London: Century Business.

Bateson, G. (1979) *Mind and Nature: A Necessary Unity*. London: Wildwood House.

Beer, M., Eisenstatt, R.A. and Spector, B. (1990) *The Critical Path to Corporate Renewal*. Boston: Harvard Business School Press.

Beer, S. (1972) *Brain of the Firm*. London: Allen Lane.

Beer, S. (1979) *The Heart of Enterprise*. Chichester: John Wiley and Sons.

Bertalanffy, L. von (1950) 'The theory of open systems in physics and biology', *Science*, 111, 23–29.

Broekstra, G. (1986) 'Organizational humanity and architecture: Duality and complementarity of papa-logic and mama-logic in managerial conceptualizations of change', *Cybernetics and Systems: An International Journal*, 17, 13–41.

Broekstra, G. (1991) 'Consistency, configuration, closure and change', in R.J. in't Veld (ed.), *Autopoiesis and Configuration Theory: New Approaches to Societal Steering*. Dordrecht: Kluwer, pp. 113–126.

Broekstra, G. (1992) 'Toward a theory of organizational change: The chaos hypothesis', in R. Trappl (ed.), *Cybernetics and Systems Research '92*. Singapore: World Scientific, pp. 1023–1030.

Broekstra, G. (1993) 'Chaos, the fifth environment and the revolution of inter-organizational cooperation', in R. Glanville and G. de Zeeuw (eds), Problems of Support, Survival and Culture, Special Issue, *Systemica*, 9 (1–6), Amsterdam: Thesis Publishers, pp. 21–31.

Broekstra, G. (1995) 'Organizations are closed systems', in R. Glanville and G. de Zeeuw (eds), Problems of Excavating the Foundations of Cybernetics, Special Issue, *Systemica*, 10 (1–6), Amsterdam: Thesis Publishers, pp. 1–6.

Business Week Reporters (1986) 'What's in – what's out', *Business Week*, 27 January, 30–39.

Cardamone, M.A. (1986) 'The likeness of mind', in R.K.Ragade (ed.), *General Systems: Yearbook of the Society for General Systems Research*, Louisville, KY: SGSR, pp. 49–61.

Chandler, A.D. (1962) *Strategy and Structure: Chapters in the History of the Industrial Enterprise*. Cambridge, MA: MIT Press.

Chandler, A.D. (1977) *The Visible Hand: The Managerial Revolution in American Business*. Cambridge, MA: Belknap Press.

Drucker, P.F. (1994) 'The theory of the business', *Harvard Business Review*, Sept.–Oct, 95–104.

Eccles, R.G. and Nohria, N. (1992) *Beyond the Hype: Rediscovering the Essence of Management*. Boston: Harvard Business School Press.

Galbraith, J.R. (1973) *Designing Complex Organizations*. Reading, MA: Addison-Wesley.

Gilder, G. (1989) *Microcosm: The Quantum Revolution in Economics and Technology*. New York: Simon & Schuster.

Gustavsson, B. (1992) *The Transcendent Organization*. Stockholm: University of Stockholm.

Harman, W. (1988) *Global Mind Change: The Promise of the Last Years of the 20th Century*. Indianapolis: Knowledge Systems.

Hock, D.W. (1995) 'The chaordic organization: Out of control and into order', *World Business Academy Perspectives*, 9 (1), 5–18.

Janov, J. (1994) *The Inventive Organization: Hope and Daring at Work*. San Francisco: Jossey-Bass.

Jantsch, E. (1973) 'Forecasting and systems approach: A frame of reference', *Management Science*, 19 (12), 1355–1368.

Jantsch, E. (1980) *The Self-Organizing Universe: Scientific and Human Implications of the Emerging Paradigm of Evolution*. Oxford: Pergamon.

Jones, R.S. (1982) *Physics as Metaphor*. New York: Meridian.

Kanter, R.M. (1980) 'Building the parallel organization: Creating mechanisms for permanent QWL', *Journal of Applied Behavioral Science*, 16 (4), 371–388.

Kauffman, S.A. (1993) *The Origins of Order: Self-Organization and Selection in Evolution*. Oxford: Oxford University Press.

Kelly, K. (1994) *Out of Control: The New Biology of Machines, Social Systems and the Economic World*. Reading, MA: Addison-Wesley.

Lawrence, P.R. and Lorsch, J.W. (1967) *Organization and Environment: Managing Differentiation and Integration*. Boston: Harvard University Press.

Lewin, R. (1992) *Complexity: Life at the Edge of Chaos*. New York: Macmillan.

Limerick, D. and Cunnington, B. (1993) *Managing the New Organization: A Blueprint for Networks and Strategic Alliances*. San Francisco: Jossey-Bass.

MacLean, P.D. (1990) *The Triune Brain in Evolution*. New York: Plenum Press.

Miles, R.E. and Snow, C.C. (1978) *Organizational Strategy, Structure, and Process*. New York: McGraw-Hill.

Miles, R.E. and Snow, C.C. (1984) 'Fit, failure and the Hall of Fame', *California Management Review*, XXVI (3), 10–28.

Miles, R.E. and Snow, C.C. (1986) 'Organizations: New concepts for new forms', *California Management Review*, XXVII (3), 62–73.

Miles, R.E. and Snow, C.C. (1992) 'Causes of failure in network organizations', *California Management Review*, Summer, 53–72.

Miles, R.E. and Snow, C.C. (1994) *Fit, Failure, and the Hall of Fame: How Companies Succeed or Fail*. New York: Free Press.

Morgan, G. (1986) *Images of Organization*. Beverly Hills, CA: Sage Publications.

Nevis, E.C. (1987) *Organizational Consulting: A Gestalt Approach*. New York: Gardner Press.

Nicolis, G. and Prigogine, I. (1989) *Exploring Complexity: An Introduction*. New York: Freeman.

Nonaka, I. (1988) 'Creating organizational order out of chaos: Self-renewal in Japanese firms', *California Management Review*, Spring, 57–73.

Nonaka, I. and Takeuchi, H. (1995) *The Knowledge-Creating Company: How Japanese Companies Create the Dynamics of Innovation*. New York: Oxford University Press.

Orton, J.D. and Weick, K.E. (1990) 'Loosely coupled systems: A reconceptualization', *Academy of Management Review*, 15 (2), 203–223.

Pascale, R.T., Goss, T. and Athos, A. (1993) 'The reinvention roller coaster: Risking the present for a powerful future', *Harvard Business Review*, Nov.–Dec., 97–108.

Ray, M. and Rinzler, A. (eds) (1993) *The New Paradigm in Business*. New York: Putnam.

Sloan, A.P. (1963) *My Years with General Motors*. New York: Doubleday.

Toffler, A. (1985) *The Adaptive Corporation*. London: Pan Books.

Trist, E.L., Higgin, G.W., Murray, H. and Pollock, A.B. (1963) *Organizational Choice*. London: Tavistock Publications.

Tushman, M.L. and Romanelli, E. (1985) 'Organization evolution: A metamorphosis model of convergence and reorientation', in L.L.Cummings and B.M. Staw (eds), *Research in Organizational Behavior*, Vol. 7. Greenwich, CT: JAI Press, pp. 171–222.

Varela, F.J. (1979) *Principles of Biological Autonomy*. New York: North Holland.

Varela, F.J., Thompson, E. and Rosch, E. (1991) *The Embodied Mind: Cognitive Science and Human Experience*. Cambridge, MA: MIT Press.

Waldrop, M.M. (1992) *Complexity: The Emerging Science at the Edge of Order and Chaos*. Harmondsworth: Penguin Books.

Zand, D.E. (1981) *Information, Organization, and Power: Effective Management in the Knowledge Society*. New York: McGraw-Hill.

4

Metaphors in Organizational Research: Of Embedded Embryos, Paradigms and Powerful People

Stewart R. Clegg and John T. Gray

In the beginning was the word

One word. The word was "embryonic". We began with a metaphor. At the outset it was almost all we had. Although we were to live with it intimately for a period of three to four months it was not a word of our choosing. Unlike the fictitious consumer sovereign we were not "free to choose". The word was already writ. Our role was to dwell in the word, not to deconstruct it. The house of language, defined through this one word, connected to the sign of the dollar, held us, as research consultants to Government, if not exactly captive, at least in thrall for the period of our research.

In other words: The metaphor of "embryonic industry" had been chosen by the Taskforce, yet the Inquiry that it mounted did not define what it meant by this term. Consequently we, as consultants to the Inquiry into Australia's Leadership and Management Needs into the 21st century, commissioned to discover these needs for embryonic industry, were to define embryonic industry as

> new and emerging. Its novelty lies in the application of distinctive practices to production, service or problem resolution in ways that are discontinuous with existing technologies, values and knowledge. The root metaphor is that of an "embryo". If there is not something that is new and discontinuous then there would be no new conception, nothing in embryo. At the core are innovation in products and processes. Innovation is not just technical; it is also organizational and managerial. (Clegg et al., 1995: 6)

One might say that we blurred the metaphor without ever losing its sense. As we were to discover, in all our discussions, the title was more significant than the definition. It provided a means for reasonable address, and research, of a topic that fitted our interpretation of what we took to be the intentions of our patrons.

Several metaphors affected the research in addition to the chief metaphor of embryos. The metaphor (and the practicalities) of specialist knowledge in "compartments", the "tyranny" of an impossibly short "deadline", the embodiment in the Taskforce of "the Government". Each of these influenced the schema of the project team and, accordingly, its symbols, language and interpretations. Consequently its various representations – to respondents to the research; to senior international academics who advised the research team; to the entrepreneurs, financiers and officials who contributed data, insight and focus to our deliberations – were all riven through with these artefacts.

The research design ensured that reflective dialogue was commonplace between researchers and the respondents. The major empirical method consisted of "Focus Groups" in which insights from various literatures were exposed, discussed, affirmed and corrected. The process of preparing a large amount of analytical material for presentation and discussion with the focus groups demanded considerable effort in a short period of time, but the value of such open discourse was that it enabled critical, frequent and reflexive revision of interpretations. Chief of these were a shifting focus on the importance of the market, the embeddedness of industry and the criticality of management education.

The research report is structured around various metaphors, constituted with a Government and Public Service audience in mind and written in what its principal author constituted as an accessible style. To some readers the style offends the myth of "The Report to Government", whilst to others it seems refreshingly direct, readable and accordingly influential. Metaphors vitally affected this research in all of its stages and in the thinking of all of its key players. This chapter explores the most significant of these stages and players and provides background and detail sufficient to judge their power. Our presentation of the report begins where we did not: already deeply imbued in metaphoricality, represented through a poem – Australian, of course.

A commencing metaphor

All their lives in a box! What generations,
What centuries of masters, not meaning to be cruel
But needing their labour, taught these creatures such patience
That now though sunlight strikes on the eye's dark jewel
Or moonlight breathes on the wing they do not stir
But like the ghost of moths crouch silent there.
Look it's a child's toy! There is no lid even,
They can climb, they can fly, and the whole world's their tree;
But hush, they say in themselves, we are in prison.
There is no word to tell them that they are free,
And they are not; ancestral voices bind them
In dream too deep for wind to find them.

This is an extract from 'The Silkworms' by Douglas Stewart (1967), of which the poet is reported to have said, 'Oh, it is just a minor piece about some insects.' It was D.H. Lawrence, of course, whose injunction was always to trust the tale, not the teller. On this occasion at least, it might be wise to do so.

Readers interpret much more into the work than a descriptive piece about the habits of insects. The text is seen as metaphorical; the insects' prison analogous to the ideational prisons that humans create. Yet the open-lidded box does not contain the silkworms, their behaviour does. Their understanding of their world constitutes their world. Where there is no word to tell them they are free then they are trapped. Organizational analysts, when they first read Stewart, often find the metaphor reminiscent. The complete poem is replete with metaphors that are commonplace in organization theory. It includes the prison, means of domination, language games, organism, and also dreaming. Only the latter, perhaps, is less than common currency in the vernacular.

How do we react when confronted with such a piece? What sense do we make of it? Does it improve our reflection and analysis? Does the ready realization that the poem, like organizational analysis, is an effect of metaphor disturb us? Does it disturb us that its art is no less than our science? Is all science and language metaphor?

Stewart cleverly uses a commonplace child's pastime to make us reminiscent, then encourages interpretation. He uses metaphor as a means of focus rather than embellishment. His poems seem elusively multi-paradigmatic and touch a wide readership. His text "belongs" to the reader; encouraging interpretation, challenging varying ways of seeing the "real" meaning.

In counterpoint to the rich range of the poet, Morgan (1980: 605) reminds us of a description given by Mannheim. The son of a peasant lives trapped in and impoverished by his rural world view. His experience is so limited, his discourse so dependent on the native soil that he can conceive of no alternative. Then he visits the city. Here, he discovers an alternative reality when first he leaves the country, or as we would say "the bush", and visits the city. Now he has two world views which he can consciously apply. Stewart's poem hints at similar disjunctures. There are alternatives but one must have power to find them and that power can be found only in experience and its language. Morgan's (1980) piece similarly explores the value of the explicit recognition of alternative paradigms.

There is little that is original in what Morgan (1980) has to say. In many ways he trades off the restricted habitat that his presumed audience is wont to cultivate. The novelty is in straying into the paddock cultivated by the historians, and philosophers, of science.

Frequently, after Kuhn (1962), it is argued that science emanates from underlying assumptions. Such differing assumptions, if strongly framed, may constitute alternative realities or paradigms. For Kuhn their framing and its strength is a matter of historical linearity. Rarely do we see mutually exclusive and strong paradigmatic assumptions occupying the same chronological space.

Within paradigms we construct metaphors. These function as the basis for schools of thought that employ consistent technologies to analyse and interpret data or to puzzle solve. Whilst Morgan seems sanguine concerning the temporal co-presence of alternative realities, as underlying assumptions to science, Kuhn's original explanation of a paradigm was as a dominant assumption accepted by a community. This dominant paradigm defined normal science. 'Discovery commences with the awareness of anomaly, i.e., with the recognition that nature has somehow violated the paradigm-induced expectations that govern normal science' (Kuhn, 1962: 65). Further, he argues that such anomaly brings on scientific revolution. (Kuhn appears here to express a decidedly objectivist view of nature, though he is not consistent in that stance.) This explanation of scientific domination (see Phillips, 1973: 28–31) seems to express the notion of a battle of paradigms with only one declared victor at any time by the consensus of a scientific community.

Morgan implicitly contests that point. In doing so, his reference is rather more Feyerabendian (cited in Phillips, 1973) than Kuhnian. He suggests that it is possible that there exist several paradigms from within which different and contemporary subcultures within a scientific community might develop. Whilst he limits his description to currently powerful paradigms, there is no suggestion that the future will differ. No future paradigmatic unity, a state of discursive grace, is presumed. Morgan's diagram (see Figure 4.1), which, in a poetic image, seems faintly to represent a parent gathering children, quickly describes the connections between Kuhn's paradigms and puzzle solving. The important link device is that of metaphors.

Handily, in the same place, he suggests that four paradigms are influential in organizational analysis (Figure 4.2). On this occasion he elaborates the metaphors that are attached to them.

Before we discuss further the use of metaphors in research it is worthwhile to revisit this well-used matrix. It divides between cells which are more or less objectivist or subjectivist on one axis and more or less conservative (regulatory) or critical (radical) on the other. These axes reflect major debates of social science during the 1960s and 1970s which are here appropriated to report metaphors in use by organizational analysts.

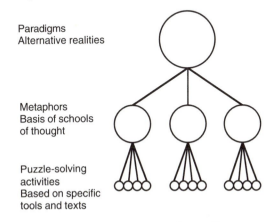

Paradigms
Alternative realities

Metaphors
Basis of schools
of thought

Puzzle-solving
activities
Based on specific
tools and texts

Figure 4.1 *Paradigms, metaphors and puzzle solving: Three concepts for understanding the nature of organization science.* Source: Reprinted from G. Morgan, 'Paradigms, Metaphors and Puzzle solving in Organization Theory', published in *Administrative Science Quarterly*, 25(4): 606, by permission of *Administrative Science Quarterly*.

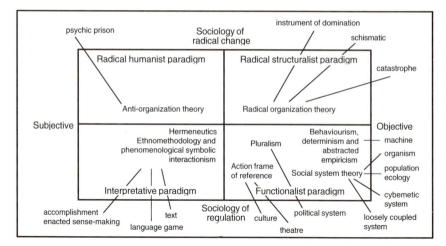

Figure 4.2 *Paradigms, metaphors and related schools of organizational analysis.* Source: Reprinted from G. Morgan, 'Paradigms, Metaphors and Puzzle solving in Organization Theory', published in *Administrative Science Quarterly*, 25(4): 608, by permission of *Administrative Science Quarterly*.

The functionalist paradigm assumes 'that society has a concrete, real existence, and a systemic character oriented to produce an ordered and regulated state of affairs' (Morgan, 1980: 608). Metaphors commonly used in this paradigm include that of the organism or machine. The interpretative paradigm is based on a view that 'the social world has a very precarious ontological status, and what passes as social reality does not exist in any concrete sense, but is the product of . . . experience of individuals' (Morgan, 1980;608). Metaphors commonly found within this paradigm include text, discourse or language game. These paradigms are in distinct counterpoint as 'the interpretative theorist . . . view[s] the functionalist's attempt to establish an objective social science as an unattainable end' (Morgan, 1980: 609). This dichotomy deserves marking as it is germane to our later extended discussion of metaphors in research as well as being the subject of a well-known debate between Morgan (1980, 1983) and Bourgeois and Pinder (1983; Pinder and Bourgeois, 1982).

The radical humanist paradigm is similarly sceptical of the ontological status of the social world and adopts a critical view of the ideational constructs which are experienced. Metaphors commonly found within this paradigm include the psychic prison and the Panopticon. To provide the symmetry we expect, the radical structuralist paradigm aligns with functionalism in its view on the concrete nature of social reality but is critical of dominating institutions within it. Metaphors commonly found within it include catastrophe, crisis and instruments of domination.

Morgan argues that metaphors reveal underlying assumptions. Thus a researcher who uses organic metaphors, such as embryonic industry, will have proceeded, *de jure*, from an objectivist paradigm. We shall argue that this is not necessarily so, even in the given circumstances in which we found ourselves unwittingly in thrall to the metaphoricality of absent others.

Metaphors are of course a means of suggesting that an item has some of the qualities of another item which is the metaphor. Thus to say that an organization is a garbage can is not to say that it has all the qualities of a garbage can, yet that it can be represented as having some of them.

The simplest of distinctions can elude the shrillest of critics. Pinder and Bourgeois (1982: 644) produce an argument that is particularly silly concerning the garbage can and decision-making. Congruence is sought between the metaphor, garbage can, and the organizational phenomena. Thus they note that the age of decision-makers may be analogous to the time of garbage decomposition, urgency may be analogous to heat caused by decay in the garbage can. They express dismay that other features of the metaphor such as the amount of biodegradable contents and the air-tightness of the lid create problems for the reader. It all depends. How literal is the reader? How poetic is his/her imagination? The vivacity or turgidity of the reader's imagination, regrettably, can be no more prescribed by the organization theorist than by the poet. For many of our colleagues, unmoved by an inkling of the muse even when visibly animated and exercised by it, this may be no problem. For others, particularly the rare philosopher-poets like Jim March, it presents certain insuperable barriers to understanding.

Pinder and Bourgeois argue that poetic or metaphorical inexactitude causes the 'reader ... to analogize, ... to gain an appreciation for the complexity and indeterminacy ... in the process' (1982: 644). Of course they do. That is a constitutive part of the purpose of metaphors. It is, one might say, their form of life. 'Effective metaphor is a form of creative expression which relies upon constructive falsehood as a means of liberating the imagination' (Morgan, 1980: 612). Indeed, it does.

Discussion need not be so literal, so dull, as Bourgeois and Pinder would have it be. Recall the dichotomous views concerning the ontology of social reality that Morgan suggests. In the interpretative perspective we can say that language is the phenomenon under investigation. Wittgenstein put it aptly:

> So you are saying that human agreement decides what is true and what is false?
> – It is what human beings say that is true and false: and they agree in the language they use. That is not agreement in opinions but in form of life. (1953: 28)

The test of "truth" of interpretations is acceptance of a scientific community which depends on ideological commitment learned within a culture of language. Therein metaphors are means of expression, liberation and innovation. From the point of view of our region of the dismal sciences they are part of that language game by which organizational analysts define the science that they do.

On the one hand the concrete view of social reality is that 'there is pure experience. Facts that are recorded from nature' (Phillips, 1973: 33). Within this rubric metaphors are inextricably woven into our common speech and embellish natural facts. To reach the facts unadorned by metaphor, to capture them in all their brutish nature, this should be the goal. Pinder and Bourgeois (1982) warn that administrative science borrows metaphors from other sciences and walks of life. Such sequestration (they argue) embellishes fact and obscures or distorts meaning. They call for a science which eschews metaphors in its creation of theory, or at least openly recognizes their use and preferably creates a clean terminology, metaphorically unpolluted, one based only on natural facts. This is reminiscent of the fantasy-island of pure speech that Wittgenstein carried around in his knap-sack in the Austrian trenches of the First World War, only to question and abandon it subsequently.

Morgan (1983) disposes of these positivist prescriptions sufficiently without us needing to add our wit or weight, yet the debate should be noted: doubtless some of its premises will recur. None the less, in arriving at their conclusions, Pinder and Bourgeois (1982: 647–649) traverse interesting territory concerning metaphors; not least they ask 'why do we use metaphors?' It is conceivable that a more interesting question might be 'how do we not use metaphors discursively?'

Pinder and Bourgeois' reasons for using metaphors include the following:

1. language is inherently figurative;
2. metaphor usage demonstrates cleverness;
3. borrowing metaphors from other disciplines brings legitimacy;
4. metaphoricality is a result of being multi-disciplinary;
5. when we ignore existential presuppositions we will use metaphors;
6. finally, metaphor use is expedient.

To this we would add Morgan's (1980: 610–611) list:

7. metaphors are central to the way in which humans forge their experience;
8. through metaphor we develop language;
9. not only are metaphors essential to the development of language, but, what amounts almost to the same thing, they are essential to develop cognition;
10. through metaphor we generate an image of data.

With the exception of borrowing to bring legitimacy, which seems an example of scientific cultural cringe, each of these aspects of the use of metaphor might be said to have played some part in our recent research.

Metaphors in research

How do we use metaphors in organizational research? As the debate sketched above reminds us, metaphors are part of our means for forging experiences. It may be that they can be traced back to underlying assumptions or dominant paradigms or that the device can be used to switch analysis from one school of thought to another. Typically, however, we use them in explanation of phenomena we have experienced. We attach them to phenomena to shape and interpret them. Researchers review their data and detect some patterns and then they use metaphors to explain these patterns.

Most metaphors are attached to processes *post hoc*. A prime example of this behaviour is represented by Bolman and Deal (1991) in their explanations of the different frames that one may use in conducting organizational research. They identify patterns of understanding organizational behaviour and symbolism and attach metaphors to these patterns. Thus the structuralist or determinist view of an organization is typified as the factory; the people management approach as the family; the political approach as the jungle; the symbolic approach as theatre. Deal and Bolman use the organization as their unit of analysis and do so in a reflexive attitude. These *post hoc* analytical formulae have found favour with practitioners. Dunford and Palmer (1995) have tested these analytical metaphors with practising managers and report that the metaphors were easily understood, that managers were able to switch frames to reflect upon data; further, that the managers reported that this improved their decision-making. Researchers might note the potential of such a scheme for their interpretation of data.

Other authors adopt a more individual focus. They investigate the use of metaphors in unravelling organizational dilemmas and as a means of interpreting the 'mental chart' of the manager. Hampden-Turner (1990) is a prime example of such an approach. His work, rich with metaphors, portrays the manager as 'standing at the helm' charting the organizational craft between the rock (Scylla) and the whirlpool (Charybdis). His research uses metaphors to explain phenomena described by respondents and iterated to others. As Hampden-Turner reminds us, Lévi-Strauss once described a metaphor as 'the likeness of unlike categories' and goes on to explain that managers create a mental construct laden with metaphor to interpret organizational affairs. Managers thereby use metaphors in the process of managing organizational meaning, as artefacts in the culture of the organization.

All the authorities to whom we have so far alluded agree that metaphors enable the creation of mental constructs within either a scientific community, practising managers or research respondents. All agree that they are inevitable and all but Pinder and Bourgeois see them as valuable devices for research. All agree, though in different fashions, that they are applied after the event.

Recently we were involved in a major piece of research into leadership and management commissioned by the Australian Government. In that research the metaphor was *ante hoc* and it affected all work and relations. The fact that the metaphor was applied before data collection and at the request of the patron makes it a special case. If we were to follow Morgan's (1980) logic, our use of an organic metaphor would reveal us as functionalists, whereas our writing (Clegg et al., 1995) concerning embryonic industry is decidedly interpretative. The metaphor of embryo permeated language and symbols and structured respondents' constructs. The ambiguity of the metaphor provided a device that permitted respondents to find coherence, to find likeness in unlike categories, during the process of data collection.

After the research was complete we did choose to indulge in some *post hoc* metaphoricalizing; yet this had a specific strategic purpose (Clegg and Gray, 1994). We presented our views to a national conference on strategic management education but intentionally chose different metaphors; those relating to a scientific voyage of discovery in which interesting specimens were found, in order to contribute to an extended debate in the academy. In this instance we felt competing responsibilities. Our patron demanded and deserved confidentiality of findings until its full report had been discussed by Cabinet. Yet the observations we had made were separate neither from other research, nor from the debate in Australia concerning the roles of management education in industry development. Our paper to the conference scrupulously avoided revealing final conclusions and recommendations to the Taskforce but openly discussed intriguing phenomena we had seen on the voyage which related to the debate. Thus we used "metaphor" to preserve the patron's needs while serving the academy's need for discussion.

Researchers will thus find significant use for metaphors; particularly when they are sufficiently understandable to focus respondents yet sufficiently ambiguous to permit latitude in that focus. We found in our brief, quite serendipitously, such a metaphor. At first we played with it in our team discussions, but increasingly we became more and more serious about the metaphor and its use in gathering, interpreting and reporting data. It affected the cognitive constructs of the researchers and consequently interpretations which used the metaphor gained relatively more prominence than those which did not. It affected our discourse. It became the grammatical basis for our mode of rationality, our way of making sense of the scenes that we, and others, constituted ourselves as being enveloped within. The research team came to use language, symbols and other artefacts, which drew from the base metaphor to structure understandings and interpret these to respondents.

In this instance the metaphor was *ante hoc* to the research and had a significant effect on its outcomes. The metaphor was used as a liberating, creative device to focus discussion within an arena.

The research process

This story relates to research which we conducted for the Australian Government from September 1993 to January 1994. The Government had established a National Taskforce of Inquiry into Australia's Leadership and Management Needs into the 21st Century. The Taskforce commissioned a number of bids for research projects. We made two bids for projects, initially for another project, but we were steered towards the 'embryonic industry' commission as the Taskforce sought to reserve the project that we first bid for as an enclave for an internationally renowned consulting group named after a North-Eastern city in the United States.

Several powerful metaphors affected the research, for good and ill, that related to the research topic, the perceptions of the researchers, the respondents and the readers. The route the research took needs to be sketched quickly before we discuss the effects of metaphors. The method contained several parts: some were cumulative and some were iterative; for our purposes they can be divided as follows:

- Literature Analysis;
- International Hubs of Advisers which we formed around influential and respected colleagues in the UK, USA, Canada, Hong Kong;
- Focus Groups which we formed, comprising high-level executives, entrepreneurs, officials, financiers, academics in the major East Coast Cities of Australia;
- Invited Submissions;
- Reviews of the many Draft Reports which were provided by international hubs, some focus group members and faculty;
- Interviews with entrepreneurs in embryonic industry;
- Inquiry Mentor Discussions.

It can be seen that the research was busy work. There were many sites, some literally thousands of kilometres apart and others metaphorically close; yet all of them related, both metaphorically and by spatial proximity. From beginning to end the research had to be completed to penultimate draft stage within three months; to final draft stage within four.

Metaphorical metamorphism

The topic, 'What are the leadership and management needs of Embryonic Industry?', had been chosen by the Taskforce. There are no records for the basis of this nomenclature. Yet it may have been a very different study if we had been asked to investigate emerging industry or growing industry. No, we were not asked to investigate the baby, nor the growing child, nor even the foetus, but the embryo. The definition which is now accepted by the Industry Taskforce and the Australian Government is the one that we provided.

Here, perhaps, is a first effect of metaphors in research; their ambiguity provides capacity for ingenuity and creativity which, if properly managed, can be most effective. The consultant in the team, perhaps cynically, felt that the best brief is the one defined by the consultant and agreed by the patron. It was to be so in this instance due to some exceptionally fine project management by our Research Manager. She held the sword of Damocles above us, reminded us of deadlines but gave us sufficient space to be creative. We defined embryonic industry, and, in the process, as remarked above, blurred the metaphor without ever losing its sense. Thus was conceived a topic which could be reasonably researched; moreover, it was one that fitted our interpretation of the intentions of our patron that we never had to call to further account.

Indeed there was a sense of hermeneutics in the topic definition. We can recall that hermeneutics requires of the learners that they know of the universe of data before they know of the subset; but that the subsets build the universe. Thus there is a circle of hermeneutics and the process of topic definition was exemplary of this "hermeneutic circle". The Taskforce asked us to investigate embryonic industry but never defined what it meant by the term. After literature research and field discussions we developed a definition. The circle was completed some months later, when the Task-force's Research Manager published a research lexicon for all the Taskforce's deliberations. Included therein were the expected and well-known definitions of topics for the several commissioned projects, including our definition of embryonic industry. If Molière's *bourgeois gentilhomme* was surprised to discover that he had always spoken in prose (much as a later Bourgeois might express similar surprise on a not unrelated topic), these researchers were pleased to see that an elective affinity comprised a goodness of fit between authorities that defined embryonic industry!

But hermeneutics is more than this romanticist circle; it also implies (Gadamer, 1989) that the real meaning of the text is determined by the reader and is beyond the fiat of the author. This metaphor of embryonic industry had been determined by our main reader, the Taskforce, to be identical with our conception. It was determined by our respondents (not only the Taskforce) as understandable, ambiguous yet broadly focused, while liberating in terms of the negotiated order researched.

The first group transformed by the metaphor was the researchers. We formed a core project team which included expertise in organizational analysis, economics, public policy analysis, sociology and commercial consultancy. This was neither entirely accidental nor totally planned. We were committed to the notion of a multi-disciplinary project and, given the time constraints, were fortunate to acquire the talented team that we did. Having said this, one must immediately mention that some of the researchers took a considerably different role than first expected. Our original plan involved much economic analysis and forecasting. This was not to be. Particularly in public policy areas, economics has had a disproportionately powerful role in Australian industry debate. Yet, whilst the original design was simple, it was too simple.

Our original plan was to base insight on economic analysis of global trends in embryonic industry and to posit Australia's competitive advantages in those industries identified. Once these were defined we would define leadership and management needs in industry sited at these trend lines. This plan omitted the complexities of society. Industry does not innovate, a firm does. Moreover, this innovation does not occur separately from other influences. Public agencies, the market, aggregating groups, institutional practices, labour groups and others enable or deny the firm's innovation and growth. Our initial view was, in these respects, under-socialized. After further research and interpretation we concluded that our focus was, most appropriately, to be the firm, embedded in a complex.

Typically, one considers the influences on one's analyses in reflection. Why did we so rapidly learn that our original design should be improved? Did the nice fit of the notion of market embeddedness with the metaphor of an embryo embedded in a nourishing medium affect our rapid acceptance and modification of our initial under-socialized views? Clearly this fit with our construct and its consistency with artefacts that members of the team had previously made their own was powerful. As was the tyranny of a very short deadline.

We used a diagram to represent this notion of an embryonic firm embedded in a complex (Figure 4.3). The process of rendering this diagram was uneven: it began as a representation of work first seen in an unpublished chapter for a book of one of the team members and rapidly transformed into an artefact in its own right.

Embedded embryos

The notion of the embryonic firm swirling in its search for a medium in which to nourish is the centre point of the complex (described above) and our research. Innovators identify opportunity which has the potential to bring to market new concepts, products and services and they seek allies which can assist development. These might be, for example, venture capitalists, public agencies, networks or established firms. Thus one innovating firm might discover nurture from an alliance with a venture capitalist, whilst another might find a corporate parent in an established firm.

Proceeding from this schema we found some European analyses of successful innovation particularly useful. Fairtlough (1994) described the processes which his firm, Celltech, used to foster innovation. Fairtlough was Managing Director of Shell Chemicals UK, where he learned that the traditional functional management paradigm stifled innovation. He made significant changes at Shell but his views were given full rein when he formed Celltech, eventually a spectacularly successful firm. This firm became renowned for its biotechnological breakthroughs and market success. Its staff adopted an approach which was considerably different to the prevailing managerialist paradigm, one more attuned to virtuous circles that empower the workforce to innovate. Several of his concepts were particularly powerful in our understanding of phenomena in embryonic industry.

Fairtlough (1994) talks of compartments as a means of growing innovation. His argument is that the organization should rigorously debate the innovation, process it, make the innovator champion it against critics, but once it is accepted place it in a compartment with elements which nurture it. He is a biologist who consistently uses the biological metaphor in his explanations of innovation, yet, despite Morgan's (1980) advice, this does not reveal, we believe, underlying determinist assumptions. Hence, he accepts the possibility of the nurturing of allies during compartmentalization who may in later development become competitors for resources. These notions of compartments and collaboration fitted nicely with our concepts and were readily explained to respondents within our metaphor.

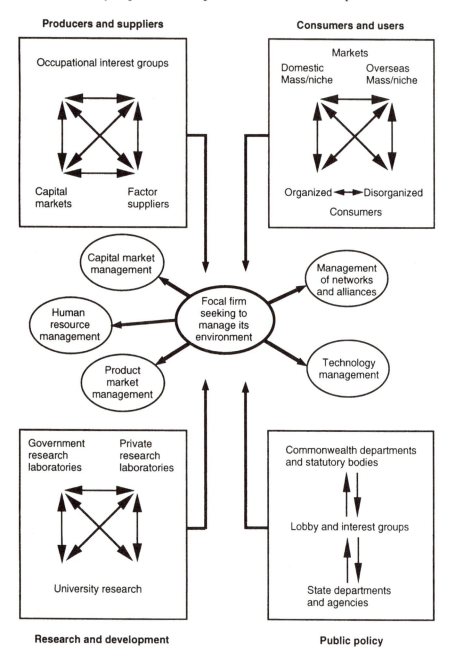

Figure 4.3   *The embryonic industry complex and a focal firm*

Paradigms: Blind alleys and blinkers

During our literature analysis we took a traditional approach to the problem and found ourselves searching the obvious keywords, embryonic industry, with little success. When we broadened this to include innovation, technology, industry growth, a literature presented itself; yet it was one considerably economic and predominantly technological. Enter the metaphor of the scientist bravely innovating through technology. As argued elsewhere (Gray, 1994), one can become blinkered and misled by a discipline; yet the task of researchers is to look around such blinkers, take wide counsel and remain focused upon the brief.

The literature of technology is voluminous and influential in policy-making circles. It led us to an initial definition of embryonic industry and to a series of tentative propositions that we took to focus groups in each of the capital cities on the East Coast of Australia.

We were seduced by Freeman's (1987) eloquent argument that there are periodic innovations in technology which are so influential that they supersede traditional technology and produce a new techno-economic paradigm which significantly alters society. Accordingly, we posited that embryonic industry would be sited near radically transforming technology. We immersed ourselves in the literature of technology and produced a series of proposals that connected leadership and the management needs of embryonic industry with technology. Now that our journey of research is concluded we can look back on these initial propositions as planned routes, all of them readily found in the literature and well argued, yet inadequate to our brief. Initially the focus groups, then subsequently the hubs, advised us that we were concentrating upon one part of the picture at the expense of the whole. The device of the embryonic industry complex was influential to these advisers. It provided a chart by which to navigate and a *patois* in which to debate our technological bias. We discussed this, and similar issues, with our respondents, modified our views, tested them and continued; always using the original propositions; seeking congruity, noting agreement to modifications.

Once these blinkers were removed, once this blind alley was abandoned, the research (itself embryonic) flourished. Our respondents enabled us to connect notions of cultural innovation, organizational innovation and ecological values with embryonic industry and to determine means by which the management and leadership needs of this industry could be better served.

A valuable lesson had been learned by the researchers. Paradigms present presuppositions concerning data which should be doubted. Researchers should seek alternative realities which may explain the data or else they may be trapped. Here we can analogize between the research team and the learning organization (Senge, 1990). Our initial design proceeded from a techno-economic paradigm only, one which imposed a form of single-loop learning (Kromer, 1993). Breaking from that design, accepting other paradigms (and their associated metaphors) permitted double-loop learning in which we learned of our fundamental processes and became a learning organization.

Powerful people: Respondents

The second important group to be affected by the metaphor were the respondents, our focus groups, hubs and field study interviewees.

To each of the focus groups we took views found in the literature expressed in terms of our chief metaphor and its diagrammatic representation. These groups were a blend of influential entrepreneurs, policy-makers, academics, financiers and others with whom we found metaphorical language and symbols useful. They provided a commencing focus which was sufficiently colourful, ambiguous and yet recognizable, so that researchers and respondents could quickly gain rapport and extend each other's thinking about the matter.

Without doubt the groups were singularly useful in their task of focus. We have subsequently explored the use of focus groups in grounding research propositions; they are seen as risky, advantageous and rapid.

Two examples of the impact of focus groups may suffice; particularly as each of these outcomes was probably due to metaphor. A focus group is a group interview with most participants meeting for the first time. Thus an important task is to present information which is sufficiently bounded to limit outrageous side-tracking but not so limited as to allow only the authors' viewpoints. As we have mentioned, we used metaphor for this task; it was a feature of our team language and accordingly in all of our presentations. The first focus group was able to use the metaphor and refer to market intelligence as a vital nutrient. The embryo could not flourish without nutrition and this nutrient was critical. The trend lines of technological revolution may not be sites where the market nutrient was present in this country (we were advised metaphorically). Subsequent focus groups returned to this theme, emphasizing that the strategic control exerted over technology by multinational alliances may preclude certain Australian embryonic industries. The trajectory of our research was then adjusted to seek Australian competitive advantage and we came to propose means by which Australia's cultural diversity could be used to develop embryonic cultural industry. Extending from this analysis, which presented society as composed from a macrocosm of ethnic subcultures, we introduced the notion of intellectual subcultures and sought sites where these might have competitive advantage. It was in this way that we introduced the advantages Australia holds in terms of green values and its global perception as a developed yet relatively unpolluted nation. We do not say that these findings would not have occurred without focus groups using metaphors, but we suspect they would have taken longer.

We produced drafts of our deliberations and sent them to the international hubs for analysis. The language and symbols of these drafts and final report were similar to our focus group presentations, though obviously developing.

Our hubs found them useful with their advisers and replied, indeed extended, the metaphorical argot. Thus insights were enriched, clarified and enlivened. Their contributions were invaluable, if more reflective. Our research design had the strengths of immediacy with focus groups and analytical reflection with hubs and was facilitated by the team's language and symbols, laden as they were with metaphors. We would argue that if the occasional response from hubs was metaphorically overwrought or inconsistent, wherein was the hurt to that? The language games were liberating and at times playful. The time for rigorous metaphorical consistency was not during data collection, nor even initial analysis, but in final reportage. The task of research seems therefore to be an engagement of researchers and respondents in which understandings are explored and interpretations applied and the conversational circle continued. Thus our report distils much of the research conversation and is the end of one major cycle and the beginning of subsequent cycles.

We found metaphors similarly useful in the interviews which the research team conducted for our field studies. These were completed with successful innovators whose endeavours had spawned embryonic industry. Here the metaphor was less intrusive as respondents did not proceed from much more than our definition of embryonic industry and a non-directive interview protocol. None the less the interviewees described their circumstances in terms of metaphorical language and were able to focus on our metaphor and use it to describe their experiences in ways which were similar to the focus groups.

Powerful people: Readers

As the research developed, we had several readerships. The first were the hubs which received our numerous drafts (some before they had dispensed with the previous draft), but also our Research Manager, the Inquiry Mentor appointed by the Taskforce as our Panopticon, and the Taskforce itself. The report evolved from the research, was intrinsic to the research, was a device of the research. Accordingly in its various stages it was cast at different readerships.

We were reminded of our eventual readership, the Taskforce, when our appointed Mentor from the Taskforce was given an early draft. The research proceeded in such a way that our nascent ideas were rapidly drafted and circulated for comment, which, whilst tiring, gave opportunity for broad opinion. Our Mentor, viewing the Taskforce as the patron and major reader, sought strategy which could be implemented, policy which could be devised and advised, yet found in this early draft institutions, agencies, complexes, paradigms. 'Where are the people?' 'What do we do to improve management in embryonic industry?' 'What should management education and training do?', were questions which came back from the Mentor.

Through valuable comments such as the above we were introduced to the politics of the Taskforce and its vision of the whole task. The hermeneuticians among us enjoyed the circle of understanding that was being extended. Our text interpreted, fed back, redirected in ways that would increase prospects of implementation.

We had commenced our work with the metaphor of the embryo, to which we had added project team language and artefacts. Many of these were circular, which could relate to the powerful myth of the circle as a representation of fertility (Campbell, 1988: 108ff.). They may also relate to our underlying presuppositions on the nature of knowledge and were comfortably littoral to our commencing metaphor. Many of these metaphors reflected the idea of the virtuous circle as a means of improving innovation. This was originally seen in the work of Hampden-Turner (1990) and it suggests that one should be open, involve others and build trust. From such an approach comes commitment, which, due to openness, can produce new insights. We found the virtuous circle in play during all our research. It was particularly so during our reporting stage, as new insights added by our respondents were drafted in.

Circles are creative, troublesome, demand attention, take time and are vital for effective research. None of the circles would have operated as effectively as they did without our research language being laden with metaphor, developed through intensive drafting and reflection. We lost count of the drafts but we do recollect that there were three final drafts before the (really) final draft. By some reckoning, that of the drafter, this was about the fifty-fifth draft. Of course, the first drafts were very slight; the final draft was a 60,000-word manuscript.

Yet there was one more metaphor to be faced: that of the Official Government Report. We decided that the language which had developed the research was the text of the research. If readers were to interpret the dealings that had preceded, then they required insight into the project language. In this final stage we involved readers outside the original hundred and fifty or so in the respondent group (confidants who had experience in such matters, who could read the material and offer honest appraisal).

Their advice we interpreted as, "If the style stays then some lobbying should proceed with it." We saw the report as extending the negotiation and took that option; discussing it with our Research Manager, our Mentor and finally the gathered Taskforce, which pronounced it professional and lucid. Perhaps our advisers misread policy-makers. Perhaps the policy-makers with whom we dealt were different than the norm. The learning from this aside is that metaphors of readership can blinker one as easily as the dominating research paradigm might.

And in the End

The research was affected in each of its stages by the use of metaphors. Metaphors permeated the research team's artefacts and were communicated to the many respondents to the research. This was a liberating and creative process which permitted people from various perspectives to focus in an area for discussion and negotiation that formed the research. Concrete facts were not discovered hidden in the field for us to find by our scientific endeavours. Our scientific endeavours interpreted and defined the "facts" through an extended process of scholarship, discussion and negotiation. In all of this the literature's comments on metaphors that have been alluded to in this chapter were partially borne out. Clearly Morgan's (1980) advice that metaphors are devices to enhance (not embellish) research data was found accurate. His notion that the use of a metaphor necessarily reveals the underlying assumption of the researcher was not accurate, however, and here one pauses to worry about the interpretations analysts sometimes place on organizational language.

When we say that language reveals underlying assumptions in organizations, how exact are we in enumerating institutional reasons as to cause? Our patron had supplied the metaphor that was used in our research yet the fact that it was organic did not reveal that we, the researchers, proceeded from a determinist perspective.

Indeed the research experience confirmed that Pinder and Bourgeois' advice to speak exactly, eschew metaphor and produce objective organization science was faintly risible and pragmatically impossible (Bourgeois and Pinder, 1983; Pinder and Bourgeois, 1982). We used metaphors for several of the reasons they identify but never saw the need to objectify our language. Nor do we know how we might have done so, other than through determining some hermeneutic in which others must move. At least our method had the benefit of an unfolding, open-ended conversation, rather than one foreclosed monologically. We reject their notion of objective concrete social reality and argue rather that we find negotiated, interpreted order in data. Accordingly any attempt to introduce a science which uses special, "exact" language and eschews metaphors would be simply a peculiar form of language game in its own right, one that prevents understanding at worst, and which, at best, is merely deleterious to it.

Metaphors are used widely by researchers, respondents and readers. In "ordinary" discourse the metaphor liberates ideas, enlivens discussions and texts and provides an arena for negotiation. Why should matters be different during research? Of course they should not. As Morgan (1980) warns, the constant use of an inhibiting metaphor may limit actors. That is not our proposal: rather we seek for researchers to be alive to the liberating possibility of metaphor. We recognize that researchers may be boxed in (like the silkworms) by their language and seek means to fly beyond such limits, to loose, occasionally, the metaphorical fly from the metaphorical bottle of stunted imagination.

Metaphors are inevitable and useful. They are not embellishments. No pure space exists outside their spell. They are part of our craft. They form our life as researchers. Without them we would be nowhere that we could know.

A concluding metaphor

We conclude with the final stanzas of Douglas Stewart's poem, which, on one level, talks to researchers about the limits that they bring to their understanding and their science:

They stir, they think they will go. Then they remember
It was forbidden, forbidden, ever to go out;
The Hands are on guard outside like claps of thunder,
The ancestral voice says Don't, and they do not.
Still the night calls them to unimaginable bliss
But there is terror around them, the vast, the abyss,
And here is the tribe that they know, in their known place,
They are gentle and kind together, they are safe forever,
And all shall be answered at last when they embrace.
White moth moves closer to moth, lover to lover.

There is that pang of joy on the edge of dying.
Their soft wings whirr, they dream that they are flying.

References

Bolman, L.G. and Deal, T.E. (1991) *Reframing Organizations: Artistry, Choice and Leadership*. San Francisco: Jossey-Bass.

Bourgeois, V.W. and Pinder, C.C. (1983) 'Contrasting philosophical perspectives in administrative science: A reply to Morgan', *Administrative Science Quarterly*, 28 (4), 608–613.

Campbell, J. (1988) *The Power of Myth*. New York: Doubleday.

Clegg, S.R. and Gray, J.T. (1994) 'The strategic implications to management education of the leadership and management needs of Australia's embryonic industries: A voyage on the Beagle'. Paper presented to the Strategic Management Educators' Conference, Queensland University of Technology, Brisbane, April.

Clegg, S.R., Dwyer, L., Gray, J.T., Kemp, A., Marceau, J., and O'Mara, E. (1995) 'Management and leadership needs of embryonic industries', *DEET Report of the Taskforce into Australia's Management and Leadership Needs*. Canberra: AGPS.

Dunford, R. and Palmer, I. (1995) 'Claims about frames: Practitioners' assessment of the utility of reframing', *Journal of Management Education*, 19 (1), 96–105.

Fairtlough, G. (1994) *Creative Compartments: A Design for Future Organizations*. London: Adamantine Press.

Freeman, C. (1987) 'The challenge of new technologies', in OECD, *Interdependence and Co-operation in Tomorrow's World*. Paris: OECD, pp. 204–236.

Gadamer, H.G. (1989) *Truth and Method* (2nd edn). London: Sheed and Ward.

Gray, J.T. (1994) 'Desperately seeking diversity: Paradigms in research'. Paper presented to the International Organizational Behaviour Teaching Conference, Otago University, Dunedin, December.

Hampden-Turner, C. (1990) *Charting the Corporate Mind*. Oxford: Blackwell.

Kromer, G.H. (1993) 'Perspectives on organizational learning: A critique and extension'. Unpublished dissertation, St Andrews University.

Kuhn, T.S. (1962) *The Structure of Scientific Revolutions*. Chicago: University of Chicago Press.

Morgan, G. (1980) 'Paradigms, metaphors, and puzzle solving in organization theory', *Administrative Science Quarterly*, 25 (4), 605–622.

Morgan, G. (1983) 'More on metaphor: Why we cannot control tropes in administrative science', *Administrative Science Quarterly*, 28 (4), 601–607.

Phillips, D.L. (1973) 'Paradigms falsification and sociology', *Acta Sociologica*, 16 (1), 28–42.

Pinder, C.C. and Bourgeois, V.W. (1982) 'Controlling tropes in administrative science', *Administrative Science Quarterly*, 27 (4): 641–652.

Senge, P.M. (1990) *The Fifth Discipline: The Art and Practice of the Learning Organization.* New York: Doubleday.

Stewart, D. (1967) 'The silkworms', in *Collected Poems, 1936–1967.* Sydney: Angus and Robertson, pp. 66–67.

Wittgenstein, L. (1953) *Philosophical Investigations.* Oxford: Blackwell.

PART II

METAPHORS OF ORGANIZING: LANGUAGE AND DISCOURSE

5

Metaphors in Popular Management Discourse: The Case of Corporate Restructuring

Richard Dunford and Ian Palmer

The use of metaphors to understand organizational processes has been a matter of development and debate within organization theory (e.g. Bolman and Deal, 1984, 1991; Morgan 1980, 1986, 1993; Pinder and Bourgeois, 1982; Reed, 1990; Tsoukas 1991, 1993). Metaphor-based analysis has spread to a range of different areas of organizational practice, including strategy (Peters, 1992), organization development (Akin and Schultheiss, 1990), information technology (Kendall and Kendall 1993), organizational culture (Brink, 1993), organizational change (Lundberg, 1990; Marshak, 1993), policy (Dobuzinskis, 1992), human resource development (Marx and Hamilton, 1991), industrial relations (Dunn, 1990), group development (Srivastva and Barrett, 1988), decision-making (Connolly, 1988) and leadership (Bensimon, 1989).

A relatively undeveloped aspect of the application of metaphors to organizational processes is the use of metaphorical language in popular management discourse. This chapter addresses this issue by investigating the identity of metaphors used in the popular management literature to explain and describe corporate restructuring through downsizing.

What do metaphors do?

When Pfeffer states that 'language is a powerful, if not the most powerful method of social influence' (1994: 109), he is restating the position expressed earlier by Morris that 'sharing a language with other persons provides the subtlest and most powerful of all tools for controlling the behavior of these other persons to one's advantage' (1949: 214).

Received knowledge with regard to metaphors is that they are both descriptive and generative. They 'name' a situation, they 'frame' it, they 'set the problem' (Schön, 1993), and then 'provide a familiar structure for guiding inferences, sanctioning actions and setting goals' (Boland and Greenberg, 1988: 19). Language is important because 'the way people talk about the world has everything to do with the way the world is ultimately understood and acted in' (Eccles and Nohria, 1992: 29). Similarly, Tsoukas argues that metaphors 'do not simply describe an external reality; they also help constitute that reality and prescribe [both] how it ought to be viewed ... and a mode of behaviour' (1991: 570). The metaphor may define the nature of the situation, the respective roles of the key actors and the proper procedures or even outcomes to be followed/attained (Hirsch and Andrews, 1983). Srivastva and Barrett expressed this view as follows:

> Naming also directs actions towards the object you have named because it promotes activity consistent with the related attribute it carries. To change the name of an object connotes changing your relationship to the object and how one will behave in relationship to it because when we name something, we direct anticipations, expectations and evaluations towards it. (1988: 34–35)

Common to all these arguments is the assertion that metaphors matter, that is, that, far from being neutral and descriptive, they materially affect practice. Some authors, including Czarniawksa-Joerges and Joerges (1990), Evered (1983), Hirsch and Andrews (1983), Marshak (1993), Meyer (1982), Pondy (1983), Sapienza (1985), Schneider and Dunbar (1992) and Wilson (1992), have specifically focused on organizational contexts. For Pfeffer 'managerial language is critical [and] both reflects and determines how people think about the managing process' (1994: 112); for Czarniawksa-Joerges and Joerges, linguistic artefacts are used for the management of meaning with 'power in organizations belong[ing] to those who can define reality for others' (1990: 339). For Evered (1983: 141) 'reality-defining words, symbols and metaphors' are so fundamental that organizational change necessitates a language change if it is to be successful. This is expanded on by Marshak:

> underlying, usually inarticulated understandings about a situation are often shaped and revealed metaphorically. Furthermore, because these understandings are critical to how people assess the need for change – and indeed their conception of change itself – paying attention to managing the metaphors of change becomes a critical competency for leaders and change agents. (1993: 44)

Pondy (1983) argues that metaphors facilitate change because they make the strange familiar; that is, they link something novel and potentially threatening to familiar situations. Similarly, Hirsch and Andrews argue that metaphors provide 'reference to established and favoured values at the more generalized level of common culture' (1983: 150).

In her study of top managers' decision-making, Sapienza (1985) found that their actions fitted with dominant metaphors in their organizations. She argues that decision-making

> entailed a response to the intersubjective reality created in part by managers' shared beliefs and depicted in metaphoric imagery. Strategy was designed in some measure to adapt the institution to a metaphorical reality. (1985: 82)

Metaphors direct attention to certain interpretations of situations and away from others. In doing so, 'accounts become persuasive by virtue of not representing alternative formulations and the act of re-presentation also becomes an act of re-pression of alternatives' (Linstead, 1993: 56). This is a subtle process:

> One of the sources of a metaphor's power is its transparency at the point at which it becomes a familiar part of one's mental world. We are typically not aware of our thoughts as such, nor are we aware of their arbitrary (although sometimes helpful) character. This lack of awareness prevents us from realizing what the metaphor is pointing toward, what it is highlighting and what it is obscuring. (Ng and Bradac, 1993: 140–141)

The net effect of this is that while metaphors can give insight and aid comprehension, they may also lead to the attribution of inappropriate characteristics and, hence, mislead (Ortony, 1975).

Metaphors provide a central role in defining action as legitimate, necessary, maybe even as the only "realistic" option for a given situation. These characteristics have the effect of depersonalizing actions. That is, they distance actors from their actions so that 'judgements about the propriety of particular actions can be made implicitly and indirectly with a significant degree of detachment from the particular situation' (Hirsch and Andrews, 1983: 149). A positive interpretation of this process is that metaphors facilitate action; a negative interpretation is that metaphors may lead to managers not directly confronting the implications of their decisions. By providing new ways of seeing, metaphors may make one 'more accepting and open' (Srivastva and Barrett, 1988: 54), but also may produce simplistic analyses.

The centrality and significance of metaphors constitutes the core assumption upon which the following study is founded. The study examines the metaphors used in the popular management literature to describe corporate restructuring through downsizing. Specifically, it is the premise of this chapter that this literature contains a range of metaphors which structure the way in which issues, debates and outcomes are framed. Supposing that language has such significance, what are the images that are constituent parts of the popular management discourse on downsizing?

Corporate restructuring through downsizing

Downsizing, as Freeman and Cameron note, 'is a term that has arisen out of popular usage rather than precise theoretical construction' (1993: 12). However, its origins in "pop management" discourse should not blind us to the significance of the phenomenon to which it refers. Corporations are operating in a context where a pervasive belief is that the world economy faces a sustained period of slow, low-inflationary expansion and global over-capacity, an era in which they cannot easily raise prices to expand profit margins (Richman, 1993: 54). At the same time corporations have had to cope with the effects of (1) deregulation, which has blurred product and geographic market boundaries and produced new competitors, (2) global competition and (3) pressure for short-term results, especially from institutional investors (Frohman and Johnson, 1993: 6–8). One central element of corporate restructuring in response to this situation has been substantial reorganization of the workforce based on the reduction of employee numbers (Useem, 1992: 46). Downsizing is a generic term to refer to this form of restructuring.

Academic caution is a valuable counterpoint to the uncritical proclaiming of new eras, most commonly found in the evangelism of "pop management" writers. However, in the case of downsizing there does seem to be considerable evidence that it is a significant phenomenon in the United States, the United Kingdom, Canada, Germany and to a lesser extent Japan (Baggerman, 1993). In the United States more than 85 per cent of the Fortune 1000 firms reduced their white-collar workforces between 1987 and 1991, affecting more than 5 million jobs (Cascio, 1993: 95). One of the striking characteristics of restructuring since the mid-1980s is the extent to which it has affected white-collar rather than blue-collar employees. For example, while middle managers make up between only 5 and 8 percent of the US workforce, they accounted for 17 per cent of all layoffs between 1989 and 1991 (Cascio, 1993: 95).

A significant aspect of downsizing is its applicability to both decline and growth (Freeman and Cameron, 1993). It is not restricted to being a cost-driven response, associated mainly with corporations burdened with debt as a result of borrowing excesses of the mid-1980s. It is also a pre-emptive strategy to improve the competitive position of organizations. Even some corporations with record profits have downsized 'in anticipation of a continuing intensely competitive market' (Cascio, 1993: 102). However, the intended performance improvements have at times proven to be elusive. Whether the measure is cost, profit, productivity, return on shareholders' funds, share price, quality or innovation, there is accumulating evidence that downsized firms often fail to achieve intended outcomes (Cascio, 1993, 1994; *Economist*, 1994; Freeman and Cameron, 1993; Tomasko, 1993).

Methodology

The sample that provided the data for this chapter was produced through an electronic literature search for articles on downsizing that were published between 1991 and 1994 in the popular management literature. Popular management literature was defined for these purposes as material primarily designed to be read by management practitioners, and as such excluded journals with a primarily academic audience. This produced 74 articles from 43 different journals. To this have been added two popular management books on downsizing (Tomasko 1993; Tylczak, 1991). These 76 sources comprise the database for the following analysis.

Each source was analysed in terms of the metaphors that it contained. Metaphors were listed and categorized in two ways:

1. according to the aspect of downsizing which they addressed;
2. where several of the metaphors seemed to derive from a root metaphor, that root was identified and used as a basis for categorization.

Neither of these categorizations was established a priori but each emerged from the analysis of metaphors. Categorization was undertaken by two coders for whom an inter-rater reliability of 0.95 was established using a standard formula (Holsti, 1969). Because each metaphor is listed in Tables 5.1–5.4, readers are also able to make their own independent assessment of the appropriateness of the categorization.

Metaphors in downsizing

The data revealed that the metaphors used in descriptions of downsizing addressed the following four aspects:

1. the external conditions within which organizations operate;
2. the internal conditions of pre-downsized organization;
3. the process of downsizing;
4. the negative effects of downsizing.

The metaphors describing the external conditions within which organizations operate centre on themes which present a picture of turbulence and uncertainty (see Table 5.1). Organizations are represented as facing a hostile environment with the physical environment to the fore in the imagery: 'the wolf is at the door'. Firm action is necessary, this being portrayed through imagery with strong military/violence overtones, that is not uncommon in the strategy literature (Hirsch and Andrews, 1983). It is time to 'declare war'.

The second category of metaphors deals with how organizations are placed to cope with the external conditions. The popular management literature is unequivocal. There is one overwhelmingly dominant image – the organization as body. This root metaphor is represented by a wide range of metaphors almost exclusively about being overweight or unwell (see Table

Table 5.1 *Metaphors for external conditions and strategic responses*

Metaphor	Inference
Physical environment	
the wolf is at the door (Lee 1992: 23)	The environment
the edge of a cliff with no handrail (Faltermayer, 1992: 84)	is threatening.
facing stormy seas (Lawrence and Mittman, 1991: 34)	
economic storms (Lester, 1992: 72)	
battering by environment (Lester, 1992: 72)	
Military/Violence	
declare war on competitors (Newman, 1991: 10)	Strong action is
combat tenacious global competitors (Richman, 1993: 55)	necessary.
combat rising costs (Baggerman, 1993: 27)	
turn up the heat on competitors (Richman, 1993: 56)	

5.2). Indeed the difference between these two states is scarcely differentiated, perhaps reflecting a societal level juxtaposition of images – "lean is healthy" and "fat is unhealthy". The message is clear: Organizations must respond to a hostile environment, yet they are in 'poor shape'. The inference is that drastic action must be taken.

Three root metaphors express how the process of downsizing is undertaken (see Table 5.3). One is body/medical in orientation. Managers are described as 'trimming the fat', 'unclogging blocked arteries' and 'using the

Table 5.2 *Metaphors for internal conditions of pre-downsized organizations*

Metaphor	Inference
Body/Medical	
haemorrhaging (Huey, 1993: 39)	
bloated (Plunkett, 1993: 64)	The current state of
overweight (Lee, 1992: 20)	organizations can be seen as
fat (Jayne, 1992: 68)	akin to an overweight
laggard (Richman, 1993: 55)	person. Organizations are
excess clothes (Bernasek, 1994: 8)	over-staffed, slow-moving
diseased (Tomasko, 1992: 13)	and, as such, inappropriately
dead weight (Tomasko, 1992: 15)	placed to meet
flab (Faltermayer, 1992: 80)	environmental changes.
ill (Lesly and Light, 1992: 100)	
ailing (Baggerman, 1993: 27)	
rotund (Skagen, 1992: 1)	
portly (Skagen, 1992: 1)	
frozen (Horton and Reid, 1991: 43)	
constipated (Horton and Reid, 1991: 44)	
slothful (Reich, 1994: 8)	
bulge (Denton, 1992: 5)	
healthy* (Lesly and Light, 1992: 101)	

* This apparently anomolous image reflects the fact that some high performing organizations have downsized proactively, that is, in anticipation of the future competitive situation (see, e.g. Cascio, 1993).

surgeon's scalpel'. This is not surprising given the dominance of this theme in descriptions of the pre-downsizing state of organizations. The military/ violence root metaphor, originally noted in Table 5.1, also re-emerges . As the response to being 'overweight' moves into prescription, and the realm of strategic decision-making, the language of the latter is adopted for use along with that from the diagnostic stage (the body/medical imagery). The third root metaphor to appear was that using horticultural imagery, exhorting us to prune and slash and get 'rid of deadwood'.

The rise of counter-metaphors

Alongside the metaphors that present images of why and how organizational downsizing should occur there has been a growth of counter-metaphors, that is, metaphors which present negative images of downsizing (see Table 5.4). Some of these refer to organizational performance in a general sense while others specifically refer to effects on remaining employees. Some of the counter-metaphors turn an original metaphor 'back on itself'. For example, 'slimming' is now associated with becoming 'too thin', 'anorexic', 'anaemic', with 'muscle as well as fat' being lost. The 'medical intervention' is portrayed as leaving survivors 'dazed', even 'paralysed', with 'scars that take a long time to heal'. 'Survivors', rather than being overwhelmed with relief and gratitude, are portrayed as 'deeply wounded' 'casualties' whose experience of downsizing has left them with the outlook of 'mercenaries' or shocked into a 'bunker mentality'. Horticulturally, we are reminded that we 'reap what we sow'. New root metaphors appear, including those with a nautical focus – 'abandoning ship' and 'hanging around the lifeboat instead of helping to steer'.

Discussion and conclusions

This chapter has identified a range of metaphors and counter-metaphors which characterize the popular management discourse on downsizing. The data reveal the dominance of specific root metaphors, in particular those based on body/medical imagery and military/violence imagery. These are associated with particular diagnoses of the external conditions within which organizations operate, and the internal conditions of these organizations. They are also associated with descriptions of how organizations downsize and the unanticipated consequences that may emerge. Received knowledge as to the effect of metaphors would suggest that the nature of these metaphors has a material effect on downsizing practice. The nature of the dominant root metaphors would suggest a reinforcement of strategies based upon reduction of workforce numbers. McKinley et al. (1995) see the portrayal of downsizing in the popular management literature as having played a key role in establishing it as a desirable practice.

The root metaphors through which we conceptualize a situation may be central to the courses of action that we consider. It is important to identify

Table 5.3   *Metaphors for how organizations downsize*

Metaphor	Inference
Body/Medical	
slimming down (Wrubel, 1992: 50)	The organization can be
using the surgeon's scalpel (Train, 1991: 17)	seen as akin to a body that
paring to the bone (Lee, 1992: 20)	needs to become more lean
shrinking (Newman, 1991: 10)	in the interests of good
get rid of bulge (Donath, 1992: 8)	health. The organization's
having radical surgery (Reich, 1994: 7)	performance will be
unclogging blocked arteries (Jayne, 1992: 72)	improved by identifying and
getting fit (Thomas, 1992: 70)	removing staff who are
crash diet (Lee, 1992: 19)	excess to requirements.
curing (Baggerman, 1993: 28)	
improving health (Train, 1991: 19)	
slenderizing (Faltermayer, 1992: 80)	
having tummy tucks (Skagen, 1992: 1)	
trimming the fat (Heitman and Zahra, 1993: 10)	
becoming lean (Pilarski, 1992: 36)	
shed a few pounds (Lee, 1992: 20)	
surgically rightsizing (Lee, 1992: 20)	
wasting (Pullinger, 1992: 329)	
belt tightening (Newman, 1991: 10)	
vaccinating (Tylczak, 1991: 62)*	
practicing preventive medicine (Tylczak, 1991: 62)*	
Military/Violence	
killing fields (Faltermayer, 1992: 80)	
slaughtering (Faltermayer, 1992: 84)	
bloodletting (Wallfesh, 1991: 179)	The organization can be
bonfire (Capell, 1992: 44)	seen as subject to action that
tossing managers overboard (Lester, 1992: 72)	is akin to decisive, violent
the firing squad (Horton and Reid, 1991: 42)	military action to remove
predator (Horton and Reid, 1991: 44)	staff who are excess to
lopping heads (Labich, 1993: 25)	requirements.
hacking (Skagen, 1992: 1)	
hitlist (Jayne, 1992: 66)	
hatchetman (Richman, 1993: 54)	
cutting deeply (Heenan, 1992: 19)	
frontal assault (Tomasko, 1992: 13)	
biting the bullet (Boronson and Burgess, 1992: 44)	
thinning the ranks (Cappelli, 1992: 60)	
the firing line (Newman, 1991: 10)	
heads roll (Lee, 1992: 17)	
use a machete to slash employee head count (Lee, 1992: 17)	
quick hit (Lee, 1992: 18)	
use the axe (Train, 1991: 17)	
purging (Lawrence and Mittman, 1991: 36)	
slashing (Newman, 1991: 11)	
slash and burn (Hass, 1993: 23)	
cutting heads (Faltermayer, 1992: 71)	

Table 5.3 *Continued*

Horticultural

scything (Faltermayer, 1992: 84)	The organization can be
pruning (Heenan, 1992: 19)	seen as akin to a tree or
shedding (Lorinc, 1991: 86)	shrub needing to be 'cut
chopping (Jayne, 1992: 66)	back' to improve its health.
rid of deadwood (Moskall, 1992: 18)	Organizations do this by
slash and burn (Thomas, 1992: 73)	removing staff who are
mowing (Faltermayer, 1992: 71)	excess to requirements.

Miscellaneous

to pack parachutes (Lawrence and Mittman, 1991: 36)
leakage (Syedain, 1991: 46)

* These prescriptions relate to proactive downsizing (see Table 5.2)

and discuss the root metaphors present in a given discourse because they are often 'buried deep in the idiom and tend to act subliminally in our conceptual faculties' (Dunn, 1990: 14). The military/violence metaphor directs attention towards strategies that trade on the dominance of macho/ male imagery and language. Wilson (1992) argues that the use of metaphor in organizations reinforces patriarchal power relations, citing in particular the common use of militaristic metaphors for their highlighting of male experiences. The medical/body metaphor is centred on body image and the societal value attached to being lean.

Counter-metaphors may help to increase the level of awareness of issues to be considered in the management of the restructuring process and its aftermath. At the very least, the counter-metaphors help articulate a case for the more careful management of downsizing, for example as described by Brockner (1992). They may find a receptive audience, not just amongst survivors, but also among managers contemplating corporate restructuring, because there is accumulating evidence that downsizing often does not lead to the performance improvements expected by those who initiate it within organizations.

While the counter-metaphors articulate the nature of problems associated with downsizing, they do not by themselves present an alternative. This occurs when alternative root metaphors are proposed. Reich (1993, 1994) characterizes the dominant root metaphor as the 'butcher' strategy, that is, one which emphasizes 'cutting away the fat'. He contrasts this with the 'baker' strategy, which involves 'enhancing the value of all the ingredients'.

The baking metaphor means that attention is directed towards actions such as employee involvement, profit-sharing, training and employment security (Reich, 1993, 1994). It is a metaphor that is consistent with the characterization of the approach to managing which Pfeffer (1994) has identified as highly correlated with sustained competitive success. The baking metaphor directs attention away from redundancies towards actions such as hiring

Table 5.4   *Counter-metaphors*

Metaphor	Inference
Body/Medical	
too thin (Newman, 1991: 11)	Staff reductions can leave an
down to the bare bones (Lee, 1992: 18)	organization insufficiently
bulimic management (Richman, 1993: 55)	resourced to perform
anaemic management (Tomasko, 1993: 24)	effectively.
cutting muscle as well as fat (Tomasko, 1993: 24)	
organizational anorexia (Pullinger, 1992: 330)	
loss of well being (Pullinger, 1992: 330)	
paralyzed (Lee, 1992: 19)	
scars that take a long time to heal (Lee, 1992: 17)	Downsizing can cause
dazed (Lee, 1992: 17)	damage to morale, sense of
	trust and commitment.
management addiction (Labich, 1993: 25)	Downsizing can become a
downsizing binge (Lesly and Light, 1992: 100)	pattern of action disengaged
fetish (Newman, 1991: 11)	from rational case-by-case
knee-jerk reaction (Lesly and Light, 1992: 101)	analysis.
mourning (Moskall, 1992: 17)	Survivors often take a while
grieving (Marks, 1992: 44)	to deal emotionally with a
	sense of loss.
burn out (Baggerman, 1993: 27)	Downsizing may cause
stress skyrockets (Lee, 1992: 18)	increased work pressure to
	the extent that staff may not
	be able to cope.
Military/Violence	
shooting oneself in the foot (Lee, 1992: 22)	Downsizing may remove or
deeply wounded (Moskall, 1992: 15)	undermine its key
casualties (Skagen, 1992: 1)	competitive resources.
carnage (Lee, 1992: 22)	
mercenaries (Horton and Reid, 1991: 44)	
blow their brains out (Bernasek, 1994: 1)	
bunker mentality (Lyons, 1991: 72)	Staff may become self-
morale is annihilated (Lee, 1992: 18)	interested and risk-averse.
run the gauntlet (Moskall, 1992: 16)	
grenade approach (Lee, 1992: 18)	Downsizing is often
	insufficiently selective as to
	whom is affected.
Miscellaneous	
abandoning/jumping ship (Lawrence and Mittman, 1991: 35)	Staff may focus more on
hanging around the lifeboat instead of helping to steer	getting out than on their
(Horton and Reid, 1991: 44)	current job.
like waiting for the next earthquake in Los Angeles	Staff morale is undermined
(Lee, 1992: 17)	as they wait for the expected
	next round of downsizing.

Table 5.4 *Continued*

less willing to go the extra mile (Reich, 1994: 7)	Loss of commitment
like slaves on an auction block (Tomasko, 1992: 10)	Staff see senior management as treating them like assets to be disposed of at their whim.
constantly covering their ass (Tomasko, 1992: 11) playing it close to the chest (Lee, 1992: 21) protecting turf (Lee, 1992: 20)	Staff become defensive, self-protective, conservative.
reaping what you sow (Lee, 1992: 20)	How the downsizing is handled determines its outcome.
parachutes are lined with gold but covered in blood (Moskall, 1992: 20)	Staff are often disillusioned by senior management getting generous treatment and not sharing the 'pain'
lemming-like (Lesly and Light, 1992: 101)	Companies often follow the lead of others rather than rationally assessing the situation.
like a deer caught in the headlights (Lorinc, 1991: 86) like driving a car without shock absorbers, therefore you feel every bump (Lorinc, 1991: 86) babies have been thrown out with the bath water (Horton and Reid, 1991: 43) falling through the cracks (Boronson and Burgess, 1992: 45) reinventing the wheel (Tomasko, 1993: 24)	Downsized organizations can have lost key knowledge and skills, performance begins to suffer, mistakes are made and there is no margin for error.
putting the cart before the horse (Drucker, 1993: 10)	Downsizing should follow a reappraisal of corporate strategy, not vice versa.

freezes, salary freezes, shortened work weeks, job-sharing, early retirement and reduced use of contract staff.

A number of issues concerning the way metaphors operate emerge from this analysis. First, to what extent is the language of popular management discourse also that of managers? The importance of this is that if the former is an artefact distinct from the world of management practice, it is much less significant in terms of understanding this practice.

Second, when popular management writers use downsizing metaphors it is not clear whether they consciously select them because they feel them to be appropriate to the situation they seek to describe, or whether this is largely a subconscious process. This brings to attention the issue of whether or not popular management writers are aware of, and select, the framework through which they view downsizing, or whether they are carried along by dominant metaphors without being fully aware of how they frame their perceptions of downsizing.

Third, how do metaphors become established as mainstream descriptors of organizational events? Why is it that some get taken up with more fervour than others? As Srivastva and Barrett have argued, 'metaphors are like bone or skin grafts, some "take" and some do not' (1988: 54). The significance of this is that if metaphors are generative, then having an understanding of how they become embedded is central to being able to influence the metaphors that carry a particular discourse.

Fourth, a question arises about the relationship of metaphors to counter-metaphors. For example, what are the conditions which lead to the emergence of counter-metaphors? To be "heard", do they have to invert the dominant root metaphors and create new inferences, or is a more effective approach to produce a completely new root metaphor such as the baking metaphor? The significance of this is that those wishing to highlight the limitations of a dominant metaphor may need to know whether it is likely to be more productive to seek to undermine a metaphor from within the terms of its own root metaphor or to move completely outside it. This is an issue in the management of meaning (Morgan, 1986). The process whereby discourses develop over time, and the way in which metaphors and counter-metaphors are formed, used and discarded remains unexplored. For example, does a metaphor as language give 'birth to its own image in a play of mirrors that has no limits' (Foucault, 1977)? Hence, does one metaphor lead to the development of a counter-metaphor? Alternatively, do counter-metaphors only emerge once a critical mass of mainstream metaphors has taken hold?

Finally, the limits of the power of language need to be considered. While language may contribute to specific courses of action being taken, this need not mean that in its absence those actions would not occur. As Thompson has argued, 'it is one thing to claim that language is an important resource for the way that power is identified, shaped and fought out and another to say that *of necessity* it is brought into being by, and is indissolubly linked to, language' (1993: 199). This is an important issue to investigate because it questions the priority to be attached to language in efforts to understand organizational practices. It suggests the need for more research on the effect of language on action.

References

Akin, G. and Schultheiss, E. (1990) 'Jazz bands and missionaries: OD through stories and metaphor', *Journal of Managerial Psychology*, 5, 12–18.

Baggerman, L. (1993) 'The futility of downsizing', *Industry Week*, 18 January, 27–28.

Bensimon, E.A. (1989) 'The meaning of "good presidential leadership": A frame analysis', *Review of Higher Education*, 12, 107–123.

Bernasek, A. (1994) 'The poisoning of work', *Sydney Morning Herald*, 29 January, Spectrum Section 1, 8.

Boland, R.J., Jr. and Greenberg, R.H. (1988) 'Metaphorical structuring of organizational ambiguity', in L.R. Pondy, R.J. Boland and H. Thomas (eds), *Managing Ambiguity and Change*. New York: John Wiley and Sons, pp. 17–36.

Bolman, L.G. and Deal, T.E. (1984) *Modern Approaches to Understanding and Managing Organizations*. San Francisco: Jossey-Bass.

Bolman, L.G. and Deal, T.E. (1991) *Reframing Organizations: Artistry, Choice and Leadership*. San Francisco: Jossey-Bass.

Boronson, W. and Burgess, L. (1992) 'Survivors' syndrome', *Across the Board*, November, 41–45.

Brink, T.L. (1993) 'Metaphor as data in the study of organizations', *Journal of Management Inquiry*, 2, 366–371.

Brockner, J. (1992) 'Managing the effects of layoffs on survivors', *California Management Review*, 34 (2), 9–28.

Capell, P. (1992) 'Endangered middleman', *American Demographics*, January, 44–47.

Cappelli, P. (1992) 'The impact of managerial layoffs', *Chief Executive*, June, 58–60.

Cascio, W.F. (1993) 'Downsizing: what do we know? What have we learned?', *Academy of Management Executive*, 7, 95–104.

Cascio, W. (1994) 'The cost of downsizing', *HR Monthly*, February, 8–13.

Connolly, T. (1988) 'Hedge-clipping, tree felling and the management of ambiguity: The need for new images of decision-making', in L.R. Pondy, R.J. Boland and H. Thomas (eds), *Managing Ambiguity and Change*. New York: John Wiley and Sons, pp. 37–50.

Czarniawksa-Joerges, B. and Joerges, B. (1990) 'Linguistic artifacts at service of organizational control', in P. Gagliardi (ed.) *Symbols and Artifacts: Views of the Corporate Landscape*. Berlin: de Gruyter, pp. 339–364.

Denton, K. (1992) 'Delayered, downsized and demotivated', *Business Forum*, Summer, 5–8.

Dobuzinskis, L. (1992) 'Modernist and postmodernist metaphors of the policy process: Control and stability vs. chaos and reflexive understanding', *Policy Sciences*, 25, 355–380.

Donath, B. (1992) 'Going flat out for flat organizations isn't easy', *Marketing News*, 7 December, 7–8.

Drucker, P. (1993) 'Restructuring middle management', *Modern Office Technology*, January, 8–10.

Dunn, S. (1990) 'Root metaphor in the old and new industrial relations', *British Journal of Industrial Relations*, 28, 1–31.

Economist (1994) 'When slimming is not enough', 3 September, 63–64.

Eccles, R.G. and Nohria, N. (1992) *Beyond the Hype: Rediscovering the Essence of Management*. Boston: Harvard Business School Press.

Evered, R. (1983), 'The language of organizations', in L.R. Pondy, P.J. Frost, G. Morgan and T.C. Dandridge (eds), *Organizational Symbolism*. Greenwich, CT: JAI Press, pp. 125–143.

Faltermayer, E. (1992) 'Is this layoff necessary', *Fortune*, 1 June, 71–86.

Foucault, M. (1977) *Language, Counter-Memory, Practice*. Ithaca, NY: Cornell University Press.

Freeman, S.J. and Cameron, K.S. (1993) 'Organizational downsizing: A convergence and reorientation framework', *Organization Science*, 4, 10–29.

Frohman, A.L. and Johnson, L.W. (1993) *The Middle Management Challenge: Moving From Crisis to Empowerment*. New York: McGraw-Hill.

Hass, N. (1993) 'Flashdance', *Financial World*, 16 February, 22–23.

Heenan, D.A. (1992) 'Here today, gone tomorrow', *AIM*, August, 19–20.

Heitman, E. and Zahra, S.A. (1993), 'Examining the U.S. experience to discover successful corporate restructuring', *Industrial Management*, January–February, 7–10.

Hirsch, P.M. and Andrews, A.Y. (1983) 'Ambushes, shootouts and knights of the round table: The language of corporate takeovers', in L.R. Pondy, P.J. Frost, G. Morgan and T.C. Dandridge (eds), *Organizational Symbolism*. Greenwich, CT: JAI Press, pp. 145–155.

Holsti, O.R. (1969) *Content Analysis For the Social Sciences and Humanities*. Reading, MA: Addison-Wesley.

Horton, T.R. and Reid, P.C. (1991) 'Have CEOs forgotten their managers?', *Chief Executive*, March, 42–45.

Huey, J. (1993) 'Managing in the midst of chaos', *Fortune*, 5 April, 38–48.

Jayne, V. (1992) 'The purging of middle management', *Management*, December, 66–79.

Kendall, J.E. and Kendall, K.E. (1993) 'Metaphors and methodologies: Living beyond the systems machine', *MIS Quarterly*, 17, 149–171.

Labich, K. (1993) 'The new unemployed', *Fortune*, 8 March, 24–31.

Lawrence, A.T. and Mittman, B.S. (1991) 'What kind of downsizer are you?', *Management Review*, January, 33–37.

Lee, C. (1992) 'After the cuts', *Training*, July, 17–23.

Lesly, E. and Light, L. (1992) 'When layoffs alone don't turn the tide', *Business Week*, 7 December, 100–101.

Lester, T. (1992) 'Metamorphosis of the manager', *Management Today*, August, 72–75.

Linstead, S. (1993) 'Deconstruction in the study of organizations', in J. Hassard and M. Parker (eds), *Postmodernism and Organizations*. London: Sage Publications, pp. 49–70.

Lorinc, J. (1991) 'Managing when there's no middle', *Canadian Business*, June, 86–94.

Lundberg, C.C. (1990) 'Towards mapping the communication targets of organizational change', *Journal of Organizational Change Management*, 3, 6–13.

Lyons, M. (1991) 'Staff depression can remain long after retrenchments', *Business Review Weekly*, 12 April, 69–72.

Marks, M.L. (1992) 'The Perot syndrome', *Across the Board*, November, 44–45.

Marshak, R.J. (1993) 'Managing the metaphors of change', *Organizational Dynamics*, 22 (1), 44–56.

Marx, R.D. and Hamilton, E.E. (1991) 'Beyond skill building: A multiple perspectives view of personnel', *Issues and Trends in Business and Economics*, III, 1–4.

McKinley, W., Sanchez, C.M. and Schick, G. (1995) 'Organizational downsizing: Constraining, cloning, learning', *Academy of Management Executive*, 9 (3), 32–55.

Meyer, A. (1982) 'How ideologies support formal structures and shape responses to environments', *Journal of Management Studies*, 19, 45–61.

Morgan, G. (1980) 'Paradigms, metaphors, and puzzle solving in organization theory', *Administrative Science Quarterly*, 25(4), 605–622.

Morgan, G. (1986) *Images of Organization*. Beverly Hills, CA: Sage Publications.

Morgan, G. (1993) *Imaginization: The Art of Creative Management*. Newbury Park, CA: Sage Publications.

Morris, C.W (1949) *Signs, Language and Behavior*. New York: Prentice Hall.

Moskall, B. (1992) 'Managing survivors', *Industry Week*, 3 August, 15–22.

Newman, G. (1991) 'The death of middle managers', *Across the Board*, April, 10–11.

Ng, S.H. and Bradac, J.J. (1993) *Power in Language*. Newbury Park, CA: Sage Publications.

Ortony, A. (1975) 'Why metaphors are necessary and not just nice', *Educational Theory*, 25: 45–53.

Peters, T.J. (1992) *Liberation Management: Necessary Disorganization for the Nanosecond Nineties*. New York: Macmillan.

Pfeffer, J. (1994) *Competitive Advantage Through People*. Boston: Harvard Business School Press.

Pilarski, A.M. (1992) 'Downsizing and outsourcing', *Business Forum*, Fall, 36.

Pinder, C.C. and Bourgeois, V.W. (1982) 'Controlling tropes in administrative science', *Administrative Science Quarterly*, 27 (4), 641–652.

Plunkett, S. (1993) 'If you have always done it that way, think again', *Business Review Weekly*, 7 May, 64–67.

Pondy, L. (1983) 'The role of metaphors and myths in organization and in the facilitation of change', in L.R. Pondy, P.J. Frost, G. Morgan and T.C. Dandridge (eds), *Organizational Symbolism*. Greenwich, CT : JAI Press, pp. 157–166.

Pullinger, D. (1992) 'Slimming down and wasting away: Case for the process doctor', *Management Education and Development*, 23, 328–332.

Reed, M. (1990) 'From paradigms to images: The paradigm warrior turns post-modernist guru', *Personnel Review*, 19, 35–40.

Reich, R.B. (1993) 'Companies are cutting their hearts out', *New York Times Magazine*, 19 December, 54–55.

Reich, R.B. (1994) 'Of butchers and bakers: Does anyone profit from downsizing?', *Chemtech*, March, 7–9.

Richman, L.S. (1993) 'When will the layoffs end?', *Fortune*, 20 September, 54–56.

Sapienza, A.M. (1985) 'Believing is seeing: How culture influences the decisions top managers make', in R.H. Kilmann, J.J. Saxton and R. Serpa (eds), *Gaining Control of the Corporate Culture*. San Francisco: Jossey-Bass, pp. 66–83.

Schneider, S.C. and Dunbar, R.L. M. (1992) 'A psychoanalytic reading of hostile takeover events', *Academy of Management Review*, 17, 537–567.

Schön, D. (1993) 'Generative metaphor: A perspective on problem setting in social policy', in A. Ortony (ed.), *Metaphor and Thought* (2nd edn). Cambridge: Cambridge University Press, pp. 135-161.

Skagen, A. (1992) 'The incredible shrinking organization: What does it mean for middle managers?', *Supervisory Management*, January, 1–3.

Srivastva, S. and Barrett, F. (1988) 'The transforming nature of metaphors in group development: A study in group theory', *Human Relations*, 41 (1), 31–64.

Syedain, H. (1991) 'Middle managers: An endangered species', *Management Today*, May, 46–50.

Thomas, T. (1992) 'Fitness trainer to the service industry', *Business Review Weekly*, 6 November, 70–75.

Thompson, P. (1993) 'Postmodernism: Fatal distraction', in J.H. Hassard and M. Parker (eds), *Postmodernism and Organizations*. London: Sage Publications, pp. 183–203.

Tomasko, R.M. (1992) 'Restructuring: Getting it right', *Management Review*, 81, 10–15.

Tomasko, R.M. (1993) *Rethinking the Corporation: The Architecture of Change*. New York: AMACOM.

Train, A.S. (1991) 'The case of the downsizing decision', *Harvard Business Review*, March–April, 14–30.

Tsoukas, H. (1991) 'The missing link: A transformational view of metaphors in organizational science', *Academy of Management Review*, 16 (3), 566–585.

Tsoukas, H. (1993) 'Analogical reasoning and knowledge generation in organization theory', *Organization Studies*, 14, 323–346.

Tylczak, L. (1991) *Downsizing Without Disaster*. London: Kogan Page.

Useem, M. (1992) 'Corporate restructuring and organizational behaviour', in T.A. Kochan and M. Useem (eds), *Transforming Organizations*. New York: Oxford University Press, pp. 44–70.

Wallfesh, H.M. (1991) 'Downsize by design to get the intended results', *Employment Relations Today*, Summer, 175–183.

Wilson, F. (1992) 'Language, technology, gender and power', *Human Relations*, 45, 883–904.

Wrubel, R. (1992) 'Lean management: Nucor', *Financial World*, 29 September, 50.

6

Metaphor in Organization Theory: Following in the Footsteps of the Poet?

Dawn E. Inns and Philip J. Jones

This chapter aims to compare the use of metaphor in poetry with its use within the field of organization theory. We do not suggest here that the aims of the two disciplines are the same, nor that the way metaphor is used within each subject is uniform. However, and to use Mangham's terminology (see Chapter 1), the two ought, at the very least, to share a 'nodding aquaintance'. Thus we suggest that there are certain core functions of metaphor that can be discerned in both areas. In the spirit of metaphor, we hope that by bringing together two apparently disparate realms, a clearer understanding of our subject of interest may be gained: the relevance of metaphor to organization theory.

Our comparison reveals both similarities and differences in the use of metaphor across the two fields. This leads to consideration of the different aims of poetry and organization theory and how these translate into different demands placed on metaphors. These will be examined using examples from both domains.

The chapter reviews metaphorical awareness as a means of recognizing the cultural walls of human existence; a realization that the interpretation we may have of a situation is only one of several that are possible. Changing a metaphor can open up a whole set of unexplored areas which were obscured by a rival interpretation. For example, Lakoff and Johnson (1980) describe how the metaphors: "Time is Money" and "Life is a Journey" dominate Western attempts to find meaning in life. The very use of these metaphors to interpret life brings with it a set of associated concepts and vocabulary: notions of progress, direction and purpose are given centre stage (Lakoff and Johnson, 1980: 92), and ideas of "wasting time", "making the most of time" and establishing "career paths" provide bench-marks by which we evaluate activities. As anthropological accounts of non-industrial societies reveal, very different interpretations of time and life are possible, and in such societies these metaphors would be inappropriate to life as it is experienced.

The importance of metaphor and its pervasiveness in language and thought has been explored for some time by literary critics, philosophers and educational theorists who have been interested in *how* metaphor functions. In contrast, explicit acknowledgement of the importance of metaphor in organization theory is a relatively recent phenomenon. This may be explained by the fact that metaphor has traditionally been seen as the domain of literature and not part of science, in spite of the fact that science owes its development in part to the use of metaphors elaborated into models (Brown, 1977). Organization theory, drawing from social science, has been heavily influenced by the scientific ethos of objectivity and logic in spite of the input from such schools as the social constructionists and the symbolic interactionists.

However, the relevance of such research on metaphor for the social sciences is increasingly receiving attention. Miles and Huberman (1994) provide a useful summary of the main functions of metaphor which they believe are relevant to conducting research in the social sciences. These are briefly listed here because they are consistent with some of the themes explored in this chapter and therefore serve as an introduction.

Drawing on various works on metaphor, they review metaphors as: 'data-reducing devices', compactly conveying many connotations and ideas; as 'decentering devices', enabling people to see beyond their existing conceptual frameworks and models; and as a technique for theory development. This latter point follows from Lakoff's (1987) assertion that abstract ideas can best be understood by representing them initially in concrete terms and that metaphors can therefore be the starting point for the development of theory. Finally, they explore metaphors as a qualitative methodological tool, offering the researcher access to participants' interpretations of situations as they are revealed through participants' use of metaphors. This accords with the ethnographer's desire to penetrate the socially defined meanings of events.

We are specifically concerned in this chapter with exploring Morgan's claim that metaphor can be a useful creative tool for research and analysis in organizations. Morgan advances this claim using the concept of 'imaginization', whereby metaphor is used to conduct thought in a 'creative yet disciplined' way (1986: 17) and so opens up new avenues of perception which suggest new modes of action. Here we examine the process by which this might be achieved and, also, look at some of the demands placed on metaphor in organization theory if it is to be used to 'imaginize'.

The chapter also examines metaphor as a means of access to, and expression of, intuitive, embryonic perceptions and understanding. These may be easier to grasp as people attempt to describe their experiences in novel and unconventional ways. By articulating ideas through metaphors, individuals can often expand the concepts and expressions available through language. Metaphors may therefore offer concepts useful for further exploration and theory development, as well as increasing an organizational researcher's understanding of a situation from the participants' perspective.

The rapidly growing interest in metaphors in organization theory appears to be connected to wider developments in the field and to dissatisfaction

with the dominant models. One of these developments is the acknowledgement that language and discourse in organizational life are worthy of as
much attention as structures and systems.

A contemporary development which has explicitly confronted the importance of language and discourse in organizational life is postmodernism.
A postmodern perspective views language as a lens through which "reality",
as a deeply problematic concept, is mediated. Interpretations of reality are,
therefore, always located within a specific framework. From the diversity of
meanings possible, one is privileged in accounts and it is necessary to retrace
and uncover alternative and conflicting ones that have been silenced. The
study of metaphors seems to lead necessarily to an examination of some of
the debates that have structured writing on postmodernism, and where
relevant these form a part of this chapter.

Other recent developments in organization theory have looked specifically
at language and rhetoric as a hegemonic tool; structuring perceptions and
buttressing power structures. The work of Burrell (1988) and his interpretation of Foucault's work on knowledge and discourse, and the work of
Gergen (1992), and that of Legge (1991), are all examples of studies in this
vein. Dunford and Palmer in Chapter 5 of this volume explore directly ways
in which metaphors can function as powerful hegemonic tools, portraying
events in particular ways which are consistent with a specific ideological
context.

In the light of such contemporary research and theorizing it seems likely
that the study of language and discourse will become one of the main areas
of interest in organizational analysis and theory in the next decade. Further,
it appears likely that the use of metaphor, as a cornerstone of language, and
as a research tool, will inevitably become an increasingly important area of
study if we are to develop the theoretical underpinnings necessary to
understand this area.

Metaphor has a history of study in poetry and it therefore seems fruitful
to analyse the use of metaphor in organization theory by applying the
analytical tools and concepts developed in poetry. It is to this comparative
analysis, which seeks to identify similarities and differences in the use of
metaphor in poetry and organization theory, that we now turn.

Similarities and differences: Metaphor in poetry and organization theory

At first sight, metaphors appear to be used in poetry and organization theory
in quite different ways. Some initial similarities are, however, discernible.
For example, that metaphors function as a conceptual tool, not merely as an
illustrative device in both areas, and that the three functions of metaphor
identified by Ortony (1975) appear equally valid in both fields. These are:
vividness, compactness and overcoming the "inexpressibility" problem of
conveying unfamiliar phenomena to the reader. By briefly examining one

example from poetry and one from organization theory we are able to see how these three functions are at work in both domains.

Ted Hughes (1978), in the poem 'The Thought-Fox', describes the creative act of writing; how a poem forms and emerges in the poet's mind. To do this, he uses the metaphor of a fox moving into a clearing. Imprints in the snow and a glimpse of the fox's green eyes 'brilliantly, concentratedly, coming about its own business' foreshadow 'a body that is bold to come'. A half-glimpsed image and trail finally transforms itself into a fox/poem:

> *Till, with a sudden sharp hot stink of fox*
> *It enters the dark hole of the head.*
> *The window is starless still; the clock ticks,*
> *   The page is printed.* (1978: 20)

It is difficult to imagine how the act of creating a poem could have been described so well except by recourse to a metaphor. Conveying the "inexpressible" through metaphor is clearly illustrated here, as is the ability to achieve greater compactness and vividness.

Similarly, Mangham and Overington's (1987) use of the metaphor of theatre to understand organizational life illustrates these three functions. The metaphor of theatre describes vividly and concisely aspects of organizational life that may be difficult to express so well except through the theatrical metaphor. These include: the creation and management of image, the ritual nature of interaction, the importance of "personal" and "situational" scripts in determining action, and the use of props (space, decor, costumes) to convey and build up an understanding of the situation. These ritualistic aspects of behaviour in organizations can fruitfully be apprehended through the metaphor of theatre.

However, in spite of these similarities, it appears that a distinction can be made. In poetry, metaphors seem to be used primarily to generate a gestalt, emotive and holistic understanding of the subject. In organization theory, they may initially do this but are then used with the aim of enabling a rational, reductionist understanding, focusing on the analysis of one aspect of organizational life at the expense of another. This partiality is an unavoidable characteristic of a metaphoric perspective used for analysis, but Morgan (1986) argues that it is precisely by adopting a variety of perspectives, each in itself partial, that a complete picture of the complexity of organizational life can be built up. Partiality, then, is only a problem if a single metaphor is used in isolation, or if exploration is superficial.

By stating that insight appears to be the primary focus in poetry, and insight leading to analysis the concern in organization theory, we are forced to consider the different aims of the subjects. Whilst poetic metaphors can justifiably function as aesthetic devices or ends in themselves, it could be argued that organization theory uses metaphor in a more purposive, utilitarian way as a means to an end.

When Ted Hughes tries to convey the violence of a storm in the poem 'Wind' (1978), for example, the metaphor: 'The tent of the hills drummed and strained its guy-rope' (1978: 34) evokes a holistic visual image of tension which captures the strength of the storm and the fragility and insecurity felt by humans caught in it.

When a similar metaphor is used in organization theory by Hedberg et al. (1976), and organizations are portrayed as 'tents', the aim is to convey one aspect of organizational life: the uncertainty and instability that characterize organizations. This instability forces organizations to accept their structure and design as only temporary, and emphasizes the need to build in flexibility. In this organizational example an initial image is used to analyse the implications for organizations in terms of design. Metaphor is used for analysis and to guide future actions, and not merely to generate a gestalt understanding of the subject under study.

In poetry, the "gestalt" can be traced to the fusion or accumulation of images, associations and emotions that constitutes a poem. Metaphors within poems are part of this evocative fusion and function as parts of the whole, all of the parts being used to build up a desired atmosphere and effect. Metaphors as part of this effect may act as 'objective correlatives' (Cuddon, 1991: 647). This is a term which refers to the artist's need to find a set of expressions, a situation or object which can capture, transmit or distil an experience of emotion that the writer has had and which he or she wishes to convey to the reader. Symbols and images become the "containers of emotion".

In organization theory, a metaphor is used primarily in isolation; intensity or fusion are not the main focus, nor is the metaphor to act primarily as a "container of emotion" but rather as a problem-solving and analytical tool. An evocative image may be necessary to waken the reader to the strangeness of the comparison, as in Cohen et al.'s metaphor for decision-making processes in organizations as a 'garbage can' approach (1972); or Skinner's 'big hat, no cattle' (1981) to describe human resource management. However, the problem-solving and utilitarian demands on organization theory require that these initial images be carried forward and explained and investigated as fitting images.

This is not to say that reason is absent from the use of metaphor in poetry, and that we find only emotion. Seventeenth-century metaphysical poetry perhaps shows most explicitly that this is not the case. However, in organization theory, the emphasis seems to be primarily on metaphors as tools for analysis, and, in order to carry out this function, they must somehow be "literalized" and made less implicit. What is considered an effective metaphor in poetry is essentially different from what is considered an effective metaphor in organization theory. This can be clearly demonstrated by making a comparative analysis of examples from both fields.

In W.H. Auden's 'Twelve Songs', metaphors are used to convey the experience of death and the huge impact of the loss of a loved one:

He was my North, my South, my East and West,
My working week and my Sunday rest,
My noon, my midnight, my talk, my song. (1966: 92)

The fusion of images and associations conveys the desired emotion. Metaphors are used as powerful descriptive devices, functioning within the poem as a whole to express how the whole universe for the writer has been affected by this death. The metaphors in the poem act implicitly and there is no attempt made to make them more explicit.

If we take an example from organization theory, Morgan's (1986) metaphor of organizations as brains, we see something very different at work. In this example, the image is carried forward to enable rational analysis. Morgan describes how organizations can be likened to brains in their capacity as information-processing systems. He describes how, by seeing organizations as brains, we can look at ways of improving organizational capacity for intelligence, flexibility and inventiveness through organizational design. For example, by designing organizations along holographic principles so that an awareness of the whole is contained in each part, a greater rapidity of responses is obtained than in an organization designed along bureaucratic principles, where knowledge of the whole process is fragmented. By using this metaphor and by seeing organizations as brains, we can begin to consider how organizations might 'learn to learn' and speed up their information-processing capacity (Morgan, 1986).

The function of the metaphor of 'organizations as brains' is, then, to suggest solutions and to help envisage new ways of thinking about organizational design. To do this, metaphor must be used as a rational tool for exploration and be somehow "literalized" and made less implicit. This fits with the Western empirical tradition of scientific progress. Metaphor in this scenario becomes an analytical tool with which to achieve "progress".

The distinction is that metaphor is used primarily for gestalt understanding in poetry, and essentially for rational reductionist analysis in organization theory. This seems true for many examples and may in part be explained by the different aims of the two disciplines.

However, in making such a distinction there appears to be a tendency to fall victim to a common flaw; that is, to emphasize the dichotomy between art and science, cognition and emotion, creativity and disciplined analysis. Highlighting such differences in the use of metaphor might perpetuate the idea that poetry is the domain of imagination and creativity and science and social science are the domain of cognition and rational exploration. This is a view which is being increasingly challenged and indeed a recent article suggests that: 'The way science imagines the world and the way poets imagine the world are not so far apart' (Irwin, 1995: 2). We see the reasoning behind this view and, in order to avoid this trap of false dichotomy, we found that it proved fruitful to explore in more detail the similarities in the use of metaphor across social science and poetry.

We suggest that the similarities run much deeper than might be suggested by a prima facie examination. In order to examine this hypothesis it is worth considering for a moment the relative importance of metaphor within poetry. Why is it that metaphor is suggested to be 'the basic figure in poetry' (Cuddon, 1991: 542)? The compactness of images and associations achieved by metaphor is important, given the brevity of the standard poem. However, it is equally likely that the answer is to be found in the way metaphor functions to increase imaginative perception. The poet uses metaphor to convey creative, imaginative insights generated in his/her mind in an attempt to alter the everyday, worldly consciousness of the reader. This has been seen as the function of the poet:

> Baudelaire and his followers created the image of the poet as a kind of seer or voyant, who could see through and beyond the real world to the world of ideal forms and essences. Thus the task of the poet was to create this "other world" by suggestion and symbolism. (Cuddon, 1991: 941)

In 'The Thought-Fox', for example, it is through metaphor that Ted Hughes is able to apprehend and convey something the rational mind is only dimly aware of – the workings of creative thought and inspiration. The poet, then, 'instructs ... by metaphor ... creates forms that did not exist' (Cuddon, 1991: 326). The above quotations from Cuddon may be said to exaggerate the visionary powers of the poet. The emphasis made here, however, is not on some mysterious, mystic power the poet might possess, but on how the poet, by using the creative possibilities offered by metaphor, can on the one hand attain understanding and create meaning, and on the other communicate these insights to others.

It is in this capacity for creative freedom and imaginative insight that a crossover point can be seen between the use of metaphor in organization theory and in poetry. By 'imaginizing', Morgan (1986) argues that the organizational researcher can explore creative solutions to problems. This is because metaphor helps to reframe experience in new ways. The correlate of Morgan's 'imaginizing' in relation to literature is expressed in what Levin (1979: 114) calls 'phenomenalistic construal'. This term refers to the way the reader, in order to make sense of the metaphor, reinterprets the world in terms of the image offered by the poet. For the metaphor to be successful it must connect to the reader's experience and must be taken seriously for a time, as exploration occurs within the frame offered.

As Levin argues, this exploration actually constructs reality in a different way and entails a reinterpretation of the 'literal' or a 'shift in world orientation' (1977: 127) in order to explore the similarities imagined by the poet. Once this has been achieved, the perception of the phenomena has altered. Thought and language are dynamic and the mind cannot revert to 'not seeing' something in terms of the frame offered by the metaphor, given that exploration was fruitful. The 'capacity for perception and understanding' (Brown, 1977: 87) generated by a successful metaphor changes the phenomena under study and an enhanced perception must incorporate the new perspective.

An apparent similarity in the way metaphor functions in poetry and in organization theory lies, then, in this process of 'imagization' or 'phenomenalistic construal'. Levin (1979: 114) argues that this process entails what Coleridge referred to as the 'willing suspension of disbelief'; a mental state necessary for a reader to plunge into the world of poetry. This may be described as 'that state of receptivity and credulity desirable in a reader. . . . The reader must "grant" that he or she is about to read a story' (Cuddon, 1991: 1044). It is through this process that the reader is able to contemplate his/her "taken-for-granted" reality in a different light. Lakoff and Johnson (1980) argue that in facilitating this, metaphor draws attention to the interaction between the individual's conceptual framework and the external world of physical properties and social structures. These are presented as distinct and separate entities by both the 'Myth of Objectivism' and the 'Myth of Subjectivism' (Lakoff and Johnson, 1980). The 'Myth of Objectivism' claims that a "real" world exists, detached from subjective interpretation. The 'Myth of Subjectivism' argues that there is an entirely personal world, unique to the individual and the domain of the imagination. The two are equally erroneous, denying the interaction between the outer world and the personal world (Lakoff and Johnson, 1980).

Metaphors are, we suggest, important because they signal to us and make explicit that there is no absolute world "out there", but that we are actively engaged in constructing meanings from our own frame of reference and experience. The way we interpret phenomena determines our actions (Lakoff and Johnson, 1980; Morgan, 1986; Mangham and Overington, 1987). This view of human experience has been put forward by the symbolic interactionist and social constructionist schools, but the implications of this for use of metaphor in organization theory have been explored in depth by a relatively small number of writers.

We believe that it is in its contribution to "phenomenalistic construal" that metaphor offers great promise in developing organization theory. This is in terms of an organizational researcher using metaphor to guide analysis and explore solutions through a variety of perspectives; in terms of using metaphor to communicate insights to others; and in terms of people in organizations using metaphors to describe their experience and to gain a greater understanding of behaviour.

Metaphor and postmodernism

This discussion leads us to some of the concerns of postmodernism in organization theory. Postmodernism is a term which has been applied to many different writers and various works, and it would be impossible to do justice here to the complete range and complexity of views that come under this "label". However, an examination of metaphor within organization theory seems to lead inevitably to some of the pertinent debates, terms and areas of interest in postmodernism. Our aim here is not to provide the reader with a comprehensive or exhaustive analysis of postmodernism in organization theory per se, but to provide "edited highlights" in order to focus attention and stimulate further discussion within this area.

We follow Hassard in taking postmodernism here to refer to an 'epistemology' rather than an 'epoch':

> Postmodern epistemology suggests that the world is constituted by our shared language and that we can only "know the world" through the particular forms of discourse our language creates. (1994: 305)

Humans, then, by experiencing the world through a given set of words and concepts, are faced with the feelings of instability and insecurity that this occasions (Cooper and Burrell, 1988).

This is in direct opposition to a modernist viewpoint which sees language as a tool to describe a reality which is already "out there" (Cooper and Burrell, 1988). The aim of modernism is to accurately portray this reality by using increasingly sophisticated and rigorous methods (Hassard, 1994). If, however, reality is necessarily mediated by and depends on language, it is clear that this goal is impossible and that any form of unity of meaning or stability that modernism might aspire to is unattainable. Thus, as Cooper and Burrell suggest, there will always be spaces for multiple interpretations: 'The world is not already there, waiting for us to reflect it' (1988: 100). From a postmodern perspective, then, multiple interpretations are an asset rather than a problem. The deliberate use of metaphors in organizational research offers a way out of the cage of thought and language constructed by the dominance of a few paradigms within the subject, and encourages the exploration of alternative perspectives.

Gergen (1992) stresses the need to encourage the 'generative' potential of language and theory and to challenge the "taken-for-granted" in organizational life. Similarly, Cooper and Burrell (1988), drawing on Foucault's work, state the importance of trying to make 'the familiar strange', thereby achieving a new perspective and highlighting the extent to which Man is 'suspended in webs of significance he himself has spun' (Geertz, 1973: 5).

The way this can be achieved by use of metaphor can be seen, for example, in the use of metaphor offered by Latour (1988) and Law (1992): Organizations as 'actor-networks'. Both writers see organizations as a heterogeneous network of interactions between human and non-human elements. This metaphor has the potential to radically alter our perspective on organizations in many ways.

For example, the actor-network metaphor gives an equal importance to human and non-human elements in organizations. For Latour (1988), 'actors' can be either, and both play an important role in interaction. Such interaction means, for instance, that computers as 'non-humans' have now become such an intrinsic part of organizational life that any failure on the part of the computers to play their allocated 'role' will be no less catastrophic to an organization than a human failing.

Furthermore, the notion of organizations as 'actor-networks' challenges the traditionally accepted belief that organizations are fixed in one place as if an invisible boundary surrounded them. It changes our conception of an organization to incorporate all of the elements "inside" and "outside" which constitute the organization's activity, and to see the taken-for-granted boundaries established between "inside" and "outside" as an act of representation (Cooper, 1992).

The importance of metaphor to postmodernism also becomes apparent through Gergen's (1992) work. He argues that language has often mistakenly been represented as the 'slave' to the 'master' of concrete reality (1992: 212), having only the function of 'messenger' from the 'real' world. Metaphors remind us that, on the contrary: 'Our concepts structure what we perceive. . . . Our conceptual system thus plays a central role in defining our everyday realities' (Lakoff and Johnson, 1980: 3). Metaphors link thought and action and can provoke insights that often allow us to act in ways that we may not have thought possible before (Morgan, 1986: 343). For example, seeing organizations as theatre stresses the tenacity of familiar roles and scripts and may help us to understand and overcome resistance to change and the lack of creativity. It implies that we should become aware of the 'scripts' that guide behaviour and the need to challenge and rewrite these in some cases (Mangham and Overington, 1987).

How metaphor fits within the postmodern ethos, then, relates to the way in which postmodernism puts language and discourse on centre stage for research, and emphasizes that there are no absolute truths and comforting single way of viewing "reality". Acknowledging conflicting and suppressed meanings or 'other voices' (Gergen, 1992) is important for organizational researchers, and metaphors provide us with a route to this.

Furthermore, if postmodernism challenges modernism's claim to use language to describe a reality and depict a world "out there", it also casts doubt on the contention that a scientific or "literal" discourse is more fruitful than poetic language in depicting reality. The French philosopher Ricoeur criticizes the 'verificationalist concept of truth' and 'positivist concept of reality' (1978: 306) as the only possibility, and asks whether 'poetic language does not break through to a pre-scientific, ante-predicative level, where the very notions of fact, object, reality and truth, as delimited by epistemology, are called into question' (1978: 254). In comparison with scientific or "literal" discourse, Ricoeur questions whether poetic discourse may not more accurately capture how we *experience* the world. This view is also expressed by Miles and Huberman (1994), who position metaphor in-between empirical facts and the significance they have for the people concerned. They consequently offer researchers a valuable interpretative tool.

An example of poetic language capturing and conveying experience is found in 'The Jaguar' (Hughes, 1982: 15). In this poem the lethargy of the zoo atmosphere *as it is experienced* by the zoo visitors is conveyed through metaphor:

Fatigued with indolence, tiger and lion
Lie still as the sun. The boa-constrictor's coil is a fossil. . . .
It might be painted on a nursery wall.

Access to a "deeper" level of understanding through poetic language has been a claim made historically for poets and goes back to the notion of Muses and divine inspiration which speak through poets. Access to our "irrational" or "primordial" nature, which may hold insights, has been mentioned by various poets. Ted Hughes (1978), for example, talks of the necessity for poets to clutch at elusive 'irrational', fleeting thoughts that may foreshadow a deeper understanding of phenomena. He uses the metaphor of fishing to describe this; the necessity of 'catching' thoughts and drawing them out of the cloudy interior of the mind. It could be argued that metaphors help to do this in both poetry and organization theory. Metaphors suggest themselves for reasons which may not at first be apparent. It is important to explore and capture these intuitive impressions.

In organization theory, Srivastva and Barrett (1988), for example, show how metaphors used in speech by group members to describe the group's development give clear indications of inner reactions and feelings. They argue that by concentrating on these metaphors and developing them, it may be possible to gain a better understanding of feelings which are difficult to articulate.

The question which poses itself here is whether the positivist and managerialist factions of organization theory will be willing to take on the implications that postmodernism, poetry and metaphors draw attention to. In other words, and as Ricoeur (1978) states, 'reference', 'reality' and 'truth' are deeply problematic concepts. If this view is accepted, some organizational researchers may find it difficult to define such a clear role for themselves. There is no doubt that the role of organizational researcher will continue to be important, but we support Gergen (1992) in suggesting that this may need to be reviewed.

When we read a poem we have expectations of being able to "suspend" literal reference and be allowed to indulge in playful, imaginative fancies. This is what is meant by Coleridge's 'willing suspension of disbelief'. In fact, it is possible that poetry is effective because, in this unguarded state, we are more open to suggestion. This, together with the emotional power of poetry created by the fusion of images and associations, of which metaphors are a part, increases our receptivity to the ideas put forward by the poet. Even if we do not always recognize them initially as such, these ideas are, of course, culturally relative and inevitably embedded in ideas of the time and society as experienced by the poet.

Marvell's poem 'To his Coy Mistress' (Hollander and Kermode, 1973), for example, challenges the dominant moral and religious views of his day and is far from being escapist. However, in setting itself up as fiction, Ricoeur (1978) argues that poetry may have the flexibility to portray the world as it is experienced more accurately than "literal" reference.

In contrast to this freedom that poetry enjoys, to what extent do many readers of organizational texts expect a show of the "literal" and a writer who never veers far from the concrete and who is solution-driven? The expectations readers have may explain why organization theorists are tempted to try to capitalize on metaphors, as Wilson (1992) argues they do. Authors may feel compelled to expand and almost "literalize" metaphors in attempts to improve their utility as frameworks for analysis.

This discussion brings to mind the positivist versus qualitative methodology debate which is extensively examined by Easterby-Smith et al. (1991). When examining the 'usefulness' or 'validity' of metaphors in organization theory, we must consider whether we are to look at validity from a quantitative and positivist perspective, or from a qualitative and phenomenological perspective. Easterby-Smith et al. (1991: 27) define the former as a focus on facts, hypotheses, causality and fundamental laws, and the latter as the ability of the researcher to accurately convey the richness of experience of the observed: 'Has the researcher gained full access to the knowledge and meanings of informants?' (1991: 41)

Organizational metaphors seem to be evaluated on the basis of whether they are effective as tools for analysis and as a means to an end. This is contrasted with the evaluation of poetic metaphors, which seems to be whether they convey with richness and fidelity the experience of the poet. We would suggest therefore that there seems to be a tendency to evaluate organizational metaphors using the rules of positivism, and poetic metaphors using the rules of phenomenology. We are now at the heart of the debate around the division of art and science which seems to gravitate essentially around problems of method.

Authors drawn from a positivist tradition may have a mental schema of what constitutes "good" organization theory drawn from the positivist tradition, that is, solution-driven and never veering far from the concrete, the observable and objective "facts". The assumptions which drive this model of "good" research writing may tempt writers into expanding and literalizing their metaphors in an attempt to improve their utility as frameworks for analysis. However, as Chia (Chapter 7) in this volume notes, literalizing them too much or making them too 'concrete' may ultimately destroy their power. Zemke also supports this view: 'Any metaphors, have their limits. Blow the bubble gum too hard and it explodes' (1988: 31). Attempts to "literalize" metaphors in organization theory also place stringent demands on metaphors which will now be examined.

Demands placed on metaphor in organization theory

Because they are used not only for insight but also as a framework within which to conduct analysis, we suggest that greater demands are placed on metaphors in organization theory than in poetry. Metaphors which are used as tools for analysis must undergo greater testing of their viability than poetic metaphors.

Evidence in support of this hypothesis falls broadly into three areas: first, relating to the similarity/difference tension in metaphor between subject and metaphoric image; second, the problem of "pseudo-gestalt", that is, false or superficial understanding of metaphor; third, the issue of metaphor emerging from and operating within an ideological framework which may be as constraining as it is liberating. In the following three sections these three issues are explored in greater depth.

The similarity/difference tension

Brown (1977), Morgan (1980), and Alvesson (1993) all refer to the similarity/difference tension in metaphor. When doing so, they suggest that, for a metaphor to be effective, it must unite a subject and image which are similar enough for exploration of points of comparison, yet different enough to be inventive and offer new insight. Lakoff and Johnson (1980) go further and argue that metaphor does not so much illustrate similarities as create them. If these two premises are accepted, we might conclude that it is in the juxtaposition of two disparate but compatible areas that similarities are actively generated by researchers.

Similarly, Ricoeur (1978), in his work on metaphor, describes how metaphor increases our understanding by extending our categories and enabling us to see previously unseen similarities between two things. This insight opens on to a world of ambiguity and paradox, however, as the object is both like and unlike the thing it is compared to: 'In metaphor, "the same" operates in spite of the "different" ' (1978: 196). In poetry, a metaphor's validity in terms of this similarity/difference tension is scarcely explored. This may be because, as Levin, quoting Frege (1970), argues: 'in poetry the sense of an expression may be sufficient for one's purposes . . . since it is the feelings and images aroused that are of importance' (1977: 125). Therefore, when Ted Hughes describes November as 'The month of the drowned dog' (1982: 51), he is using a metaphor to convey only an image of gloom and dankness, and not to suggest there are other similarities that could be explored for purposive ends.

In organization theory, a metaphor's validity in this respect must be directly confronted when metaphors are used for analysis and an initially seductive metaphor may be abandoned because there are not sufficient potential similarities to make research within the frame of the metaphor productive. The criteria used to evaluate a successful metaphor in organization theory seem to be whether the metaphor is capable of supporting analysis and increasing understanding, with a view to anticipating events.

Pseudo-gestalt

The term "pseudo-gestalt" is used to describe the superficial or false understanding of the sense of a metaphor. It has been argued so far in the chapter that metaphor can generate a flash of understanding. The question arises: How do we know that metaphor has done what it was supposed to do? Ortony (1975) raises this point, saying that unless understanding is tested we cannot be sure a metaphor has helped a person to understand an unfamiliar or 'inexpressible' topic. However, because of the emotive impact of metaphor a person may think they have understood it in the way it was intended, when in fact they have only inadequately grasped the sense which the author meant to convey.

It could be argued that in poetry there is less concern to direct a certain interpretation of a metaphor. There may be a variety of images and associations readers have with the phrase 'The month of the drowned dog', but all will probably convey an adequate impression of winter gloom for the poem by Ted Hughes to be successful. In organization theory, it may be more important to ensure that there has been mutual understanding of a metaphor and that meaning has been reliably conveyed before a metaphor is used to guide in-depth analysis of organizations.

Wilson's (1992) scepticism about the prolific use of metaphors in organizational texts is brought to mind here. He believes that metaphor is increasingly used in managerial writing as a 'shorthand device' (1992: 80) to communicate research findings. The underdeveloped use of metaphor in certain managerial texts betrays a naive assumption that a metaphor is always insightful, and is interpreted in the same way by everyone. Instead, it may be necessary to unpack a metaphor for its meaning and check understanding before it is used for analysis. Whilst this is not necessary in poetry, an organization theorist behaving like a poet may be accused of naively or superficially employing metaphors.

Miles and Huberman (1994) also warn of the dangers of using metaphors to make sense of data too early in research, thereby constraining understanding; or of over-using them, that is, carrying likenesses revealed through metaphor too far and failing to acknowledge the dissimilarities between the subject and the metaphoric image.

Metaphors: Liberating or constraining?

The extent to which a metaphor is as constraining as it is liberating must be examined in terms of the wider ideological viewpoint and associations which underpin the metaphor.

Alvesson (1993) describes how metaphor incorporates a 'first' and a 'second level' of meaning. The first level is its apparent, initial meaning. The second level, which must be entered into if the metaphor is not to remain too broad to be useful for analysis, inevitably incorporates deeper connotations, associations and often a 'world view' or paradigm. When exploring the second level of metaphor, ontological assumptions that were implicit must become explicit.

Thus, for example, Mangham and Overington's (1987) metaphor of organizations as theatre stems from a social constructionist perspective. Similarly, Morgan's (1980) metaphor of organizations as 'psychic prisons' is informed by a 'radical humanist' perspective.

Alvesson (1993) argues that this second level of metaphor is important because without it the metaphor may be too broad to be useful. Yet, to what extent should organization theorists make this second level explicit? Too explicit and it may constrain creative exploration by the reader. However, if the second level remains entirely implicit, the metaphor may be being used in a manipulative way, luring the reader into the writer's 'world view', and with the appealing nature of metaphor reducing reflective distance. This highlights the difficulty of stimulating thought without directing it in an inhibiting way, and the problem of telling people what to look for without telling them what to see!

This point is illustrated by Pages et al. (1979). They use the metaphor of religion to analyse modern organizations as 'churches', in order to understand the psychological hold modern organizations can sometimes have over employees via a strong corporate culture. They use this framework to examine, for instance, the mission statement of a company as credo, evaluation interviews as confessions, and the values expressed in company manuals as taking on the aspect of holy scriptures for company devotees. However, they are cautious of the appealing nature of metaphor which may encourage 'hasty and unreflective assimilation' (1979: 216).

Reading Pages et al., it becomes apparent that not only does an author's attitude towards a metaphoric image inform the metaphor, but also the reader's own attitude and experience will determine how a metaphor is used. Choosing such an emotive topic as religion as a metaphor to understand organizations will probably entail a carrying over of emotional feelings from one domain to the other, and these emotional reactions may determine how the metaphor is developed.

Consequently, just how liberated are we from the "webs of significance" we have spun? Given that we necessarily bring associations of the metaphoric image to the subject, how much is the claim for new insight valid? As Alvesson (1993) states, from the diversity of meanings opened up by the metaphor, we choose one that is in line with our existing cognitive framework. This raises a wider issue of just how difficult original and creative thought is. Metaphors may not be perfect in enabling us to be aware of, and expand, the concepts that guide our behaviour, but they offer a great deal of potential.

It would be idealistic to expect anything more than this partial path to creativity and insight. The way metaphors function in both organization theory and poetry would, therefore, seem to express a fundamental aspect of the human condition which is illustrated in Mangham and Overington's work (1987): Man is neither a victim of fate, nor totally self-controlling. Meanings are given, but modified through negotiation and interaction. The role of metaphors is similarly ambivalent: they are liberating and constraining at the same time. Thus in examining the liberating or constraining effect of metaphors, we find further support for the widely cited propositions that language is necessarily restrictive but makes thought possible, and that past experience restricts interpretation but makes comprehension of the new possible.

Conclusions

A comparison of how metaphors are used in poetry and organization theory provides support for the proposition that metaphors can function as important tools for conducting research in organization theory.

Levin (1979: 117) talks of the poet as traditionally viewed as 'seer' of the new. By imagining, poets enter a world of greater possibilities. Metaphor encourages this creative exploration, and it is for this reason that metaphor is a fundamental aspect of poetry.

However, if it is accepted that metaphor does not just generate insight but can be carried further, as it 'unites reason and imagination' (Lakoff and Johnson, 1980: 193), then it appears capable of stimulating imaginative insight and acting as a framework for conducting analysis. The root meaning of analysis is 'to undo' (Cuddon, 1991: 222). In using metaphor to analyse organizations, it appears necessary to pass from a holistic, gestalt understanding to a rational, reductionist mode of thought, in order to purposively unpack the compressed meaning within the metaphor.

The poetic metaphorist may have left footprints that the organization theorist can walk in when trying to understand how metaphor can function. Yet, for the poetic, the pleasure of metaphor appears to reside primarily in the journey. The utilitarian demands placed on the organizational metaphorist may mean that the pleasure lies not so much in the journey but in safely arriving at the desired destination.

References

Alvesson, M. (1993) 'The play of metaphors', in J. Hassard and M. Parker (eds), *Postmodernism and Organizations*. London: Sage Publications, pp. 114–131.

Auden, W.H. (1966) *Collected Shorter Poems 1927–1957*. London: Faber and Faber.

Brown, R.H. (1977) *A Poetic for Sociology: Toward a Logic of Discovery for the Human Sciences*. Cambridge: Cambridge University Press.

Burrell, G. (1988) 'Modernism, postmodernism and organizational analysis 2: The contribution of Michel Foucault', *Organization Studies*, 9 (2), 221–235.

Cohen, M.D., March, J.G. and Olsen, J.P. (1972) 'A garbage can model of organizational choice', *Administrative Science Quarterly*, 17 (1), 1–25.

Cooper, R. (1992) 'Formal organization as representation: Remote control, displacement and abbreviation', in M. Reed and M. Hughes (eds), *Rethinking Organization: New Directions in Organization Theory and Analysis*. London: Sage Publications, pp. 254–272.

Cooper, R. and Burrell, G. (1988) 'Modernism, postmodernism and organizational analysis: An introduction', *Organization Studies*, 9 (1), 91–112.

Cuddon, J.A. (1991) *The Penguin Dictionary of Literary Terms and Literary Theory* (4th edn). London: Penguin Books.

Easterby-Smith, M., Thorpe, R. and Lowe, A. (1991) *Management Research: An Introduction*. London: Sage Publications.

Frege, G. (1970) *Translations from the Philosophical Writings of Gottlob Frege* (2nd edn). Oxford: Basil Blackwell.

Geertz, C. (1973) *The Interpretation of Cultures: Selected Essays*. New York: Basic Books.

Gergen, K.J. (1992) 'Organization theory in the postmodern era', in M. Reed and M. Hughes (eds), *Rethinking Organization: New Directions in Organization Theory and Analysis*. London: Sage Publications, pp. 207–226.

Hassard, J. (1994) 'Postmodern organizational analysis: Toward a conceptual framework', *Journal of Management Studies*, 31 (3), May, 303–324.

Hedberg, B., Nystrom, C. and Starbuck, W. (1976) 'Camping on seesaws: Prescriptions for a self-designing organization', *Administrative Science Quarterly*, 21(1), 41–63.

Hollander, J. and Kermode, F. (1973) *The Literature of Renaissance England*. Oxford: Oxford University Press.

Hughes, T. (1978) *Poetry in the Making* (5th edn). London: Faber and Faber.

Hughes, T. (1982) *Selected Poems 1957–1981*. London: Faber and Faber.

Irwin, A. (1995) 'Poetic breakthrough', *The Times Higher Education Supplement*, 24 March, 2.

Lakoff, G. (1987) *Women, Fire and Dangerous Things: What Categories Reveal about the Mind*. Chicago: University of Chicago Press.

Lakoff, G. and Johnson, M. (1980) *Metaphors We Live By*. Chicago: University of Chicago Press.

Latour, B. (under pseudonym of J. Johnson) (1988) 'Mixing humans and non-humans together: The sociology of a door closer', *Social Problems*, 55, 297–310.

Law, J. (1992) 'Notes on the theory of the actor-network: Ordering, strategy, and heterogeneity', *Systems Practice*, 5 (4), 379–393.

Legge, K. (1991) 'Human resource management: A critical analysis', in J. Storey (ed.), *New Perspectives on Human Resource Management*. London: Routledge, pp. 19–40.

Levin, S.R. (1977) *The Semantics of Metaphor*. London: Johns Hopkins University Press.

Levin, S.R. (1979) 'Standard approaches to metaphor and a proposal for literary metaphor', in A. Ortony (ed.), *Metaphor and Thought*. Cambridge: Cambridge University Press, pp. 112–122.

Mangham, I.L. and Overington, M.A. (1987) *Organizations as Theatre: A Social Psychology of Dramatic Appearances*. Chichester: John Wiley and Sons.

Miles, M.A. and Huberman, A.M. (1994) *Qualitative Data Analysis: An Expanded Sourcebook* (2nd edn). Thousand Oaks, CA: Sage Publications.

Morgan, G. (1980) 'Paradigms, metaphors, and puzzle solving in organization theory', *Administrative Science Quarterly*, 25(4), 605–622.

Morgan, G. (1986) *Images of Organization*. London: Sage Publications.

Ortony, A. (1975) 'Why metaphors are necessary and not just nice', *Educational Theory*, 25, 45–53.

Pages, M., Bonetti, M. and Gaulejac, V. de (1979) *L'Emprise de l'organisation*. Paris: Presses Universitaires de France.

Ricoeur, P. (1978) *The Rule of Metaphor: Multi-disciplinary Studies of the Creation of Meaning in Language*. London: Routledge and Kegan Paul.

Skinner, W. (1981) 'Big hat, no cattle: Managing human resources', *Harvard Business Review*, 59, September–October, 106–114.

Srivastva, S. and Barrett, F. (1988) 'The transforming nature of metaphors in group development: A study in group theory', *Human Relations*, 41 (1), 31–64.

Wilson, D.C. (1992) *A Strategy of Change: Concepts and Controversies in the Management of Change*. London: Routledge.

Zemke, R. (1988) 'Raiders of the lost metaphor', *Training (USA)*, 25 (4), 8 April, 26–32.

7

Metaphors and Metaphorization in Organizational Analysis: Thinking Beyond the Thinkable

Robert Chia

Examine language, what, if you except some primitive elements of natural sound, what is it all but metaphors, recognized as such or no longer recognized; still fluid and florid or now solid-grown and colourless? If these same primitive garments are the osseous fixtures in the Flesh-Garment Language then are metaphors its muscle and living integument.

S.J. Brown, The World of Imagery (1927)

But if this is indeed the case – if metaphor, taken in this general sense, is not just a certain development of speech, but must be regarded as one of its essential conditions – then any effort to understand its function leads us back, once more, to the fundamental form of verbal *conceiving*.

E. Cassirer, Language and Myth (1946)

since everything becomes metaphorical, there is no longer any literal meaning and, hence, no longer any metaphor either.

J. Derrida, Dissemination (1981)

Writing about metaphors is always a precarious enterprise. For one thing, it is about using language to write about the phenomenon of language itself – an invitation to get oneself entangled in the problems of reflexivity. For another, it does prima facie presuppose the possibility of conveying the meaning of metaphors literally, thereby raising into focus the uneasy relationship between the literal and the metaphorical. Finally, it is by no means entirely clear how metaphors work in the evocation of thought. Are metaphors specific features of language or are all languages inherently metaphorical? What exactly is the relationship between the literal and the metaphorical and which of them enjoys epistemological primacy, or is there something else more fundamental? Are metaphors a phenomenon of the general communication process, so much so that a specific metaphor is said to work if and only when the addressee recognizes it as being used metaphorically (a view adopted by pragmatists)? Or are metaphors purely linguistic phenomena created by the structuring of language and thereby largely independent of speech-acts (a semantic view)? These represent important clusters of concern which have deep and immediate implications for any discussion of the role of metaphor in organizational analysis. It is by no means clear which of these alternative strands of thought (or for that matter any others) is more likely to throw light on the issue of metaphors in organization theory. Yet it is patently obvious that the use of metaphors is clearly widespread; permeating not just academic texts and contexts, but the very core of our everyday existence. Metaphors are what we 'live by', according to Lakoff and Johnson (1980).

Writing about the significance of the process of metaphorization in the context of organizational analysis poses an additional and more perplexing set of problems. It invites an initial complicity with the popular "using metaphors" discourse in organization theory. There is the necessary situating of such an inquiry within the latter's circumscribed orbit of concerns only to then almost immediately take it as a convenient point of departure for demonstrating the wider significance of the process of metaphorization in organizational inquiry.

The underlying issue is that if metaphors are very much an inextricable part of our lives, can we actually "use" them as analytical tools in organizational analysis or are we, by orienting our concerns thus, already unwittingly obscuring the possibility of the more radical hypothesis that language itself is always already entirely metaphorical in character? Our strategies for inquiry and the conclusions we arrive at would therefore be substantially shaped by such primary assumptions. Paying undue attention and priority to only the more significant and obvious generative metaphors and their avowed "usefulness" in illuminating organizational situations diverts attention away from the *process* of metaphorical analysis to a preoccupation with the *content* images evoked through the use of such metaphors. In so doing metaphors are paradoxically treated literally as convenient conceptual windows which help the organizational analyst gain better access to rich avenues of meaning. Yet the a priori distinctions between what counts as literal and what counts as metaphorical are generally taken as unproblematic and the complex relationship between the two remains essentially unexplored.

To study the character of metaphor and to critically examine its applications is, therefore, to be confronted with the hidden aspects of one's own presuppositions, one's own culture and one's own language and logic of organization. An attempt to gain some insight into metaphors and metaphorization in organizational analysis ought to begin by recognizing the precarious nature of such an enterprise, and to acknowledge at the start the inherent difficulties associated with the imposition of language on thought. A critical examination of the nature of the relationship between language, thought and reality is, therefore, a central concern of this chapter. Only after such an examination might we begin to appreciate the extent to which metaphors shape and influence our modes of thought.

Brown (1927), for instance, argues persuasively that metaphors may be 'dead' (i.e., forgotten as such) but they are nevertheless still very dominant (albeit often in ossified form) in everyday language. This view is implicit in much of the language of poetry and contemporary literary criticism which sets itself the task of reinvigorating language and rediscovering the meta-phorical character of knowledge. As Nowottny, writing in reaction to the classical interpretative view of literary criticism, asserted:

> Current criticism often takes metaphor *au grand sérieux*, as a peephole on the nature of transcendental reality, a prime means by which the imagination can see into the life of things ... this attitude makes it difficult to see the workings of those metaphors which deliberately emphasize the frame, offering themselves as deliberate fabrications, as a prime means of seeing into the life not of things but of the creative human consciousness, framer of its own world. (1962: 89)

For Nowottny, for Brown and for other contemporary postmodern writers such as Derrida (1982) and Gasche (1986), metaphors do not then simply provide a readily available window on to reality. Rather they are themselves (often worn-out) artefacts of our own creative framing processes. Indeed, as Gasché wrote:

> Let us recall that both metaphor and concept (i.e., the literal) are philosophical concepts. If a general metaphorology claims that all concepts are worn-out metaphors, then the same must be true of the philosophical concept of metaphor. Yet this *metaphor of metaphor* must remain anathematized if a general metaphor-ology is to succeed at all (and thus to fail). The metaphor of metaphor is therefore the 'founding' trope of the project of metaphorology. (1986: 309; my emphasis)

The metaphor of metaphor is, as it were, the "originary" metaphor and as such comes before the concept of metaphor. Metaphor metaphorized – the double jump outside convention 'breaks the hold of convention and enables us to become aware of the subjectivity of objects and the objectivity of subjective processes' (Nowottny 1962: 86). It is this process of *metaphoriz-ation* in organizational analysis which holds the key to re-conceptualizing the latter as an intellectual strategy for de-ossifying thought and dismantling conventional wisdom in management and organization studies.

This approach to viewing metaphor in organization theory, however, runs counter to that adopted by those who continue to take a more popular view of metaphors as a special and restricted feature of language. The meaning of metaphor is, so to speak, taken literally in this instance and analysed as such. Metaphors' value as effective mediators of reality is accentuated and emphasized. Black, for instance, argues that:

> Metaphors that survive ... critical examination can properly be held to convey, in indispensable fashion, insight into the systems to which they refer. In this way, they can, and sometimes do, generate insights about "how things are" in reality. (1979: 41)

Within organization studies, Morgan (1986) has done much to popularize the use of metaphors in organizational analysis. For him, our theories and explanations of organizational life are based on metaphors that lead us to understand organizations in distinctive yet partial ways. Metaphors frame our understanding of the phenomena we apprehend in such a way as to produce a partial but insightful understanding of the latter. This creative role, attributed to the ability of various metaphors to produce multiple possible readings of the same situation, makes it an attractive proposition for organizational analysts. It is this latter perspective of metaphors which dominates contemporary discussions on metaphors in organizational analysis. This, however, is in contrast to the style of metaphorical thinking adopted in this chapter, which privileges the process of metaphorization over these multiple static images generated through the use of metaphors. Such contrasting theoretical priorities throw up in stark relief the ontological and epistemological commitments informing subtly different intellectual attitudes towards the significance of metaphor in language. They, in turn, have dramatic consequences for our understanding of metaphorical analysis in general and organizational analysis in particular.

Clearly, debate on these issues is by no means insignificant to a chapter which purports to argue that the use of metaphor is better appreciated as a triggering point in the process of metaphorization rather than as an end in itself. From this perspective, established and hitherto unproblematic categories of thought (including the literal/metaphorical distinction) are subjected to critical scrutiny and systematically "loosened" in order to induce cognitive rearrangement thereby stimulating a crucial reassessment of intellectual priorities. It is this feature which facilitates paradigm-shifting.

Here it is argued that instead of the currently popular idea of organizational analysis and research as seeking to gain knowledge of an already constituted organizational reality using new and novel metaphors, the emphasis on metaphorization forces us to confront our own habituated ways of ordering our experiences. This is achieved by directing attention onto the recursively implicated organizing logic that we consistently depend upon in generating categories of thought for the purpose of analytical comprehension. Conceived thus, organizational analysis becomes the revised intellectual project of systematically scrutinizing our own all-too-familiar modes of ordering with a view to sensitizing us to the manner in which social order is forged out of the chaos of initially undifferentiated sensations.

Sensitizing ourselves to our own peculiar (and often idiosyncratic) patterns of ordering provides us with the opportunity to re-evaluate our personal circumstances and to thereby open up new possibilities for consideration. Many contemporary managerial and organizational situations require managers to have a keen and subtle appreciation of these dominant ordering codes and consequent logics of action driving business attitudes and shaping decisional priorities. It is the cultivation of this *subliminal* aspect of managing which has been significantly overlooked in much of contemporary management education.

From this line of argument, the purpose of using metaphors in organizational analysis is not so much about whether organizations are better understood as 'machines', 'cultures' or 'psychic prisons' (Morgan, 1986), but about relaxing the boundaries of thought. Nor is it about generating a rich plethora of alternative ways of viewing organizational situations;

rather it is about a slow and stratified deconstructing of deeply entrenched and therefore "taken-for-granted" modes of ordering, concepts, categories and priorities, all of which collectively work to circumscribe the outer limits of contemporary managerial discourse. Conceiving of the use of metaphors as part of this process of metaphorization removes these outer limits and is therefore essential to the cultivation of intellectual entrepreneurship and the managerial imagination.

The literal and the metaphorical in organizational analysis

One of the dominant presuppositions of contemporary organization theory is that the accurate description and explanation of organizational reality is a respectable and worthwhile academic enterprise. As an academic discipline engaged in "theory building", it is expected to be characterized by precision, parsimony and the absence of ambiguity in describing and explaining organizational situations (Bourgeois and Pinder, 1983; Pfeffer, 1982, 1992; Pinder and Bourgeois, 1982; Sandelands and Drazin, 1989; Warriner et al., 1981). It is argued that the language of organization science should therefore be correspondingly precise, literal and unambiguously clear.

In an illuminating exchange with Morgan (1980, 1983) on the use of metaphor in organizational analysis, Pinder and Bourgeois (1982) and Bourgeois and Pinder (1983) recommended the 'development of an analytical taxonomy of organizations' as a first step towards achieving the ideal of scientific precision in the administrative sciences. They argued that the development of a 'literal' language, which enabled the connection between observable phenomena and theoretical constructs to be made, would greatly enhance the progress of the discipline. More recently, Sandelands and Drazin, in an interesting discussion on the role of language in organization theory, maintained that 'an objection must be raised to words that name no entity or process whatsoever' (1989: 472). For them, words referring to objects or processes that cannot be observed or verified must be rigorously questioned since they tended to impede progress in theory building.

Faith in the literal use of language has manifested itself in many ways in the social and human sciences. It reflects the unwavering belief and confidence in a "representationalist" view of the world. According to this representationalist view, reality can be precisely described through the medium of language in a way that is clear, unambiguous and, in principle, testable. Representationalism as a set of metaphysical commitments flows logically from the recently challenged but still dominant epistemological premise of 'transcendental realism' (Putnam, 1981).

Transcendental realism, and its methodological counterpart, representationalism, continue to circumscribe the intellectual priorities of much of contemporary organizational research and theorizing. The representationalist commitments include: (1) the belief that reality exists external to human perception in the form of entities, attributes and essential causal relationships; (2) the belief that research and inquiry are constructive attempts to accurately mirror (however problematic this is acknowledged to be) and describe reality in itself; (3) the belief that "truth" is attained when correspondence occurs between our theories and the real world; (4) the belief that the study of organizations like any other academic discipline is essentially a cumulative "theory-building" process; and (5) the belief that the use of precise terminology to describe specific entities, attributes, events, and processes, will greatly enhance the likelihood of theory building. These five representationalist "instincts" drive the research priorities of much of contemporary organization theory.

Recently there have also been clarion calls to adhere rigorously to the well-established 'scientific' criteria of 'parsimony, logical coherence, falsifiability, clarity and consistency with empirical data' (Pfeffer 1982: 259) in organizational research. However, the issues of interpretation and social construction have, within the last decade in particular, increasingly become pivotal features in organizational research and theorizing. The post-Kuhnian "crisis" in epistemology, initiated in the 1960s, finally got through to what was a hitherto narrow and highly insulated field of study.

Morgan's (1986) *Images of Organization*, riding on a trend of emerging concerns with the question of interpretation in organization studies, provided a timely impetus for catapulting the metaphors "agenda" onto the centre stage of organization theory. Such "weaker" variants of representationalist epistemology now readily accept the theory-ladenness of observation (Morgan, 1983; 1986; Outhwaite, 1983) and, therefore, acknowledge a more 'loosely coupled' (Weick, 1979) set of causal relations linking organizational phenomena to one another. They also concede to the inherently ambiguous nature of theoretical attempts at describing and explaining organizational reality (Canella and Paetzold, 1994).

Notwithstanding significant concessions, vestiges of representationalist commitments remain, in that many researchers and theorists, whilst borrowing the language of interpretation and social construction, continue to unreflexively make nuanced representationalist claims about organizational reality. In other words, the language of interpretation and social construction is explicitly used in framing the actions of organizational actors but not in framing the accounts generated by organizational researchers and theorists themselves. As Knights perceptively points out:

> insofar as they fail to acknowledge their own participation in the constitution of social reality, qualitative researchers, who claim a distance from positivist beliefs, also have a tendency to be unreflexive about the representations they produce. Whether quantitative or qualitative methods are used, representational approaches to knowledge production rest on a privileging of the consciousness of the researcher who is deemed capable of discovering the 'truth' about the world of management through a series of representations. (1992: 515)

This 'limited' interpretative approach has been called 'first-order' social constructionism (Steier, 1991: 4), whereby the notion of interpretation or social construction is used in the research process, but not 'turned back' onto the researchers/theorists themselves. Their own accounts are presented as if, through the use of "appropriate" methodology, they have been somehow able to avoid socially constructing the claims being made.

This self-privileging tendency is widespread in contemporary organization theory. However, more recently the postmodern reflexive "turn" has rendered first-order social constructionism problematical, thereby causing some organizational writers to begin to more seriously examine the strategic implications of the problem of reflexivity for organizational theorizing. Such writers (Gergen, 1992; Van Maanen, 1989; Weick, 1989) now readily accept that both their own accounts and the accounts generated by those they research are first and foremost linguistic constructions. Theories of organization are, therefore, deemed to be self-justifying "intelligible narratives" rather than systematic attempts at making transcendental truth claims. As Gergen puts it most succinctly:

> If there is one theme that unites most of those confronting the postmodern irony, it is a certain sense of ludic humility. The view of knowledge-making as a transcendental pursuit removed from the trivial enthralments of daily life, pristinely rational and transparently virtuous, becomes so much puffery. We should view these bodies of language we call knowledge in a lighter vein – as ways of putting things together, some pretty and others petty. (1992: 215)

Irony, self-reflection and 'playful seriousness' replace the rational quest for certain or even 'partially-true' knowledge of an externally constituted organizational reality. This 'second-order' theorizing renders all forms of organizational research and theorizing as the activity of 'telling ourselves a story about ourselves' (Steier, 1991: 3). It is within the context of this shifting set of epistemological commitments and intellectual priorities from representationalism to first- and then second-order social constructionism that the current use of metaphor in organization theory and behaviour can be better appreciated.

Theories of metaphor

In line with the shifting sets of ontological and epistemological commitments in organizational analysis previously discussed, it is possible to distinguish between three significant intellectual attitudes towards the role of metaphor in language. For the purpose of brevity, these will be called "depreciators", "appreciators" and "metaphorizers".

Depreciators

Depreciators view metaphors as deviant and parasitic upon the normal literal usage of linguistic terms. Metaphors are a feature of linguistic aberration which serves to obscure meaning in communication and to encourage muddled thinking. This negative view of metaphors goes back to the Aristotelian paradigm of metaphor as a form of catharsis. However, there has been a strong line in Western philosophy, especially in the strain running from British empiricism through to the Vienna circle logical positivists, which has consistently and strenuously denied any philosophical seriousness to the study of metaphor. Metaphors, according to this view, are frivolous and inessential, if not dangerous and logically perverse. They do not have any connection with facts of the world and therefore have little capacity to transmit useful knowledge about the world. Serious intellectualism involves ridding oneself of a reliance on the use of metaphors and other linguistic tropes. In *Essay*, for instance, John Locke writes:

> if we would speak of things as they are, we must allow that all the art of rhetoric, besides order and clearness, all the artificial and figurative application of words eloquence has invented, are for nothing else but to insinuate wrong ideas, move passions and thereby mislead the judgement, and so indeed are perfect cheats, and, therefore . . . wholly to be avoided. (Locke, in Cohen, 1978: 120)

Such an intellectual attitude prevails in much of the mainstream organization theory, where the emphasis on the proper and literal use of language circumscribes the form of intellectual rigour acceptable in organizational theorizing. Because of their confidence in the capacity of literal language to precisely describe reality in clear, unambiguous terms, depreciators are clearly committed to a representationalist view of the world.

Appreciators

Within the broader human sciences, however, the classically negative view of metaphor taken by depreciators has been challenged and is increasingly losing its credibility. With the increasing displacement of positivistic epistemology by a constructionist frame of reference, the issue of interpretation has become a central question in the human sciences. Metaphors, particularly within the last decade, have gained much more acceptance and respectability in academic discourses. They are now increasingly regarded as essential characteristics of the creativity of language. As Paivio succinctly puts it, metaphors 'highlight the phenomenon of semantic creativity, the capacity of language users to create and understand novel linguistic combinations that may be *literal nonsense*' (1979: 150).

ESSO Petroleum's 'Put a tiger in your tank' is one example of a nonsensical statement if taken literally. However, taken metaphorically, it has the ability (at least in its initial novel stages) to excite the imagination. This is the intellectual attitude adopted by appreciators of the role of metaphor in language. It is a view consistent with those who have come to recognize that reality in itself is not directly accessible but that we construct our own social realities on the basis of the constraining influences of language and our pre-existing stock of knowledge. Our knowledge of reality, therefore, arises through the complex interaction of a piece of information with the context within which it is presented.

Knowing is always context-dependent. As such, alternative ways of seeing and knowing are fundamental to the process of cognition. It is within this adjusted epistemological scheme of things that metaphor finds its current popularity. Metaphors are deemed to be useful linguistic handles which afford different ways of perceiving the world and hence have the capacity to provide new insights not previously possible. This positive view of metaphors emanates from a reconstituted realist epistemology. Putnam (1981) calls this 'internal realism'.

Internal realism entails the realization that the question "What does the world consist of?" makes sense only within a particular theory or description. There are no theory-independent observations of the world that can be made. From this epistemological position, "truth" does not imply correspondence to reality. Rather it entails a form of coherence between our belief systems and our experiences of reality. However:

> Internalism does not deny that there are experiential *inputs* to knowledge; knowledge is not a story with no constraints except internal coherence; but it does deny that there are any inputs *which are not themselves to some extent shaped by our concepts.* ... The very inputs upon which our knowledge is based are conceptually contaminated. (Putnam, 1981: 54)

By acknowledging the theory-ladenness of all inputs, internal realism conflates epistemology (what we can know) with ontology (what reality is), fact with value and truth with what conventionally works. Although internal realism is a form of realism, its more modest position permits the possibility of alternative, incompatible conceptual schemes to coexist, without necessarily subscribing to extreme relativism since it acknowledges the limits imposed on it by the material world. Internal realism, or, as Lakoff (1987) calls it, 'experiential realism', is what provides the epistemological justification for appreciators of metaphors.

Metaphorizers

The third intellectual attitude, referred to as metaphorization, represents the position favoured in this chapter. Metaphorizers effectively invert the literal/ metaphorical couplet by maintaining that what we call "literal" results from the "domestication" and stabilization of a term initially used metaphorically. Here it is argued that it is the metaphorical and not the literal which is of primary importance to language and the world. Thus, the poet Ernesto Fenollosa writes:

> Relations are more real and more important than the things which they relate. The forces which produce the branch-angles of an oak lay potent in the acorn. Similar lines of resistance, half curbing the out-pressing vitalities, govern the branching of rivers and of nations. Thus, a nerve, a wire, a roadway, and a clearing house are only varying channels which communicate force for itself. Nature furnishes her own clues. Had the world not been full of homologies, sympathies, and identities, thought would have been starved and language chained to the obvious. ... *Metaphor, the revealor of nature, is the very substance of poetry. The known interprets the obscure, the universe is alive with myth ... it is a mistake to suppose ... that art and poetry aim to deal with the general and the abstract ... Art and poetry deal with the concrete of nature, not with rows of 'separate' particulars.* (1969: 214; my emphasis)

Metaphors are primary precisely because they are better placed to allude to the ephemeral and changing relational character of concrete reality. The literal merely deals with "rows" of abstracted particulars generated from rendering static an essentially fluxing and changeable reality through the analytical processes of dissecting, categorizing, classifying and ordering our phenomenal experiences. Yet the insistent demands for precision, definition, clarity and parsimony as well as logical linear expositions in the theorizing process remain fundamental cornerstones of modernist thought. They reflect the advanced state of the technique of analysis which Toffler in his foreword to Prigogine and Stengers' (1984) *Order out of Chaos* observed to be the most highly developed skill in contemporary Western thinking. In a similar vein, the sociobiologist Francisco Varela noted that

> the best description of our tradition is 'abstract': nothing characterizes the units of knowledge that are deemed most 'natural'. It is this tendency to find our way toward the rarefied atmosphere of the general and the formal, the logical and the well-defined, the represented and the planned, that makes our Western world so distinctively familiar. (1992: 110)

The primacy accorded to literal meaning in the orthodox tradition results from the dominance of a scientific grammar governing such Western thought. This emphasizes the selective abstraction, dissection and averaging out of social and material phenomena. The literal meaning of a term is precisely that – creating a "mean" out of the fluxing and transforming world through the process of "averaging out" the term's usage. Once conventionalized, analogies, homologies, metaphors and resemblances lose their evocative virility, becoming ossified and apparently unproblematic literal terms.

The term "individual", for instance, as conventionally used today, conceptually implies distinctiveness, separateness, autonomy, and most importantly connotes a conceptually isolatable social phenomenon. It is frequently used in organization theory to refer to a stabilized and identifiable social entity with imputed agentic capabilities. Etymologically, however, the term "individual" implies that which cannot be separated or divided out. Individual implies the "indivisible". Boethius, writing in the twelfth century, used 'steel' to describe this property of indivisibility associated with the concept of the 'individual'. This is in vast contrast to the contemporary usage of the term. The point of this brief detour into the etymology of the word is to demonstrate that most literal terms in language are metaphorical in that their meaning has tended to "drift" over time. Through repeated usage, they become convenient and overly familiar linguistic surrogates that allow large chunks of our thought processes to be punctuated, gathered together and given legitimate expression.

The economy of expression achieved by metaphorical allusion is what prompts metaphors' widespread proliferation and sustenance. They enable us to talk about complex and intimate experiences which cannot be easily described because of linguistic and grammatical constraints. Metaphors provide a useful "short-hand" way of drawing attention to the less accessible aspects of our experiences. As Harris put it:

> Metaphors speak of what remains absent. All metaphor that is more than an abbreviation for more proper speech gestures towards what transcends language. Thus metaphor implies lack. (1978: 182)

Metaphors point to the limitations and inadequacies of the language through which thought must be expressed.

Language, thought and reality

That language imposes its own logic and structure on to thought and consequently restricts our comprehension of reality is an argument well rehearsed by philosophers of language and more recently reinforced by post-structural writers. Wittgenstein (1961), for example, in the *Tractatus-Logico Philosophicus*, attempted to articulate a picture theory of meaning that would adequately justify a representationalist epistemology. According to this argument, the world and the way in which language depicts the world must be of a certain similar form if thought as a representational activity is to be possible at all. His account was an attempt to show that the character of the world and the language used to describe it must somehow match so as to make propositions meaningful. Wittgenstein, however, was unable, in the *Tractatus*, to reconcile the problem of meaning and reference, so much so that he was forced to conclude that:

> My propositions serve as elucidation in the following way: Anyone who understands me eventually recognises them as nonsensical, when he has used them – as steps – to climb up beyond them. (1961: 6.54)

Like Nietzsche, Heidegger and Saussure, Wittgenstein was led to realize that 'The limits of my language means the limits of my world' (1961: 5.6). The reflexive problem faced by Wittgenstein in the *Tractatus* is that the theory he was attempting to articulate as one describing the relationship between language and the world appears to transgress the very limits of language which his own theory specifically denies the possibility of. In other words, if thinking is only possible through language, how can we make any justifiable claim that language, in fact, makes some grounded connection with an already constituted reality "out there". Thus, as Heidegger reminds us, we cannot know language 'according to the traditional concept of knowledge defined in terms of *cognition as representation*' (1971: 134; my emphasis). Instead, 'it is in words and language that things first come into Being and are' (1959: 13). Social entities, events and attributes do not first pre-exist and then suffer descriptive distortion through language. Instead language actively configures and brings into existence such social phenomena in the very acts of representing. However, in doing so the brute and undifferentiated character of primordial experience is systematically denied legitimacy. Yet this refusal is never complete, as post-structural writers remind us.

Foucault, in his discussion of the attempts at classical representation, points to the inevitable gap between *saying* and *seeing*. He writes:

it is in vain that we say what we see; what we see never resides in what we say. And it is in vain that we attempt to show, by the use of images, metaphors, or similes, what we are saying; the space where they achieve their splendour is not that deployed by our eyes but that defined by the sequential elements of syntax. (1970: 9)

Likewise, in *Writing Degree Zero*, Barthes (1967: 19) points out that 'at the very moment of choosing the words' the writer observes a 'tragic disparity between what he does and what he sees'. The logic of grammar determines the possibilities of what can be named, conceived and spoken. What cannot be named or spoken of is, therefore, relegated to a status of relative unimportance. However, what is unspoken of is crucially fundamental to the understanding of what is literal and explicit. Thus, in the ancient Chinese text the *Tao Te Ching*, the first lines read:

> The Tao that can be named is not the Tao
> The name that can be named is not the eternal name
> The nameless is the origin of Heaven and Earth
> The Named is the Mother of all things
> (Translated in Chan, 1963: 139)

What is implicit remains elusive and can only be alluded to yet it is none the less fundamental to our comprehension. It can only be indirectly accessed and not directly confronted and investigated. The use of metaphors in comprehending organizational reality reflects this intuitive appreciation of the limitations of language in general and the English language in particular.

In *Wholeness and the Implicate Order*, the theoretical physicist David Bohm (1980) points out that the tendency to thinking in self-identical and literal terms is directly traceable to the logical structuring of the English language. Bohm begins by noting that much of our current thinking is literal and fragmented and he identifies the subject–verb–object grammatical structure of sentences as a significant part of the problem. This structure promotes a style of thinking which

> implies that all action arises in a separate entity, the subject, and that in the cases described by a tentative verb, this action crosses over the space between them to another separate entity, the object. (Bohm, 1980: 29)

As an example, Bohm uses the sentence "It is raining" to illustrate the nature of the problem created. He asks 'Where is the "It" that would according to the sentence, be the "rainer that is doing the raining"?' (1980: 29). Clearly, it would be more appropriate to say (as the Chinese do) 'falling rain', thus emphasizing action rather than accomplished states. However, since this subject–verb–object structure is so pervasive it tends to promote a style of thinking which accentuates the dividing out of our experiences into static and isolatable events and phenomena. These then conveniently lend themselves to *literal* descriptions using readily available categories of thought. Such a static thought style is, however, unable to account for the *becoming* of social phenomena, things, events and situations.

The couplet "is/is not" is the archetypal example of the inability of the English language to accommodate changing situations and shades of experiences because of the either/or logic it embraces. By their allusive capability metaphors are better equipped to deal with the "in-between" of what *is*, and what *is not*. It is precisely in this project of redirecting our attention to the spaces between what is seen and what is said that metaphors play a crucial role. To retain their metaphorical potency, metaphors must not be allowed to solidify into literal structures. Metaphors must be constantly metaphorized in order that they retain their power to remind us of the precarious and artificially constructed nature of everyday experiences. This realization is what enables the human imagination to break out and flourish. It is this connection between the process of metaphorization and the human imagination which provides the central thrust of this chapter.

Metaphorizers are committed to a form of realism inspired by Heraclitus and the Chinese philosopher Chuang Tzu, developed by the twelfth-century Chinese philosopher Chi Tsi, reintroduced into modern Western thought by Leibniz and more recently proposed by the French philosopher Henri Bergson and the British philosopher Alfred North Whitehead. Whitehead (1985) called it the philosophy of organism. For the purpose of comparison, the term *organismic realism* will be used to make the ontological distinction between the latter and internal realism. For Whitehead, the realist (both transcendental and internal) tendency to view the world as being made up of a succession of discrete configurations of matter (i.e. 'things', 'social entities', 'states', 'events', etc.) is a result of what he called the 'Fallacy of Misplaced Concreteness' pervasive in modern Western thought. This tendency, as Bohm (1980) convincingly demonstrated, is built into the very grammatical structure of the English language.

In truth, the real world itself is but a 'dull affair, soundless, scents, colourless; merely the hurrying of material, endlessly, meaninglessly' (Whitehead, 1985: 69). Nature or reality far exceeds the limiting logical structures imposed by language. Moreover, it is always in the process of becoming. It is for this reason that internal realists are right to recognize the possibilities of multiple and incompatible conceptual schemes since reality can never be fully captured in any singular static descriptive frame. However, internalists, like transcendental realists, are wrong in believing that reality comprises already-formed entities prior to our appearance on the scene. Lakoff, in defending Putnam's internal realism, writes:

> Putnam, being a realist, does not deny that objects exist. Take, for example, the chair I am sitting on. It exists, if it didn't, I would have fallen on the floor. But that chair can be viewed *correctly* in many ways. From the molecular point of view, it is an enormous collection of molecules and not a single undifferentiated bounded entity. From the point of view of wave equations in physics, there is no chair, but only wave forms. From a human point of view, it is a single object. Thus, whether a chair is a particular object – a single bounded entity – or a bunch of molecules or a wave form is not a question that can have a unique correct answer. All the answers can be correct, but correct within different conceptual schemes. (1987: 262)

There appears to be a certain ambivalence in Lakoff's position. On the one hand he sees Putnam as being firmly committed to the existence of real objects in the world, even though it would never be possible for us to know what they are "in themselves". On the other he is suggesting that the chair can be just wave forms, thereby denying the "entity-like" characteristic of matter. This ambivalence can be attributed to an excessive preoccupation with epistemological questions (what it is possible for us to know) and not enough attention on the age-old question asked by the Ionians: "What is the world made of?" (an ontological question). This conflation of epistemology with ontology is unfortunate because it makes it difficult for internal realists to explain why it is that not only do all theories not work all the time, but that even a specific limited theory does not work all the time. An ontology of *becoming* which takes reality to be ephemeral precisely because it is always in process is better suited for explaining this anomaly. For Whitehead (1929, 1932) and those subscribing to an organismic view of reality the reason for our inability to accurately describe reality is clear. Reality is always changing and becoming, and each explicate "entity" is but a stabilized moment of the implicate movement of flux and transformation.

Metaphorizers implicitly or explicitly recognize that by making our thinking move along we become more "in-tune" and hence "in-touch" with the rhythms of the world. It is also for this reason that Bohm proposed a new language which he called *rheomode* (i.e. a language of movement) in which the verbal function is accentuated, thereby giving ontological priority to actions and movements which 'flow into each other and merge, without sharp separation of breaks' (1980: 30). Things, social entities and events can then be viewed as epiphenomena of these processes to be secondarily considered as the relatively 'invariant side or aspect of this movement' (Bohm, 1980: 47).

Metaphorization, the metaphorizing of dead metaphors, is the endless intellectual task of de-ossifying thought. It undertakes the critical task of systematically re-examining hitherto taken-for-granted concepts and categories and revealing the hidden tensions and contradictions inherent in every literal attempt to adequately represent reality. This intellectual exercise, by showing us the inadequacies of such concepts and thereby going beyond them, leads us closer to the undifferentiated "real" of brute experience. It is this re-enchantment with the concrete which lies behind the drive towards metaphorization. Organizational analysis, as this deconstructive process of de-ossifying and "emptying-out" literal meanings, has much to offer to the educational process in general and to the education of managers in particular.

Metaphorization and paradigm-shifting

Both depreciators and appreciators, despite their vastly different attitudes towards metaphor in organizational analysis, nonetheless agree that metaphors are a special feature of language. For depreciators, their use is to be avoided, whilst for appreciators their use is deliberately encouraged. A special effort is required to generate unique insights of specific organizational situations using the power of metaphors. In this latter perspective, the cognitive significance of metaphor is relatively restricted to probing those aspects not immediately accessible to analytical inquiry. Metaphorizers, on the other hand, challenge this view.

For metaphorizers, the use of metaphor is central to the process of acquiring new insights. Whilst appreciators direct attention to the similarities between two different situations (e.g. thinking of organizations as machines draws attention to the machine-like characteristic of organizational relationships), metaphorizers emphasize the constructed and conventionalized character of these apparent similarities. The comparative approach to metaphor adopted by appreciators, because it assumes the unproblematic existence of similarities between two distinct phenomena, can only add knowledge which extends but at the same time reinforces the existing conceptual framework. Radically new insights, on the other hand, create knowledge that arises out of experiencing a conceptual "jolt" to the prevailing system of comprehension and result in a requirement to substantially reconfigure the latter so that perceived anomaly can be more adequately accommodated. Petrie draws out this distinction in his discussion of metaphors and the learning process:

> Literal language [depreciators] requires only assimilation to existing frameworks of understanding. Comparative metaphors [appreciators] require simple extensions of the framework in the light of a more comprehensive framework. Accommodation of an anomaly requires changes in the framework of understanding. (1979: 606)

The literal (depreciators) approach may be compared to a *problem-solving* orientation whilst the comparative approach (appreciators) emphasizes an extended *problem-finding* mode of thought in which issues of informational clarity, variations in meaning, and the perception of complex networks of causal relations appear to thwart the efficacy of a straightforward problem-solving approach. More innovative ways of dealing with such contingent and complex situations are perceived to be necessary. The approach adopted by metaphorizers, on the other hand, is eminently suited for effecting *paradigm-shifting* in that it works to deliberately dislodge the very existing cognitive framework (including the deeply entrenched and taken-for-granted concepts and categories) used to comprehend social phenomena such as organizations. This is achieved by drawing attention to the problematical character of the framework itself and the conceptual categories associated with it. Moreover, it helps create a conceptual "space" for new distinctions to be made and therefore leads to the development of new insights.

Whilst appreciators emphasize the adding on of new knowledge to old making descriptions and explanations "thicker" and "richer", metaphorizers argue that the careful and meticulous dismantling or deconstruction of old knowledge is a far more fruitful and worthwhile enterprise since it works to strip off the "dead" layers of abstracted and ossified knowledge that make our contemporary world appear so immediately necessary and familiar. The project of metaphorization, by revealing the arbitrary nature of hitherto unchallenged ideologies and dogmas which put a gloss over the particularities of human experiences, momentarily liberates us from this modern tyranny of signs. It initiates a process of unforgetting and of resensitizing us to the concretedness of our everyday experiences. As such it is a process that opens up genuine alternatives in a postmodern world increasingly saturated by floating and endlessly deferring regimes of signification.

Paradigm-shifting is a constant and vigilant intellectual strategy whereby we remind ourselves of the "abstracted" and hence metaphorical character of contemporary forms of knowledge. The tendency to *efface* and then *forget* such arbitrary framing of knowledge is well documented by poets and philosophers of the past. Whitehead (1985, but first published in 1926) maintains that the modern tendency to reify, invert and then forget leads to our viewing the world as comprising a succession of discrete configurations of matter. What he describes as the 'Fallacy of Misplaced Concreteness' is best encapsulated in Wordsworth's *The Prelude*. Wordsworth writes of a 'false secondary power' by which we 'multiply distinction' and then 'deem them to be things that we perceive and not that which we have made'. Wordsworth, like Whitehead, was clearly aware of the debilitating effects of this abstractive and disembodied way of thinking so characteristic of modernity and it was of great concern to both of them. Whitehead, for example, wrote:

> And yet it is quite unbelievable. This conception of the universe is surely framed in terms of high abstraction, and the paradox arises *only because we have mistaken our abstractions for concrete realities.* (1985: 69; my emphasis)

The apparent concretedness of the categories and qualities we perceive (such as "individuals" and "organizations") are in effect attributes which we impute to what we apprehend as a way of making sense through arbitrarily punctuating (thereby rendering static) and subsequently ordering our experiences. None the less, Whitehead recognized that we cannot think without such abstractions. Therefore, he maintained that it is of utmost importance that we remain vigilant in constantly and critically revising our *modes of abstraction.* It is precisely this vigilant thought-style which best describes the deconstructive strategy of some postmodern writers. In this sense, Whitehead can be regarded as a precursor of postmodern thought.

It is this vigilant intellectual practice of critically revising our modes of thought that is alluded to by the term 'paradigm-shifting'. Paradigm-shifting does not merely entail shifting from one paradigm to another that is better, 'roomier' (Popper, 1970) or more 'interesting' (Kuhn, 1962). Rather it is about privileging the activity of *moving* from one paradigm to another. For it is through this moving in-between such paradigms that we are able to catch a fleeting glimpse of the subliminal features of the real. The subliminal as such lies "in-between" concepts, categories and paradigms of thought, not "in" them.

Metaphors, by speaking of what remains absent, draw our attention to the significance of the empty spaces in-between literal concepts. As "transport vehicles" (derived from the Greek word *metaphorikos*, meaning transportation), metaphors are eminently suited to carry our thinking along this endless journey of intellectual discovery. Such movements in thinking resonate with the becoming of nature, thereby enabling us to sensitize ourselves to the ways of the natural world – a world in which allusions, recursion, resonance, reverberations, homologies and the "harmony of wills" prevail and take precedence over an essentialist philosophical dogma of causal determinism. It is this heightening of the aesthetic sensibilities that paradigm-shifting accomplishes through the process of metaphorization.

Conclusions

Metaphors are not linguistic aberrations or mere "figures of speech". Instead they are quintessentially features of language. What we call "literal" is merely the momentarily arrested, stabilized (and conventionalized) sense of a metaphorical expression. Metaphors are more primary and fundamental than literal terms, and precise conceptual categories. Metaphorization involves drawing attention to the intrinsically metaphorical nature of language and the pervasiveness of "dead" metaphors that dominate "taken-for-granted" concepts and theoretical frameworks. It involves the de-ossification of literal categories with the purpose of revealing the movement-generating (hence *metaphorikos*) character of metaphors. Using metaphors in organizational analysis is not about revealing static insights into the nature of organizational reality, but about overcoming the "inertia" of thinking in categorical terms so endemic to modern Western thought. It is about shifting styles of thinking from *being* (i.e. thinking in terms of "states", "entities", "events", "attributes") to *becoming* (i.e. thinking in terms of the primacy of "movement", "unfolding", "emergence", "flux" and "transformation"). Following Whitehead (1929, 1985), it is this organismic form of thinking which is more in keeping with a processual reality.

As Bohm (1980) convincingly demonstrated, it is grammatical logic (particularly in the English language) which renders static an otherwise changing and transforming reality. Metaphors accentuate action, movement and relationships rather than entities and their attributes. Metaphorization is the process of accentuating the verbal function and reminding us that nouns and objects are stabilized and conventionalized moments of an essentially movement-driven language. By engaging metaphors to make thinking "move", we sensitize ourselves to the workings of reality and direct our attention to the arbitrary acts of abstractive framing that we constantly use in order to generate explanatory schemata.

Demonstrating the arbitrary but conventional nature of such explanatory schemata, in turn, allows us to break away from such dominant mind-sets. It is this paradigm-shifting capability of metaphors which is crucial to the analysis of organizations and the cultivation of the managerial imagination.

In a world characterized by unpredictability, volatility and dynamism, the ability to think beyond the thinkable is a crucial capability for today's managers. By directing attention to the conventionalized logic of ordering over and above the content meaning of terms, the metaphorization of metaphors helps cultivate our aesthetic sensitivities and enables us to open up new and previously unthought possibilities for consideration.

References

Barthes, R. (1967) *Writing Degree Zero*. London: Jonathan Cape.

Black, M. (1979) 'More about metaphors', in A. Ortony (ed.), *Metaphor and Thought*. Chicago: University of Chicago Press, pp. 19–41.

Bohm, D. (1980) *Wholeness and the Implicate Order*. London: Routledge and Kegan Paul.

Bourgeois, V. W. and Pinder, C.C. (1983) 'Contrasting philosophical perspectives in administrative science: a reply to Morgan', *Administrative Science Quarterly*, 28 (4), 608–613.

Brown, S.J. (1927) *The World of Imagery*. London: Kegan Paul, Trench, Trubner.

Canella, A.A. and Paetzold, R.L. (1994) 'Pfeffer's barriers to the advance of organizational science: A rejoinder', *Academy of Management Review*, 19 (2), 331–341.

Cassirer, E. (1946) *Language and Myth*. New York: Harper and Brothers.

Chan, W.T. (1963) *A Sourcebook in Chinese Philosophy*. Princeton: Princeton University Press.

Cohen, T. (1978) 'Metaphor and the cultivation of intimacy', in S. Sacks (ed.), *On Metaphor*. Chicago: University of Chicago Press, pp. 107–140.

Derrida, J. (1981) *Dissemination*. Chicago: University of Chicago Press.

Derrida, J. (1982) *Margins of Philosophy*. Chicago: University of Chicago Press.

Fenollosa, E. (1969) 'The Chinese written character as a medium for poetry', in E. Pound (ed.), *Instigations*. Freeport, NY: Books for Libraries Press, pp. 202–227.

Foucault, M. (1970) *The Order of Things*. London: Tavistock.

Gasché, R. (1986) *The Tain of the Mirror*. Cambridge, MA: Harvard University Press.

Gergen, K. (1992) 'Organization theory in the postmodern era', in M. Reed and M. Hughes (eds), *Rethinking Organization: New Directions in Organization Theory and Analysis*. Beverly Hills, CA: Sage Publications.

Harris, K. (1978) 'The many uses of metaphor', in S. Sacks (ed.), *On Metaphor*. Chicago: University of Chicago Press, pp. 180–202.

Heidegger, M. (1959) *Introduction to Metaphysics*. New Haven: Yale University Press.

Heidegger, M. (1971) *On the Way to Language*. New York: Harper and Row.

Knights, D. (1992) 'Changing spaces: The disruptive impact of a new epistemological location for the study of management', *Academy of Management Review*, 17 (3), 514–535.

Kuhn, T.S. (1962) *The Structure of Scientific Revolutions*. Chicago: University of Chicago Press.

Lakoff, G. (1987) *Women, Fire and Dangerous Things: What Categories Reveal about the Mind*. Chicago: University of Chicago Press.

Lakoff, G. and Johnson, M. (1980) *Metaphors We Live By*. Chicago: University of Chicago Press.

Morgan, G. (1980) 'Paradigms, metaphors, and puzzle solving in organization theory', *Administrative Science Quarterly*, 25 (4), 605–622.

Morgan, G. (1983) 'More on metaphor: Why we cannot control tropes in administrative science', *Administrative Science Quarterly*, 28 (4), 601–607.

Morgan, G. (1986) *Images of Organization*. Beverly Hills, CA: Sage Publications.

Nowottny, W. (1962) *The Language Poets Use*. London: Athlone Press.

Outhwaite, W. (1983) 'Towards a realist perspective', in G. Morgan (ed.), *Beyond Method*. Newbury Park, CA: Sage Publications, pp. 321–330.

Paivio, A. (1979) *Imagery and Verbal Processes*. Hillsdale, NJ: Lawrence Erlbaum Associates.

Petrie, H.G. (1979) 'Metaphor and learning', in A. Ortony (ed.), *Metaphor and Thought*. Chicago: University of Chicago Press, pp. 579–609.

Pfeffer, J. (1982) *Organization and Organization Theory*. Englewood Cliffs, NJ: Prentice Hall.

Pfeffer, J. (1992) *Managing with Power: Politics and Influence in Organizations*. Boston: Harvard Business School Press.

Pinder, C.C. and Bourgeois, V.W. (1982) 'Controlling tropes in administrative science', *Administrative Science Quarterly*, 27 (4), 641–652.

Popper, K.R. (1970) 'Normal science and its dangers', in I. Lakatos and A. Musgrave (eds), *Criticism and the Growth of Knowledge*. Cambridge: Cambridge University Press, pp. 51–58.

Prigogine, I. and Stengers, I. (1984) *Order out of Chaos*. Bantam: New York.

Putnam, H. (1981) *Reason, Truth, History*. Cambridge: Cambridge University Press.

Sandelands, L. and Drazin, R. (1989) 'On the language of organization theory', *Organization Studies*, 10 (4), 457–478.

Steier, F. (1991) *Research and Reflexivity*. Beverly Hills, CA: Sage Publications.

Van Maanen, J. (1989) 'Some notes on the importance of writing in organization studies', *Harvard Business School Research Colloquium*. Boston: Harvard Business School.

Varela, F. (1992) 'The reenchantment of the concrete', in J. Crary and S. Kwinter (eds), *Incorporations*. New York: Zone, pp. 96–119.

Warriner, C.K., Hall, R.H. and McKelvey, B. (1981) 'The comparative description of organizations: A research note and invitation', *Organization Studies*, 2 (2), 173–180.

Weick, K.E. (1979) *The Social Psychology of Organizing* (2nd edn). Reading, MA: Addison-Wesley.

Weick, K.E.(1989) 'Theory construction as disciplined imagination', *Academy of Management Review*, 14 (4), 615–631.

Whitehead, A.N. (1929) *Process and Reality*. New York: Macmillan.

Whitehead, A.N. (1932) *The Aims of Education*. London: Williams and Norgate.

Whitehead, A.N. (1985) *Science and the Modern World*. London: Free Association Books.

Wittgenstein, L. (1961) *Tractatus-Logico Philosophicus*. London: Routledge.

PART III

METAPHORS IN ORGANIZATIONAL SETTINGS: IMPACT AND OUTCOMES

8

Metaphors, Metaphoric Fields and Organizational Change

Robert J. Marshak

While this chapter intends to increase awareness about metaphors and organizations, its real purpose is to suggest the instrumental power of metaphors and metaphorical analysis in organizational change. The chapter is in three parts. The first part reviews recent trends in organization theory in order to then propose a meta-theory of organizational change that can be used to address an organization's symbolic meaning system. The second part explores the dimensions of such systems and introduces the more specific concept of an organizational "metaphoric field". The final part addresses the use of metaphors in organizational diagnosis and intervention.

Cognition, culture and the unconscious in organizational change

Beginning in the 1980s the literature related to organization theory and organizational change began to pay increasing attention to three newer approaches, or "schools", for thinking about organizational behaviour. For our purposes we will name these the cognitive, cultural and unconscious or psychoanalytic schools. While they are quite distinct from one another, theoretically, each emphasizes the importance of subjective social meaning in determining perception and response. It is for this reason that they all help form the theoretical foundation for our discussion of metaphors and organizational change.

The cognitive school

The cognitive school advances the premise that problem-solving and/or adaptive behaviour in individuals and organizations is guided by sets of conscious, but usually implicit, governing beliefs. Governing beliefs are technically referred to as schemata (DeRubeis and Beck, 1988; Lau and Woodman, 1995; Markus and Zajonc, 1985), but also include such terms as 'paradigm' (Kuhn, 1970), 'frame' (Goffman, 1974), 'theory-in-use' (Argyris and Schön, 1978), 'cognitive map' (Bougon et al., 1977), 'template' (Bartunek and Moch, 1987) and 'prism' (Marshak and Katz, 1991). To avoid routine, repetitive and/or self-defeating behaviour requires "getting out of the box" created by these governing schemata. Questioning and then changing governing beliefs will achieve this since such processes are presumed to lead to creativity and innovation, and the possibility of fundamental rather than marginal change. Argyris (1985) has noted how an absence of reflection about these implicit beliefs can leave an organization's focal system "trapped" in a cycle of familiar, but useless or even dysfunctional routines. Drawing on cybernetic theory (e.g. Ashby, 1952, 1960; Beer, 1959, 1972; Morgan, 1982), the "cognitive revolution" in psychology (e.g. Beck, 1967, 1970; Dobson, 1988; Ellis, 1962, 1970; Guidano and Liotti, 1983; Mahoney, 1974, 1977; Mahoney and Thoreson, 1974; Markus, 1977; Meichenbaum, 1973, 1977) and their own research and thinking, a range of organization theorists have advanced versions of this model (e.g. Argyris, 1990, 1992; Daft and Weick, 1984; Gray et al., 1985; Mitroff, 1983; Morgan and Ramirez, 1984; Senge, 1990).

Perhaps because new behaviour is presumed to result from rational change of beliefs, the favoured metaphor of this school, especially among writers about organizational change, appears to be "organizations as learning systems" (e.g. Argyris, 1990, 1992; Senge, 1990). This metaphor, discussed in considerable detail by Døving in Chapter 10, includes action learning and single-loop, double-loop and even triple-loop learning (Argyris et al., 1985; Nielsen, 1993). The distinction between single-loop and double-loop learning is particularly important in organizational change. In single-loop learning organizational problem-solving or change initiatives are carried out within the framework of existing assumptions, beliefs, theories-in-use, paradigms, etc. Double-loop learning, on the other hand, requires first understanding, and then altering the existing framework in order to generate new thought and behaviour patterns. This distinction has also been used to separate what some have called first-order change from second-order change (e.g. Bateson, 1972, 1979; Goldfried and Robins, 1983). According to Bartunek and Moch: 'First-order changes are incremental modifications that make sense within an established framework or method of operating.

Second-order changes are modifications in the frameworks themselves' (1987: 484). The various theoretical approaches that make up the cognitive school are classified by Morgan (1986) under the metaphor of 'organizations as brains'.

The cultural school

Following the lead of cultural anthropologists, organization theorists began to posit that behaviour in organizations was influenced or governed by multi-layered systems of collective beliefs called "cultures" (Davis, 1984; Deal and Kennedy, 1982; Frost et al., 1985; Kilmann et al., 1985; Schein, 1985). Even though they may be visible and manifest themselves in many ways, the most influential of these beliefs, or basic assumptions, tend to be "forgotten", preconscious, or what has otherwise been termed as out-of-awareness (see, for example, Schein, 1985). Unlike the cognitive school, where governing beliefs are assumed to be expressed literally, cultural beliefs are assumed to be most powerfully expressed through symbolic modalities such as myths, stories, rituals and, of course, metaphors (Martin, 1982; Pondy et al., 1983). An organization's multi-layered system of beliefs, and therefore its culture, is considered to be a primary determinant of organizational behaviour and success by providing implicit control over individual and organizational choice (Peters and Waterman, 1982).

In terms of organizational change, any significant change in the environment or business situation facing an organization might bring into question the continued applicability of its traditional assumptions and beliefs, and therefore its culture. While different theorists have argued whether or not organizational cultures can be changed (Kilmann, 1985; Kilmann et al., 1985; Schein, 1985), most agree that significant organizational change in response to new conditions, such as new technologies, markets, competitors, business paradigms, etc., requires changing the controlling organizational culture. In essence, second-order organizational change is required, or, in terms of Kuhn's (1970) paradigm theory of scientific revolutions, there has to be a "cultural revolution". The various concepts and theories that make up this approach to organization theory and change are classified by Morgan (1986), not surprisingly, under the metaphor of 'organizations as cultures'.

The unconscious or psychoanalytic school

Interest in the influence of unconscious dynamics in organizations began to gather momentum in the 1980s and 1990s as psychoanalytically trained writers turned their attention to corporate life (Baum, 1987, 1989; De Board, 1978; Diamond, 1986; Gabriel, 1991; Hirschorn, 1988; Katz, 1983; Kets de Vries and Miller, 1984; Levison and Rosenthal, 1984; Schwartz, 1987). Drawing on the seminal ideas of both Freud and Jung, a major premise of this school is that unconscious dynamics influence perception, meaning and action in organizations. This may result from unconscious dynamics within the psyche of a key individual such as the organization's leader (Kets de

Vries, 1990; Mazlish, 1990), or from the collective unconscious of the group (Bion, 1959) and/or organization (Mitroff, 1983). Unconscious forces are presumed to control individual, group and organizational behaviour to varying degrees and significant change may not be possible without addressing controlling unconscious elements. In most psychoanalytic traditions, and especially in the work of Jung, symbols are considered the primary medium for communication with the unconscious (Campbell, 1971; Fontana, 1993; Jung, 1964). According to Jung (1968), symbols are expressions of underlying psychic patterns, called archetypes, that give form and meaning to 'reality'. For purposes of this discussion, archetypal patterns are, in essence, unconscious schemata that are revealed symbolically, including metaphorically (Siegelman, 1990).

From the perspective of the psychoanalytic school, individual and organizational change result from addressing the schemata of the unconscious and/or ameliorating its consequences or expression. Addressing the unconscious is considered necessary for second-order change in organizations by Olson, who argues that 'to reach the deep levels of second-and third-order change, organizational change agents should understand and address the unconscious' (1990: 70). While comparatively under-represented, interest in addressing organizational change issues using an orientation that deals with unconscious dynamics is on the rise (Barry, 1994; Katz and Marshak, 1995; Kets de Vries, 1991; Marshak and Katz, 1992; Merry and Brown, 1987; Mitroff, 1983; Olson, 1990). Morgan (1986) classifies this set of theories and approaches under the metaphor of 'organizations as psychic prisons'.

Common elements

These three schools or approaches are normally thought of separately, probably because they are based on different theoretical traditions and social units of analysis. Those differences notwithstanding, they also all suggest a singular meta-theory of organizational change that incorporates the following features:

1. Organizational behaviour is influenced by out-of-awareness schemata. These schemata may be underlying theories-in-use, cultural assumptions and beliefs, and/or unconscious material or archetypes.
2. Organizational schemata may be accessed and modified. Different methods are suggested depending on whether or not the schemata are considered to be conscious, pre-conscious or unconscious.
3. Second-order organizational change requires modification of controlling schemata in order to create innovative behaviour that is different from "automatic" or "habitual" patterns.

What also unites the cognitive, cultural and unconscious/psychoanalytic schools are metaphors. Metaphors are unifying in two ways. First, metaphors are themselves schemata that structure or mediate meaning and response (Lakoff and Johnson, 1980). Consequently, the ability to diagnose and then modify the metaphors that may be controlling how an organizational situation is perceived and understood becomes a primary instrument of organizational change (Marshak, 1993). In short, metaphors are schemata that play a crucial role in structuring organizational reality and response. To significantly change organizational behaviour may well require accessing and modifying controlling metaphorical constructs.

The second way metaphors are unifying is through their ability to serve as the communications bridge between the literal and the symbolic as well as the conscious and the unconscious (Marshak, 1993; Siegelman, 1990). Consequently, metaphors can serve as the common medium for diagnosing and addressing theories-in-use, cultural assumptions and beliefs, and unconscious dynamics. The ability to use metaphors for diagnosis and intervention is therefore critical for successful second-order change in organizations. When we consider that the most important changes facing postmodern organizations all require second-order change (e.g. from industrial to post-industrial paradigms), the instrumental role for metaphors should be clear. Organizations are not just 'brains' or 'cultures' or 'psychic prisons'. They are multi-layered systems of symbolic meaning operating at individual, group and organizational levels simultaneously.

Organizational change and symbolic meaning systems

It is appropriate at this point to expand on what is meant by a "multi-layered symbolic meaning system" and the function of metaphors in it. Broadly conceived it implies a whole or system that has depth, breadth, inter-relationships and coherence among its various symbolic components.

- *Depth* implies that aspects of symbolic meaning are at relatively deep and/or tacit levels providing the foundation or "root" for symbolic meanings and manifestations at more surface and/or explicit levels (Guidano, 1988).
- *Breadth* implies there is a range of symbols and symbolic meanings covering the extent of the organization's domain. There will be symbols and symbolic manifestations for the organization as a whole as well as for different organizational functions, components and dynamics.
- *Inter-relationship* means that the various symbolic components do not exist independently in isolation from each other. Instead, they are linked from "top to bottom" (surface to root), and also from "side to side" through entailments and overlaps in extended meaning (Lakoff and Johnson, 1980). Increasing aggregates of symbols and symbolic manifestations organized around a core theme may be considered to form symbolic sets, clusters and constellations within the total system.
- *Coherence* is said to exist when there is overall thematic integrity and/or consistency among most, or all, of the various components that make up

the symbolic meaning system (Lakoff and Johnson, 1980). Even though there may be more than one primary symbol or set of symbols involved, all will be informed by one or a related set of core symbolic themes. If multiple core themes exist in isolation or opposition to each other, the organization could be considered to be "unintegrated" or even "schizophrenic".

Metaphoric fields

Metaphors are, of course, a principal component of an organization's symbolic meaning system. In fact, if other manifestations of a symbolic meaning system, such as art, spatial arrangements, myths, etc., were ignored, one might substitute the phrase "metaphoric field" without much loss of meaning. The metaphor of "field" is particularly apt since it conveys depth, breadth, inter-relationship, coherence and, of course, domain. It also conveys in its scientific sense an invisible "force" that can powerfully influence or determine behaviour, as in the gravitational field (Gregory, 1988). An organization's metaphoric field is considered to be an inter-related set of conscious to unconscious, explicit to tacit, core to peripheral, organizing themes that are expressed metaphorically and which structure perception and behaviour. These themes inform conscious, pre-conscious and unconscious assumptions, beliefs and patterns. They are therefore analogous to Jungian archetypes.

The image of an organizational metaphoric field is also intended to imply that organizational dynamics are influenced by "internal programming" (organizations as brains) and are mediated by "layers of inter-related symbolic meaning" (organizations as cultures), including "invisible, unconscious" dimensions that, *in toto*, "bound" or "restrict" perception and behaviour (organizations as psychic prisons). The metaphoric field may be said to define reality and response for the organization, and thereby both enable and block innovation and action. Organizational change and change strategies that are consistent with the operative theme(s) of the metaphoric field will be readily engaged because they will be coherent and easily understood, even if not fully accepted. Organizational changes and change strategies that are fundamentally inconsistent with the core theme(s) of the organization's metaphoric field will appear incoherent, be easily misunderstood, and will be quickly discarded (Marshak, 1993). Members of the organization "just won't get it". Whereas the metaphoric field helps define and enable first-order change, in second-order change the field itself is the restricting element that must be addressed. If an organization's metaphoric field contains a strong symbolic theme that "business is like war", perhaps including "all's fair in love and war", it will be difficult to introduce changes related to emphasizing fairness, integrity and spiritual values. The typical response might be something like: "What does that have to do with business?" Unless or until the metaphoric field is modified to include or accentuate a different core theme(s), the organization's reality and response will be driven by a "wartime mentality".

Metaphoric fields and organizational change

To further illustrate the concept of metaphoric fields in relation to organizational change let us examine a potential organizational change in terms of the questions: What will be changed, why, how and by whom? While these questions do not necessarily invoke all aspects of an organization's metaphoric field, they do invite consideration of multiple inter-related factors pertaining to the question of change in organizations.

To begin our analysis, and borrowing from Morgan (1986), let us consider that an organization's metaphoric field might contain the image that the organization is like a *machine, living organism, brain,* or *pattern of political alliances.* Next, let us consider some metaphors that might be used to understand organizational change. Changes intended to maintain current operations or to develop, transition or transform an organization are frequently distinguished in the professional literature (e.g. Ackerman, 1986). In the metaphoric field these "technical terms" might be understood as requests to *fix and maintain, build and develop, move and relocate* or *liberate and re-create* (Marshak, 1993). Very different actions and responses would be evoked depending on which metaphor was shaping perception. Yes, we need to change but should we "build and develop" sales, "move from" a centralized sales force "to" a decentralized sales force, "free-up" our thinking and "invent" a new sales strategy, or perhaps just "fine tune" the sales operation?

Thematic coherence

Table 8.1 shows that when the four metaphorical types of organizations are related thematically to the four types of organizational change, they assume an underlying thematic coherence. In short, a picture of what might be included in a metaphoric field begins to emerge.

Reviewing Table 8.1 makes it clear that, depending on the operative core theme(s) and its associated metaphors and symbols, quite different perceptions and actions related to organizational change will occur. In the examples that follow consider how different themes and metaphors shape the experience of organizational change and what is highlighted or overlooked. Consider also the implications if only one of the themes existed or was the dominant theme providing coherence to the organization's metaphoric field.

Mechanical If the metaphoric field is rooted in mechanistic themes and symbols, then the organization will be perceived to be some type of machine made up of independent parts, put together by design. It will therefore be run by engineers or operators who set commands and controls and who will be assisted by mechanics and repair workers who use their tool kits to fix

Table 8.1   *Examples of thematic coherence in the metaphoric field*

	Core theme			
	Mechanical	Biological	Cognitive	Relational
Organization as:	Machine	Organism	Brain	Pattern
Leader as:	Engineer or operator	Survival needs and instincts	Reason and logic	Fashioner and maker
Assisted by:	Mechanics and repair workers	Healing agents	Teachers and experts	Cutters and tiers
Fix and maintain:	Repair breakdowns	Cure sickness	Correct errors	Mend tears
Build and develop:	Enhance output	Grow in ability	Learn knowledge	Strengthen bonds
Move and relocate:	Replace with better model	Adjust to new life stage	Switch methods	Reconfigure interests
Liberate and re-create:	Re-engineer capacity	Metamorphosis	Rethink premises	Re-compose design

anything that is broken. Sometimes enhancements will be made to the machine to increase productivity or ease of use. Other times machine operators and workers will have to learn how to use a new machine that replaced the previous one because it is faster, cheaper or more productive. On rare occasions the machine may need to be totally re-engineered in order to incorporate new technologies. This may also require operators to work in completely new ways.

Biological   If the thematic coherence of the metaphoric field is based on biological symbols, then it is likely that the organization will be understood to be some type of organism living in an environment. It will have to rely on its instincts and natural abilities to adapt and respond to the opportunities and threats in its environmental niche. When sick it will seek out a healing agent to be cured. When healthy it will grow and develop into something that is bigger, faster, quicker and more powerful. It will transition from one stage in its life-cycle to another and each transition may be awkward and/or traumatic, requiring an adjustment period. Certain organisms may even be able to radically alter their form and essential being through a transformational process called metamorphosis.

Cognitive   If the metaphoric field is organized around the implicit theme of cognition, then mediating symbols and metaphors related to thinking, knowing, reasoning, calculating, learning, awareness and so on, will shape organizational reality and response. Strategies will need to be calculated based on solid intelligence and careful reasoning in order to avoid any errors in judgement. If an error does occur it should be corrected quickly in order not to compound the mistake. The organization may engage trainers to help develop abilities to think more clearly and creatively, while also avoiding the misperceptions and mental blocks associated with group-think. For certain problems, where things just don't add up, there may be a need to switch methods and use a different calculus or equation. If mistakes or miscalculations are consistent and persistent, it may become necessary to re-examine fundamental premises and assumptions in the hopes of arriving at a more satisfactory solution. This may require rethinking based on height-ened awareness of the real facts and figures.

Relational   If the organizing theme of the metaphoric field is based on the imagery of a pattern of political alliances, then organizational experience may well be mediated through symbols and metaphors emphasizing relation-ships, bonds, ties and connections. These are often rooted in textile imagery, including weaving, sewing, pattern making, fabric cutting, knitting, knotting and linking. Within the organization a pattern of alliances may need to be fashioned in order to create the common bonds necessary to hold together the different components. This may require sewing up support, possibly by cutting a deal that ties down loose ends. Being clear about the fundamental organizational pattern will help bind together the different lines of work and ensure everyone stays in the loop. Work in different components should be carefully interwoven to avoid any gaps or holes while ensuring a seamless appearance to customers. If important relationships become frayed or torn it is important to mend or patch them quickly so things don't unravel. Sometimes weak ties or weak links will need to be more securely fastened. Other times it may be necessary to reconfigure the existing relationships in order to bring together new interests that better cover the issues. At certain times it may even be necessary to take things apart or loosen and unwrap everything in order to start over and compose a new mosaic or tapestry.

As is readily apparent, the organizational answer to "what is going on here?" will be quite different depending on which metaphors of organization and change are operative. Are we "fixing" the situation by "repairing", "curing", "correcting" and/or "mending" the problem? How dramatic do the required changes need to be? Do we need to "repair", "enhance", "replace" and/or "re-engineer" the production system? When people say: "If it ain't broke, don't fix it", they are undoubtedly speaking from a metaphoric field that implies the organization is a machine that should be repaired only when broken. Consequently, requests to "get out of the box" (rethink premises) might be ignored simply because they are incoherent within the metaphoric framework of "fixing a machine".

Metaphoric diagnosis and intervention in organizational change

From an instrumental point of view there are primarily three questions worth answering with respect to organizational change: (1) what is going on presently; (2) what should be going on; and (3) what needs to be done to make things the way they should be? The answers to these questions are mediated by the metaphoric fields of the involved individuals, groups and/or organization. Furthermore, both the questions and their answers are frequently expressed, explicitly and implicitly, through metaphors (Keidel, 1994; Morgan, 1993). The first two questions are basically diagnostic, while the last pertains to intervention. The following discussion, therefore, will address key considerations in the use of metaphors in organizational diagnosis and intervention. The principal thesis is that symbolic expressions and especially metaphors are an integral part of second-order organizational change efforts (Barry, 1994; Katz and Marshak, 1995; Marshak and Katz, 1992; Olson, 1990).

Metaphors and diagnosis

Working with metaphors as an integral part of organizational diagnosis requires the ability to track literal and symbolic communication simultaneously. This process is guided by four basic premises and an overriding principle (Marshak and Katz, 1992). The four basic premises are as follows:

1. Communication is complex and expressed through multiple modalities. All messages contain literal, conscious components, as well as symbolic dimensions which may be out-of-awareness.
2. Messages conveyed through symbolic expression, such as metaphors, communicate real and legitimate issues, just as do those conveyed through literal language.
3. Symbolic, metaphorical communication provides people with a way in which to express aspects both of themselves and of situations about which they may not be consciously aware, nor be able to express analytically and/or literally.
4. More is known than what is in a person's conscious mind and is often communicated symbolically through metaphors regardless of what they consciously say or think.

With these premises serving as a reminder to constantly pay attention to the symbolic aspects of communications, a paradoxical principle informs the diagnostic process: *Explore literal messages symbolically, and symbolic messages literally.* This principle requires the diagnostic process to remain open to the potential multiple meanings that may be conveyed by a seemingly single communication.

Explore the symbolic literally   When metaphors are listened to for their literal as well as symbolic meaning a wider range of diagnostic speculation and/or inquiry is revealed. For example, if someone in an off-handed comment uses the metaphor "This office is like a prison", it can be heard as a symbolic way of expressing the range of feelings and thoughts they have about their workplace. In this instance they may be conveying a sense of little or no freedom, confinement, isolation, punishment and the like. Pursued literally, however, would mean following up on the metaphorical comment as if it were actually true. Therefore, appropriate diagnostic follow-up could include inquiry as to: How exactly is this place like a prison? Who are the inmates, guards, and the warden? Why are you here? All of these, and other inquiries, serve to expand understanding of the original metaphor by treating it as if the person were literally telling you: "I am in prison." Expanding the inquiry to include closely related images in the metaphoric field, or to explore root images, are also aspects of metaphoric diagnosis. For example, images related to law enforcement, justice, freedom, escape and so on, might also be explored. Deeper images related to being wrong and/or being unfairly punished might also be operative and worth inquiry.

Explore the literal symbolically   Conversely, seemingly literal statements should also be read or listened to symbolically. For example, if people say: "You can't tell the truth around here because too many people would get hurt", or "You can tell the boss the truth, but only if you are willing to take your lumps", or "We need to be brutally honest", it is appropriate to hear that telling the truth can be difficult and painful. It is also appropriate to speculate about what is being communicated symbolically. What implicit and/or unconscious metaphoric image would lead people to talk about telling the truth in such a way? In other words, at a symbolic level these people are talking as if telling the truth is like a __ ? In this instance it could be reasonable to hypothesize that people in this organization symbolically experience truth as a weapon, or that honesty brutalizes people. If so, what are the implications of such a message? Needless to say, it would be difficult to imagine much honesty in an organization that consistently evokes such strong images and feelings. In sum, to receive the full range of data and messages available for organizational diagnosis it is important to be able to pay attention to both the literal and symbolic levels of communication.

Metaphors and interventions

There are six major types of interventions that can be used in working with metaphors and organizational change, especially second-order organizational change (Marshak and Katz, 1990). Within each major type of intervention there are a wide variety of specific methods and techniques that can be used when working with individuals, groups and/or organizations. The following discussion includes vignettes drawn from the author's experiences as an organization change consultant, and is intended to briefly present and then illustrate each of the major types of interventions. They are: (1) recognizing, (2) repudiating, (3) reframing, (4) replacing, (5) releasing and (6) reintegrating. Three of these interventions – repudiating, reframing and replacing – might also be considered subsets of a single broader category of intervention called *rethinking*. Each of the interventions may be used separately in organizational work, but more frequently they are employed in some combination. While in any particular organizational change situation the exact order may not matter, often a rough sequence of moving from recognizing to rethinking followed by releasing and reintegration is a natural progression.

Recognizing   The first step towards second-order change is to be able to identify the metaphor and/or theme(s) in the metaphoric field (the schemata) that is influencing perception and action. Just identifying or naming the metaphor is often all that is required for the focal system to realize how reaction and response has been limited, and to then select another mental model, image or set of beliefs to guide future actions. Recognition alone is more likely to be all that is necessary when the controlling metaphor is more surface and/or more peripheral to the core theme(s) in the system's metaphoric field.

An example of a recognizing intervention occurred during a strategic planning session with the training department of a governmental agency responsible for watching over the operations of other agencies for various forms of malfeasance or inefficiencies. The team of top training managers was stuck trying to decide the proper balance among technical-, managerial-, and people skills-oriented courses. Although there were no specific comments during the discussions, the participants were clearly concerned about the degree of emphasis on people skills in the training curriculum. Being familiar with the agency's culture, the consultant working with them played a hunch and asked: 'What's the dominant image or phrase people use to describe this agency?' The quick response was, 'We're the government's watchdog!' The consultant then suggested, 'You must therefore be planning the curriculum for an obedience school for watchdogs. How is that impacting your discussions?' Several of the participants were quick to realize that the unspoken organizational fear of being seen as a "lapdog" might be influencing perceptions of courses designed to increase trust, caring and collaboration. Recognizing a metaphor that may have been implicitly shaping their discussions, the team re-engaged the curriculum question by explicitly asking: 'What should be the proper mix of courses to best prepare individuals to lead or be members of project teams doing professional analytic work?'

Repudiating   Recognizing that an implicit or explicit metaphor in the metaphoric field may be guiding how a situation is perceived may not be enough to change the situation. Instead, interventions intended to challenge or raise questions about the appropriateness of the metaphor, in whole or in part, are often necessary. The ways in which the metaphor has prevented the system from resolving some situation of importance may need to be highlighted or exposed in order for the controlling metaphor or theme to be abandoned, even temporarily. The more central or core the metaphor in the metaphoric field, the more difficult, but ultimately impactful, the task of repudiation.

The following situation demonstrates the value and impact of a repudiating intervention. Repudiation arose during a planning meeting with an executive task force that had been charged with developing strategies to support a major change initiative in a high tech corporation. The intended change was to become less "bureaucratic" and to encourage operating across organizational boundaries in ad hoc, cross-departmental teams. The effort was bogged down with middle managers who either 'couldn't get it' or were reluctant to give up direct authority or control over their people and projects. The executive task force had been talking about the idea of a two-hour slide presentation as the way to explain to middle managers what to do. When the consultant working with them suggested a range of other more involved or involving options, the uniform reaction was negative. 'Our people are too smart for that.' 'That would be like playing kiddie games.' 'They don't need that much time, they're quick students.' 'Only really smart people work here, so we don't want to insult their intelligence.' Finally the consultant observed: 'You often describe this company as like a college campus or an elite graduate school. What I can't figure out is why so many really smart people just can't get it? Maybe they need remedial management. Maybe they are a group of engineers having a hard time in a poetry course. Maybe they haven't had any of the prerequisites for this course. All I know is that acting as if they are really bright, quick students just doesn't seem to fit the facts of this situation.' After a short pause, the meeting resumed with different members of the task force offering new perspectives. 'Maybe we need to bring them along more slowly.' 'I'll bet none of them have had any management training – what can you expect.' 'We could put them through a series of workshops, sorta like in building block fashion.'

Reframing   Sometimes a metaphor and its associations need only be looked at differently, rather than abandoned entirely. This may include considering alternative ways to apply the metaphor and/or bring into focus an overlooked component or aspect of the broader metaphor set, cluster or constellation.

An example is the reframing of an organizational change effort from that of "fixing" to "re-engineering" a machine. During a meeting with a task force that had been given the task of designing and implementing a whole new way of doing business, certain phrases kept coming up throughout the discussion. 'Look, if it ain't broke, let's not fix it.' 'Remember, we have to minimize down time and get this up and running quickly.' 'Maybe we only need to tinker with what we're doing.' 'That's been running well for twenty years. I don't see why we need to fix it now.' Such statements made it appear that the task force was operating from an implicit shared metaphor – that the organization was a machine that was somehow broken. This was consistent with their discussions, which invariably seemed more focused on making small incremental changes (tinkering), rather than the more funda-mental shifts that appeared to be called for in the situation. Hypothesizing that the group might be constrained by an unexpressed limiting belief ("We're here to fix the machine"), the consultant working with the task force intervened directly, but implicitly, by reframing the suspected underlying metaphor. 'You know, maybe what you are doing is designing a fundamentally new model of the organization that incorporates the latest technology and achieves higher performance standards.' The invitation to think in terms of designing a higher performance machine (re-engineering) rather than trying to repair an old outdated one (fixing) worked as different members of the task force began to see their assignment in a new way. Soon they were talking about making fundamental changes that they had earlier not addressed because those aspects of the organization were 'still working OK and therefore did not need fixing'.

In part, the effectiveness of reframing interventions such as that illustrated by the last vignette rests on their ability to alter the way things are perceived without having to directly challenge a deeply held core metaphor or theme itself. This, of course, is also one of its limitations. One might reframe what needs to be done to the machine, but it is still a machine that does not need emotional or spiritual attention.

Replacing When the controlling metaphor or part of the metaphoric field cannot be repudiated or reframed in a way that invites new perceptions and behaviours, it may be necessary to replace the metaphor or theme with another. This is done by attempting to substitute a metaphor or metaphor set, cluster or constellation from a less central or less potent part of the metaphoric field. Another approach would be to import a new metaphor/theme into the focal system's metaphoric field. Sometimes new themes or metaphors that have recently become part of the field can serve as effective substitutes. However, and as the following example shows, it is important that the metaphor or theme selected as a replacement is appropriate to the circumstances in which it is applied.

The example of a replacement intervention occurred at a large manufacturing-based corporation. The organization found itself having to cope with the need to shift from industrial to post-industrial business paradigms and practices, for example global strategies, mass customization, horizontal work processes, self managed teams. Although this invited re-examining and possibly changing fundamental values and premises, a key divisional vice-president none the less tended to use mechanical "fix and maintain" or "build and enhance" metaphors in meetings devoted to working the changes. 'We need to take apart and clean up our operation.' 'We need to reduce tolerances and achieve a zero-defect way of doing business.' 'Everything has to be tightened up and made to run more efficiently.' The consultant working with the vice-president considered reframing the situation from "fixing" or "enhancing" to "re-engineering". This was not pursued, however, because "re-engineering" might tend to emphasize an exclusive focus on operating differently when there was also the need to "think" differently.

Given this need to think differently, metaphors related to religious or ideological "conversion" were briefly considered as replacements because they connote a re-examination and eventual change in fundamental thinking patterns. These too were not pursued. They were deemed as inappropriate and too controversial, despite the fact that aspects of the religion metaphor cluster such as "vision", "creed", "faith", "ten commandments" or "our bible" are routinely used in most organizations. Instead the metaphor of computer "reprogramming" was tried as a replacement for the "fix and maintain" mechanical imagery. 'We need to change not only what we do, but the programming that tells us how to think about what we do.' 'Our old program is hopelessly out-of-date; we need to develop a cutting edge program to guide our operations into the future.' The reprogramming metaphor was tried because it was related through computer imagery to mechanistic metaphors and themes, and might therefore be more readily accepted as a substitute. It was also selected because it placed emphasis on cognitive processes ("software") rather than structural components ("hardware") which is often the case with the "re-engineering" metaphor (e.g. Hammer and Champy, 1993).

In this instance, then, attempting to replace a mechanistic fix or maintain metaphor with a cognitive reprogramming one appeared the appropriate course of action. Further, it would undoubtedly have been much harder, and inappropriate, to try to apply the metaphor of "religious conversion". Asking someone to metaphorically "change their religious faith" as opposed to asking them to "use a different calculus or program to solve a problem" may well have turned out to be the difference between a successful and unsuccessful replacing intervention.

Releasing Following repudiating, reframing and especially replacing, interventions intended to assist or support the focal system in letting go of previously held perceptions, interpretations and feelings about a situation are often necessary. This is especially true when the metaphor represents a core or defining theme in the organization's metaphoric field. Interventions to help the organization learn how to better use the new, less familiar image system, that reinforce any new perceptions and interpretations that reveal new options, and that monitor attempts to return to using the previous metaphor(s) are all forms of releasing interventions. Additionally, because metaphors evoke affect as well as analysis, attention to emotional release may also be needed.

Take, for example, a chief executive's sense of self-worth. As a "captain of industry" issuing commands that control complex operations, they might feel threatened, consciously or unconsciously, by an invitation to become a "master weaver" responsible for pulling together many different organizational strands into a harmonious pattern that is both functional and aesthetically pleasing. Analytically, shifting to a metaphor cluster that emphasizes patterns over parts, interdependence over independence, and pleasing the customer over productive capacity may all be quite appropriate and needed. Nevertheless, unless the emotional affect such metaphors evoke is also addressed, it is unlikely there would be a change from a more to a less emotionally attractive metaphorical image.

Reintegrating   Repudiating, reframing, replacing and releasing impact the structure and relationships of the symbolic themes and metaphors contained within the metaphoric field. This will necessitate some modification of the existing system of thematic coherence, or, in the extreme, require reorientation around a new system of coherence. The more dramatic the changes in the metaphoric field, the greater the need for thematic reintegration to restore systemic coherence. Emotional as well as cognitive realignment must occur for reintegration to be successful. The structure of meaning provided by the "re-cohered" metaphoric field must "make sense" and "feel right" before it can be said that the organization is fully reintegrated, that is, has fully achieved second-order change.

For instance, a large corporation was engaged in a change effort to develop long-term dedicated relationships with key suppliers. This involved work on a new vision, design of new work processes and a variety of training programmes. Implementation was slow, however, as managers reported difficulty "feeling safe" with the proposed new relationships. During interviews, imagery related to being vulnerable to thieves came up repeatedly. 'We've got to be careful or they will steal us blind.' 'It's in their interest to take whatever they can get.' 'Rule number one is to remember they are out for themselves.' This prompted an explicit effort to replace the metaphor of "suppliers as thieves" with that of "suppliers as strategic allies". Suppliers became 'allies in our efforts to win new customers' and part of a 'strategic partnership' needed to keep costs down. The new imagery also led to the development of "strategic alliance" workshops between managers of the organization and various supplier organizations. The president of the organization felt a major corner had been turned when a purchasing manager remarked after one of the workshops, 'That's the first meeting I've had with them when I didn't feel like I needed to check to see if I still had my watch and wallet.'

Conclusions

Second-order change in organizations requires addressing and modifying controlling organizational schemata. These include conscious, pre-conscious and unconscious assumptions, beliefs and patterns held by individuals, groups and the organization. Symbols, especially metaphors, are the common building blocks and forms of expression for conscious, pre-conscious and unconscious elements of an organization's schemata. The organization's system of symbolic meaning, or more specifically its metaphoric field, is therefore a principal, but implicit, framework that structures organizational reality and response. In order to diagnose an organization's metaphoric field it is necessary to explore literal communications symbolically, and symbolic communications literally. Only then is it possible to address and/or alter the metaphoric field for purposes of second-order organizational change. This can be accomplished using some combination of recognizing, rethinking, releasing and reintegrating interventions.

References

Ackerman, L. (1986) 'Development, transition, or transformation: The question of change in organizations', *OD Practitioner*, 18 (4), 1–8.

Argyris, C. (1985) *Strategy, Change, and Defensive Routines*. Marshfield, MA: Pitman Publishing.

Argyris, C. (1990) *Overcoming Organizational Defenses: Facilitating Organizational Learning*. Boston: Allyn and Bacon.

Argyris, C. (1992) *On Organizational Learning*. Cambridge, MA: Blackwell.

Argyris, C. and Schön, D. (1978) *Organizational Learning*. Reading, MA: Addison-Wesley.

Argyris, C., Putnam, R. and Smith, D.M. (eds.) (1985) *Action Science*. San Francisco: Jossey-Bass.

Ashby, W.R. (1952) *Design for a Brain*. New York: John Wiley and Sons.

Ashby, W.R. (1960) *An Introduction to Cybernetics*. London: Chapman and Hall.

Barry, D. (1994) 'Making the invisible visible: Using analogically-based methods to surface unconscious organizational processes', *Organization Development Journal*, 12 (4), 37–48.

Bartunek J.M. and Moch, M.K. (1987) 'First-order, second-order, and third-order change, and organization development intervention: A cognitive approach', *Journal of Applied Behavioral Science*, 23 (4), 483–500.

Bateson, G. (1972) *Steps to an Ecology of Mind*. New York: Ballantine.

Bateson, G. (1979) *Mind and Nature: A Necessary Unity*. New York: Bantam.

Baum, H.S. (1987) *The Invisible Bureaucracy*. Oxford: Oxford University Press.

Baum, H.S. (1989) 'Organizational politics against organizational culture: A psychoanalytic perspective', *Human Resource Management*, 28, 191–207.

Beck, A.T. (1967) *Depression: Causes and Treatment*. Philadelphia: University of Pennsylvania Press.

Beck, A.T. (1970) 'Cognitive therapy: Nature and relation to behavior therapy', *Behavior Therapy*, 1, 184–200.

Beer, S. (1959) *Cybernetics and Management*. New York: John Wiley and Sons.

Beer, S. (1972) *Brain of the Firm*. New York: Herder and Herder.

Bion, W.R. (1959) *Experiences in Groups*. London: Tavistock.

Bougon, M.G., Weick, K.E. and Brinkhorst, D. (1977) 'Cognition in organizations: An analysis of the Utrecht Jazz Orchestra', *Administrative Science Quarterly*, 22 (4), 609–639.

Campbell, J. (ed.) (1971) *The Portable Jung*. New York: Penguin.

Daft, R.L. and Weick, K.E. (1984) 'Toward a model of organizations as interpretation systems', *Academy of Management Review*, 9, 284–295.

Davis, S.M. (1984) *Managing Corporate Culture*. Cambridge, MA: Ballinger.

Deal, T.E. and Kennedy, A.A. (1982) *Corporate Cultures: The Rites and Rituals of Corporate Life*. Reading, MA: Addison-Wesley.

De Board, R. (1978) *The Psychoanalysis of Organizations*. London: Tavistock.

DeRubeis, R.J. and Beck, A.T. (1988) 'Cognitive therapy', in K.S. Dobson (ed.), *Handbook of Cognitive-Behavioral Therapies*. New York: Guilford Press, pp. 273–306.

Diamond, M.A. (1986) 'Resistance to change: A psychoanalytic critique of Argyris and Schön's contributions to organization theory and intervention', *Journal of Management Studies*, 23 (5), 543–562.

Dobson, K.S. (ed.) (1988) *Handbook of Cognitive-Behavioral Therapies*. New York: Guilford Press.

Ellis, A. (1962) *Reason and Emotion in Psychotherapy*. New York: Stuart.

Ellis, A. (1970) *The Essence of Rational Psychotherapy: A Comprehensive Approach to Treatment*. New York: Institute for Rational Living.

Fontana, D. (1993) *The Secret Language of Symbols: A Visual Key to Symbols and Their Meaning*. San Francisco: Chronicle Books.

Frost, P.J., Moore, L.F., Louis, M.R., Lundberg, C.C. and Martin, J. (1985) *Organizational Culture*. Beverly Hills, CA: Sage Publications.

Gabriel, Y. (1991) 'Organizations and their discontents: A psychoanalytic contribution to the study of organizational culture', *Journal of Applied Behavioral Science*, 27 (3), 318–336.

Goffman, E. (1974) *Frame Analysis*. New York: Harper.

Goldfried, M.R. and Robins, C. (1983) 'Self-schemas, cognitive bias, and the processing of learning experiences', in P.C. Kendall (ed.), *Advances in Cognitive-Behavioral Research and Therapy*, Vol. 2. New York: Academic Press.

Gray, B., Bougon, M.G. and Donnellon, A. (1985) 'Organizations as constructions and destructions of meaning', *Journal of Management*, 11, 83–95.

Gregory, B. (1988) *Inventing Reality: Physics as Language*. New York: John Wiley and Sons.

Guidano, V.F. (1988) 'A systems, process-oriented approach to cognitive therapy', in K.S. Dobson (ed.), *Handbook of Cognitive-Behavioral Therapies*. New York: Guilford Press, pp. 307–356.

Guidano, V.F. and Liotti, G. (1983) *Cognitive Processes and Emotional Disorders: A Structural Approach to Psychotherapy*. New York: Guilford Press.

Hammer, M. and Champy, J. (1993) *Re-engineering the Corporation*. New York: Harper Collins Publishers.

Hirschorn, L. (1988) *The Workplace Within*. Cambridge, MA: MIT Press.

Jung, C.G. (ed.) (1964) *Man and His Symbols*. New York: Dell Publishing.

Jung, C.G. (1968) *Analytical Psychology: Its Theory and Practice*. New York: Vintage Books.

Katz, G.A. (1983) 'The noninterpretation of metaphors in psychiatric hospital groups', *International Journal of Group Management Review*, 31 (1), 53–67.

Katz, J.H. and Marshak, R.J. (1995) 'Re-inventing OD theory and practice', *Organization Development Journal*, 13 (1), 63–70.

Keidel, R.W. (1994) 'Rethinking organizational design', *The Academy of Management Executive*, 8 (4), 12–30.

Kets de Vries, M.F.R. (1990) 'Leaders on the couch', *Journal of Applied Behavioral Science*, 26 (4), 423–431.

Kets de Vries, M.F.R. (ed.) (1991) *Organizations on the Couch: Clinical Perspectives on Organizational Behavior and Change*. San Francisco: Jossey-Bass.

Kets de Vries, M.F.R. and Miller, D. (1984) *The Neurotic Organization*. San Francisco: Jossey-Bass.

Kilmann, R.H. (1985) *Beyond the Quick Fix*. San Francisco: Jossey-Bass.

Kilmann, R.H., Saxton, M.J., Serpa, R. and Associates (1985) *Gaining Control of the Corporate Culture*. San Francisco: Jossey-Bass.

Kuhn, T.S. (1970) *The Structure of Scientific Revolutions* (2nd edn). Chicago: University of Chicago Press.

Lakoff, G. and Johnson, M. (1980) *Metaphors We Live By*. Chicago: University of Chicago Press.

Lau, C.M. and Woodman, R.W. (1995) 'Understanding organizational change: A schematic perspective', *The Academy of Management Journal*, 38 (2), 537–554.

Levison, H. and Rosenthal, S. (1984) *CEO: Corporate Leadership in Action*. New York: Basic Books.

Mahoney, M.J. (1974) *Cognition and Behavior Modification*. Cambridge, MA: Ballinger.

Mahoney, M.J. (1977) 'Personal science: A cognitive learning therapy', in A. Ellison and R. Grieger (eds), *Handbook of Rational Psychotherapy*. New York: Springer, pp. 280–302.

Mahoney, M.J. and Thoreson, C.E. (1974) *Self-Control: Power to the Person*. Monterey, CA: Brooks/Cole.

Markus, H. (1977) 'Self-schemata and processing information about the self', *Journal of Personality and Social Psychology*, 35, 63–78.

Markus, H. and Zajonc, R.B. (1985) 'The cognitive perspective in social psychology', in G. Lindzey and E. Aronson (eds), *The Handbook of Social Psychology*, Vol. 1. New York: Random House, pp. 137–230.

Marshak, R.J. (1993) 'Managing the metaphors of change', *Organizational Dynamics*, 22 (1), 44–56.

Marshak, R.J. and Katz, J.H. (1990) 'Covert processes and revolutionary change', in M. McDonald (ed.), *Forging Revolutionary Partnerships: Proceedings of the 1990 National OD Network Conference*. Portland, OR: National OD Network, pp. 58–65.

Marshak, R.J. and Katz, J.H. (1991) 'Covert processes at work', *Chesapeake Bay Organizational Development Network Newsletter*, 6 (2), 1–5.

Marshak, R.J. and Katz, J.H. (1992) 'The symbolic side of OD', *OD Practitioner*, 24 (2), 1–5.

Martin, J. (1982) 'Stories and scripts in organizational settings', in A. Hastorf and A. Isen (eds), *Cognitive Social Psychology*. New York: North Holland, pp. 255–305.

Mazlish, B. (1990) *The Leader, the Led and the Psyche*. Middletown, CT: Wesleyan University Press.

Meichenbaum, D.H. (1973) 'Cognitive factors in behavior modification: Modifying what clients say to themselves', in C.M. Franks and G.T. Wilson (eds), *Annual Review of Behavior Therapy, Theory, and Practice*. New York: Brunner/Mazel, pp. 218–230.

Meichenbaum, D.H. (1977) *Cognitive Behavior Modification*. New York: Plenum.

Merry, U. and Brown, G.I. (1987) *The Neurotic Behavior of Organizations*. Cleveland, OH: Gestalt Institute of Cleveland Press.

Mitroff, I.I. (1983) *Stakeholders of the Organization Mind*. San Francisco: Jossey-Bass.

Morgan, G. (1982) 'Cybernetics and organization theory: Epistemology or technique?', *Human Relations*, 35, 521–538.

Morgan, G. (1986) *Images of Organization*. Beverly Hills, CA: Sage Publications.

Morgan, G. (1993) *Imaginization: The Art of Creative Management*. Newbury Park, CA: Sage Publications.

Morgan, G. and Ramirez, R. (1984) 'Action learning: A holographic metaphor for guiding social change', *Human Relations*, 37, 1–28.

Nielsen, R.P. (1993) 'Woolman's "I am we" triple loop action-learning: Origin and application in organization ethics', *Journal of Applied Behavioral Science*, 29 (1), 117–138.

Olson, E.E. (1990) 'The transcendent function in organizational change', *Journal of Applied Behavioral Science*, 26 (1), 69–81.

Peters, T.J. and Waterman, R.H. (1982) *In Search of Excellence: Lessons from America's Best-Run Companies*. New York: Harper and Row.

Pondy, L.R., Frost, P.J., Morgan, G. and Dandridge, T.C. (eds) (1983) *Organizational Symbolism*. Greenwich, CT: JAI Press.

Schein, E.H. (1985) *Organizational Culture and Leadership: A Dynamic View*. San Francisco: Jossey-Bass.

Schwartz, H.S. (1987) 'Anti-social actions of committed organizational participants: An existential psychoanalytic perspective', *Organization Studies*, 8 (3), 327–340.

Senge, P.M. (1990) *The Fifth Discipline: The Art and Practice of the Learning Organization*. New York: Doubleday/Currency.

Siegelman, E. (1990) *Metaphor and Meaning in Psychotherapy*. New York: Guilford Press.

9

Telling Tales: Management Consultancy as the Art of Story Telling

Timothy Clark and Graeme Salaman

Organizations of all kinds are increasingly turning to management consultancies for assistance with a wide range of management issues and problems. Indeed, during the latter part of the 1980s the management consultancy industry was one of the fastest growing sectors of the UK economy. For instance, between 1985 and 1992 it expanded by a little over 200 per cent (Business Statistics Office, 1985, 1992). Despite this growth a number of researchers have noted that the market provision of management consultancy services is inherently problematic (Clark, 1995; Holmstrom, 1985; Mitchell, 1994). These writers point out that clients and consultants collaborate and interact in an atmosphere of uncertainty. This arises primarily from the interplay between two factors: (1) the structural characteristics of the management consultancy industry; and (2) the characteristics of the service being offered.

Management consultancy is characterized by low barriers to entry which have underpinned its recent expansion. Entry is in effect "free". This situation has two important implications for clients. First, they have a wide range of suppliers from which to choose. Second, the lack of any effective barriers to entry means that clients are responsible for determining the quality and value of consultancy work prior to contracting with a particular supplier. However, determining the relative quality and value of management consultancies is made difficult by a number of service characteristics. In particular, intangibility implies that a service does not take on a physical form. Ascertaining the quality and relevance of a service prior to purchase is therefore problematic. Indeed, intangibility may imply that clients view consultancies as perfectly substitutable since they are unable to determine the relative quality of the alternatives they may be considering. Furthermore, the characteristic of interaction suggests that there is nothing to evaluate until the client and consultant meet to produce the service. As a consequence, service production is inherently social. This underpins the heterogeneity of services since the centrality of client–consultant interaction ensures that no two assignments will be the same. Each service purchase is therefore unique, implying that past performance may not be repeated in the future. When seeking to purchase a management consultancy service a client must therefore seek to overcome these endemic problems.

Given these problems, this chapter seeks to answer the questions: How do consultants convince clients of their value and quality? What do consultants do for clients?

The chapter is structured as follows. The first section identifies the major structural features of the management consultancy industry in order to provide an overall context for the later discussion and to determine the implications of these features for the client–consultant relationship. The second section is specifically concerned with identifying the key character- istics of the service sector industry. As with the first section, it examines the implications of these characteristics for the client–consultant relationship. The final section considers how management consultants convince clients of their expertise, knowledge and value. Elsewhere we have argued that management consultancy can be examined using a 'dramaturgical' meta- phor, that is, that it can be seen to be about the nature of the consultant's performance in front of the client (Clark and Salaman, 1996). Here we develop this theme even further. It is argued that consultants successfully satisfy and retain clients by telling strong stories. They can be seen as purveyors of myths, constructing meaning via the manipulation of rhetoric and symbols. In this respect the client–consultant relationship and how it works is best understood by extending the dramaturgical metaphor into "the art of story telling".

Some features of the management consultancy industry in the UK

This section examines a number of structural features of the management consultancy industry. It provides a backdrop from which the argument in subsequent sections emanates in addition to considering how these market features impact on the client–consultant relationship. Three key structural features are identified – barriers to entry, heterogeneity and turbulence.

Barriers to entry   Barriers to entry are those obstacles which prevent potential entrants from disturbing the character of existing market competi- tion, that is, they isolate the market from potentially disruptive forces. In the case of the management consultancy industry, barriers to entry prevent potential entrants from obtaining assignments. Once an assignment has been awarded to an organization, regardless of its patrimony, it is deemed to have entered the industry. Barriers to entry are an important determinant of the structure of any industry. By governing the manner and rate of entry they determine both the shape and competitive character of an industry. The explosion in the number of management consultancies in recent years indicates that both the method and speed of entry have been significant determinants of the industry's structure. For example, Bryson et al. indicate that 57 per cent of management consultancies operating in 1990 had entered since 1980 (1993: 121).

The explosive growth of the management consultancy industry in the 1980s was facilitated by the prevalence of low barriers to entry. Economists identify five types of barrier to entry:

1. Legal, or structural, barriers set the parameters for entry. They define which firms have the necessary requisites for entry. In the management consultancy industry no specific legal entry restrictions exist.
2. Absolute cost barriers refer to established firms having lower average cost curves compared to potential entrants. Since the management consultancy industry is not characterized by asset specificity, these barriers are low. For example, the intellectual assets of consultants, researchers and secretaries can be applied to a wide range of industries. Similarly, physical assets which include office space, telephones, etc., are not industry-specific.
3. Initial capital requirement barriers refer to the cost of obtaining "start-up" capital. These too are low for management consultancies. All they require is a telephone, fax, stationery, secretarial support and an office.
4. High-scale barriers may occur where firms have to enter at a large size and producing a large proportion of industry output (Bain, 1956). With regard to management consultancies in the UK, the majority are small, with 77 per cent of firms employing less than 12 consultants (Bryson et al., 1993).
5. Product differentiation barriers arise when buyers prefer the products of incumbent firms over those of potential entrants, and this certainly appears relevant to management consultancy in the UK. A number of studies have reported that the reputation of a consultancy and its consultants is the most important criterion identified by clients in selecting between consultancies (Askvik, 1992; Clark, 1993; Dawes et al., 1992; Stock and Zinszer, 1987). It would therefore be expected that this barrier might be high. If it were not, new consultancies would enter the high-quality, high-price end of the market by charging lower fees and forcing existing fee levels down. O'Farrell et al. (1993: 44) suggest three reasons to explain why this is a difficult entry strategy to pursue.

   First, creating a reputation can be costly and time-consuming. A track-record is a prerequisite for the development of a high-quality reputation.

   Second, new entrants have to convince clients that their quality matches that of incumbent consultancies. This is difficult since a major transaction cost is buyer uncertainty resulting from the imbalance of information between buyers and sellers (Holmstrom, 1985). The seller is better informed about the quality of the service than the buyer. Buyer ignorance means that they are unable to distinguish between the relative qualities of different consultancies. Even if a new entrant were able to deliver a high-quality service, from the clients' viewpoint their service would be indistinguishable from that of a low-quality producer.

Third, and related to the previous point, the nature of services, particularly intangibility and perishability (these are discussed more fully in the next section), reinforces the importance of reputation as a primary selection criterion. Hence, incumbent consultancies maintain their stock of "goodwill" with clients by investing heavily in signalling their quality to existing and potential buyers. This creates not only additional costs for new entrants but also certain rigidities in that buyers may prefer transacting with known consultancies rather than risk the new and unfamiliar (Nayyar, 1990). Established consultancies are therefore able to charge higher fees and reap higher returns than new entrants who may be of equal quality.

Heterogeneity The overall low barriers to entry detailed above have enabled a wide variety of firms to enter the management consultancy industry. Clark (1995) has reported from an analysis of entry patterns between 1960 and 1990 that 52 per cent of management consultancies were cross-entrants (i.e. already established firms in other industries such as accountancy and advertising). This implies that a major structural characteristic of the industry is the heterogeneity of firms offering management consultancy services. Indeed, the industry is characterized by low levels of exclusiveness (the extent to which firms offer a single service and so are present in a single market) and high levels of specialization (the extent to which firms offer a range of services and so are present in more than one market) (Evely and Little, 1960: 31–32). As a consequence, two main types of management consultancies operate in the UK. These are as follows:

1. Specialist management consultancies – they are distinguished from the other types in that their primary source of income is from management consultancy assignments. Peet has suggested that the services offered by these consultancies can be divided into four general areas: (a) strategy; (b) traditional; (c) human resources; and (d) specialist (e.g. executive recruitment) (1988: 7).
2. Multi-service firms – this refers to those organizations who offer a range of services of which management consultancy is one. Management consultancy activities are therefore secondary to their principal, and defining, activity. In the main these organizations include:
    (a) the consultancy divisions of the large accountancy firms – the diversification of large accountancy firms into management consultancy, and related services, has been well documented (Daniels et al., 1988). In the UK in 1992/3 Arthur Andersen derived a little over 56 per cent of its total fee income from consultancy fees. Coopers and Lybrand, KPMG Peat Marwick and Price Waterhouse earned in excess of 20 per cent of their total fees from consultancy

activities (*Accountancy*, 1994: 13). The position of accountancy firms in management consultancy is now so dominant that according to Abbot they account for 6 of the 10 largest management consultancies in the UK, with Andersen Consulting, Coopers and Lybrand, and Price Waterhouse occupying the first three places (1994: 24).

(b) the consultancy divisions of large communications groups – during the 1980s a number of large communications groups diversified into the management consultancy industry via acquisition. Some of the most well-known examples include Saatchi and Saatchi's purchase of Hay-MSL, Moxon Dolphin and Kerby, and Harrison Cowley; the purchase of Accountancy Personnel, a specialist recruitment consultancy, by the Hays Group (primarily a transport and distribution company); and the establishment of 3i Consultants by 3i, the leading UK source of venture capital (Underwood, 1989). More recently Cray Electronics has purchased PE.

Turbulence   A further indicator of the extent to which entry is free in an industry is the measure of industry turbulence. Turbulence indicates the 'flux created in an industry's total composition by flows of births and deaths' (Beesley and Hamilton, 1984: 220). An industry's turbulence, expressed as a *T* value, is calculated as the sum of births and deaths in an industry divided by the stock of firms in the base year. A *T* value indicates the percentage of firms which have entered or exited an industry between two points in time. Hence, turbulence measures the degree to which an industry's total composition changes over time.

Keeble et al.'s (1994) study of the management consultancy industry suggests that turbulence is particularly prevalent amongst smaller consultancies. They report a *T* value for the industry between 1985 and 1990 of 36 per cent. This figure confirms the existence of low entry and exit barriers within the management consultancy industry, but on closer scrutiny such figures reveal that turbulence relates, in part, to the size of the consultancy. In the five-year period 1985 to 1990 the *T* value for firms employing no more than two consultants was 51 per cent, with a *T* value of 42 per cent for those consultancies employing between three and five consultants, a *T* value of 27 per cent for those consultancies employing between six and twelve consultants, and a *T* value of 23 per cent for those consultancies employing between thirteen and twenty-five consultants. In contrast, no consultancy employing more than 100 consultants closed over the period.

Implications of market features on the client–consultant relationship

The previous discussion has sought to identify the main structural features of the management consultancy industry. Three structural features were examined in turn – barriers to entry, heterogeneity and turbulence. It was argued that the low level of barriers to entry has underpinned the rapid expansion of the industry in recent times. New consultancies can enter the industry with ease. Entry is in effect free. For clients of management consultancy services this means that any assessment of a consultancy's quality and value has to be made once entry has been effected since there is no formal mechanism relating to the certification of consultancy skills thereby providing some indication of potential quality prior to entry. Since there is no certificating body, the responsibility for pre-judging the value and quality of a consultancy's service falls on the clients. Hence, their ability to ascertain the value of a consultancy's service prior to purchase is of crucial importance.

The low level of entry barriers underpins the high level of heterogeneity within the industry. Ease of entry has enabled a large number of organiz-ations from the accountancy, advertising and public relations industries to offer management consultancy services. This suggests that the pre-contractual stage is not simply characterized by a condition of large numbers bidding. In addition, clients have a wide range of alternatives from which to choose. They must therefore determine the pros and cons associated with using different kinds of suppliers of management consultancy services. This adds a further level of complexity to the initial selection decision.

Finally, the high level of industry turbulence – particularly among smaller consultancies – implies that there is no certainty that clients will be able to transact with the same supplier at some point in the future. The industry is constantly being regenerated by the influx of new consultancies and the death of existing participants. Consequently, clients may encounter difficulty developing a continuous, long-term relationship with a single supplier. Where this is the case, clients may have to switch between alternative suppliers. This is not a simple matter; depending on the extent of the changes to the composition of the industry, their information banks on suppliers may have little relevance to the new selection context. Where their information banks fail to reflect the current state of the market, clients, even experienced ones, will in effect be first-time purchasers since they will be selecting between consultancies that are unknown to them. To avoid this, clients need to refresh their information banks before each purchase deci-sion. Since this can be a costly and lengthy procedure, the purchasers of management consultancy services will wish to find a mechanism which enables them to circumvent this problem. Our argument is that this desire to circumvent the problem has led to the adoption of what, on the face of it, appears to be a rather subjective process by which to select a consultant. It is a process whereby the consultant is allowed to convince the client of their quality and indispensability by telling them of their past endeavours. It is for this reason that we believe it is appropriate to apply the metaphor of the consultant as a story teller when analysing the client–consultant relation-ship.

Service characteristics

We have suggested that a number of features of the management consultancy industry impact on the nature of the client–consultant relationship
in such a way as to make the metaphor of the consultant as story teller highly
appropriate. However, before we go on to apply this metaphor in detail, it is
as well to look at how service sector characteristics can be applied to the
management consultancy industry. These too have important implications
for the client–consultant relationship and therefore the metaphor we use to
describe it.

Management theorists have argued that services share a number of
common characteristics which differentiate them from goods. The most
commonly distinguished characteristics are intangibility, interaction, heterogeneity and perishability.

Intangibility This is perhaps the most commonly identified characteristic
of services and as such is considered by some commentators to be the factor
which best distinguishes them from material goods. At its simplest it means
that whilst services are intangible goods are tangible. Hence, prior to the
purchase of a service a consumer is unable to perceive a complete physical
form. There is nothing which can be seen, touched, tasted, heard or smelled.
Oberoi and Hales write 'this means that there is no complete physical form
which can be perceived by the consumer at the pre-purchase stage, as an
object or thing' (1990: 701–702). Similarly, Walker suggests that services
and goods primarily differ in that services 'do not take the intervening form
of a material product' (1985: 48).

Interaction A further distinguishing feature of service delivery is that it is
primarily a process of interaction between the buyer and seller. In order for
the production and consumption of a service to be completed, the buyer and
seller frequently have to interact directly. The delivery of a service may
therefore be characterized as a relational activity based upon social inter-
course between the two parties (Mills and Margulies, 1980: 260).

Heterogeneity This refers to the extent to which the production and
delivery of services can be standardized. From the customer's point of view
it specifically relates to consistent quality. Customers seek a high-quality
level of service each time a purchase is made. The degree to which services
are heterogeneous depends on what can be termed their 'plasticity'. This
refers to the amount of discretion available to a service provider when
fulfilling the terms of a contract (Alchian and Woodward, 1988: 69). For
instance, an ice cream vendor has little discretion when supplying their
product to the public. Similarly, the ability of a computer software supplier
to modify a particular package is limited by the original programmers'
intentions in addition to legal constraints. In contrast, management consultancies have considerable discretion since they are not selling a pre-

defined package. Rather they are selling a bundle of services which can be modified and adapted in response to the idiosyncrasies of clients' problems and the interaction process. As Oberoi and Hales write: 'This means that a service is unique to the consumers' requirements, and that standardization of service is difficult or impossible' (1990: 702).

Perishability   This characteristic implies that services are destroyed in the process of consumption and cannot be stored. It also implies that goods are more durable than services. A management consultancy report, a legal contract or a piece of music written by a composer may all have much longer lives than many so-called durable manufactured goods (e.g. confectionery, fuel, paper). Some services, though, are more perishable than others. Greenfield (1966), who introduced the concept of perishability in the context of business services, argued that much depended on the time span used to distinguish between perishable, semi-durable and durable. Commercial cleaning services, for example, may be classified as a perishable business service since the premises must be cleaned at regular intervals. Semi-durable services would include advertising and marketing activities since these may undergo periodic review and change. Durable business services are those classified as being concerned with the strategic direction of the firm, such as those provided by management consultancies, market research consultancies and R and D projects. These survive so long as they contribute to the strategic intentions of senior management.

Implications of service characteristics on the client–consultant relationship

The previous discussion has argued that services differ from goods in a number of important respects. In particular, services are characterized by high levels of intangibility, interaction, heterogeneity and perishability. These service characteristics have a number of implications for the users and suppliers of management consultancy services. Intangibility suggests that purchasers will have difficulty selecting between alternative consultancies since there is no material form which can be evaluated beforehand. This suggests that services, such as management consultancy, are low in search qualities – attributes which can be ascertained prior to purchase (Nelson, 1970). Since services do not take on a complete physical form there is little which can be directly evaluated beforehand. The buyer is therefore ill informed about the relative quality of the alternatives they are considering. Indeed, they may view them as perfectly substitutable since high- and low-quality suppliers will appear identical.

   Intangibility further implies that convincing clients of their worth is a vital part of consultants' work. Because clients are not fully cognizant of the nature of the service they have purchased there is an opportunity for consultants to create and project a particular image of the service they are supplying by controlling and managing the way in which it is delivered (i.e.

the interaction process). In other words, intangibility enables consultants to take command of the process by which images, impressions and perceptions of their value and service quality are created. Clients subsequently use these tailored and controlled images as the basis on which to evaluate the value and quality of the service they have received. This is a crucial factor in the client–consultant relationship. It enables consultants to convince clients that they are delivering a service which is both valuable and high quality. In effect, the assignment process allows the consultant ample opportunity to persuade clients of their high quality based on their special expertise, talents and skills. Impression management is therefore at the core of much consultancy work. Consultants devote considerable time and effort to managing the expectations and overall experience of the client in order to foster and convey the impression that they are delivering a high-quality service. This is in keeping with Alvesson's assertion that service organizations, such as management consultancies, are essentially 'systems of persuasion' (1993: 1011). Their work centres on the creation and management of impressions, that is, convincing clients of their "know how" and that they have something of value to offer. Indeed, he suggests that their rationale for existing and their economic fortunes are dependent upon the extent to which they are able to successfully apply this process.

Impression management in consultancy is further reinforced by the characteristic of interaction. Production and consumption do not occur separately. Services are sold then produced and consumed simultaneously. This can mean that at the pre-purchase stage there is nothing to evaluate until the client and consultant interact to produce the service. Furthermore, it suggests that the quality of what is produced, and therefore evaluated after delivery, is to a large extent dependent upon the outcome of the interaction between the client and consultant. Hence, clients are likely to place considerable emphasis on the quality of the interaction process when selecting between alternative consultancies. For this reason, when choosing a consultancy, clients will tend to spend some time evaluating previous interactions which are based on their prior experiences. Therefore, for consultants to persuade clients of their quality, and convince them of their value, they must actively manage and manipulate the interaction process in order to create favourable impressions of their service.

The ability of consultants to manage and manipulate the interaction process is further enhanced by the heterogeneity of services. Consultants are not able to deliver a standardized service. Whilst this might imply variable quality to clients, it offers consultants the opportunity to tailor their services to the particular requirements of individual clients. They are able to modify the service they offer in order to meet the particular needs of each client and at the same time convey the "right" impression. Heterogeneity therefore gives rise to the possibility that consultants are able to manage the interaction process in many and various ways. There are, then, a wide range of devices, mechanisms and tools available to consultants when seeking to create, manage and manipulate client impressions of their service.

Telling a strong story

How, then, are we to understand and analyse the key task of management consultants – the way in which they convince clients of their knowledge, expertise and value? We wish to engage with this question by examining the work of management consultants in terms of a metaphor which focuses on the active management of the client–consultant relationship. We use a metaphor which tries to catch and characterize the way consultants typically resolve the real problem they face, that is, the way in which they seek to portray themselves as indispensable to clients. In what follows we depict management consultants as story tellers attempting to create a reality for their audience (i.e. clients) which captures their imagination and commitment. Hence, the key question becomes: How do management consultants develop and tell strong stories which convince clients of their value?

To be successful and to survive in the management consultancy industry consultants must convince clients of their expertise, knowledge and indispensability. To achieve this they must appear authoritative, must behave confidently and must be in command of something which clients seek and value.

But in command of what? We suggest that it is the *apparent* possession by consultants of something that client managers value which leads them to bestow high status upon consultants. Therefore, consultants' authority vis-à-vis clients depends on mastering techniques which convey the *impression* that they possess authority and expertise in areas which clients value. They do this by encouraging clients to make their judgements about the value and quality of their service on the basis of the 'generic *symbols of expertise*' which they provide (Starbuck, 1992: 887). These include qualifications, quality of data, client base, demeanour, style, confidence, etc. In short, consultants manipulate symbols of their authority – their "symbolic outputs".

It appears, then, that the foundations for consultants' success cannot be discovered in the professional knowledge-base of the activity. Although this view is one which metaphorically has been asserted and perpetuated by the consultants themselves (see Clark and Salaman, 1996), it is clearly invalid, for consultancy knowledge is a social product. Instead, consultancy success is achieved through "knowledge" which is produced and displayed through what Callon and Latour have described as a process of translation:

> By translation we understand all the negotiations, intrigues, calculations, acts of persuasion and violence, thanks to which an actor or force takes, or causes to be conferred on itself, authority to speak or act on behalf of another actor or force. "Our interests are the same", "do what I want", "you cannot succeed without going through me". (1981: 40)

Translation is achieved through 'problematization' (Callon, 1986). In such circumstances one actor (i.e. a management consultant) convinces another actor (i.e. a client) that their interests coincide – "I want what you want" –

by redefining the "problem" in terms of a solution owned or within the orbit of the former.

It therefore seems that knowledge is important in the work of management consultants, but it is a particular sort of knowledge – one that can be defined as the consultant's ability to identify and manipulate the symbols of knowledge in the course of giving authoritative performances. This is achieved through the consultant telling strong stories.

Alvesson (1993) notes that the 'knowledge' of knowledge workers in general – and we would argue management consultants can be classified as such – cannot be defined on a neutral, formal, theoretical basis. Not only are the results of knowledge-intensive work ambiguous (i.e. highly uncertain, very difficult to evaluate and without agreement on boundaries, clear principles or solutions), but it is also the case that the role knowledge plays in knowledge-intensive organizations is ambiguous. This lack of a clear role means that organizations demanding expert assistance from knowledge-intensive organizations (i.e. management consultancies) cannot rely upon accessing formal, rational bodies of knowledge and expertise. Instead, the impact of consultants is dependent upon beliefs about them being able to offer something of value to clients. These beliefs are formulated not by an objectivistic and functionalist knowledge-base, but by the manipulation of myths and symbols through language. Indeed, 'Ambiguity means that the possibility of rationality – clarifying means–ends relationships or exercising qualified judgement – becomes reduced. A space is thereby created for . . . the adoption of institutionalized myths' (Alvesson, 1993: 1002–1003).

Building on the previous point, Meyer and Rowan (1977) argue that management consultants operate as organizational myth makers. These myths act as *rationality-surrogates*. They are taken-for-granted beliefs that compensate for the uncertainties generated by the absence (impossibility) of "true" rationality – an absence which follows from the difficulties in establishing clear means–ends linkages. Consultants therefore provide these institutionalized myths. As Alvesson writes:

> To use or be connected to agents which are highly visible and sanctioned in terms of knowledge and expertise is important in adapting to the institutional environment in the contemporary Western world. Knowledge-intensive service organisations [management consultancies] thus become vital symbols for client organisations' elaboration of rules and requirements for rationality. The well-run company utilizes expertise from recognised knowledge-intensive firms for education, personnel, recruitment, management development, computer development projects, market research, advertising, managerial advice, strategic planning, etc. . . . An implication is that the focus changes from an emphasis on formal knowledge to persuasive strategies in convincing all concerned about expertise and superior rationality. (1993: 1004)

The important feature of knowledge for management consultants is therefore its symbolic quality – what is important is to give the sense of being knowledgeable by persuading clients of one's knowledge. To put it another way, being perceived as knowledgeable is more important than being knowledgeable. The knowledge required to achieve this is knowledge of the management of meaning, of myths and of rhetoric. Hence, if, as Jackall suggests, consultants are 'virtuosos in symbolic management' (1988: 137), impression management becomes not incidental, but, as we are arguing, central to consultancy work. Accordingly, rhetoric becomes a distinctive feature of consultancy work so that 'the degree of elaboration of the language code through which one describes oneself and one's organisation regulates client-orientations as well as identity' (Alvesson, 1993: 1007). The focus of this language is the claim to have mastery of, and expertise in, valued managerial behaviours, skills and knowledge.

The inherently ambiguous nature of consultants' expert knowledge allows them to present it as a range of stories. In doing so they can manage meanings and therefore the way in which they display their expertise to clients. In short, they tell tales. They tell tales about organizational processes and functions and about mythical manager heroes. They tell tales about miraculous strategic virtuosity, of heroic organizational turn-rounds and of battles with organizational monsters (poor quality, poor service levels, huge inventories, etc.). They tell tales about the necessary virtues for organizational success and how these virtues may be gained. One could continue with such examples, but the point is that consultants construct a sense of their value, knowledge, insight and skill through stories which allow them to manipulate language and symbols. How is this achieved?

In the remainder of this chapter we wish to suggest that the consultants' success lies in the telling of inspiring, powerful stories which generate knowledge for the client and resolve the client's ignorance and uncertainty. But the consultant's tales not only describe the organization to the client, they also define the client him- or herself, and in so doing they represent the identity of the consultant. Hence, consultants create and demonstrate their value by *creating* the manager in the course of a joint enterprise to know the organization. As a consequence, the ultimate subject of consultancy work is not the client's *organization*, but the client *as a manager*. The consultants' role, and their appeal to managers, is that consultants' stories simultaneously centre on and celebrate a new hero – the manager as corporate leader, as strategist, as saviour, etc.

A major reason for consultants being able to succeed with managers through the expert management of meaning is that management itself is concerned with the management of meaning. Consultants not only define the role and nature of management, they also demonstrate the *key skills* of senior managers. Consultants appeal to managers because they display mastery in skills which are central to the task of management. Their appeal, in part, therefore lies in their sharing with clients – and showing mastery with – a shared set of symbols about effective management.

Jackall (1988) points out that managers work within a symbolic world. He argues that mastery of the management of meaning is not just external to the core of management, it is at its core. In a similar vein, Mangham writes: 'Actors and senior managers are involved in performing, not in a performance: stars, particularly in the theatre and within business enterprises, appear live before their audiences and must elicit appropriate responses moment by moment, *reading* the situation so that they get it "right on the night"' (1990: 106). Furthermore, he notes that 'Managing is itself a form of performance: to manage is to engage in the art of performing . . . a process that involves the reading and interpretation of events and circumstances and the expression and embodiment of that reading in action on the part of the manager' (1990: 110). Management consultants may therefore support managers by simultaneously enhancing their skills and displaying the skills managers need and admire: 'Managers' use of certain kinds of expertise, namely that generated by management consultants of various sorts, themselves virtuosos in symbolic manipulation, aptly illustrates their peculiar symbolic skills' (Jackall, 1988: 137).

Management consultants convey their expertise to managers through language. Management consultants do what managers do: They use language to help their clients understand, know, classify and therefore be able to act on the world. Czarniawska-Joerges identifies three elements:

> Managers tell their subordinates what is what (they *label* things), what things are like or what they could be like (they use *metaphors*), they tell them what is normal or acceptable (they utter *platitudes*). Labels, metaphors and platitudes are building blocks for more complex control machinery: world views, philosophies, ideologies, cosmologies, business ideas. (1990: 139)

One major reason for the power of these labels, metaphors and platitudes is that they resonate with powerful values and discourses of the external world. Du Gay and Salaman, for example, argue that the notion of 'enterprise' is central to many programmes of organizational restructuring and is prevalent in many consultants' prescriptive remedies. These authors remark that 'the significance of enterprise as a discourse resides in its ability to act as translation device, a cipher "between the most general *a priori* of political thought", and a range of specific programmes for managing aspects of economic and social existence' (1992: 629).

A further reason for the appeal of consultants' words lies in their strangeness and their familiarity – their capacity to be simultaneously banal and challenging. They surprise, they comfort, they disguise, they make connections between words and actions and deny the connection or present it as natural. They show that we know – better than the client, the same as the client, differently from the client; they surprise. These labels are then used to generate insight – "that's right!" These stories work in two ways: solving mysteries or deconstructing certainties. Both indicate mastery and add value. As March writes:

> good consulting, like good theory and good art, emphasizes aspects of events and interpretative schemas that may be, by themselves, quite misleading or overstated, but that lead in combination with what is accessible to ordinary knowledge to improvements in understanding. From this perspective, the extent to which speculation is non-redundant in an interesting way is likely to be as important as whether it is precisely true. . . . Thus, it calls for an appreciation of the role of surprise, evocativeness and beauty in interpretation. (1984: 31, quoted in Czarniawska-Joerges, 1990: 149)

Words work by identifying necessary types of associated actions – costs (*reduce!*), value (*add!*), quality (*improve!*), clients (*cherish!, increase!*), etc. As a consequence, labels and words remove uncertainty and anxiety. It has been argued that labels and words familiarize and make acceptable practices such as lean production, cost control and culture change (Czarniawska-Joerges and Joerges, 1990). Dunford and Palmer (Chapter 5 of this volume) go one step further, noting how the labels and words used to describe the practice of downsizing are often underpinned by key metaphors. They note that such metaphors may therefore have played an important role in portraying downsizing as both desirable and necessary to organizational survival and competitiveness. In sum, and as Czarniawska-Joerges and Joerges have pointed out, labels and words:

> objectivize, make strange into familiar, doubtful into obvious, and by involving values close the gaping door of the unknown. They can be seen as verbal rituals, utterances whose meaning lies in the act of repetition. They familiarize by relating concrete things or happenings to commonsensical generalizations. These characteristics of their functioning suggest a similarity between platitudes and rituals, both of them being linkages between a specific present and the accumulated past. (1990: 347)

Consultants' words and stories *constitute*, make up, the world they describe to managers. As such, their seemingly knowledgeable descriptions of organizational structures, processes and purposes become authoritative exercises in power – indeed, knowledge and power are similar and inter-related. But the situation is not one where consultants impose meanings on managers; it is more one of negotiation where consultants' success lies in reflecting and modifying managers' meanings. As Mangham remarks of managers' performance: ' A successful performance is the result of a triadic collusion between author, actor and audience . . . it must be remembered that the *process* is not one of interpreting followed by expressing, but a co-mingling of the two' (1990: 107). The production (by consultants) and consumption (by managers) of consultancy knowledge by organizations and managers occurs simultaneously. 'Thus meaning is as much a product of acts of consumption as it could be of acts of production' (Jeffcutt, 1993: 23).

Following on from the previous point, consultants' knowledge offers representations of organization structures, processes and purposes to managers. Within these representations is an identity for managers themselves – a positive description stressing the importance of the manager's role. The process of client–consultant interaction is not therefore simply about the managers' being supported in their work (see below) but also about them being favourably reconstituted and redefined. Indeed, one of the unremarked aspects of the successful consultant is the way in which consultancy work carries a conception of the nature and importance of the manager in a way that would have been inconceivable twenty years ago when managers and management were, if anything, regarded negatively. They were the subject of mimicry or associated with power-game dramas, whereas today the modern manager is a hero or heroine, and some business leaders enjoy a near cult status.

Following Gergen's (1991) work, Jackson (1994) has argued that management consultants need to be able to: (1) resolve identity dilemmas for managers; and (2) reduce 'information anxiety' among managers – the ever-widening gap between what we understand and what we should understand. Jackson is basically saying that managers are increasingly uncertain of: (1) who they are, and therefore that which they should manage; and (2) the possibilities open to them in order to secure a more stable role. Enter the consultant to resolve both at once.

These meanings and identities are produced and consumed through the interaction between consultant and client. The manager does not docilely consume; the consultant does not autocratically produce. Consultancy activity, as Bloomfield and Vurdubakis note, constitutes (but does not 'reflect') reality for consultants and their clients. Consultancy talk and consultancy reports function as intermediaries between the actors in the relationship 'defining and associating heterogeneous entities (humans, technologies, institutions etc.) and thereby construct the form and the substance of the relations set up between them' (1994: 456). The organization realities (structures, strategies, environments, scenarios, competencies, etc.) which consultancy talk makes available for and accessible to management action and understanding are textually constructed, known and described realities. The knowledge practices inherent in consultancy talk set up specific relations between, and actions on, the organizational features they describe. Hence, the talk is believable because it claims to describe reality. Consultancy talk and activity is the means through which management can understand, know and calculate organizational structures and processes, and is thus the basis on which they act to achieve compliance with their business objectives. As a consequence, the process of management is itself re-defined.

Consultancy work introduces managers to ways of knowing organizations and their role within them. It enables managers to make sense of the confusion of undifferentiated events and factors. As Bloomfield and Vurdubakis (1994) note, this involves using consultancy talk and reports to achieve a textual ordering and classifying of the organization or the situation it is facing. For example, what type of organization is it or what opportunities or weaknesses exist? While such textual ordering and classification may appear to make the consultant reflect upon the "real" world of the client manager's organization, it is in fact regulating what the organization's management do since they are working within the textual framework described by the consultant.

It remains to consider the properties necessary for consultants to achieve credibility in this milieu. Consultants' stories claim authority by types of authoritative referencing often to other famous, successful, senior clients (war stories) or to accepted values and assumptions within the political environment (enterprise), etc. Legge (1994), following Latour (1987), argues that good consultancy stories are self-fortifying and well positioned. They anticipate and answer potential objections in advance; they link claims to ideas the client already accepts; they develop the elements in the story progressively building on earlier assertions; and they ensure that the client draws the necessary and inevitable conclusions. There can be no room here for ambiguity. As Bloomfield and Vurdubakis (1994) have remarked, a first step in making an issue manageable (subject to management understanding and action) is to frame it in words and analysis in such a way that the problem and its solution are clear and can be read by anyone who follows the argument. The benefit of consultants' stories must be either clear and immediate or capable of being seen as contributing ultimately to problem solving. In line with this argument, Legge writes:

> the consultant might seek to build a client base by doing away with potential clients' explicit interests: by redefining the problems presented; by inventing new problems; by seeking new clients and endowing them with problems for which the consultancy already has a packaged solution; by using strong rhetoric to render any detour invisible; by becoming indispensable. (1994: 6)

Therefore, consultancy knowledge is inseparable from the rhetoric of persuasion (Alvesson, 1994). Labels introduce order and certainty by giving names to things, and metaphors break through the banal and commonplace and create the promise of the new.

Talk and reports within consultancy achieve credibility and value by a variety of techniques. Bloomfield and Vurdubakis note the brevity, layout and style of consultancy language and consultancy reports ('the ubiquitous overheads'). The aim is to suggest economy, directness, 'to the point' non-wordy, 'strict economy in matters of communication, no verbiage, waffle, or waste just plainly stated fact: reading a report takes time, time is money'. A useful finding must be stated in a way that it can be grasped immediately. By capturing the world of the organization succinctly and economically the consultant demonstrates their commitment and capacity to achieve control over their subject matter in the same way that the manager aspires to achieve such mastery – in talk and in 'reality' (1994 : 456). If it is true, as Jackson (1994) argues, that the modern manager is beset with 'information anxiety' and doubt, then the consultant's success lies in the apparently confident grasp of, and dominance of, these ambiguities and uncertainties which he or she can resolve and dissipate through concise, economical and resolute texts and talk. In other words, putting together a strong story often requires brevity on the part of the consultant story teller.

Conclusions

This chapter has demonstrated that the combination of industry character-istics (particularly barriers to entry) and service characteristics (particularly intangibility) creates a situation in which: (1) clients have difficulty in ascertaining the quality and value of suppliers of consultancy services prior to purchase; and (2) consultants must convince clients of their worth. The inability of clients to determine the quality of individual suppliers means that management consultancies must in some way convey to their clients that they have something valuable to offer. Because clients do not know what they are getting until they get it, consultants are able to take control of the process by which impressions and perceptions of their service are created. A client–consultant relationship emerges which is best understood by using the metaphor of the consultant being highly adept at the art of story telling. Successful consultants exhibit an ability to tell strong stories. In so doing they are able to create a favourable impression among management of their value and worth. Management consultancies are therefore "systems of persuasion" *par excellence* and mastery of the management of meaning is not just external to the core of management, it is at its core.

In arguing that consultants' role and success lies in their supporting management work and reducing uncertainty in terms of their competence at managing meanings, the chapter has sought to emphasize that this is a quality managers admire because this is the essence of their work too. By telling strong stories which resonate with managers' values, and which describe what organizations are like, how they work, and how they must be managed, consultants offer a conception of management itself in virtuous, heroic, high-status terms. The work of management consultants therefore not only constitutes organizational realities, it constitutes managers themselves.

References

Abbot, P. (1994) 'Survey: Andersen retains its stranglehold', *Management Consultancy*, July/August, 24–32.

Accountancy (1994), 'News', *Accountancy*, July, 13–14.

Alchian, A.A. and Woodward, S. (1988) 'The firm is dead; long live the firm: A review of Oliver E. Williamson's "The Economic Institution of Capitalism" ', *Journal of Economic Literature*, 26, 65–79.

Alvesson, M. (1993) 'Organizations as rhetoric: Knowledge-intensive firms and the struggle with ambiguity', *Journal of Management Studies*, 30, 997–1015.

Alvesson, M. (1994) 'Talking in organizations: Managing identity and impressions in an advertising agency', *Organization Studies*, 15 (4), 535–563.

Askvik, S. (1992) 'Choosing consultants for OD assignments'. Paper presented to the International Organization Development Association World Conference, University of Coventry, November.

Bain, J.S. (1956) *Barriers to New Competition*. Cambridge, MA: Harvard University Press.

Beesley, M.E. and Hamilton, R.T. (1984) 'Small firms' seedbed role and the concept of turbulence', *Journal of Industrial Economics*, 33, 217–231.

Bloomfield, B. and Vurdubakis, T. (1994) 'Re-presenting technology: IT consultancy reports as textual reality constructions', *Sociology*, 28, 455–477.

Bryson, J., Keeble, D. and Wood, P. (1993) 'The creation, location and growth of small business service firms in the United Kingdom', *Service Industries Journal*, 13, 118–131.

Business Statistics Office (1985) *Size Analysis of United Kingdom Businesses, 1985* (PA 1003). London: HMSO.

Business Statistics Office (1992) *Size Analysis of United Kingdom Businesses, 1992* (PA 1003). London: HMSO.

Callon, M. (1986) 'Some elements of a sociology of translation: Domestication of the scallops and the fishermen of St Brieuc Bay', in J. Law (ed.), *Power, Action and Belief: A New Sociology of Knowledge?* London: Routledge and Kegan Paul, pp. 105–128.

Callon, M. and Latour, B. (1981) 'Unscrewing the big Leviathan: How actors macrostructure and how sociologists help them do it', in K. Knorr-Cetina and A.V. Cicourel (eds), *Advances in Social Theory and Methodology: Toward an Integration of Micro- and Macro-Sociologies.* Boston: Routledge and Kegan Paul, pp. 38–66.

Clark, T. (1993) 'The market provision of management services, information asymmetries and service quality – some market solutions: An empirical example', *British Journal of Management,* 4, 235-251.

Clark, T. (1995) *Managing Consultants.* Buckingham: Open University Press.

Clark, T. and Salaman, G. (1996) 'The use of metaphor in the client-consultant relationship: A study of management consultancies', in C. Oswick and D. Grant (eds), *Organization Development: Metaphorical Explorations.* London: Pitman Publishing, pp. 154–174.

Czarniawska-Joerges, B. (1990) 'Merchants of meaning: Managing consulting in the Swedish public sector', in B. Turner (ed.), *Organizational Symbolism.* New York: de Gruyter, pp. 139–150.

Czarniawska-Joerges, B. and Joerges, B. (1990) 'Linguistic artifacts at service of organizational control', in P. Gagliardi (ed.), *Symbols and Artifacts: Views of the Corporate Landscape.* Berlin: de Gruyter, pp. 339–364.

Daniels, P.W., Leyshon, A. and Thrift, N.J. (1988) 'Large accountancy firms in the UK: Operational adaptation and spatial development', *Service Industries Journal,* 8, 315–346.

Dawes, P.C., Dowling, G.R. and Patterson, P.G. (1992) 'Criteria used to select management consultants', *Industrial Marketing Management,* 21, 187–193.

Du Gay, P. and Salaman, G. (1992) 'The cult(ure) of the customer', *Journal of Management Studies,* 29, 615–633.

Evely, R. and Little, I.M.D. (1960) *Concentration in British Industry.* Cambridge: Cambridge University Press.

Gergen, K.J. (1991) *The Saturated Self.* New York: Basic Books.

Greenfield, H.I. (1966) *Manpower and the Growth of Producer Services.* New York: Columbia University Press.

Holmstrom, B. (1985) 'The provision of services in a market economy', in R.P. Inman (ed.), *Managing the Service Economy: Prospects and Problems.* Cambridge: Cambridge University Press, pp. 62–84.

Jackall, R. (1988) *Moral Mazes: The World of Corporate Managers.* New York: Oxford University Press.

Jackson, B. (1994) 'Management gurus as guarantor: The implications and challenges for management research'. Paper presented to the British Academy of Management Conference, University of Lancaster, September.

Jeffcutt, P. (1993) 'Organization studies and transformation in modern society'. Paper presented at the EGOS Conference, Paris, July.

Keeble, D., Bryson, J. and Wood, P. (1994) *Pathfinders of Enterprise: The Creation, Growth and Dynamics of Small Management Consultancies in Britain.* Small Business Research Trust Business Services Research Monograph No. 3, School of Management, the Open University, Milton Keynes.

Latour, B. (1987) *Science in Action: How to Follow Scientists and Engineers through Society.* Cambridge, MA: Harvard University Press.

Legge, K. (1994) 'On knowledge, business consultants and the selling of TQM'. Unpublished paper, University of Lancaster.

Mangham, I.L. (1990) 'Managing as a performing art', *British Journal of Management,* 1, 105–115.

March, J.R. (1984) 'Decision making and post-decision surprises', *Administrative Science Quarterly,* 29 (1), 26–42.

Meyer, J.W. and Rowan B. (1977) 'Institutionalized organizations: Formal structure as myth and ceremony' in M. Zey-Ferrell and M. Aiken (eds), *Complex Organizations: Critical Perspectives*. Glenview, IL: Scott Foresman, pp. 146–168.

Mills, P.K. and Margulies, N. (1980) 'Toward a core typology of service organizations', *Academy of Management Review*, 5, 255–265.

Mitchell, V.-W. (1994) 'Problems and risks in the purchasing of consultancy services', *Service Industries Journal*, 14, 315–339.

Nayyar, P.R. (1990) 'Information asymmetries: A source of competitive advantage for diversified firms', *Strategic Management Journal*, 11, 513–519.

Nelson, P. (1970) 'Information and consumer behaviour', *Journal of Political Economy*, 78, 311–329.

Oberoi, U. and Hales, C. (1990) 'Assessing the quality of the conference hotel service product: Towards an empirically based model', *Service Industries Journal*, 10, 700–721.

O'Farrell, P.N., Hitchens, D.M. and Moffat, L.A.R. (1993) 'Competitive advantage of business service firms: A matched pairs analysis of the relationship between generic strategy and performance', *Service Industries Journal*, 13, 40–64.

Peet, J. (1988) 'A survey of management consultancy: Outside looking in', *The Economist*, 13 February, 1–19.

Starbuck, W.H. (1992) 'Learning by knowledge-intensive firms', *Journal of Management Studies*, 29, 882–898.

Stock, J.A. and Zinszer, P.H. (1987) 'The industrial purchase decision for professional service', *Journal of Business Research*, 15 (1), 1–16.

Underwood, L. (1989) 'Management consultants look for world power', *Director*, June, 131–139.

Walker, R.A. (1985) 'Is there a service economy? The changing capitalist division of labour', *Science and Society*, 49, 42–83.

10

In the Image of Man: Organizational Action, Competence and Learning

Erik Døving

Organizational "action", "competence", and "learning" have become popular elements of organization theory (see, for example, Kogut and Zander, 1992; Levitt and March, 1988). They are three concepts that should not be regarded as real or literal, but rather as potentially powerful and appropriate metaphors that project human properties or abilities onto a non-human entity called "organization". The term used to describe this process is anthropomorphization, defined in the *Oxford English Dictionary* as the attributing of human shape or characteristics to gods, objects or animals. As noted by, for example, Kumra (1996), there is an abundance of anthropomorphic metaphors in the organizational literature, but how appropriate is their use? Allowing for some similarity between organizations and individuals is one thing; portraying them as identical is quite another. This chapter therefore examines the extent to which we can consider organizations as if they are individual human beings.

The chapter comprises two parts. Part one commences with a discussion of a number of general problems associated with the use of metaphors. It then looks at particular problems associated with the application of anthropomorphic metaphors to organization theory and behaviour. Finally, it discusses problems related to the measurement of organizational phenomena where they are described in metaphorical terms. Part two of the chapter outlines a solution to these problems, specifically where they relate to the concepts of organizational action, competence and learning.

A taxonomy of trouble

A metaphor is the application of words to something different from their literal meaning. To put it another way, it is the application of words to something in a figurative sense. This involves transferring a terminology from one domain, the source domain, to another, the target domain, where the terminology normally does not apply (Tsoukas, 1991). In short, metaphors treat things that are different as if they were not. However, while metaphors may be an efficient way of imagining a complex reality, they should not automatically be regarded as a representation of it. Strictly speaking, metaphors are linguistic mistakes and should therefore not make sense (Weick, 1979). By saying that: 'Truth is a woman', Nietzsche compared objects commonly supposed to be incommensurate and we should consequently not be able to understand such a comparison. Considered in this way, the use of metaphors can be seen as problematical.

Metaphors and some general problems

As the chapters in Part II of this volume demonstrate, metaphors are a creative, dynamic and flexible element of language (Lakoff and Johnson, 1980). Well-made metaphors may deepen and expand our understanding. In fiction, drama and particularly in poetry, metaphors are frequently used as figurative tools and are regarded as unproblematic. However, in science and philosophy metaphors have traditionally been viewed quite differently. Descartes, for example, subscribed to the belief that a "pure" scientific language free of metaphors was desirable. Metaphors were to be considered as temporary aids to be got rid of as soon as possible. Similarly, metaphors have been characterized as 'dangerous feints' (Derrida), as a 'veiling of the intellect' (Locke), as seductive (Pinder and Bourgeois, 1982), and accused of bringing too much subjectivity into the otherwise objective territory of science. Language should, it has been argued, describe things "as they are".

Organization science, possibly more than any other scientific discipline and quite contrary to the empiricists' wishes, abounds with metaphors. Some of these, such as 'garbage can' (Cohen et al., 1972), are standard elements of organizational theoretic vocabulary. Others, such as 'organizations as psychic prisons' (Morgan, 1986), while not standard vocabulary, have been the focus of considerable attention. The most important ones, for instance "organization", "system" and "structure", we hardly treat as metaphors at all. Words such as these are reified metaphors and are taken for granted as literal descriptions of concrete things (Weick, 1979).

It is hard to defend the position that we ought to pursue a literal language and view metaphors as dispensable literary devices (Pinder and Bourgeois, 1982). It is also hard to fully agree with Morgan (1986) that an unlimited production of new metaphors will benefit organizational research. Here it is posited that even if reality may be classified using an infinite number of concepts (Whorf, 1956), science – especially organization science – cannot in fact progress without some agreement on basic theoretical concepts, and these include the use and role of metaphor.

Scientific theory is constituted by (1) statements about the existence of phenomena and (2) statements about the relationships between phenomena (Bacharach, 1989). The first type of statements provide the concepts or constructs of the theory. The second type of statements are the stuff of theory: explanatory mechanisms, propositions and hypotheses. In effect this means that the second type of statement is dependent on the first in order to come into existence.

It may be argued that the two types of statements invariably go hand in hand. For example, the population ecology metaphor discussed later in this chapter encompasses concepts (e.g. population, niche, density, growth) and mechanisms (e.g. variation, selection, retention). However, since the former has primacy over the latter, metaphors in organization theory will, in this chapter, be discussed only in relation to type (1) statements.

The application of a new metaphor to a concept ought to act as a sensitizing device, helping the observer to see phenomena that otherwise would remain invisible or tacit. As research proceeds, the metaphorical language becomes far more literal in its application (Tsoukas, 1991). That is, metaphors, being primarily sensitizing devices, should be transformed into well-defined concepts with precise references.

This, though, is not a simple transition. Abstract concepts such as utility, cause, rationality, relation, function, institution, force, equilibrium or structure can claim to exist as unobservable entities. Things do not walk around with the labels "utility" or "force" attached to them. In such instances, it is very hard, perhaps even logically impossible, to empirically transform a metaphor into something that proves or disproves type (1) statements. It will therefore remain figurative.

This is not to decry the value of metphors in scientific inquiry. Scientific inquiry may be viewed as a decision process that involves alternative theories being ranked according to simplicity (parsimony), precision, generality and truth-value – with truth-value as the ultimate test of goodness. Empirical data facilitate the ranking of one theory above another. This suggests that we need an array of alternative theories to choose from. However, neither a complete set of data nor a complete set of alternative theories are ever given, both must be found or produced by the scientist (March and Simon, 1958). The larger and more diverse the set of alternatives generated, the greater the probability that the best or at least a better theory will be included in the set. In the philosophy of science the production of alternative theories is often referred to as "discovery", whereas the ranking of alternatives is referred to as "justification". These are fundamentally different processes and are both equally important parts of the overall decision process. The first process requires creativity, whereas the second requires methodological rigour. The extent to which metaphors can provide methodological rigour when constructing theory is debatable, but they play an important role with respect to creativity (Bacharach, 1989; Davis, 1971; Weick, 1979). This means that in the course of the scientific decision process some metaphors will or should be chosen as more appropriate and fruitful than other, less enlightening and less productive ones (Pinder and Bourgeois, 1982).

Metaphors may therefore be a good starting point when creating organization theory, but for us, as conscientious scientists, a metaphor, no matter how creative and elegant, ought to be far from satisfactory. The metaphor itself does not reveal what it is that makes two objects resemble each other (Pinder and Bourgeois, 1982; Tsoukas, 1991, 1993). In poetry, the reader him- or herself must imagine how two seemingly different objects are in some way similar. In science it is the other way around: explicity is our guiding star. Each metaphor must be accompanied with careful analysis that explains important dissimilarities as well as similarities. Often the process of explanation founders owing to the metaphor in question suffering from any one of four potential errors. These are the errors of commission, omission, inappropriateness and redundancy.

Errors of commission   Errors of commission occur when irrelevant information is *forced* upon the target domain (Krippendorff, 1975). Even where a metaphor appears to be a powerful image or exploratory tool, we cannot assume that all the properties in the source domain find their parallel in the target domain. Each inference about the properties or characteristics of the target domain should be tested on its own merits and not simply be assumed to work because it holds in the source domain (Pinder and Bourgeois, 1982). We must keep in mind that metaphors are constructive lies (Morgan, 1980), and we should be careful not to bring any unwanted baggage as we leave one territory and enter another (Beyer, 1992). In short, this is about the risk of pushing the metaphor too far – assuming likeness where none exists (Tsoukas, 1991, 1993).

Errors of omission   Errors of omission occur when information from the source domain does not cover everything referred to in the target domain (Krippendorff, 1975). In this case the metaphor is too restricted, it does not tell the whole story. In effect, it creates blind spots in the target domain that are very hard to detect. Important aspects of the target domain phenomena are therefore omitted from any subsequent analysis.

Errors of inappropriateness   Errors of inappropriateness occur where the source and target domains can be shown to have only trifles in common. As a result, the metaphor will be rather uninformative or completely inappropriate (Morgan, 1980). If we cannot learn anything new from the metaphor, it is both uninteresting and rather useless (Beyer, 1992; Davis, 1971), and should consequently be abolished. Moderately inappropriate metaphors may, however, prove informative by illuminating the essential similarities and dissimilarities between source and target.

Errors of redundancy   An error of redundancy occurs when all the properties covered by the metaphor are already covered by an existing concept in the target domain. In such circumstances the metaphor cannot be used to discriminate one concept from another and so becomes uninformative (Morgan, 1980). Tsoukas (1991) has argued that metaphors are used as short-hand notations for phenomena otherwise not identified with one single word or not identified at all. They are then compact ways of handling complex issues – a way of clarifying and communicating difficult concepts (Weick, 1979). Where a metaphor does not add any value as a short-hand notation it is redundant and should be abolished. This is not as simple as it seems. In practice there will be considerable disagreement about the redundancy versus conceptual value of a metaphor.

Having discussed a number of the problems associated with the application of metaphors in organization science, it is useful to introduce an example which shows how such problems manifest themselves. The example given is that of the population ecology model. It is a model that invokes the biological image of organizations being subject to demographic trends (Hannan and Freeman, 1977). Yet the model can be questioned owing to a number of weaknesses within the metaphor used to construct it.

First, unlike natural species, organizations do not have a limited life. Second, organizations cannot mate. They do not have a readily identifiable reproductive system that allows growth in numbers and secures diffusion of favourable genes to the whole population. Third, organizations do not have a breeding mechanism that secures both variation (mutation) and inertia (retention of favourable properties). In fact, the major, and perhaps only, similarity is that of selection due to competition for scarce resources and selection due to predators and parasites. Unlike natural creatures, organizations are able to migrate to another population or another niche (change competitors) and are capable of "intended mutation" (organizational redesign).

Thus, the similarities are so marginal that the metaphor becomes inappropriate, but because the model assumes a great deal of likeness, the biological metaphor forces irrelevant information upon the target domain. If selection is the only similarity, the model becomes redundant since competition is well described by existing economic literature. These problems pertain to all kinds of comparisons of seemingly different and incommensurate objects. Where the compared objects are humans and organizations and are therefore partially different, additional problems may appear. This brings us to the issue of anthropomorphic metaphors.

Anthropomorphic metaphors and problems of level

In organization theory anthropomorphic concepts can cause a lot of confusion. Some of this confusion is caused by problems common to all metaphors (see above discussion), but much of it is specific to the individual–organization relationship. This latter type of confusion is due to the fact that though organizations are inhabited by individuals it may be inappropriate to use the individual human as a metaphor for the total organization (a point also discussed by MacKechnie and Donnelly-Cox in Chapter 2).

The individual–organization relationship operates in two different ways: metaphorically and causally. While it is true that the two inter-relate, what tends to happen is that metaphorical relationships are automatically conflated with causal relationships and it is this that leads to confusion and a devaluing of the metaphor-in-use. The two should therefore be viewed as being very distinct from each other.

Metaphorical relationships assume some similarity between humans and organizations. Nevertheless, anthropomorphic phrases should be handled with care since the phrases themselves only *assume* "what" it is that makes organizations and humans resemble each other. The challenge is to clarify this "what".

Causal relationships mean that some phenomenon at the individual level produces outcomes at the organizational level, or vice versa. They may also mean that an organizational-level phenomenon is an aggregate of individuals. If the phenomena at different levels are also metaphorically related, ambiguity arises and we are dealing with some sort of *semi-anthropomorphism*. An example is Alvesson's and Billing's (1992) work, where gender is used both as a variable for explaining differences between individuals within organizations and as a metaphor for illuminating the character of organizations. In such cases this ambiguity may on the surface appear to be nothing more than a problem of linguistics, but can actually have a significant and detrimental effect on the way the research develops and tests its theory (Rousseau, 1985). Often, two detrimental effects are particularly apparent; these concern realism and confusion of level.

An *error of realism* may occur if a metaphorical relationship is treated as a causal relationship. Metaphors are conceptual tools and should not be confused with reality. Anthropomorphic concepts do not give any real or literal description of the organization, even if (as is usually is the case) the organization is inhabited by humans for whom the description is considered as literal (i.e. not metaphoric). At the organizational level the anthropomorphic terminology consists of figures of speech, whereas at the individual level we apply the terms literally. Assume (1) that there exists some individual competence and that all individuals possess some, and (2) that organizations are made up of individuals. These two premises allow us to conclude that competence exists in organizations. We cannot, however, conclude that something called "organizational competence" exists, and, if it exists, how it is related to individual competence.

Confusion of level occurs when a causal relationship together with a metaphorical relationship is mistakenly treated as an identity relationship. Even if the occurrence of some phenomenon at the organizational level (e.g. organizational learning) depends in some way upon a phenomenon at the individual level bearing a similar name (e.g. learning in organizations), the two phenomena should not be confused. Confusion of level will therefore lead to an *individualistic fallacy*, which occurs when inferences about organizational properties are drawn from individual-level data. For example, inferences about organizational competence cannot be drawn from data about individual employees' competences.

When we talk about organizations taking on human properties we are inevitably thinking of them as if they are individual well-defined actors. This can be true only in a metaphorical sense. We are then making an error of realism and confusing the levels of organization and the individual. That said, organizations do not exist independently of their members; they are products of individual behaviour (Collins, 1981; Hernes, 1976; Schelling, 1978). This view is acceptable provided that it does not drift into some extreme form of "methodological individualism" (see, for example, Elster, 1989).

Arguments for methodological individualism lead to arguments for more radical interpretations of the organization so that individual behaviour is no longer the appropriate level of analysis. Instead, chemical and physiological processes would be deemed more suitable. This would be individualism taken too far and would be tantamount to an argument against anthropomorphic descriptions of collective phenomena (Gilje and Grimen, 1993) – an argument not supported in this chapter. Rather, it is argued that human characteristics do point to the individual as the most appropriate level of analysis where, for example, we talk about the organizational phenomena of action, competence and learning (discussed below). However, anthropomorphic metaphors will only work at the organizational level where two key conditions are met:

1. the metaphor allows for a causal relationship that explains the organizational phenomenon in question as an outcome of individual behaviour; and
2. if other organizational concepts are implied or presupposed by the same metaphor, they too are justified by causal relationships that do not contradict the causal relationship under consideration.

Problems of measurement

Even if we find some satisfactory answer to the problems so far discussed, empirical investigation into a particular concept will, where a metaphor is involved, still encounter problems of measurement. These problems revolve around whether we measure the phenomenon under consideration at the organizational or individual level.

Ideally, organization-level concepts should be measured at the organizational level (Rousseau, 1985). A process of construct validation should take place that, for example, involves distinguishing organizational learning from non-organizational learning, the latter including change without learning, learning without change and non-change. Such a strategy is, though, highly questionable. The organization is an ambiguous object. Unlike people, it cannot be weighed and measured, and it cannot be interviewed about feelings, preferences or beliefs.

Most organizations do, however, produce or possess material artefacts and these might in some way be used to provide relevant measurements. They include tangible inputs and outputs, buildings and machinery, balance sheets, advertising and prices. All are important and easily observable features of the organization and its activities as a collective (Østerberg and Engelstad, 1984).

An alternative strategy is to infer organizational-level data from individual-level data. But this poses further difficulties. It requires that we have a solution to the problem of aggregation, and therefore a theory relating the two levels. To construct such a theory appears a tall order. It would need to be reliable and well specified, otherwise we could not feel confident about the validity of any organizational-level data it produced. How, for example, would one quantify each individual's contribution to their organization's ability to learn overall? In other words, theory validation would be crucial before the theory itself could be said to provide accurate measurements of organizational phenomena (Cook and Campbell, 1979; Meehl, 1990).

Resolving the problems: The cases of organizational action, competence and learning

The following sections seek to provide a new and more clearly defined framework for the analysis of organizational action, competence and learning. It is argued that this new framework goes some way to unburdening these concepts of the problems that have so far been discussed while sustaining the value of the relevant anthropomorphic metaphors.

Previous sections have posited that a concept cannot unambiguously be transferred from the individual to the organizational level. They have further posited that organizational-level phenomena should be explained as being composed of, or as being caused by, individual-level phenomena. This leads on to the proposition that organizational phenomena can be claimed to exist, but should be explained on the basis of individual actions. In other words the actions of the individual human being are assumed to be the appropriate level of analysis.

The basic model of an action is quite simple: actors find themselves in a situation or state where they are equipped with abilities or skills, and act upon this situation according to some rules, beliefs or knowledge. Knowledge and skills together make up the actors' *competence* (Nordhaug, 1993). *Learning* occurs when agents change their competence. Thus, as will become evident in the discussion that follows, action, competence and learning are inter-related, and can be neither understood nor defined independently of one another. An anthropomorphic metaphor that claims the organizational-level existence of one of them is evidence of the existence of the others.

Individual action, competence and learning

Analysis of organizational action, competence and learning requires an understanding of the thought processes and behaviour that influence these phenomena at the individual level. In this section individual action, competence and learning are considered. Subsequent sections move on to discuss these phenomena at the organizational level.

An elementary model of human action includes at least two features: the individual and the situation (Lazarsfeld, 1993). The individual is characterized by (a) some *knowledge* or belief about which actions are appropriate in which situations, and (b) the *skill* or ability to accomplish the action ("to do it right"). In addition, the individual must know which situation they are in, that is, they need (c) *information* about the situation.

If this is all that there is to human action, then we are dealing with what amounts to *obligatory action*, characterized by actors maximizing situation–action fit (March and Olsen, 1989). Information is the only endogenous variable in this model. The behaviour-guiding rules (knowledge) may incorporate norms, conventions, law, bureaucratic rules, contracts and accumulated experience. The output of such a decision is the action the actor finds most appropriate given his or her interpretation of the situation. Ideas about organization 'performance programs' (March and Simon, 1958), 'standard operating procedures' (Cyert and March, 1963), 'rules calculable in advance' (Weber, 1983), 'habitualized action' (Berger and Luckmann, 1967), 'routine' (Nelson and Winter, 1982; Silverman, 1970), 'institutions' (Jepperson, 1991) and 'habits as alternatives to thought' (Weick, 1990) all correspond well to this model.

An extended model of individual action includes future outcomes of action as well as the actor's private preference ordering of those outcomes. This model deals with *anticipatory* action (March and Olsen 1989). It calls for four types of input to an action to be considered (Grandori, 1987; Lave and March, 1975):

1. *information* about the state of the (relevant part of the) world;
2. *knowledge* or beliefs about causal relationships linking state of the world and alternative actions to future outcomes;
3. means (techniques or skills) that enable the actor to *control* or manipulate the causal relationships; and
4. knowledge (or beliefs) about the relative desirability of outcomes, also known as *preference ordering* of outcomes.

In contrast to the first model, this model makes a basic distinction between beliefs about causation and preferences. Knowledge about causal relationships helps the actor predict outcomes of different alternatives in a given situation. Such predictions must be deduced from a rule known to be valid in the situation. The validity of such a rule must be either innate or established by experience or instruction. Possession of means helps the actor to predict and control the outcomes. Means may be either skills (acquired or innate) or technology (tools, machinery). Information may be all kinds of data, objects and interpretation that define the situation. Information and means are the only endogenous variables in the model.

It is assumed that anticipatory action demands much more from the actor's decision-making capacity and that as a process of learning occurs the actor develops standard programmes for recurring decision situations (March and Simon, 1958). A sample of human behaviour is expected to be distributed along a continuum that stretches between these two extremes, with an emphasis on the type of repetitive behaviour underpinning the first model.

A theory about individual learning extends both of the aforementioned models to include knowledge and skills as endogenous variables. Knowledge and skills have already been described as forming the individual's competences. In fact there are three main sources of competence. They are inheritance (talents), the actor's own experience, and other persons (Nordhaug, 1993). The latter two qualify as models of learning. Taking *learning by experience* first, this occurs:

1. when actors' previous actions and outcomes inform decisions about the validity of assumed causal relationships or their beliefs about the appropriateness of an action in a given situation; and
2. when actors discover that repeated actions enhance their control over relevant causal relationships or their ability to accomplish the appropriate action.

Learning by instruction or example from other people is somewhat different. It occurs where other people's behaviour, the result of their behaviour, or their utterances:

1. inform actors' decisions about the validity of assumed causal relationships or their belief about the appropriateness of an action in a given situation; or
2. help actors gain control over relevant causal relationships or enhance their ability to accomplish the appropriate action.

Organizational action

Organizations do not act, people do. Organizational action is therefore defined as the sum of individual actions on behalf of the organization. An individual acts on behalf of the organization within the role they are given. Given that an organization is a set of roles and routines (Stinchcombe, 1965), it is possible to argue that the sum of organizational role behaviour constitutes the organizational routines. A single role may necessitate both goal-directed and rule-guided behaviour according to the models above.

To perform an organizational role the actor needs knowledge about appropriate behaviour and the associated skills to do it right. Part of this competence will be acquired prior to organizational membership and is what Nordhaug (1993) has termed 'firm non-specific competence'. The remaining part of the actor's competence will be acquired within the organization. Some of this knowledge will be passed on to them from other organizational members by example and instruction. Some of the knowledge will be found in the organization's documents (policy statements, charts, manuals, contracts, etc.), and will serve as examples or will give precise instructions. Finally, available tools and finished products will act – as constraints, facilitators or examples – and therefore influence behaviour.

On this basis the organization should be seen as a nexus of roles held together by interlocking micro-routines (DiMaggio and Powell, 1991; Starbuck, 1983). Taking such a perspective enables the organization to be considered as a functioning unit. Organizational action is an appropriate metaphor to the extent that the individual's behaviour can be attributed to (or explained by) their membership of the organization and the role they play in it. Were the organization to simply be viewed as an arena or as a set of exchange relations it could not be considered as a functioning unit and the idea of "organizational action" would be less appropriate.

Organizational competence

Organizational competence depends on individuals, hardware (such as machines) and documentation retaining knowledge (Krippendorff, 1975; Østerberg and Engelstad, 1984; Weick, 1979). The individual's contribution to this competence is of primary importance, as can be seen in the following example. Suppose we found organizational members had no knowledge about what to do in an organizational situation and that we found they had no documentation, skills and tools with which to execute an action correctly. We would be faced with a situation of disorganization. In such a situation the organization would lack competence.

The individual's contribution to the organization's competence is evident in a number of other ways. First, organizational competence depends, in part, on organizational members' knowledge of appropriate role behaviour and the associated skills, but in general does not depend on any single, particular individual. Second, the part of the organization's competence made up by each individual's organization non-specific competence (Nordhaug, 1993) is not affected by turnover. Third, the part made up by individuals' firm-specific competence is likely to be eroded by high turnover, but in situations of low turnover it ought to remain reasonably unaffected since newcomers will, by instruction, formal training, imitation and learning by doing, gradually acquire and replace that portion of specific competence lost by turnover (Levitt and March, 1988). Of course, transfer of competence to newcomers comes at the cost of a "learning curve", the length of which depends on the amount of specific competence needed to do a job. Where competence was not distributed among the remaining individuals or was not retained in documents or hardware, the original competence would be lost and could not be passed on to new organization members. It would have to be recovered by experimentation and experience.

The idea of organizational competence is a little discussed yet basic element of organization theory (Nelson and Winter, 1982). More specifically, it is a missing element in most conceptualizations of organizational learning. Organizational competence is what keeps an organization going, organizations function because people know what to do. So, in a sense, to describe an organization is to describe its competence, and vice versa (Kogut and Zander, 1992; Skule, 1994; Winter, 1990). Not unsurprisingly, then, it is often assumed that the competitive advantage of a firm is heavily determined by the state of its knowledge and therefore its competence.

Organizational learning

Learning is the process whereby competence is established or changed. It therefore follows that if what is learned is actioned, then we are witnessing behavioural change. For competence to change at the organizational level, the individual's knowledge about what to do must also change. Similarly, and if change does not occur by chance, there must be some kind of decision taken by its members that alters the organization's competence. Thus, by definition, organizational learning has both a cognitive and a behavioural dimension.

Definitions of organizational change revolve around types of change and the conditions necessary for them to occur. Three types of change may qualify as evidence of organizational learning. These are modification, removal or replacement of material artefacts (equipment); change of roles, rules and routines; and turnover, dismissal, recruiting and promotion (Huber, 1991; Levitt and March, 1988).

The conditions that need to be satisfied for an instance of change to qualify as organizational learning are: (1) perceived improvement, (2) intention and (3) experience. Conditions (1) and (2) are closely related. In such circumstances change can occur (a) because it is believed to be an improvement, (b) by chance, or (c) by a functional mechanism not involving intention, for example where learning within the organization and among its members occurs as the inevitable outcome of a natural and standard evolutionary process (Elster, 1983). If some change is intended, an actor must by definition believe the change will lead to some kind of an improvement. Condition (3) concerns the information upon which the decision to change something is based. This information has two sources: through experience generated within the organization or through communication with other organizations (Levitt and March, 1988).

Conclusions

This chapter has established that the application of individual-level concepts to organizational phenomena is an operation liable to encounter a range of problems. Among the most common seems to be that phenomena at different levels are confused and that primarily metaphorical relationships are automatically treated as causal relationships. The appropriateness of such anthropomorphic metaphors is seldom explicitly questioned. It is not that they are inappropriate, rather it is that a failure to question them and understand their weaknesses as well as strengths may lead to unwarranted projections of human abilities onto organizational entities. In such circumstances the insights metaphors offer to organization theory are devalued if not lost altogether.

The chapter has simultaneously acknowledged the limitations and justified the use of the anthropomorphic metaphors of organizational action, competence and learning. This has been achieved in a way that avoids confusion of level while maintaining a reasonable degree of appropriateness and non-redundancy. The framework used allows processes such as job redesign, personnel turnover and selection, experience accumulation, process innovation, technical change and diffusion of innovations – all of which are relevant at the individual level – to be classified as organizational learning. The basic argument is that an organization is not simply the sum of its parts, but comprises the actions and behaviour of its members in their appropriate roles. Organizational competence is therefore a function of organizational role structures and the way that individuals perform their roles. Organizational learning occurs only when individuals have to make changes to the way that they perform these roles.

The main challenge to researchers and practitioners of organization theory is, then, to keep organizational- and individual-level concepts analytically apart. Even where an anthropomorphic metaphor seems appropriate, we should always give a thorough account of how and why the organizational and individual levels are linked. Only then can the value of the metaphors, such as those underlying organizational action, competence and learning, be appreciated and serve a useful role in any empirically based inquiry into these phenomena.

General note

The views expressed in this chapter are my own and I alone am responsible for any errors it may contain. However, I am indebted to Odd Nordhaug for support and comments, and most importantly for giving me the idea to write this chapter. The chapter has benefited considerably from comments by Joyce Falkenberg, Willy Haukedal, Svein. T. Johansen, Torsten Nesheim and Anita Tobiassen. The Norwegian School of Economics and Business Administration provided financial and technical support.

References

Alvesson, M. and Billing, Y.D. (1992) 'Gender and organization: Towards a differentiated understanding', *Organization Studies*, 13 (1), 73–102.
Bacharach, S.B. (1989) 'Organizational theories: Some criteria for evaluation', *Academy of Management Review*, 14 (4), 496–515.
Berger, P.L. and Luckmann, T. (1967) *The Social Construction of Reality: A Treatise in the Sociology of Knowledge*. Garden City, NY: Anchor.
Beyer, J.M. (1992) 'Metaphors, misunderstandings, and mischief: A commentary', *Organization Science*, 3 (4), 467–474.
Cohen, M., March, J.G. and Olsen, J.P. (1972) 'A garbage can model of organizational choice', *Administrative Science Quarterly*, 17 (1), 1–25.
Collins, R. (1981) 'On the microfoundations of macrosociology', *American Journal of Sociology*, 86 (5), 984–1014.
Cook, T.D. and Campbell, D.T. (1979) *Quasi-Experimentation: Design and Analysis Issues for Field Settings*. Boston: Houghton Mifflin.
Cyert, R.M. and March, J.G. (1963) *A Behavioral Theory of the Firm*. Englewood Cliffs, NJ: Prentice Hall.

Davis, M.S. (1971) 'That's interesting! Towards a phenomenology of sociology and a sociology of phenomenology', *Philosophy of the Social Sciences*, 1, 307–344.

DiMaggio, P.J. and Powell, W.W. (1991) 'The new institutionalism in organizational theory', in W.W. Powell and P.J. DiMaggio (eds), *The New Institutionalism in Organizational Analysis*. Chicago: University of Chicago Press, pp. 1–38.

Elster, J. (1983) *Explaining Technical Change: A Case Study in the Philosophy of Science.* Cambridge/Oslo: Cambridge University Press/Universitetsforlaget.

Elster, J. (1989) *Nuts and Bolts for the Social Sciences*. Cambridge: Cambridge University Press.

Gilje, N. and Grimen, H. (1993): *Samfunnsvitenskapenes forutsetninger* [Philosophy of the Social Sciences]. Oslo: Universitetsforlaget.

Grandori, A. (1987) *Perspectives on Organization Theory*. Cambridge, MA: Ballinger.

Hannan, M.T. and Freeman, J. (1977) 'The population ecology of organizations', *American Journal of Sociology*, 82 (5), 929–964.

Hernes, G. (1976) 'Structural change in social processes', *American Journal of Sociology*, 82 (3), 513–547.

Huber, G. (1991) 'Organizational learning: The contributing processes and the literatures', *Organization Science*, 2 (1), 88–115.

Jepperson, R.L. (1991) 'Institutions, institutional effects, and institutionalism', in W.W. Powell and P.J. DiMaggio (eds), *The New Institutionalism in Organizational Analysis*. Chicago: University of Chicago Press, pp. 143–163.

Kogut, B. and Zander, U. (1992) 'Knowledge of the firm, combinative capabilities, and the replication of technology', *Organization Science*, 3 (3), 383–397.

Krippendorff, K. (1975) 'Some principles of information storage and retrieval in society', *General Systems*, XX, 15–35.

Kumra, S. (1996) 'The organization as a human entity', in C. Oswick and D. Grant (eds), *Organization Development: Metaphorical Explorations*. London: Pitman Publishing, pp. 35–53.

Lakoff, G. and Johnson, M. (1980) *Metaphors We Live By*. Chicago: University of Chicago Press.

Lave, C.A. and March, J.G. (1975) *An Introduction to Models in the Social Sciences*. Lanham, MD: University Press of America.

Lazarsfeld, P.F. (1993) *On Social Research and Its Language*. Chicago: University of Chicago Press.

Levitt, B. and March, J.G. (1988) 'Organizational learning', *Annual Review of Sociology*, 14, 319–340.

March, J.G.and Olsen, J.P. (1989) *Rediscovering Institutions: The Organizational Basis of Politics*. New York: Free Press.

March, J.G. and Simon, H.A. (1958) *Organizations*. New York: John Wiley and Sons.

Meehl, P.E. (1990) 'Appraising and amending theories: The strategy of Lakatosian defense and two principles that warrant it', *Psychological Inquiry*, 1 (2), 108–141.

Morgan, G. (1980) 'Paradigms, metaphors, and puzzle solving in organization theory', *Administrative Science Quarterly*, 25 (4), 605–622.

Morgan, G. (1986) *Images of Organization*. Beverly Hills, CA: Sage Publications.

Nelson, R.R. and Winter, S.G. (1982) *An Evolutionary Theory of Economic Change*. Cambridge, MA: Harvard University Press.

Nordhaug, O. (1993) *Human Capital in Organizations: Competence, Training, and Learning*. Oslo: Scandinavian University Press.

Østerberg, D. and Engelstad, F. (1984) *Samfunnsformasjonen: En innfring i sosiologi* [Introduction to Sociology]. Oslo: Pax.

Pinder, C.C. and Bourgeois, V.W. (1982) 'Controlling tropes in administrative science', *Administrative Science Quarterly*, 27 (4), 641–652.

Rousseau, D.M. (1985) 'Issues of level in organizational research: Multi-level and cross-level perspectives', *Research in Organizational Behaviour*, 7, 1–37.

Schelling, T.C. (1978) *Micromotives and Macrobehavior*. New York: Norton.

Silverman, D. (1970) *The Theory of Organizations*. London: Heinemann.

Skule, S. (1994) 'From skills to organizational practice'. Doctoral thesis, Norwegian Institute of Technology, Trondheim.

Starbuck, W.H. (1983) 'Organizations as action generators', *American Sociological Review*, 48, February, 91–102.

Stinchcombe, A. (1965) *Constructing Social Theories*. New York: Harcourt Brace and World.

Tsoukas, H. (1991) 'The missing link: A transformational view of metaphors in organizational science', *Academy of Management Review*, 16 (3), 566–585.

Tsoukas, H. (1993) 'Analogical reasoning and knowledge generation in organization theory', *Organization Studies*, 14 (3), 323–346.

Weber, M. (1983) *Max Weber on Capitalism, Bureaucracy and Religion: A Selection of Texts*. Boston: Allen and Unwin.

Weick, K.E. (1979) *The Social Psychology of Organizing* (2nd edn). Reading, MA: Addison-Wesley.

Weick, K.E. (1990) 'Cognitive processes in organizations', in L.L. Cummings and B.M. Staw (eds), *Information and Cognition in Organizations*. Greenwich, CT: JAI Press, pp. 287–320.

Whorf, B.L. (1956) *Language, Thought and Reality: Selected Writings*. New York: John Wiley and Sons.

Winter, S.G. (1990) 'Survival, selection, and inheritance in evolutionary theories of organization', in J.V. Singh (ed.), *Organizational Evolution: New Directions*. Newbury Park, CA: Sage Publications, pp. 269–297.

11

Can You Resist A Dream? Evangelical Metaphors and the Appropriation of Emotion

Heather Höpfl and Julie Maddrell

Introduction: Moses as Metaphor

It was a glorious late summer evening when Julie and her team set off for a Parfum Hypnotique training rally at the National Exhibition Centre in Birmingham. People had travelled from all over the country to be there. Julie took a mini-bus down with her distributors. She had been briefed to get them "worked up" before they arrived. They made several stops on the way and she had taken bottles of champagne to be opened en route. It created an atmosphere of opulence. They arrived at the rally to be greeted by a superb feat of stage management. The staging and setting for the event were magnificent. There were two huge silver pyramids which dominated the performance arena. Dry ice filled the spaces between the pyramids and rolled out over the audience. The scene was one of ethereal splendour, overpowering enormity: Mount Sinai in conjunction with the *son et lumière* of the Valley of the Kings. Suddenly, the founder of the organization emerged from between the pyramids and the audience went wild. Timing his moment carefully, he walked forward and raised his arms in the air, pronounced the words, 'Manna from heaven' and, at this command, hundreds of balloons were released onto the audience. The assembled gathering was enraptured. There was a palpable frenzy in the auditorium. The effects were spectacular.

Metaphor and motivation

The notion of charismatic power and rhetorical skill is considered to be consonant with the capacity to move, in various senses of the word, an audience from one state to another. In the language of everyday experience people speak of being *moved* by a performance, a visit to a particular place, a story they have heard. Such an expression suggests a change of state, a change of position, a change of experience. Something occurs in the individual's experience which brings about *movement*. The central concern in the discussion which follows is with the ways in which such movement is achieved, the role of metaphor in this process and the use of transformational metaphors in the stimulation and appropriation of the emotions for specific ends.

In the twentieth century alone, innumerable examples of powerful orators and actors come to mind – Billy Graham, Martin Luther King, Richard de Vos, Tom Peters, Winston Churchill, Adolf Hitler, Margaret Thatcher. Although widely different in their messages and overt motivations, they possess common characteristics in terms of their ability to inspire a vision, make a dream vivid and exercise considerable personal power. All of these capabilities are regarded as essential skills of the classical orator. When this type of performance is seen in relation to the emotional perturbations it creates, it can be argued that skilled rhetoric invokes the aversions, such as fear, and, at the same time, offers a vision of the satisfaction of the appetites, of sensual satiation. The skilled performer uses a range of uplifting textual metaphors, that is to say, metaphors which are concerned with feelings, in order to offer release from "burdens", or transport (again, *movement*) from their effects. Accomplished orators may offer delivery from all manner of oppression and, in doing so, they metaphorically offer themselves as *bearers* of such suffering (L. *patior*, to suffer). In their bearing, they emulate the posture and gestures of the priest and become the vicarial instrument of such suffering, the embodiment of desires, the condition for the translation of the aspirational into the tangible.

The American direct marketing company Amway is essentially redemptionist in its messages of salvation through enterprise, and its co-founder Richard de Vos is an accomplished orator. Amway markets household cleaning products yet its television programme was called *The Freedom Show* and dealt with its audience's 'dreams and hopes for the future', with the challenge 'who can resist a dream?' Distributors, presumably inspired by visions rather than the household detergents they sell, describe their experiences of visiting the organization's headquarters as '*moving*'. Put simply, they are transported from their normal world with all its pressures and cares. Distributors experience an evident sense of belonging to the organization which has done so much to confer identity and a sense of worth on them. The organization gives their lives purposes and provides the motivation for their behaviour. The ability to inspire the vision of such fulfilment is a considerable skill and can be examined via dramaturgical theories and, in particular, by recourse to an analysis of rhetoric.

The inspirational performance has a long tradition. The writings of Quintilian in the first century AD had considerable influence on theories of acting up until the middle of the eighteenth century. They are primarily concerned with styles of delivery and their effects. The predominant method of achieving propriety in acting was through rhetoric. The actor was expected to exhibit emotions as if they were his own, that is, to 'impersonate' emotion (Roach, 1985: 24). Quintilian refers to such behaviour as '*visiones*'. The *visiones* are inspirational visions, fantastic dreams based on the association between inspiration of breath and states of consciousness and with the physiological understanding of bodily humours and disposition. It affects the state of mind of the actor to the extent that simulated feelings become indistinguishable from genuine feeling. In other words, motivating an audience, in the sense of movement, depends on a capacity for impersonation. The skills of classical oratory involved the orator being energized (*enargeia*) by an image so powerful that it could be communicated to the spectators, that is, 'the spirit moves the actor, who, in the authenticity of his transport, moves the audience' (Roach, 1985: 44–45). Skilled exponents of this style are able to communicate a vision to their audiences and to do it with authority (Höpfl and Linstead, 1993). The use of evangelical metaphors, salvationist rhetoric and quasi-religious symbolism make for a bizarre pastiche of religious experience. However, in its eclecticism it produces a formulation which touches the deeply encultured dramatistic imagery of religion and its forms. By appropriating religious experience via textual metaphors, it is possible for exponents of the rhetorical style to exploit hierophantic imagery in the service of secular ends.

Metaphor and movement

In his seminal essays on figurative ingenuity, *Persuasions and Performances: The Play of Tropes in Culture*, the cultural anthropologist James Fernandez (1986) provides a forceful assessment of the contribution of metaphor and other figurative devices to human interaction and experience. Fernandez provides a basic definition of metaphor as 'the predication of a sign-image upon an inchoate subject' (1986: 31). That is to say, he takes a sign-image to be a token of communication which is replete with 'unconceptualized meanings . . . [which are] preserved in memory, rising again and again in dream or mythopoeic performance' (1986: 31). As Amway entices: 'Can you resist a dream?' Consequently, an examination of expressive behaviour is rendered more accessible via an examination of 'underlying metaphors and the subjects upon which, as sign-images, they were first predicated' (1986: 31).

It is not possible to do justice to the scope of Fernandez' ideas here, but a particularly significant contribution of the book lies in his analysis of what he terms 'the missions of metaphor' (1986: 28–70). The primary mission of metaphor, he argues, 'is to convert pronouns from their inappropriate and inchoate condition', thereby, and secondly, providing an identity for inchoate subjects and enabling movement in these subjects (1986: 62). In the discussion which follows, Fernandez' view that movement is achieved via the use of metaphor for persuasion and performance plays a central role.

It is in the relationship between movement and metaphor, with the latter as the vehicle for such movement or carriage, that the possibility of exploring motivation (as movement), emotion (as movement), passion (as bearing and as phoria) and expressive behaviour (as meta-phor) becomes apparent. Metaphor is about movement. Fernandez provides a *vehicle* for ethnographers to explore the expressive aspects of a culture. In this chapter, the concern is with an extreme variant of expressive behaviour: with rhetorical styles of delivery and evangelical metaphors. In broad terms, the argument presented here is concerned with the relationship between motivation and emotion, both of which share a common etymological root (L. *movere*, to move). Movement, therefore, is a significant aspect of metaphor as is the notion of *something moved*, something which has to be *borne or carried*. This is the *phoric* role of metaphor, where form is subjected to the weight of meaning. Metaphor bears (*carries*) meanings which confer identity on the social subject and via a series of metaphoric progressions moves the subject from one position to another. The chapter explores the significance of religious and liturgical metaphors as vehicles of transformation. Fernandez asserts that religious ritual provides a singular test to the missions of metaphor in that 'metaphors are not only rhetorical devices of persuasion . . . [but] can also lead to performance' (1986: 42). This provides the point of departure for the discussion which follows.

Liturgy and transformation

Ritual provides an important vehicle for transformation. This has significance for the transformative functions of metaphor and has particular relevance to the analysis of quasi-religious imagery and evangelical metaphors. Involvement in ritualistic behaviour is transformative. Individuals enter the ceremony in one state and leave in another. Blessings, absolution, grace and healing are sought via the experience of participation. The individual leaves the ritual site 'incorporated, empowered, activated, and euphoric' (Fernandez, 1986: 42). The use of religious imagery and symbolism in organizational life draws on the emotional associations which attach to deeply encultured imagery. The sign-images of the religious life become the means by which such associations are appropriated and by the use of textual metaphors become the transformative vehicles for contiguous associations.

However, in an investigation into the effects of transformational metaphors, the primary problem is how to gain access to inner experience. Clearly, while behaviour is observable, inner experience is more difficult to explore. In this account, an ethnographic method has been adopted in order to bring together accounts of behaviour, reflections and recollections with observations on the expressive behaviour under scrutiny (Höpfl and Linstead, 1993). Moreover, if good ethnography requires sensitivity to 'local figures of speech' (Fernandez, 1986: 28, 29) then an analysis of the use of metaphorical devices in organizational rhetoric provides a powerful insight into the mechanisms of motivation, the direction of movement and the object(s) of attraction.

In terms of the relationship between metaphor and movement and metaphor and motivation, it is interesting to consider the *passions* as motions. In fact, this provides a further consonance of ideas, since Fernandez cites Wheelwright (1962) as defining metaphor, from its Greek root, as 'change in motion' (1986: 37). Indeed, it makes transparent the correspondence between the excitation of the emotions (the passions) and metaphor as the means of movement. In relation to oratorial styles, Roach (1985) examines the historical development of theories of acting against prevailing theories of emotion in order to consider their consequences for styles of expression in dramatic performance. The book provides a useful standpoint from which to survey ways in which the passions have been understood and used in dramatic representation as an aspect of the actor's craft. In 1604 Thomas Wright's treatise on the emotions, *The Passions of the Minde in Generall*, was published. The passions of the mind were generally supposed to be of two kinds. The concupiscible (L. *con -*; *cupere*, to desire) and the irascible (L. *irasci*, to be angry). Both types of passion were concerned with the way people were drawn towards or repelled by an object which excited them. Concupiscible passions were thought to involve movement towards an object, the object which excited desire, the desire to have: greed, love, joy, whereas the irascible passions were viewed as movements away from the object which brought about the perturbation, as in fear or hate (Roach, 1985). In 1651, Hobbes described the passions in terms of appetites and aversions: attraction and repulsion. Textual metaphors are the vehicle for such movements. They provide a means for the construction of identity for social subjects and also induce movements in emotional experience. These attributes are especially apparent when considered in the context of evangelical metaphors – and evangelical metaphors are highly pertinent to the discussion that follows.

Seeing visions, dreaming dreams

In 1992, Julie Maddrell was a graduate student at Bolton Institute, UK. She had previously achieved high status in Parfum Hypnotique, then a major UK direct selling operation. One day, after class, she described her experiences of working for the organization. Subsequently, she wrote up her experiences in research notes and expressed her feelings in these terms:

They ended the presentation with the words, 'Tomorrow will be the same as today unless you do something about it now! Can you afford not to?' It was that that ensnared me into the positive thinker's nirvana. For a nominal fee I was soon on the road to building my dream and, whether I had a dream or not, I was soon to acquire one. After twelve years of working as a very committed teacher, I was drowning in despondency. Parfum Hypnotique provided me with an ideal opportunity to build my own business with no financial risk [and] to feel valued, recognized and rewarded. For the next two and a half years I committed my every waking hour to network marketing and outwardly my dreams were realized – a personalized number plate on my new Mercedes, business trips to California and family holidays aboard luxury cruise liners. The kids were delighted with the perks of mum's new business. My husband was delighted to see me so fulfilled. The local newspaper ran a story under the headline 'The Sweet Smell of Success', but for me it was all beginning to smell a little sour.

Despite invitations to return to work for the organization, Julie severed her links and became a doctoral student of the Institute.

Julie had been exposed to the persuasions of a skilled direct marketing operation and she was simultaneously part of the cycle of persuasion. She became committed to "living the dream". The power of transformational rhetoric held her captive in her own constructions and in the role of constructing such snares for others. She became overwhelmed by guilt and responsibility as she was required not only to reconstruct her own identity but also to be the instrument of initiation for others entering the process. After two and a half years, in which she had achieved considerable success, Julie became disillusioned, that is, she could no longer sustain "the dream". The aspirations which had motivated her towards the satisfaction of her appetites had become the source of her revulsion, her aversion. The power of the emblems of success no longer had any power to move her. She was de-motivated. Psychologically, she had re-moved herself outside the community. She began to deconstruct the identity she had assembled.

Direct marketing employs a range of evangelical metaphors which would be immediately recognizable by members of the non-conformist Christian churches. However, after over a decade of imported styles of corporate evangelism in the UK, the consequences of such overt manipulation and its more subtle counterparts have received scant attention in the literature. In the illustrations provided, a range of metaphors are used to move the subject from the position of his/her daily reality to an aspirational vision of the apparently achievable trappings of success. However, such aspirations are profoundly melancholic and doomed to fail. In Parfum Hypnotique, converts experienced the joy of feeling chosen, special, members of a community and people with a strong sense of direction. They were both motivated and *moved* towards the object of their desire. Julie observed:

> Once caught on the roundabout, many people become so involved that their whole life revolves around their team. Their friends are the people they recruit. Their social life revolves around company meetings. These are always fun events – bright lights, loud music, razzamatazz. For many people whose work life is routine, perhaps mundane, working in such an atmosphere of glitz becomes addictive. The alternatives cannot live up to this and even when their business is not succeeding they still pay out to go to company seminars and training sessions because their spirits are raised. They are transported out of their hum-drum existence.

This provides some clue as to the direction of the emotional change. However, it goes further. The appetite having been stirred, recruits are encouraged to "live the dream". Great emphasis is placed on the fact that the opportunity is open to anyone. Everyone is a potential recruit and once recruited a new member is introduced to the idea of commitment at an early stage. New recruits are exposed to a series of personal testimonies which are reeled off night after night around the country. Such stories are of the type, "Six months ago I was only a __ but now __". In her research notes, Julie continues:

At this point people often suffer from the hot bath syndrome, i.e. they are excited, hot, and can envisage themselves in the place of the successful. Once reality dawns, however, very quickly they go cold and so it is very important to follow with step two. Painting and re-inforcing the dream is done in many ways but several advocates of this theory encourage new recruits to experience their dream for a short period of time and the ultimate loss of it will spur them on to work harder to make the dream a reality again . . . sponsors should take their new found friend (the new recruit) to an appropriate garage (say), book a test drive in the dream machine, take sales literature and so on and then encourage their protégé to put pictures of the desired object in a prominent place in their home – the bed head perhaps.

Evangelism

The "live the dream" philosophy is primarily concerned with the construction and maintenance of illusion. For Parfum Hypnotique, the creation of illusion, the *Aufhebung* of consummatory visions and inspirational exhortation, was rooted in the use of transformational metaphors and sacerdotal stages of initiation which were designed to move the subject from the drabness of his or her quotidian experience via images of personal advancement to triumphant visions of achievement, status and power, of hierophantic transformation. The promotional events hosted by Parfum Hypnotique, with their magnificent stage management, were intended to extend the promise of such fulfilment via commitment, consummation via incorporation and, concomitant with this, ensnarement via the appropriation of emotion. Metaphors perform as the primary device of this transformation and function to *carry* the notion of transcendence of the commonplace. The immense promotional events serve to move, to motivate, to emotivate (L. *emotio* fr. *emovere*, to stir) the audience by stimulating and manipulating emotional responses to achieve a non-cognitive attachment to the organization and its objectives. The company training programmes encouraged the development of a charismatic style of leadership at each level of the hierarchy. The directors of the company portrayed themselves as "poor boys made good" and, as part of the construction of consumable biographies and the reinforcement of the mythology of heroic transformation, training sessions in the organization were normally preceded by an abundance of personal testimonies. Members of the higher reaches of the hierarchy would *offer* themselves as exemplars of successful transformation and present themselves as *transfigured*. Their appearances at such events consequently took on a profound significance so that audiences would seek the reassurances of the often told rags to riches stories which had much in common with non-conformist testimonies of personal salvation, of *amazing grace*.

Mythopoeic metaphors

The Training Director, Gregory Curtis, demonstrated his manifest wealth with ostentatious attention to detail, yet consistently reinforced his testimony by reference to his northern working-class origins and by referring to himself as a 'common working man'. His testimony proclaimed that he had *only* been an ordinary man, like them, until he had accepted the *vision* and been converted to its realization. Curtis was a man in his early forties, a practising Catholic, who drew on tales of childhood deprivation to underline his personal success story. In the folklore of the organization, Curtis had the status of a deity. In this quasi-religion of personal prosperity with its implicit transgression of the notion of an actual deity, the ultimate transformation of the initiate via the organizational hierarchy was into the Godhead itself. Curtis became the embodiment of the philosophy of success and, in transformational terms, "the Word made Flesh". His personal charisma was renowned and he was able to attract huge audiences throughout the UK. Like Tom Peters, Billy Graham and such evangelical figures, he possessed considerable charismatic and rhetorical power. His one-day training courses offered such uplift and inspiration that people would attend time after time in order to seek personal renewal and to bring new recruits for conversion. Curtis's command of rhetoric was paradigmatic. His *hagiography* was built on stories of heroic achievement, personal religious devotion and sexual potency. In other words, he was elevated by a powerful mythology rooted in earthly passions and desires. He was, perhaps rightly within the "live the dream" philosophy, the consummation of all aspirations for his followers. Rumours of his sexual generosity abounded. He was regarded with awe. On one occasion at a promotional rally in Paris, the great man expressed a desire to attend early morning Mass at Sacré Coeur and invited Julie to accompany him. Julie's team were astonished by the invitation, with its implicit conferral of sanctified intimacy and by the heightened significance of the occasion. It was regarded as an honour which could not be refused. Here the god of Mammon and God, The Almighty would be brought into communion and Julie had been invited to pass beyond the veil of the Temple in order to be present and, indeed, participate in this conjunction of sorcery and sanctity. However, it was an honour which was never bestowed. Julie can now relate with a jaundiced eye how she got up at 6.30 a.m. to keep the appointment. Curtis, however, like other returning deities, failed to appear. None the less, anxious to protect notions of his infallibility, Curtis later urged Julie to pretend that he had, in fact, turned up. He assured her that greatness by association would play an important part in the way she was viewed by her team if she kept faith with him.

Captives and converts

This recurrent religious rhetoric and imagery provided the basis of much of the proselytizing work of Parfum Hypnotique. Indeed, advice on the recruitment of a new distributor was referred to in the training handbook as 'On converting or capturing a new distributor'. The techniques are techniques of seduction and incremental commitment. The training strategy entraps the new recruit in a complex web of cognitive, connative and

affective lures. This culminates in an approach which seeks to 'commit the
family' to the same shared vision of success via the Parfum Hypnotique
razzamatazz. Curtis argued that for successful commitment the whole family
should be involved and Family Days were organized to include a Rewards
Ceremony. On one occasion, Julie was present at a rally at which two very
successful people in the organization advocated to a conference of between
three and four thousand people the benefits of *committing the children*. In
other words, ensuring that the children understood "the business", became
sellers of the philosophy and the product.

Curtis sought to inculcate a sense in which the Parfum Hypnotique
apostles saw themselves as "The Elite, The Chosen Ones". Those who saw
difficulties or who could not sustain the vision were labelled in such a way
as to be excluded from the community by their lack of understanding of
higher things. This constructed an effective inhibition against backsliding.
The all-inclusive, consensual world view of the organization rested on a
transformational rhetoric which defied contradiction. Julie made excellent
progress through the hierarchy and rapidly became a Group Director. At this
level, she found she was responsible for advancing the message and
personifying the dream for her own selling team. This required a personal
bricolage (Linstead and Grafton Small, 1990) to construct a self which could
at once characterize the *virtues* of conformity with the organization's
objectives and, at the same time, convey the image of virtue rewarded. The
noviciates came from a wide social spectrum and had varying levels of
intellectual and social skill. They shared a belief in the fulfilment of their
aspirations via dedication to the ideology of network marketing. Julie found
she had entered a priestly order. Her function was to achieve the translation
of their humdrum lives into the visions of success they were repeatedly
offered. She was to officiate at their Confirmation. This placed a burden on
her. As she began to work with her team, she realized that the only real thing
the recruits had in common was their desire to be free of their own particular
personal burden. These ranged from financial worries to difficult personal
relationships. The team began to define her role into a pastoral responsibility
and required that she attend to their various emotional concerns and
needs.

Metaphors confer identity

One example which demonstrates the way in which the passions are
manipulated is the case of a van driver from Wigan. This was a man of 29
who was single and lived at home with his mother. Harry was captivated by
visions of success and by the kinship the network gave him. He found a
purpose in the meaning structure afforded by Parfum Hypnotique which
helped to insulate him from the obvious social isolation of his daily life. In
his first month of selling he was able to exploit his immediate family,
neighbours and work associates. He achieved a profit of approximately £42
pounds over the month. This provided him with the basis of a tale of

considerable success which he subsequently presented as his personal testimony at the end of the month. However, without an obvious talent for selling, his sales rapidly diminished as his source of readily available customers dried up. Nevertheless, the story of the successes in the first month became the basis of a series of success "testimonies". While sales dwindled, his stories became more elaborate and at every meeting he would relive his moment of glory. His personal satisfaction came from recounting this "wondrous" tale of revelation and salvation, of conversion from a state of being unworthy to being worthy of notice – if only to tell the tale. Julie, who was by then Group Director, found these testimonies an embarrassment. Being part of the process of his enchantment, she also recognized the joys of the convert in his behaviour. His life had been transformed by his moment of glory and was a source of immense personal pride. However, for Julie, his roseate glow was a persistent source of guilt. She had herself been part of Parfum Hypnotique's seductive rhetoric and felt herself to be responsible for his disconcerting behaviour. She carried the burden of this guilt and, at the same time, had to cope with her concern not to betray him and his attachment to his now defunct claim to fame. Week after week he made his personal testimony and reinforced his need to feel wanted and worthy. The task of bearing this need fell on Julie.

A phoric role

Another example was that of a former policeman who had been invalided out of the police force after 19 years' service. Here was a conscientious, hard-working individual with a commitment to voluntary work whose life was relatively unglamourous and boring. For him, Parfum Hypnotique offered the allure of success and the glimpse of a different way of life. In part, his attachment to Parfum Hypnotique was personified by the charm and lifestyle of his Group Director. She came to represent the embodiment of the organization's values and rewards. Julie began to realize that the hierarchy functioned by the construction of a hierarchy of admiration, envy and opportunity. Aspects of her life which did not derive from the network became synonymous with its professed rewards in the eyes of her team and, at the same time, became available to them as part of her consumable biography. Consequently, her social standing and, later, social life became accessible to her team as if, having entered a priestly vocation, she was entirely dedicated to the fulfilment of their desires: wants which had been stimulated by the transformational metaphors of network marketing.

Perhaps inevitably, the socially skilled and middle class tended to achieve higher rank in the organization. In the minds of lower levels of field staff, the comfortable lives of Group Leaders equated with achievable success in the organization. As Julie achieved beatific status in the organization she found that she had created a team in her own image. This fitted very much into Curtis' team development philosophy. Her team was full of home-loving, warm, generally Catholic individuals who could relate to Julie and who could equate their own aspirations with her achievements and successes. Her kitchen was always full of people and at any time of the day or night the team would contact her with all sorts of problems. The reciprocity of such groups is self-reinforcing with the leader as much as the led bound by the seductions of mutual worth. However, for Julie this bond was becoming a bind. Increasingly, she found herself carrying their aspirations and the awareness that they could not be fulfilled. She found herself to be the locus of their needs and her function to both keep them true to the faith and to keep faith with them. By offering initiates a dream, the organization had established a complex network of emotional dependency in which Julie's role was increasingly phoric; a role which might be seen as the inevitable counterpart to the meta-phorical manipulations of the organizational rhetoric. She had to carry what was not carried by the metaphor: the translation of the figurative into the actual.

'The kettle was always on and the phone would ring in the middle of the night if one of them had a problem.' Initially, such sustained "busyness" had its own rewards and reinforced Julie's personal sense of being wanted and worthy. However, as her own family began to be overwhelmed by the demands and problems of strangers, she began to take stock. Her aversion to the organization and its style of operation was beginning to gnaw. Just as in dramatic representations the actor has to bear or suffer the passions that are required by the performance, in order to carry or bear the action, Julie was required to "carry off" a performance.

Insupportable roles

In the vicarial demands of her role with Parfum Hypnotique, Julie found that her mission was to "sell" a dream and to use "the vision" to move (motivate) her team. Motivational talks were scripted and rehearsed. Training manuals offered guidance on how to play the required role. She began to feel the burden of being all things to her team. An inner conflict began to open up between the need to "work up" other people and yet "hold down" her own emotions. Holding back her own feelings began to be an increasing burden and, as more and more demands were placed on her, she began to feel increasing disillusionment to the point at which she realized, 'I just couldn't carry on with it.' For over two years Julie had carried her role in Parfum Hypnotique to great effect. She supported Curtis' "leading role" very successfully and comported herself to the organization's objectives through her performance. However, once unable to sustain the appearance of a coherent, enduring, authoritative self and a commensurate commitment to the performance, she could only sustain herself by removal. Motivational devices which had once aroused her appetite were now distasteful, the rhetoric transparent and the role unsustainable. Her role as the embodiment of transformation became *unbearable*.

Insupportable meanings

The primary function of metaphor, as considered here, has been argued (after Fernandez, 1986) to be the *conversion* of the subject from one state to another. Arousing emotions in others depends on the power of the actor to initiate passions; to stir the emotions. This is achieved via the use of transformational metaphors. The type of behaviour which inspires "visions" and arouses "emotions" requires skilled performance. Competent orators can invoke both appetites and aversions and can move the audience by manipulating emotions. Direct marketing, it has been argued, functions as a type of evangelism and many of the techniques it employs would be immediately familiar to members of a range of non-conformist Christian churches. By pursing the theme of evangelical metaphors, this chapter has sought to show how, by their sales techniques and training, the specific direct marketing organization under scrutiny, Parfum Hypnotique, seeks to transport individuals from the quotidian world, with all its pressures and stresses, whilst, at the same time, establishing a complex network of emotional dependencies. The use of mythopoeic imagery and narrative is used to generate powerful associations. Over time, the objects of excitement, the inspiration of desires and appetites can become sources of dread, disgust and aversion. Parfum Hypnotique, however, is only an extreme variant of the style of corporate evangelism that has been imported into the UK over the last decade. This raises issues about the appropriation of emotions in organizational life and about the use of transformational metaphors in corporate rhetoric. Both of these issues merit further investigation.

General notes

This chapter had its origins in discussions between the authors which began in 1992 when Heather Höpfl was teaching a graduate course in Organizational Behaviour and Julie Maddrell was a member of the class. Some of the empirical material reported in Julie Maddrell's research notes subsequently contributed, with acknowledgement, to an article: H. Höpfl and S. Linstead, 'Passion and performance: Suffering and the carrying of organizational roles'. This appears in S. Fineman (ed.), *Emotion in Organizations*, London: Sage Publications, 1993.

In order to conceal their real identities, the names Parfum Hypnotique and Gregory Curtis are fictitious.

References

Fernandez, J.W. (1986) *Persuasions and Performances: The Play of Tropes in Culture.* Bloomington: Indiana University Press.

Hobbes, T. (1651) *Leviathan*. Oxford: Blackwell, 1949.

Höpfl, H. and Linstead, S.L. (1993) 'Passion and performance: Suffering and the carrying of organizational roles', in S. Fineman (ed.), *Emotion in Organizations*. London: Sage Publications, pp. 76–93.

Linstead, S.L. and Grafton Small, R. (1990) 'Theory as artefact: Artefact as theory', in P. Gagliardi (ed.), *Symbols and Artifacts: Views of the Corporate Landscape*. Berlin: de Gruyter, pp. 387–419.

Roach, J.R. (1985) *The Player's Passion: Studies in the Science of Acting*. Newark: University of Delaware Press.

Wheelwright, P.E. (1962) *Metaphor and Reality*. Bloomington, IN: Indiana University Press.

Wright, T. (1604) *The Passions of the Minde in Generall* (Reprint). Urbana: University of Illinois Press, 1971.

PART IV

METAPHOR AND ORGANIZATIONS: ISSUES AND DIRECTIONS

12

The Organization of Metaphors and the Metaphors of Organization: Where Are We and Where Do We Go From Here?

Cliff Oswick and David Grant

In their seminal work *Metaphors We Live By*, George Lakoff and Mark Johnson (1980) discuss a series of ontological and orientational metaphors. One of the metaphors singled out for particular attention is that of a journey. It is a metaphor that seems to fit all *walks of life* (no pun intended). For instance, Lakoff and Johnson (1980: 44) illustrate how it can be used to describe aspects of love:

Look *how far we've come.*
We're *at a crossroads.*
We'll just have to *go our separate ways.*
We can't *turn back now.*
I don't think this relationship is *going anywhere.*

Further examples of domains where we find journey-based metaphorical entailments include: metaphoric states as *locations* (Johnson, 1987), arguments presented as *paths* (Lakoff and Johnson, 1980), life as a *journey* and purposes as *destinations* (Lakoff, 1987). Within the field of organization science we also find the metaphor being used to portray organization development as either an *ongoing* or *discrete journey* (Oswick and Grant, 1996) and organizational change as *linear* or *cyclical* (Marshak, 1993a).

Here the notion of a journey is used as a *vehicle* for exploring the application of metaphor to organizations and organization theory. In effect, this chapter seeks to present an interpretation of *where we are now*, by reviewing the existing body of metaphor-related organizational research, and to propose some alternative *ways forward*. In doing so, the aim is to provide a broad overview, rather than detailed critique, of past work and to advocate several specific directions for future research (a "what should" approach), as opposed to attempting to discuss a fuller repertoire of possibilities (a "what might" approach).

Where are we now?

Perrow (1974) has used the metaphor of a sandpit to convey an image of the study of organizations. He describes organization theorists as being like children playing in a sandpit; each child oblivious to, and uninterested in, what the others are doing, concerned with building their own sand-castles and pausing only occasionally to destroy an alternative sand-castle that threatens to become more impressive. The vivid image of sand-castle building seems to be particularly apt when applied to much of the research pertaining to metaphor undertaken by organization theorists.

With respect to metaphor, the sand-castle built by Gareth Morgan (1980, 1981, 1983, 1986, 1993; Morgan and Ramirez, 1984) is by far the biggest and most impressive. Inevitably, it has come under considerable attack from a number of directions. Morgan's work has been criticized by Pinder and Bourgeois (1982; Bourgeois and Pinder, 1983) for *going too far* in terms of the "ways of thinking" status accorded to metaphor. Paradoxically, Mangham argues that Morgan *fails to go far enough* in describing the cognitive status of metaphor (see Chapter 1 of this volume). A number of other tangential assaults have also been launched. For example, Reed posits that one of the implications of Morgan's work is that: 'Organization theory is transformed into a supermarket of metaphors which its customers can visit to purchase and consume its conceptual wares according to their brand preferences and purchasing power' (1990: 38). Tinker (1986) argues that the organizational metaphors proposed by Morgan create a false consciousness owing to their tendency to reify and ideologically distort. And more recently, Tsoukas (1993a) has criticized metaphors in general, and Morgan's work in particular, on the grounds that they can obscure and mislead the generation of scientific knowledge. The common feature of all of these attacks is their failure to leave more than a few minor battle scars on the Morgan sand-castle.

One of the most significant aspects of Gareth Morgan's contribution to our understanding of metaphors is the *amount of ground covered*. Not only has he passed comment upon the general role and scope of metaphor (1980, 1983, 1986, 1993), he has also explored the application of specific metaphors to organizations and organizational processes (1981, 1982, 1986, 1993; Morgan and Ramirez, 1984). Morgan has, then, considered both the "organization of metaphors" and the "metaphors of organization". Viewed from this perspective his work seems to be unique. For the most part, researchers have tended to be content with limiting their analysis to one or other of these two *avenues* of inquiry.

The "organization of metaphors" track

Many researchers within the field of organizational analysis have experienced difficulty in disentangling the concept of metaphor from its original roots in philosophy and linguistics. As a consequence, the central thrust of much of the research undertaken by organization theorists during the past two decades has been geared towards exploring the "organization of metaphors" and not the "metaphors of organization".

Commentators on organizations have been preoccupied with establishing the role, and cognitive status, of metaphor. While the formulation of conceptual frameworks and the development of theoretical insights are worthy of endeavour, and indeed are an essential facet of knowledge generation, the linkage to organization theory frequently seems to be rather tenuous, almost incidental – operating as a form of illustration of, or addendum to, the main arguments. Take, for example, the following assertions: Metaphors aid understanding due to their vividness, compactness and ability to convey the inexpressible (Ortony, 1975); metaphors have a generative value (Schön, 1993); metaphors are dispensable literary devices (Pinder and Bourgeois, 1982); metaphors represent alternative ways of seeing and thinking (Morgan, 1986); metaphors have a transformational role (Tsoukas, 1991); metaphors enhance creativity (Morgan, 1993); metaphors have both a surface meaning and a deeper second level of meaning (Alvesson, 1993). All of these arguments, although appearing within the organization-related literature, are general in nature. None of them are specific to organization science. They could easily be transferred and applied to any one of a number of other fields of inquiry, and, therefore, have more to do with addressing the "organization of metaphors" than "metaphors of organization".

A further criticism of the "organization of metaphors" literature relates to the rigidity and insularity of the positions adopted by the various writers. It could be argued that an unwavering support for a particular view of metaphor illustrates a degree of polemic commitment; however, it also tends to create a false dichotomy. The reader is left to choose between a series of contrasting philosophical positions each of which is presented, to a greater or lesser extent, as the definitive interpretation. For example: Are metaphors merely fanciful literary embellishments which should be eschewed from organizational language (Pinder and Bourgeois, 1982)? Or are they a fundamental and necessary part of language (Lakoff and Johnson, 1980)?

The black and white logic which underpins statements of this kind fails to consider the contingent nature of metaphor and tends to promote an inappropriate form of compartmentalization. As an example, take the use of the journey metaphor in this chapter. Those immersed in the "organization of metaphors" debate would seek to pigeon-hole this as an either/or decision.

They might ask: Does it indicate (1) a way of thinking about research, (2) a desire to embellish an otherwise dull chapter, or (3) an attempt to overtly recognize an everyday metaphor which often passes unnoticed within most discourses? To some extent, in this particular instance, the answer to all three of the possibilities presented is – yes. References are made to: research *directions* and *trajectories*, researchers *covering the same ground*, the *way forward*, alternative *routes*, *lines* of inquiry, *departures from* previous work, and so on. However, explicitly acknowledging the use of this 'basic, everyday, conventional, conceptual metaphor' (Mangham, Chapter 1, this volume) has little to do with adding to, or strengthening, the arguments. Therefore, the underlying purpose of consciously incorporating the metaphor has more to do with embellishing, rather than extending, the text. Finally, the decision to colour the chapter using the journey metaphor as opposed to one of the other 'basic, everyday, conventional, conceptual metaphors', such as the 'container metaphor' (Lakoff and Johnson, 1980), also perhaps says something about our "way of thinking".

This simple example shows us how metaphor defies a rigid interpretation and transcends the boundaries imposed by most mainstream classifications. Metaphor can serve different purposes at different times and it can even function in different ways at the same time. If it does nothing else, one of the things postmodernism teaches us is the need to acknowledge the existence of multiple interpretations of reality (see, for example, Cooper and Burrell, 1988; Gergen, 1992; Hassard, 1994). Hence, one person's "embellishment" is another's "way of thinking".

The "metaphors of organization" track

The application of metaphors to organizations, and for that matter organizational practices and processes, has occurred in three main ways. In common with a number of other classifications (see the Introduction to this volume for details), the interpretation presented here is hierarchical. For our purposes the three levels of "metaphors of organization" are subsequently referred to as the superficial, the intermediate and the meaningful.

"Superficial metaphors" are characterized by a 'surface-level' application (Schön, 1993) to organizational phenomena. Normally only a minimal overlap between the source and target domains exists, and the nature of the relationship is often abstract or, at the very least, unclear. There are two primary motives for using this category of metaphor: first, to "dress up" speech and text in order to make it more palatable, and in some cases more memorable; second, to aid the process of making the complex appear simple, but in doing so superficial metaphors tend to oversimplify the area of application to the point that the insights generated become rather spurious.

Although superficial metaphors do not deepen our understanding or encourage us to think about the area onto which they are projected in a new way, their ability to embellish and simplify organizational concepts has endeared them to practising managers, consultants and "pop management" writers. We need look no further for examples than the work of Charles Handy, with his 'gods of management' (1978), 'boiling frogs' (1989) and 'empty raincoats' (1993). Unfortunately, using metaphor in this manner adds credence to the criticisms of organizational discourse and language made by Pinder and Bourgeois (1982) and Sandelands and Drazin (1989). Superficial metaphors have not enhanced research, instead they have clouded and constrained the generation of knowledge with regard to metaphors and organizations.

"Intermediate metaphors" have more than an isolated similarity, or fleeting resemblance, to the domain onto which they are projected. The role they are asked to play is a more sophisticated one than that of mere embellishment or simplification. They offer deeper insights into organizational phenomena and typically have a 'second order' of similarity (Alvesson, 1993). For instance, in addition to permitting an initial surface comparison to be made, the "organization as family" metaphor also accommodates a deeper form of analysis by considering second-order comparisons, such as the existence of metaphoric counterparts to the father role, the mother, the children, family feuds, family values, and so on.

It is the extension of the intermediate metaphor which stimulates further understanding, enhances creativity, and encourages new 'ways of seeing and thinking' (Morgan, 1986). Superficial metaphors do not offer the same scope. Handy's 'boiling frog' (1989), for example, does not offer sufficient scope for any further meaningful second-order insights into the nature of change to be developed.

To facilitate comparisons at a secondary level, intermediate metaphors are necessarily broad. The inherent conceptual latitude of these metaphors has spawned a plethora of "organization as" metaphors. At various times organizations have been described as analogous to machines and organisms (Burns and Stalker, 1961), garbage cans (Cohen et al., 1972), icebergs (Selfridge and Sokolik, 1975), tents (Hedberg et al., 1976), text (Mangham, 1978), churches (Pages et al., 1979), loosely coupled units (Weick, 1982), brains and psychic prisons (Morgan, 1986), theatres (Mangham and Overington, 1987), spider plants and blobs out of water (Morgan, 1993), soap bubbles (Tsoukas, 1993b) and human entities (Kumra, 1996).

Unlike intermediate metaphors, which have a premeditated conceptual base, "meaningful metaphors" are discovered rather than created. Meaningful metaphors seek to uncover the specific "metaphors-in-use" within organizations. A fundamental distinction exists between meaningful and intermediate metaphors: meaningful-level metaphors are "exposed" while intermediate-level metaphors are "imposed". Although the theoretical distinction between these two categories is fairly clear-cut, in practice "grey areas" exist. The metaphors presented by some researchers are part "imposed" (arrived at conceptually) and part "exposed" (arrived at empirically). A good example is Dunn's (1990) work on the root metaphors of industrial relations. He relies on a "quasi-empirical" content analysis of the embedded metaphors found in the past literature (the exposed element) from which his own metaphor (the imposed element) is extrapolated and conceptually refined.

When compared to superficial and intermediate metaphors, meaningful metaphors have attracted only very limited attention in the organization theory literature. As Palmer and Dunford point out: 'With a few exceptions, most applications of metaphor-based analysis to organizations involve a deductive approach in that the emphasis is on illustrating how particular metaphors can be applied to organizational situations' (1996: 10). Examples of applied work which attempts to expose the metaphors-in-use, and develop strategies for examining them, seem to be concentrated within the field of organization development and change (see, for example, Barrett and Cooper-rider, 1990; Brink, 1993; Broussine and Vince, 1996; Cleary and Packard, 1992; Keizer and Post, 1996; Marshak, 1993b; Sackmann, 1989; Srivastva and Barrett, 1988).

Where to next?

In considering where we go from here, it is perhaps helpful to briefly outline the *directions* in which future research should not go. First, we suggest the need for further research into the "organization of metaphors" is questionable. Second, no direct research benefits are likely to accrue from actively pursuing the formulation of more "superficial metaphors". In effect, both of these possible directions are *dead ends* in terms of research. Finally, the generation of "intermediate metaphors" constitutes a particularly *well-trodden path* which offers only very limited scope for further inquiry.

While arguing that more research into the "organization of metaphors" is unrequired, it is important to acknowledge that the work undertaken thus far has generally been well focused and of considerable value. Researchers in this domain have helped to *transport* and reinterpret concepts taken from philosophy, linguistics and cognitive psychology and apply them to organization theory. This process has done much to popularize metaphor-related research and, more importantly, it has been instrumental in placing parameters on, and helping to crystallize, organization theorists' understanding of metaphors.

As with most fields of inquiry, theorizing of the kind undertaken within the "organization of metaphors" *track*, is a necessary precursor to well-focused empirical work. However, we contend that the scope for fresh insights, and therefore more research, is limited. Furthermore, the body of knowledge generated is sufficiently disseminated amongst an organization theory audience that researchers immersed in metaphor are likely to turn to the rich vein of original sources which lie outside of the discipline. The external body of available literature is exemplified by sources such as Van Noppen and Hols (1990), who have produced a classified bibliography of research on metaphor which contains more than three and a half thousand references to work published between 1985 and 1990.

Having discussed where we should not go, let us now turn our attentions to the *directions* we should be heading in. In the remainder of this chapter three main research *routes* are presented, namely:

1. The need for more applied research on metaphor in organization theory and analysis.
2. Using metaphor as a *vehicle* for, rather than target of, research.
3. Greater exploration of the other tropes which are closely related to metaphor.

Route 1: More applied research

Whether we call them dominant metaphors, root metaphors, embedded metaphors or meaningful metaphors, we still have only the most partial of insights into the fundamental metaphors which underpin and shape organization theory and organizational action. It is tempting, given the paucity of research into the metaphors-in-use, to suggest that any applied research would be "good" research. However, in order to further our understanding and knowledge we particularly need empirical work that isolates and makes transparent the metaphors, and groups of metaphor, prevalent in the discourse on organizations and those to be found within organizational settings.

The theoretical assertions made within the "organization of metaphors" literature also need to be rigorously tested. For example: Do metaphors illuminate (Ortony, 1993) or obscure organizational phenomena (Pinder and Bourgeois, 1982)? Do they shape our thoughts (Morgan, 1986)? Do they influence our behaviour (Tsoukas, 1991)? Do they liberate (Barrett and Cooperrider, 1990) or reify and ideologically distort our views of organizations (Tinker, 1986)? Without further grounded research the answers to such questions remain somewhat inconclusive. More work of the kind undertaken by Clegg and Gray (Chapter 4, this volume), which goes some way to addressing several of these issues, is clearly required.

A variety of research methodologies are at hand for those wishing to capture the metaphors embedded within the "talk" and "text" of organizations. For example, Dunford and Palmer's macro-level examination of the metaphors associated with corporate restructuring (see Chapter 5, this volume) illustrates the merits of scrutinizing text using an approach based upon 'Content Analysis' (Holsti, 1969). Another example of discursive research is found in the work of Broussine and Vince (1996), who used a micro-level 'dialogical approach' (Randall and Southgate, 1981) to explore the metaphors used by a group of public sector managers to convey their feelings towards externally imposed change. Other possible methodologies include: discourse analysis (Marshall, 1994), conversation analysis (Psathas, 1994), narrative analysis (Kohler-Reissman, 1993), semiotic analysis (Manning and Cullum-Swan, 1994), case study method (Stake, 1995), action research (Whyte, 1991), and new paradigm research techniques (Reason, 1988). The approaches presented here are intended to be illustrative rather than exhaustive; there are undoubtedly other meaningful and novel ways of studying metaphors.

Route 2: Using metaphors for research

Instead of thinking of metaphors as a target of organizational research it is possible to think of them as a device for enhancing such research. In this sense, they can provide a means to an end rather than being an end in themselves.

If, as Burke suggests, the metaphors used by stakeholders in organizations 'are windows into the soul, if not collective unconscious, of the social system' (1992: 255), they represent a powerful medium for gathering data and developing new insights into organizational phenomena. Brink *goes as far* as to advocate treating 'metaphors as data' (1993: 366). Although this proposition is not without merit, we must not lose sight of the dangers and difficulties of interpretation. As Davidson points out: 'Metaphor is the dreamwork of language and, like all dreamwork, its interpretation reflects as much on the interpreter as on the originator' (1978: 99).

Ortony contends that 'vividness', 'compactness' and the 'ability to convey the inexpressible' are qualities which make metaphor a valuable aid to learning (1975: 45). These three qualities also have the potential to enhance research. First, the compactness and vividness of metaphor can help to ensure that manageable amounts of valid data are generated. Second, metaphors can provide a means of accessing the aspects of organizational life that respondents would otherwise find difficult to articulate in literal terms.

There are two main ways in which metaphors can be used for research, ways which fit in with Burrell and Morgan's classification of methodology as being either 'nomothetic or idiographic' (1979: 6). The defining characteristics of nomothetic approaches being that they 'are group centred; employ standardized, controlled environmental contexts; quantitative methods; and seek to establish general laws' (Oswick et al., 1996: 144). By contrast, idiographic approaches focus on the individual, use naturalistic environmental contexts, qualitative methods, and seek to explore the unique experiences of the individual.

The nomothetic application of metaphors involves using them as part of a standardized procedure where the metaphors available to respondents are prescribed and restricted. In its simplest form this might involve asking a group of respondents to identify which one of a specified set of metaphors best fits or describes their organization. The major advantage of this approach is that it accommodates direct comparisons between respondents and, by assigning values to the responses, also enables statistical techniques to be used to analyse the data generated. A number of possible variations exist within the basic nomothetic research framework, all of which draw upon a fixed set of metaphoric alternatives. For example:

1. Ranking – listing the metaphors in ascending (or descending) order according to "most like" and "least like" the target domain. *Example – The organization is: (1) most like a prison, (2) next most like a kindergarten, (3) like a circus, and (4) least like a marching band.*

2. Ipsative questions – forced comparison between a pair of metaphors. *Example – Is your manager more like: (a) a juggernaut or (b) a sports car?*

3. Likert-scaled questions – selecting from a range of graduated responses to a metaphorical statement. *Example – My work colleagues are like vultures. Do you: (1) strongly agree, (2) agree, (3) feel undecided, (4) disagree, or (5) strongly disagree?*

Nomothetic instruments are useful for gathering a limited amount of data from a large sample. Consequently, this methodology can be described as offering considerable "breadth", but at the expense of "depth". If we wish to gain deeper metaphorical insights we need to turn to idiographic approaches.

Rather than relying upon a cluster of metaphors fixed by the researcher, the idiographic approach encourages the participants to generate the metaphors and allows them to ascribe their own meaning to the selections made. Among the more traditional methods available for achieving these aims are interviews and questionnaires. The general format of both of these techniques should, however, incorporate the use of open questions and avoid being too structured and directive. Edgren (1990) advocates an approach to studying organizational culture, referred to as the 'commando model', which includes asking "metaphor-based open questions". Typical questions include: 'If the corporation were an animal, what animal would you choose? Describe your animal', and 'If the corporation were a season, which would you choose? Describe your season' (1990: 57). Edgren suggests the approach is a particularly useful way to collect data in situations where researchers have limited time and resources. The speed and clarity with which data can be generated and interpreted is due, at least in part, to the 'vividness and compactness' (Ortony, 1975) of expression that metaphor permits.

Another idiographic alternative which embraces metaphor is the projective process of getting subjects to draw, and then interpret, a picture which represents the target domain (Broussine and Vince, 1996). By providing a visual image, as opposed to the more common verbal representation of metaphor, this approach offers the potential for glimpses into unarticulated feelings and attitudes. As Krantz reminds us, the compelling aspect of metaphor is not the 'mental image itself but the way in which the image reaches into the subjective terrain of unconscious experience' (1990: 242).

Finally, it is possible to develop a further research technique, which is part idiographic and part nomothetic, based upon a modified version of the 'repertory grid' (Kelly, 1955). In attempting to elicit personal constructs the repertory grid technique draws upon the same cognitive foundations as metaphor, given that 'a construct is a way in which two things are alike and in the same way different from a third' (Oppenheim, 1966: 209). The set of "elements" which are randomly compared in order to generate constructs are normally concrete concepts expressed in literal terms. It is possible to substitute these elements for metaphorical ones, and thereby expand the potential for fresh, innovative 'ways of seeing and thinking' (Morgan, 1986) about organizations and organizational constructs.

Route 3: The scope for other tropes

In an age where postmodernism has shone a spotlight upon language and discourse it is rather surprising that the close relatives of metaphor (namely synecdoche, metonymy and irony) have not been subjected to greater scrutiny. If we disregard metaphor, research which examines the nature and application of the tropes within the field of organization theory is scarce. Even within the much broader field of linguistics we find that tropological research 'is not nearly so extensive as that on metaphor' (Gibbs, 1993: 253). It would appear that synecdoche, metonymy and irony have been over-shadowed by metaphor. On the limited occasions where they are deemed to have warranted discussion, it has typically been in relation to metaphor, rather than as areas worthy of attention in their own right. As suggested in the Introduction to this volume, there has been a long-standing debate both within, and outside of, organization theory on the positioning of metaphor and the other tropes in terms of their relative status and value.

Do metaphors prefigure the ground to be studied through the use of tropes (Morgan, 1983)? Are all of the tropes, including metaphor, equally abstract and illuminating (Manning, 1979)? Is metaphor less sophisticated than the other tropes (White, 1978; Winner and Gardner, 1993)? In some ways, semantic questions of this kind divert attention away from exploring the tropes-in-use within organizations. Does it really matter whether one trope is more sophisticated, or cognitively superior, to another? The limited research which has been undertaken thus far has, to coin a phrase, focused upon "the organization of tropes, rather than the tropes of organization".

There are a number of potentially fruitful lines of inquiry open to researchers. For instance: To what extent is the notion of organizational culture metonymical or synecdochic? Arguably, the concepts of "organiz-ing" and "organizational culture" are conflated within the popular manage-ment discourse (see, for example, Deal and Kennedy, 1982; Ouchi, 1981; Peters and Waterman, 1982). Organizational culture (as the part) is often used to stand for the organization (the whole). This metonymic confusion of levels has perhaps contributed to the formation of the "pop management" falsehood of cultural change as the cure for all organizational ills.

In the case of irony, the idea that it entails 'a juxtaposing of opposites' (Brown, 1977: 174) surely offers substantial scope for further investigation in organization theory. For instance, there may well be considerable potential for uncovering "the ironic" within the domain of management rhetoric. Further concrete examples of the potential for irony can be found with organizations. Take, for example, the concurrent, and somewhat paradoxical, pursuit of "empowerment" (a process which supposedly enhances autonomy), and "business process re-engineering" (which, with its Tayloristic overtones, tends to reduce discretion).

Conclusions

Having just discussed irony, it is somewhat ironic that the completeness, forcefulness and lucidity of Gareth Morgan's arguments have perhaps stifled research into metaphors in organization science. Researchers find it difficult to *move beyond* the parameters set by Morgan and hence a considerable amount of time has been devoted to challenging, reinterpreting, reproducing and applying his ideas. In order for further progress to be made in terms of knowledge generation, organization theorists need to break free from Morgan's way of thinking about metaphors and start to develop their own alternative insights.

The research *directions* presented in this chapter are necessarily broad and they may well say more about our "way of thinking" about metaphor than they actually do about future research. However, it is hoped that the *routes* outlined in this chapter may, at the very least, provide some inspiration for those wishing to break Morgan's "spell" over metaphor.

References

Alvesson, M. (1993) 'The play of metaphors', in J. Hassard and M. Parker (eds), *Postmodernism and Organizations*. London: Sage Publications, pp. 114–131.

Barrett, F.J. and Cooperrider, D.L. (1990) 'Generative metaphor intervention: A new behavioral approach for working with systems divided by conflict and caught in defensive perception', *Journal of Applied Behavioral Science*, 23 (4), 219–244.

Bourgeois, V.W. and Pinder, C.C. (1983) 'Contrasting philosophical perspectives in administrative science: A reply to Morgan', *Administrative Science Quarterly*, 28 (4), 608–613.

Brink, T.L. (1993) 'Metaphor as data in the study of organizations', *Journal of Management Inquiry*, 2, 366–371.

Broussine, M. and Vince, R. (1996) 'Working with metaphor towards organizational change', in C. Oswick and D. Grant (eds), *Organization Development: Metaphorical Explorations*. London: Pitman Publishing, pp. 557–572.

Brown, R.H. (1977) *A Poetic for Sociology*. New York: Cambridge University Press.

Burke, W.W. (1992) 'Metaphors to consult by', *Group and Organization Management*, 17 (3), 255–259.

Burns, T. and Stalker, G.M. (1961) *The Management of Innovation*. London: Tavistock.

Burrell, G. and Morgan, G. (1979) *Sociological Paradigms and Organizational Analysis*. London: Heinemann.

Cleary, C. and Packard, T. (1992) 'The use of metaphor in organizational assessment and change', *Group and Organization Management*, 17 (3), 229–241.

Cohen, M.D., March, J.G. and Olsen, J.P. (1972) 'A garbage can model of organizational choice', *Administrative Science Quarterly*, 17 (1), 1–25.

Cooper, R. and Burrell, G. (1988) 'Modernism, postmodernism and organizational analysis: An introduction', *Organization Studies*, 9 (1), 91–112.

Davidson, D. (1978) 'What metaphors mean', in S. Sacks (ed.), *On Metaphor*. Chicago: University of Chicago Press, pp. 97–128.

Deal, T.E. and Kennedy, A.A. (1982) *Corporate Cultures*. Reading, MA: Addison-Wesley.

Dunn, S. (1990) 'Root metaphor in the old and new industrial relations', *British Journal of Industrial Relations*, 28, 1–31.

Edgren, L.D. (1990) 'The commando model: A way to gather and interpret cultural data', in B.A. Turner (ed.), *Organizational Symbolism*. Berlin: Walter de Gruyter, pp. 48–75.

Gergen, K.J. (1992) 'Organization theory in the postmodern era', in M. Reed and M. Hughes (eds), *Rethinking Organization: New Directions in Organization Theory and Analysis*. London: Sage Publications, pp. 207–226.

Gibbs, R.W., Jr. (1993) 'Process and products in making sense of tropes', in A. Ortony (ed.), *Metaphor and Thought* (2nd edn). Cambridge: Cambridge University Press, pp. 252–276.

Handy, C. (1978) *Understanding Organizations*. London: Penguin.

Handy, C. (1989) *The Age of Unreason*. Boston: Harvard Business School Press.

Handy, C. (1993) *The Empty Raincoat*. London: Random House Business Books.

Hassard, J. (1994) 'Postmodern organizational analysis: Toward a conceptual framework', *Journal of Management Studies*, 31 (3), May, 303–324.

Hedberg, B., Nystrom, C. and Starbuck, W. (1976) 'Camping on seesaws: Prescriptions for a self-designing organization', *Administrative Science Quarterly*, 21 (1), 41–63.

Holsti, O.R. (1969) *Content Analysis for the Social Sciences and Humanities*. Reading, MA: Addison-Wesley.

Johnson, M. (1987) *The Body in the Mind: The Bodily Basis of Meaning, Reasoning and Imagination*. Chicago: University of Chicago Press.

Kelly, G.A. (1955) *The Psychology of Personal Constructs*. New York: Norton.

Keizer, J. and Post, G. (1996) 'The metaphoric gap as a catalyst of change', in C. Oswick and D. Grant (eds), *Organization Development: Metaphorical Explorations*. London: Pitman Publishing, pp. 90–105.

Kohler-Reissman, C. (1993) *Narrative Analysis*. Qualitative Research Methods Series (Vol. 30). Beverly Hills, CA: Sage Publications.

Krantz, J. (1990) 'Comments on the Barrett and Cooperrider article', *Journal of Applied Behavioral Science*, 26 (2), 241–243.

Kumra, S. (1996) 'The organization as a human entity', in C. Oswick and D. Grant (eds), *Organization Development: Metaphorical Explorations*. London: Pitman Publishing, pp. 35–53.

Lakoff, G. (1987) *Women, Fire and Dangerous Things: What Categories Reveal about the Mind*. Chicago: University of Chicago Press.

Lakoff, G. and Johnson, M. (1980) *Metaphors We Live By*. Chicago: University of Chicago Press.

Mangham, I.L. (1978) *Interactions and Interventions in Organizations*. New York: John Wiley and Sons.

Mangham, I.L. and Overington, M.A. (1987) *Organizations as Theatre: A Social Psychology of Dramatic Appearances*. Chichester: John Wiley and Sons.

Manning, P.K. (1979) 'Metaphors of the field: Varieties of organizational discourse', *Administrative Science Quarterly*, 24 (4), 660–671.

Manning, P.K. and Cullum-Swan, B. (1994) 'Narrative, content and semiotic analysis', in N.K. Denzin and Y.S. Lincoln (eds), *Handbook of Qualitative Research*. Newbury Park, CA: Sage Publications, pp. 86–109.

Marshak, R. (1993a) 'Lewin meets Confucius: A re-view of the OD model of change', *Journal of Applied Behavioral Science*, 27 (4), 393–415.

Marshak, R. (1993b) 'Managing the metaphors of change', *Organization Dynamics*, 22, 44–56.

Marshall, H. (1994) 'Discourse analysis in an occupational context', in C. Cassell and G. Symon (eds), *Qualitative Methods in Organizational Research*. London: Sage Publications, pp. 75–104.

Morgan, G. (1980) 'Paradigms, metaphors, and puzzle solving in organization theory', *Administrative Science Quarterly*, 25 (4), 605–622.

Morgan, G. (1981) 'The schismatic metaphor and its implications for organizational analysis', *Organization Studies*, 2 (1), 23–44.

Morgan, G. (1982) 'Cybernetics and organization theory: Epistemology or technique?', *Human Relations*, 35 (7), 521–537.

Morgan, G. (1983) 'More on metaphor: Why we cannot control tropes in administrative science', *Administrative Science Quarterly*, 28 (4), 601–607.

Morgan, G. (1986) *Images of Organization*. Beverly Hills, CA: Sage Publications.

Morgan, G. (1993) *Imaginization: The Art of Creative Management*. London: Sage Publications.

Morgan, G. and Ramirez, R. (1984) 'Action learning: A holographic metaphor for guiding social change', *Human Relations*, 37, 1–28.

Oppenheim, A.N. (1966) *Questionnaire Design and Attitude Measurement*. Aldershot: Gower.

Ortony, A. (1975) 'Why metaphors are necessary and not just nice', *Educational Theory*, 25, 45–53.

Ortony, A. (1993) 'Metaphor, language and thought', in A. Ortony (ed.), *Metaphor and Thought* (2nd edn). Cambridge: Cambridge University Press, pp. 1–17.

Oswick, C. and Grant, D. (1996) 'Organization development and metaphor: Mapping the territory', in C. Oswick and D. Grant (eds), *Organization Development: Metaphorical Explorations*. London: Pitman Publishing, pp. 1–3.

Oswick, C., Lowe, S. and Jones, P.J. (1996) 'Organizational culture as personality: Lessons from psychology', in C. Oswick and D. Grant (eds), *Organization Development: Metaphorical Explorations*. London: Pitman Publishing, pp. 137–153.

Ouchi, W.A. (1981) *Theory Z: How American Business Can Meet the Japanese Challenge*. Reading, MA: Addison-Wesley.

Pages, M., Bonetti, M. and Gaulejac, V. de (1979) *L'Emprise de L'organisation*. Paris: Presses Universitaires de France.

Palmer, I. and Dunford, R. (1996) 'Understanding organizations through metaphor', in C. Oswick and D. Grant (eds), *Organization Development: Metaphorical Explorations*. London: Pitman Publishing, pp. 7–19.

Perrow, C. (1974) ' "Zoo story" or "Life in the organizational sandpit" ', in Open University Course Team (eds), *Social Sciences: A Third Level Course in People and Organizations*. Milton Keynes: Open University Press, pp. 146–168.

Peters, T.J. and Waterman, R.H. (1982) *In Search of Excellence: Lessons from America's Best-Run Companies*. New York: Harper and Row.

Pinder, C.C. and Bourgeois, V.W. (1982) 'Controlling tropes in administrative science', *Administrative Science Quarterly*, 27 (4), 641–652.

Psathas, G. (1994) *Conversation Analysis: The Study of Talk-in-Interaction*. Qualitative Research Methods Series (Vol. 35). Beverly Hills, CA: Sage Publications.

Randall, R. and Southgate, J. (1981) 'Doing dialogical research', in P. Reason and J. Rowan (eds), *Human Inquiry: A Sourcebook of New Paradigm Research*. Chichester: John Wiley and Sons, pp. 150–172.

Reason, P. (ed.) (1988) *Human Inquiry in Action: Developments in New Paradigm Research*. London: Sage Publications.

Reed, M. (1990) 'From paradigms to images: The paradigm warrior turns post-modernist guru', *Personnel Review*, 19, 35–40.

Sackmann, S. (1989) 'The role of metaphors in organization transformation', *Human Relations*, 42 (6), 463–485.

Sandelands, L. and Drazin, R. (1989) 'On the language of organization theory', *Organization Studies*, 10 (4), 457–478.

Schön, D. (1993) 'Generative metaphor: A perspective on problem setting in social policy', in A. Ortony (ed.), *Metaphor and Thought* (2nd edn). Cambridge: Cambridge University Press, pp. 135–161.

Selfridge, R.J. and Sokolik, S.L. (1975) 'A comprehensive view of organization development', *Business Topics*, Winter, 10–14.

Srivastva, S. and Barrett, F. (1988) 'The transforming nature of metaphors in group development: A study in group theory', *Human Relations*, 41 (1), 31–64.

Stake, R.E. (1995) *The Art of Case Study Research*. Newbury Park, CA: Sage Publications.

Tinker, T. (1986) 'Metaphor or reification: Are radical humanists really libertarian anarchists?', *Journal of Management Studies*, 25, 363–384.

Tsoukas, H. (1991) 'The missing link: A transformational view of metaphors in organizational science', *Academy of Management Review*, 16 (3), 566–585.

Tsoukas, H. (1993a) 'Analogical reasoning and knowledge generation in organization theory', *Organization Studies*, 14 (3), 323–346.

Tsoukas, H. (1993b) 'Organizations as soap bubbles: An evolutionary perspective', *Systems Practice*, 6 (5), 501–515.

Van Noppen, J.P. and Hols, E. (eds.) (1990) *Metaphor II: A Classified Bibliography of Publications from 1985–1990*. Philadelphia: John Benjamin.

Weick, K. (1982) 'Managing change among loosely coupled systems', in P. Goodman and Associates, *Change in Organizations*. San Francisco: Jossey-Bass, pp. 375-408.

White, H. (1978) *The Tropics of Discourse*. Baltimore: Johns Hopkins University Press.

Whyte, W.F. (ed.) (1991) *Participatory Action Research*. Newbury Park, CA: Sage Publications.

Winner, E. and Gardner, H. (1993) 'Metaphor and irony: Two levels of understanding', in A. Ortony (ed.), *Metaphor and Thought* (2nd edn). Cambridge: Cambridge University Press, pp. 425–445.

13

An Afterword: Is There Anything More to be Said About Metaphor?

Gareth Morgan

I am delighted that David Grant and Cliff Oswick have asked me to write the closing chapter to this collection of essays. Having more or less refrained from reading and writing about metaphor in recent years, in favour of what I will call the praxis of "doing metaphor", the opportunity is very timely. It has afforded me the chance to catch up with recent contributions to the metaphor debate and pull together some of the notes, reflections and thoughts drawn from my experience of the last few years.

To begin, let us applaud the objective of the volume.

It is indeed time to take stock of our understanding of the nature and role of metaphor in the study of organization. The essays presented seem to capture a wide range of contributions and interpretations. As will become evident from what I have to say, I do not think that it is possible or productive to try to make a complete and definitive statement on the nature of the field, even if, for the sake of convenience, we limit "the field" to the essays presented in this volume. There are so many differences and nuances in what is being said. My aim in writing this closing chapter, therefore, is just to provide a point of reference that may place some of the ideas and arguments in fresh perspective.

I will start by outlining my own view of metaphor. It is inherently a personal view, since that is the only place one can ever start. I want to be explicit about this, because I feel that one of the big problems in this field rests in the fact that people often assert their own personal perspective on metaphor as "the view", or the " best view", when in point of fact it is just "a view" that happens to make sense from their perspective. It is a simple trap to fall into, and I willingly recognize that some of my own writings, especially the early ones, share this problem.

Metaphor is a process

Metaphor is a process that involves the "carrying over" or crossing of one element of experience into another. This results in metaphors (note the 's') as images or words that are used to create and express meaning. Since these images and words are found most obviously in language, metaphor is most often seen as a linguistic phenomenon. However, the linguistic aspect is just a surface expression of a deeper process. This is why I like to describe metaphor as a primal, generative process that is fundamental to the creation of human understanding and meaning in all aspects of life. We typically understand one phenomenon through another. This is the basic crossing that creates meaning as we engage, organize and seek to understand our world. We consciously use new metaphor to explore and understand the new. But, by implication, we also use what may be described as "old metaphor" to negotiate what we already know, or think we know. I thus fully agree with the authors in this volume who treat metaphor as a constitutive, generative force – as a form of life and experience rather than as an "optional extra". To quote the closing sentences from the essay by Clegg and Gray (Chapter 4): 'Metaphors are inevitable and useful. They are not embellishments. No pure space exists outside their spell. They are part of our craft. They form our life as researchers. Without them we would be nowhere that we could know.' The only point I would add is that the sentiment expressed here is even more powerful when you talk about the process of metaphor, rather than of metaphors, per se.

Obviously, there is still an enormous amount that needs to be learned about how metaphor works, and about the pervasiveness and character of its influence. My hunch is that many of the most important future break-throughs here will come from the domains of cognitive and brain research and from the field of artificial intelligence, rather than from those of linguistics and philosophy. As I reflect on the issues in my own experience, I am constantly amazed at the extent to which the basic crossing of meaning found in metaphor inhabits areas of experience and emotion that you would never expect. Consider, for example, how people may respond to remote events that touch their lives. For example, you read in the newspaper of a sick child. How is this information processed? Chances are that the news is experienced metaphorically through one's own personal experience as a parent, through empathy for a friend with a child in a similar situation, or through some other relevant frame. It may seem to be stretching the point to say that this is metaphor. But the process of experiencing the one domain through another seems to be what metaphor is all about. I do not want to get entangled in detailed discussion here. My point is that when you view metaphor as a primal human process, there is much more than meets the eye.

Metaphor is ontological and epistemological

This point is implicit in the above, but deserves to be emphasized in its own right.

Metaphor, as a primal process, is ontological. It belongs to the realm of "Being".

Metaphors (note the 's' again) are epistemological, in that they give us specific frames for viewing the world. By changing our metaphors we can learn to "see" and understand in different ways and gain different kinds of knowledge.

It seems to me that much of the debate and confusion about the role of metaphor can be clarified if we bear this distinction in mind. Many of the people who are attacking the role and usefulness of metaphor in science or organization studies are implicitly casting the attack at an epistemological level. Often, their attack is fuelled by their dislike of a particular metaphor, or by the very idea that metaphor has a role to play in serious inquiry. They worry about whether metaphors are "too pervasive", "need to be controlled", or "limited in use". When you step back from this debate, and see it from an ontological view, everything appears in a new light. It becomes clear that metaphors aren't optional; they're inevitable. The point is well made in the introductory chapter to this volume, and also by Mangham (Chapter 1), who, following Lakoff and Johnson (1980), draws attention to the way metaphor pervades ordinary language. It is in language use that we see the ontological dimension of metaphor expressed most clearly, because it is everywhere. It is impossible to avoid. Whenever we speak or write, we leave a metaphorical trail, because our speaking and writing are giving form to a metaphorical mode of experiencing the world.

Whether we are "for" or "against" the use of metaphor thus seems irrelevant. Like it or not, metaphor is something with which we all have to deal. But, more of this later.

The "metaphorical" versus the "literal"

There is a lot of talk in the metaphor debate about the distinction between literal and metaphorical modes of understanding. As I see it, the distinction is very misleading, especially when used to highlight a difference between "literal" and "metaphorical" knowledge, and to present the former as being more foundational, or more solid, than the latter. I will make my argument in two ways.

First, the concept of "literal" is itself metaphorical. The etymology of the term reflects that the word was first used in connection with letters of the alphabet. Perhaps the association would be clearer if we spelled the word as "letteral"! The word originally referred to misprints in scribal manuscripts, to the use of the alphabet in mathematical notation, and to translations that were verbally exact and faithful to an original text. Its use was extended to the idea of taking words in scripture in their natural or customary meaning and of making interpretations according to the rules of grammar, as opposed to allegorical, metaphorical or mystical interpretations.

In talking about "literal knowledge" or the idea that there is a "literal meaning" or a "literal truth" we are thus making major metaphorical leaps. They are evident in how the concept has evolved, and in the assumption that language and language use are neutral. It is one thing to say that a word has been misspelled, but quite another to suggest that words and concepts have clear, unequivocal meanings, let alone assert that there is a clear equivalence with the world they are used to describe. Yet this is precisely the kind of assumption that would-be "metaphor bashers" use to assert the priority of literal meaning. As I show below, there is a difference between the search for literal as opposed to metaphorical knowledge, but it is a complete mistake to think that one is necessarily better than another. Different, yes! Better, no!

This brings me to my second point. It seems impossible to pursue forms of literal knowledge that are independent of the metaphorical, because the domains are so intertwined. This is illustrated in the etymology discussed above, but there is another way of making the point. To do so, let's examine the field of organization studies.

What would a "literal" view of organization look like? Advocates of the literal mode (e.g. Pinder and Bourgeois, 1982) suggest that we should eradicate metaphor in favour of an empirical focus on observable organizational characteristics, so that organizations are studied as they actually are rather than through the creative frames provided by metaphor.

But how can you study organizations "as they actually are"? What would you look for? What would you see?

In order to "see" anything, you have to have concepts that will bring the phenomenon into focus, and these concepts always have metaphorical origins.

Take, for example, the concept of organization structure, which most "literal" analysts would probably concede as a key organizational characteristic. As I have shown elsewhere (Morgan, 1986), this concept is intimately connected with the metaphorical idea that the organization is a kind of a machine, or a living organism comprised of a series of interconnected parts. Both images focus on the design and connection of parts as a key to understanding the true or literal nature of organization. Over time the view of organization as a structure becomes so taken for granted that the prefiguring image disappears from view, leaving the residual concepts as seemingly literal, objective features of organization.

This process, whereby metaphor generates an image that allows us see and understand a phenomenon that can then be studied and understood in more detail through the concepts generated by the metaphor in a more reductive fashion, is key to all human understanding. Technically, it reflects the combination of two tropal operations: metaphor and metonymy (Morgan, 1983; White, 1978). Metaphor opens a domain of understanding, metonymy ties down the detail.

The role of metaphor in organization studies seems quite well understood. The role of metonymy is less appreciated. Technically, metonymy is the process whereby the name of an element or characteristic of a phenomenon is used to represent the total phenomenon, as in the well-known example of "The Monarchy" being described as "The Crown". In organization studies an organization may be represented as a structure of parts if viewed through the influence of a mechanical metaphor, as a set of rituals or beliefs if studied through a cultural metaphor, and so on. The "literal" view asserts the priority of metonymical modes of understanding without recognizing that this is the case. Metaphor and metonymy are always interconnected. You cannot have one without the other. A metaphorical image relies on some kind of metonymical reduction to make it concrete, otherwise it remains in thin air. Metonymy is entirely dependent on metaphor, for without a prefiguring image we have nothing to see. Any claim that it's possible to gain "literal" forms of knowledge that are independent of the metaphorical completely ignores how the literal is produced.

Traditional science values metonymical modes of understanding

This discussion of the relationship between metaphor and metonymy helps to put the quest for scientific knowledge in new light. Since science is committed to achieving objective forms of knowledge, the inherent tendency is to try to tame, moderate, deny or deride the metaphorical, while implicitly asserting the importance and superiority of the metonymical. Or, to put it more forcefully, science is hooked and at times obsessed by the quest for metonymical–literal modes of understanding. Even theorists who wish to act as arbiters and integrators of the different points of view (e.g. Tsoukas, 1991, 1993) are dominated by this reductive focus, and it has many unfortunate consequences.

The basic problems are clearly illustrated in the excellent essay in Chapter 6 by Inns and Jones on the difference between poetic and scientific modes of understanding. As they show, in poetry metaphor is used to generate important insights that rely on evocative, gestalt-like modes of knowing. The quest is for a kind of holistic or dramatic understanding that, at times, can completely reframe how we see and experience a phenomenon. Science, on the other hand, strives to translate the implications of a metaphor into constituent elements and relationships. The metonymic naming and measurement of parts is what's valued. That's why those scientists who recognize the inevitable role of metaphor in science usually couple this understanding with the idea that metaphors can be a source of new hypotheses, play a valuable role in the early, creative, stages of a study, or in generating a search for new "literal identities".

One cannot blame them for this, because if they want to do traditional science, they have to get into a reductive, analytical, measuring mode. But the perspective becomes completely counter-productive when they make a giant leap to the presumption that they are now engaged in some kind of objective mode of inquiry. Given that the metonymical concepts and measures that are being used to shape the science are driven by a metaphor that is usually lost from view, their objectivity is as subjective as that of the researcher who chooses to explore the implications of metaphor at a more general level.

There is too much metaphor bashing in science. Sometimes it is explicit. Sometimes it is hidden behind the guise of getting a balanced view. It arises because metaphor presents a threat to the "objective foundations" on which science seeks to build. Ironically, the attack does nothing to remove the subjectivity that lies at the heart of the problem. A "banning" or derision of metaphor, or the attempt to convert the implications of metaphor into "literal identities", certainly doesn't make metaphor and its influence go away, or make science any more objective.

As I suggest below, the real challenge facing science is to embrace the metaphorical basis of scientific inquiry, and learn how to deal with the many constructive implications that can unfold. In my view, the significance of the position of those who recognize the key role of metaphor in science is not that they wish to replace the reductive–metonymical mode of understanding with the poetic. Under that scenario, science would no longer be scientific! Rather, it is to suggest that a full understanding of metaphor will help science become more consciously aware of its limitations, and help it deal with the fact that its objectivity is a socially constructed objectivity in a more growthful, positive way.

Metaphor creates partial "truths"

The most important aspect of metaphor for this purpose rests in recognizing that whenever we focus on a domain of study through metaphor, we engage in a process that, at best, creates "partial truths". In bringing an image, idea, concept or element of experience from one domain and applying it to another, and understanding the one through the other, we are engaged in a creative process that always has strengths and limitations. The strengths rest in the insights created through the metaphor. The limitations rest in the fact that no metaphor ever captures the totality of experience to which it is applied. In creating one set of insights it excludes others. As it is sometimes put, a way of seeing is also a way of not seeing.

Also, we have to remember that all metaphor creates a kind of "constructive falsehood". The phenomenon captured through the metaphor is not strictly what the metaphor asserts it to be. The man is not a lion! The organization is not a machine! Even though these metaphors may be useful in helping us to see and understand characteristics of the man and the organization, they are not strictly "true".

Metaphor has an inherently dialectical quality that binds truth and falsehood into the same process, creating powerful insights that, if taken too literally, or too far, can become counter-productive. I am not entirely comfortable with using the words true and false to characterize metaphor in this way. I prefer talking about insights and strengths or weaknesses and limitations. But the terminology does serve to dramatize an important point, especially when talking within the context of basic epistemology.

It is in this respect that science has a lot to learn from metaphor. To the extent that science is based on metaphor, it's best seen as a process that creates partial truths that exclude other partial truths. Take the famous scientific example: Is light a wave or a particle? If scientists study light as a wave, it reveals itself as a wave. If it is studied as a particle, it reveals itself as a particle. Each image or way of seeing generates distinctive insights; distinctive "truths".

It seems to me that if we approach science, and our understanding of science, with this perspective consciously in mind, we are able to develop a much more open and constructive view of the basic enterprise. In recognizing science as a metaphorical enterprise that uses metonymical reductions to create a guise of objectivity, we are obliged to recognize that any given perspective or approach always has its limits, and that to go beyond these limits, new approaches and perspectives are necessary. This opens the way to a science that is much more tentative in its claims, multidimensional in its approach, and much more open to new lines of development.

It also encourages a science that places the whole process of falsification on a completely new level. As is well known, the role of falsification in establishing the validity and merits of a particular scientific theory or approach is well established at the level of hypothesis testing (Popper, 1958). An appreciation of the role of metaphor in theory generation requires us to go one step further, and recognize the inevitable limitations and biases of the theoretical models that are generating the hypotheses in the first place. It encourages us to be consciously sceptical of our fundamental theories and to avoid being seduced by them. If nothing else, it requires the scientist to raise his or her head above the data, or the quest for new hypotheses or literal identities, and appreciate the processes of social construction that are shaping and limiting what's being studied. In recognizing that every view of the world has inherent strengths and limitations, an awareness of the role of metaphor has fundamental implications for how all knowledge should be regarded.

Scientific objectivity is as much a part of the scientist's perspective as of the object observed. An understanding of the role of metaphor in this process brings a new twist to the basic problem, and reinforces the importance of self-awareness and self-reflection in all knowledge generation. If science could position itself more modestly as a metaphorical form of knowledge that uses metonymical reduction to gain rigorous understandings, the stage would be set for a much broader, deeper, more open and more holistic enterprise that integrates and builds on insights from many different domains.

The metaphor of metaphor

Given the argument outlined above, I think that this is an appropriate place to recognize that the concept of metaphor must also be recognized as a metaphor. After all, as everyone recognizes, metaphor was first identified and discussed as a linguistic phenomenon. In this volume and related work it is now being "carried over" to a new domain, the study of "organization", and is being used in a relatively new way. When we view the concept of metaphor in this manner we are obliged to recognize that it too creates partial truths, and has both strengths and limitations!

Much of the current debate on metaphor reflected in this volume, and in the above discussion, hinges on the fact that different contributors are seizing on different strengths and limitations. By recognizing this, we can begin to put the metaphor debate in fresh perspective, and create an opportunity to go forward in a new way.

Let us begin by looking at the strengths. The metaphor concept provides a way of explaining the creative manner in which humans forge meaning in all aspects of life. It provides a way of explaining how language and highly conventionalized social constructions of reality emerge and develop, and how we can deliberately stretch the conventional to develop creative ways of seeing, understanding and acting on the world. In this regard, metaphor can be seen as having a liberating, empowering dimension that encourages people to take control of their lives and of the meanings they impose on the world. Instead of living through other people's social constructions they are encouraged to live through their own.

The inherent "falsity" of metaphor also encourages a healthy scepticism in the way we view knowledge, and opens our social constructions of reality to the kind of continuous deconstruction and reconstruction for which many postmodernist theorists call. Metaphor is truly postmodern, because the dialectical tension between truth and falsehood implied in any metaphor demands a self-critical form of imagination and understanding. Metaphor is both evocative and tentative. Those who understand its role and functioning in the creation of knowledge are obliged to be consciously aware of this, and the blindspots and biases that use of metaphor creates. Metaphor invites humility and tolerance.

Metaphor opens the way to new modes of theorizing and new modes of understanding that are ideally suited to the flux and change of an electronic world. Just as the world of literacy and print has created a bias towards the concretization and fixing of reality through metonymical modes of under-standing, metaphor opens the way to more fluid forms of discourse. Indeed, it both demands and promotes discourse. No metaphor can ever bring closure because its inherent falsity and limitations define frontiers for new debate and new insight. Metaphor, in this sense, invites opposition and its own deconstruction. Its limitations can be catalysts for further development. In metaphor we find an organic, self-organizing concept that's ideally suited for exploring the nature of an organic, self-organizing world. As the hold and legitimacy of mechanistic thinking decline, we can expect the import-ance of metaphor to rise.

Against these strengths, as many critics have pointed out (e.g. Alvesson, 1990, 1993; Reed, 1990; Tinker, 1986; Tsoukas, 1991, 1993), there are important weaknesses. Unbridled use of metaphor can carry the user away on flights of fancy that may have little to do with "reality". Metaphor can be amorphous and difficult to tie down. It underplays the role and significance of other tropes. It can be "too relativist". It is too subjective. It is too voluntarist. It is too idealistic. It can be superficial, creating surface rather than depth understanding. It can privilege one viewpoint over another. It undermines "rational" explanations of social life. It can mystify and create ideological distortions. It ignores the role of power in society. It suggests that people have more power over the social construction of reality than they actually do. It ignores the fact that knowledge is class-based, and that certain metaphorical constructions are more enduring and more powerful than others. It focuses attention on a technique through which knowledge is created, instead of the context in which knowledge is created. It thus deflects attention from societal processes of domination and control that play a key gate-keeping role in the social structuring of knowledge. It ignores that bias in the social context is reflected in the bias of the metaphors and knowledge that achieve prominence.

All these points are important, and must be embraced.

In developing the implications of metaphor for organization studies and the pursuit of knowledge more generally, gains can be made by developing the strengths, and overcoming the weaknesses. Interestingly, as in the use of all metaphor, it is vital to note that the weaknesses and limitations do not negate or eliminate the strengths. Rather, they define new challenges that must be addressed.

Thus, to elaborate the critique offered above, the use of metaphor may be seen as having unfortunate consequences in terms of its lack of rigour from a scientific viewpoint, and because of potential ideological bias. The former problem can be addressed by adopting a rigorously metonymic transform-ation of the implications of favoured metaphors into sets of literal identities, as advocated by Tsoukas (1993). This will help to advance the cause of traditional science through conventional forms of hypothesis testing. This, however, in no way negates other means of using metaphor to create exploratory theory and more organic, self-organizing patterns of insight, for example, as I have demonstrated in my approach to "imaginization" (Morgan, 1993). The processes are not exclusive, and there is absolutely no reason why one should be reduced to the other.

Similarly, the fact that use of metaphor is open to all kinds of ideological bias does not negate the utility, role and function of metaphor in both traditional and more novel modes of inquiry. The critique of metaphor from an ideological point of view does, however, oblige us to bear this in mind in doing metaphorical work. It also opens up a vital frontier for research. It is vital to understand how different metaphors have come into prominence, and how they may advance certain social constructions and social interests over others. This agenda defines an enormous piece of work, and, without question, it needs to be done.

Some closing remarks

If there is one thing that I have learned about academic work it is that every piece is implicitly or explicitly biased and incomplete. Metaphor symbolizes this, because whenever we engage the world through metaphorical modes of experience we are always engaging the world in partial, biased ways. This has been well recognized in relation to how language shapes reality. An explicit recognition of metaphor lends the process a special poignancy, because metaphor relies on a degree of distortion to create its effects.

Applying this principle to my own work, it is clear that I have placed emphasis on the "liberating potential" of metaphor in creating new insights and extending the boundaries of organization and management theory. I have been less interested in using metaphor to create new metonymical reductions for empirical investigation, though I recognize this as a worthwhile task. I have sought to challenge thinking in organization theory at an epistemological level, using the inherent bias and partiality of metaphor to justify a broader pluralism, rather than by attacking it through the lens of ideological and political bias, though I recognize that this is also worthwhile. I have sought to challenge the way we develop organization theory as a quasi-objective and rigorous process by modelling an alternative through my concept of imaginization.

Through all this I have consciously sought to develop and model a postmodern approach to organization and management that thrives on continuous construction, deconstruction and reconstruction, without adopting the intellectual trappings of the professional postmodernist. I have consciously sought to develop the dialectical aspect of metaphor, using the paradoxical relationship between insights and limitations as a means of creating springboards for new development. I have specialized in trying to create a mode of metaphorical imagination that is open to continuous self-organization through an open-ended construction and deconstruction of meaning. I have sought to see the power of particular metaphors not in the content of the metaphors per se, but in the mode of engagement they create. Indeed, I have acted on the principle that no metaphor has an objective character, since the meaning and significance of a metaphor always depend on what is evoked for the user. Increasingly, I have sought to develop theory through practice rather than as an abstract intellectual endeavour, and throughout all these endeavours I have been driven by a desire to develop ways of thinking that recognize paradox and contradiction as a defining feature of social life.

I can be critiqued on all these dimensions, since my position creates a series of counter-positions from which to respond. We see many of these in earlier chapters of this volume. For the most part, I accept what is said, because, as I have discussed at length, every position has its weaknesses. And by understanding our weaknesses we learn and grow.

There are, however, three points of criticism that deserve detailed attention.

The first is offered by Iain Mangham, who uses a detailed discussion of my work to illustrate the unconscious use of metaphor through language, and to suggest that I trivialize the role of metaphor by ignoring what he calls "basic", "deep", "fundamental" conceptualizations in favour of idiosyncratic metaphor. He presents me as using "jokey titles", "childlike sketches" and "fleeting" metaphors to divert attention from what is fundamental: the highly conventionalized metaphor that shapes everyday discourse.

Given what I have said in this chapter, I endorse his central point about the role of metaphor in language and conventional discourse, and the major contribution of Lakoff and Johnson (1980), but his central point could be made much more easily.

As I read his contribution, I was struck by an experience I had thirty years ago in visiting a London theatre where a play called *The Bedsitting Room*, an innocuous comedy featuring British comedian Spike Milligan, was being performed. Outside the theatre were two picture frames. One contained a famous painting of a nude, minus all her "private parts". The other picture frame presented the missing parts mounted on a background of white paper. The two frames were counter-posed to show how the censor had trivialized and changed the meaning of the production by eliminating key elements.

I had the same feeling in reading Mangham. Like the censor, he has snatched and highlighted the "juicy" parts of my work that suit his purposes and presented them completely out of context. He could have saved himself a lot of work by just selecting random paragraphs from any of my writings, the paragraphs that he quotes from Lakoff and Johnson and Johnson, or, indeed, those from his own work. As in this chapter, they are full of metaphor and metaphorical arguments that shape the overall text.

The substantial point that must be addressed, however, is that Iain Mangham's argument is profoundly conservative. We are advised to confine our attention to the deep conventional structures of meaning, because that's where substantial analysis must focus. But where do the conventional meanings come from, if not from what was once regarded as an idiosyncratic way of looking at the world? Life, as Mangham points out, is now often conceived in a taken-for-granted manner as a journey into the future, with all kinds of obstacles on the way. The journey is indeed a metaphor of our time. But we do not have to return very far in human development to find a conception of time where there was no past or present. The idea of thinking about life and time as "a journey" in this context would have seemed extremely idiosyncratic. But it has proved to be a breakthrough of enormous power.

I would not claim that the new metaphors that I have developed are likely to have anything like this status. But I do know that people and organiz-ations who learn to recognize when they are "looking through the rear-view mirror" can be deeply affected by the insight that they are adapting to a reality that has already passed. Similarly, organizations struggling with problems of decentralization have been able to create very different styles of operation by thinking of themselves through the image of a "spider plant". The managers that I have persuaded to analyse their organizations as "yogurt" have often generated penetrating insights about how they are reproducing desired and undesired characteristics. The metaphor has also helped them find their own creative power in dealing with the problems they face. These, indeed, seem like idiosyncratic metaphors when presented out of context. But in an appropriate context, they can generate enormous insight.

Since Iain Mangham specializes in conducting and writing about organizational interventions (Mangham, 1978), I am amazed that he chooses to ignore the live, dynamic aspect of this kind of metaphor. It is so central to the dramaturgical view of organization that he has spent so much time developing. But, obviously, it does not quite fit what he wants to put into the "picture frame" that he has selected for the purpose of critiquing my work.

I stand firmly behind the contributions of what, at first sight, may seem as idiosyncratic metaphor, not that I would ever recommend the generation of idiosyncrasy as an end in itself. As I have gone to great lengths to point out (Morgan, 1993), it is the "resonance" or ability of a metaphor to link subject and object in a meaningful new relationship that's key. All my accounts of imaginization in practice demonstrate this. Readers who want to explore this further, and how the limitations of metaphor can be systematically used to create organic, self-organizing processes of inquiry that constantly generate new insight, need look no further than the writings on the spider plant (Morgan, 1993), which Mangham chooses to present in a flat, static way.

My second major critical comment in relation to some of the ideas presented in earlier chapters relates to the way various authors position the status and intent of my book *Images of Organization* (1986). For example, Robert Chia suggests that it offers a series of 'static images' of organization with a view to producing multiple readings of situations, as opposed to advancing his agenda of 'metaphorization' – a process that recognizes the deeper role of metaphor in everything we do. I agree with most of what Chia says, except that I think he misinterprets the true significance of *Images*. My conscious aim was to position the book in a way that was accessible to a wide audience, framing it within the context of a managerial orientation that stressed the utility of using different metaphors for capturing different aspects of organizational reality, and for diagnosing and acting on organizational problems. Undoubtedly, it "privileges" a managerial point of view. But the deeper aim of the book is to model a way of thinking that uses metaphor to confront and deal with the complex, and paradoxical, character of organizational life.

Superficially, *Images of Organization* presents eight metaphorical views of organization, analysing the domain of organization theory to make its point. But its real power, and this I think is one of the major reasons why it has been so influential, rests in the fact that each metaphorical frame has the effect of deconstructing the others. As such, it is a perfect example of Chia's metaphorization in practice. Organizations are successively examined as machines, organisms, brains, cultures, and so on, without asserting that they are ultimately any of these things. The reader is constantly thrust back on his or her own powers of interpretation in determining how he or she can best make sense of organizational reality. The fundamental stance is distinctly postmodern. It embraces paradox and contradiction as a fundamental feature of our world.

Clearly *Images of Organization* is a book that is itself rooted in a dominant metaphorical frame stressing the social construction of reality. But it is not a "solipsist" work that denies an objective reality. Rather, its position is that objective reality can only be grasped subjectively through the metaphors that shape our thinking.

I capture the basic problem through the well-known analogy of the blind men trying to understand an elephant, with the added dimension that insofar as organization and organizations are concerned, we have no certainty that we are dealing with anything as clear-cut as an elephant. It is not, as MacKechnie and Donnelly-Cox suggest in Chapter 2, that the essence of organization or organizations always 'remains beyond the reach of metaphor', so much as that there is no certainty about this essence beyond what we can capture through metaphor. There is no definitive "master-metaphor", though there are good contenders for this role. Some, on the basis of nineteenth- and twentieth-century experience, would opt for the machine. For radical theorists, domination is the uniting theme. Others would argue for the overriding influence of culture. Those with their eye on the electronic revolution and the twenty-first century may opt for the brain. Where is the "master-metaphor"? It seems to me that you can take your choice!

This brings me to my third and final point. As I started this chapter, I want to return to the difficulties of determining "THE VIEW" insofar as metaphor is concerned. In the previous chapters we have been exposed to discussion of types of metaphor, hierarchies of metaphor, deep metaphors, surface metaphors, fundamental conceptual metaphors, poetic metaphor, scientific metaphor, idiosyncratic metaphor, conventionalized metaphor, live metaphor, dead metaphor, dormant metaphor, resonant metaphor, "fields" of metaphor, and master metaphors, to name just a few of the concepts evoked in developing different points of view. My point: We use metaphors to talk about metaphor. The process may be instructive and helpful in creating insight and understanding about different perspectives. A particular argument may even lead us to change our point of view and act differently in relation to the metaphor debate, This, after all, is one of the things that metaphor helps us do. But we should not pretend that our favoured point of view on metaphor is "THE" view.

As I have suggested in this chapter, my favoured view is to see metaphor as a distinctively postmodern concept that has an inherent tendency to deconstruct itself and the knowledge that it generates. For some, this may appear to be a real problem. But I see it as a strength, because it provides us with a distinctly self-organizing and organic mode of knowing ideally suited for dealing with what I believe to be a self-organizing organic world.

In line with the ideas of writers like Marshall McLuhan (1964), it seems clear that the desire to transform the metaphorical into reductive, metonymical modes of understanding is fostered by a literacy based on the printed word. As we move into our electronic age, all this is likely to change, creating a context in which metaphor and metaphorical thinking will become more and more powerful. The electronic world is one where fundamental realities have no firm ground. It is a world where images and more oral, multidimensional modes of discourse flourish. It is a world where foundational literal science will probably always have a role to play. But it will probably not be recognized as the pre-eminent mode of knowing. We already see some of the transformations that are likely to occur by the way in which new modes of scientific thinking are using artificial intelligence to make conceptual breakthroughs and to model and understand the realities that they wish to explore (Kelley, 1994; Lewin, 1992). Metaphor is the explicit medium of this world.

In my current work I am consciously aligning myself for this emerging reality: by practising and "doing metaphor", rather than trying to make my case in strictly intellectual terms. This seems to offer at least one interesting frontier for development that can help to meet Oswick and Grant's desire (Chapter 12) to see more radical innovation in the metaphor field.

References

Alvesson, M. (1990) 'Organization: From substance to image', *Organization Studies* 11 (3), 373–394.

Alvesson, M. (1993) 'The play of metaphors', in J. Hassard and M. Parker (eds), *Postmodernism and Organizations*. London: Sage Publications, pp. 114–131.

Kelley, K. (1994) *Out of Control: The New Biology of Machines, Social Systems and the Economic World*. Reading, MA: Addison-Wesley.

Lakoff, G. and Johnson, M. (1980) *Metaphors We Live By*. Chicago: University of Chicago Press.

Lewin, R. (1992) *Complexity: Life at the Edge of Chaos*. New York: Macmillan.

McLuhan, M. (1964) *Understanding Media*. New York: New American Library.

Mangham, I.L. (1978) *Interactions and Interventions in Organizations*. Chichester: John Wiley and Sons.

Morgan, G. (1983) 'More on metaphor: Why we cannot control tropes in administrative science', *Administrative Science Quarterly*, 28 (4), 601–607.

Morgan, G. (1986) *Images of Organization*. Beverly Hills, CA: Sage Publications.

Morgan, G. (1993) *Imaginization: The Art of Creative Management*. London: Sage Publications.

Pinder, C.C. and Bourgeois, V.W. (1982) 'Controlling tropes in administrative science', *Administrative Science Quarterly*, 27 (4), 641–652.

Popper, K. (1958) *The Logic of Scientific Inquiry*. London: Hutchinson.

Reed, M. (1990) 'From paradigms to images: The paradigm warrior turns post-modernist guru', *Personnel Review*, 19, 35–40.

Tinker, T. (1986) 'Metaphor or reification: Are radical humanists really libertarian anarchists?' *Journal of Management Studies*, 23, 363–384.

Tsoukas, H. (1991) 'The missing link: A transformational view of metaphors in organizational science', *Academy of Management Review*, 16 (3), 566–585.

Tsoukas, H. (1993) 'Analogical reasoning and knowledge generation in organization theory', *Organization Studies*, 14 (3), 323–346.

White, H. (1978) *The Tropics of Discourse*. Baltimore: Johns Hopkins University Press.

Index

abstractions, 7, 8, 136, 142
Ackerman, L., 153
action, organizational, 7, 10, 16, 185–97
action learning, 148
action research, 219
actor-networks, 118
adaptive behaviour, 148
adaptive cycle, 62
adaptive organizations, 63–4
administration, 38, 39–40
Administrative Science Quarterly, 77–8
Akin, G., 95
Alchian, A.A., 172
Allen, R.F., 68
Alvesson, M., 7, 122–4, 174, 176–7, 181, 190, 215, 217, 234
Amway, 201, 202
analogies, 7, 8, 46
Andrews, A.Y., 96, 97, 99
anomalies, 8
ante hoc metaphors, 81, 82
anthropological metaphor, 11, 40–3, 45–9, 51
anthropomorphic metaphors, 16, 185, 189–91, 192, 196–7
anticipatory action, 193
appreciators, 134–5, 140, 141
archetypes/archetypal patterns, 150, 152
Argyris, C., 148
artificial intelligence, 70, 228, 240
Ashby, W.R., 62, 148
Askvik, S., 168
Auden, W.H., 114
autonomy, 61, 63–5, 67
autopoietic system, 65

Bacharach, S.B., 186, 187
Badaracco, J.L., 63, 64
Baggerman, L., 98, 100, 102, 104
Bak, P., 56
baking metaphor, 103, 106
Bamforth, K.W., 2
Barnard, C., 38–9, 41–2, 44, 48, 50
Barrett, F.J., 2–4, 7, 10, 22, 95–7, 106, 120, 218, 219
barriers to entry, 166–9, 171
Barry, D., 150, 156
Barthes, R., 138

Bartlett, C.A., 63
Bartunek, J.M., 148
base domain, 2, 5, 7–8, 26–8, 185, 188, 216
basic metaphors, 11, 21–9, 31–5, 216, 228, 236
Bateson, Gregory, 69, 148
Baum, H.S., 149
Bedsitting Room, The (play), 237
Beer, Michael, 54
Beer, Stafford, 4, 12, 54, 67, 148
Beesley, M.E., 170
beliefs, 192, 193, 230
    governing (schemata), 148–51
Bensimon, E.A., 95
Berger, P.L., 3, 193
Bergson, Henri, 139
Bernasek, A., 100, 104
Bertalanffy, Ludwig von, 61
Beyer, J.M., 188
"big hat, no cattle" metaphor, 114
Billing, Y.D., 190
biological metaphors, 42, 47, 49, 51, 85, 189
biological thematic coherence, 154
Bion, W.R., 150
Black, M., 3, 7, 129
Bloomfield, B., 180, 181
blueprint metaphor, 42
body metaphors, 99–101, 102, 103, 104
Bohm, David, 138, 139, 140, 143
'boiling frogs' metaphor, 217
Boland, R.J., Jr., 96
Bolman, L.G., 81, 95
Boronson, W., 102, 105
Bougon, M.G., 148
Boulding, K.E., 4
Bourgeois, V.W., 4, 78–81, 84, 91, 95, 131, 186–8, 214–15, 217, 219, 230
Bradac, J.J., 97
brain metaphors, 29, 47, 50, 115
    triune-brain evolution, 10, 12, 53–71, 150
Brink, T.L., 4, 10, 95, 218, 220
Brockner, J., 103
Broekstra, G., 57, 60, 62, 64–6, 69
Broussine, M., 10, 218, 219, 221
Brown, G.I., 150
Brown, R.H., 4, 111, 116, 122, 222

Brown, S.J., 9, 127, 128, 129
Bryson, J., 167, 168
Bunge, M., 4
bureaucracy, 58, 59, 64
Burgess, L., 102, 105
Burke, W.W., 220
Burns, T., 2, 40, 217
Burrell, G., 112, 118, 216, 220
business cycle, 12
business fads, 53, 54–6, 58
Business Process Re-engineering, 55–6,
    159, 160, 161, 223
Business Statistics Office, 166
business unit, 61, 64, 65, 67
Business Week, 54
buyer uncertainty, 168–9

Callon, M., 175
Cameron, K.S., 98
Campbell, D.T., 192
Campbell, J., 90, 150
Canella, A.A., 132
Capell, P., 102
Cappelli, P., 102
captives (evangelical metaphor), 207–8
Cardamore, M.A., 69
Cascio, W.F., 98, 100
case study effect, 219
Cassirer, E., 127
causal relationships, 50, 191, 193–4
centralization, 58, 59, 60
Champy, J., 161
Chan, W.T., 138
Chandler, Alfred, 59, 60
change, paradigms of, 57–66
chaos theory, 55–6, 65–6, 68
charismatic style, 200–1, 206–7
Chen, K., 56
Chia, Robert, 238
Chi Tsi, 139
Chuang Tzu, 139
Clancy, J.J., 22
Clark, T., 166–9, 175
Cleary, C., 218
Clegg, S.R., 74, 81, 82, 88
client–consultant relationship, 10, 15,
    166–7, 170–81
closed system, 58
cognition
    in organizational culture, 147–51
    as representation, 137
cognitive map, 148
cognitive nature of metaphors, 6, 11, 22–3,
    35, 214, 215
cognitive revolution, 148

cognitive thematic coherence, 154–5
Cohen, M., 186
Cohen, M.D., 114, 217
Cohen, T., 134
Coleman, H., 48
Coleridge, T.S., 116, 120
collaborative individualism, 63
collective unconscious, 68
Collins, R., 191
combining metaphors, 32–4
command-and-control imperative, 59
'commando model', 221
commission, errors of, 188
communication, 156–7, 162
compactness (of metaphor), 220, 221
competence, organizational, 7, 16, 185–97
complexity, 55–7, 64–5, 70
conceptual metaphor, 11, 23–4, 26–35, 216
concupiscible passions, 204
connectionism, 66
Connolly, T., 95
consciousness, 68–9, 70–1
consistency model, 62
construct validation, 191
content analysis, 219
content images, 128
contingency theory, 2, 40–2, 44
conventionalization parameter, 29
conversation analysis, 219
converts (evangelical metaphor), 207–8
Cook, T.D., 192
Cooper, R., 118, 216
Cooperrider, D.L., 2–4, 10, 22, 218, 219
corporate consciousness, 12, 68–71
corporate culture, 124
corporate persons, 48
corporate restructuring, 10, 13, 219
    counter-metaphors, 101, 103–6
    downsizing, 98–106
    metaphors in, 95–8
counter-metaphors, 13, 101, 103–6
creativity, 187
cross-domain mapping, 23
Cuddon, J.A., 114–17, 125
Cullum-Swan, B., 219
cultural school (organizational culture),
    147–51
culture
    corporate, 124
    metaphor, 47, 51, 130, 230
    organizational, 95, 147–51, 222
Cunnington, B., 63, 65
Curtis, Gregory, 206–10 *passim*
cybernetic theory, 148
Cyert, R.M., 193

Czarniawksa-Joerges, B., 96, 178, 179

Daft, R.L., 148
Daniels, P.W., 169
Davidson, D., 220
Davis, M.S., 187, 188
Davis, S.M., 149
Dawes, P.C., 168
dead metaphors, 9, 128, 140, 143
Deal, T.E., 81, 95, 149, 222
De Board, R., 149
decentralization, 59, 60–1
decision-making, 79, 95, 97, 114
decoupling, 65
deductive metaphors, 10
deep metaphor, 6–7, 215, 236
Deetz, S., 22
Denton, K., 100
depreciators, 133–4, 140–1
Derrida, J., 127, 129, 186
DeRubeis, R.J., 148
Descartes, R., 186
design strategies, 44, 114, 115
de Vos, Richard, 201
diagnosis, metaphors and, 155–62
dialogical approach, 219
Diamond, M.A., 149
Dickson, W.J., 2
DiMaggio, P.J., 43, 194
direct marketing, 16, 200–11
discourse analysis, 219
discourse and language
    organizational analysis, 14, 127–44
    organizational theory and poetry, 13–14,
        110–25
    popular management discourse, 10, 13,
        95–106
discovery (alternative theories), 187
Dissemination (Derrida), 127
division of labour, 11, 12, 50–1, 58
divisional organization, 12, 57, 60–1
Dobson, K.S., 148
Dobuzinskis, L., 95
'doing metaphor', 227, 240
domain similarities (source/target), 7–8
domination metaphors, 47, 50, 219
Donath, B., 102
dormant metaphors, 9, 10, 128
double-loop learning, 87–8, 148
downsizing, 13, 95, 97–106, 179
dramaturgical metaphor, 167, 201–2, 238
Drazin, R., 37, 46, 50, 131, 217
dreams, 201, 202, 204–6, 210
Drucker, P.F., 54, 105
Du Gay, P., 178

Dunbar, R.L.M., 96
Dunford, R., 10, 81, 218
Dunn, S., 7, 95, 103, 217
durable business services, 173
Durant, William, 60

early theorists, 38–40
Easterby-Smith, M., 121
Eccles, R.G., 54, 96
Edgren, L.D., 221
efficiency–effectiveness dilemma, 54–5
Einstein, Albert, 70
elaborated metaphors, 32–4
Ellis, A., 148
Elster, J., 191, 196
embedded metaphors, 85–6, 219
embryonic metaphors, 12–13, 74–91
emotion, 161, 162
    appropriation of, 16, 200–11
    poetry and, 14, 114, 120
emotions of limbic system, 67
empowerment, 53, 55, 223
'empty raincoats' metaphor, 217
Engelstad, F., 191, 195
enterprise, 178
entry barriers, 166, 167–9, 171
environment, 41, 42, 43
epistemological metaphor, 17, 130–5, 228–9
epistemology, 131–5, 137, 140, 232
    postmodern, 117–18
equilibrium, 67
    paradigms of change, 58, 62
errors of commission, 188
errors of inappropriateness, 188
errors of omission, 188
errors of realism, 190
errors of redundancy, 188–9
ethnographic research method, 16, 203
Etzioni, A., 2
evangelical metaphors, 16, 200–11
Evely, R., 169
Evered, R., 96
everyday experience, 25–9, 31, 200
everyday metaphors, 23–9, 31
everyday phrases, 25–9
evolution of living organization, 12, 53–71
evolutionary paradigm, 53, 57–8, 65–6,
        69–70
experience, 25–9, 31, 200
experiential realism, 135
expertise, 175–81
extended metaphors, 32–4

failed-change syndrome, 53–4
Fairtlough, G., 85

'Fallacy of Misplaced Concreteness'
   (Whitehead), 139, 142
false consciousness, 6, 214
falsification, 233
Faltermayer, E., 100, 102, 103
family metaphor, 217
Fayol, H., 2, 38
Fenollosa, Ernesto, 135
Fernandez, James, 202–4, 211
figurative language, 4–6, 22, 186–7
Fillmore, C., 25
firm, theory of, 45, 46
first-order change, 148, 152
first-order cybernetics, 62
flux metaphor, 47, 51, 140
focus groups, 75, 83, 87, 88–9
Fontana, D., 150
formal organizations, 38–40, 48
Foucault, M., 106, 112, 118, 137
'frame', 148
Fraser, B., 9
Freedom Show, The (TV programme), 201
Freeman, C., 87
Freeman, J., 42, 189
Freeman, S.J., 98
Frege, G., 122
Freud, Sigmund, 149
Frohman, A.L., 98
Frost, P.J., 149
Frye, Northrop, 46
functional intelligence, 67–8
functional organization, 12, 57, 59–60
functionalist paradigm, 78

Gabriel, Y., 149
Gadamer, H.G., 84
Galbraith, J.R., 44, 45, 62
game playing metaphor, 46, 49, 50
garbage-can approach, 79, 114, 186
Gardner, H., 222
Gasché, R., 129
Geertz, C., 118
General Motors, 44, 60
Gentner, D., 7
Georgiou, P., 2
Gergen, K.J., 112, 118–20, 133, 180, 216
Gestalt, 69, 113–15, 125, 231
Ghoshal, S., 63
Gibbs, R.W., Jr., 8, 25, 222
Gilder, G., 70
Gilje, N., 191
'gods of management' metaphor, 217
Goffman, E., 148
Goldfried, M.R., 148
Gouldner, A.W., 2

governance system, 46, 49
governing beliefs, 148, 149, 150–1
Grafton Small, R., 208
grammar, 136–7, 138, 139, 143
   metaphor, 43–4, 49, 50
Grandori, A., 40, 193
Grant, D., 4, 7, 213
Gray, B., 148
Gray, J.T., 82, 87, 88
Great Depression (1870s), 58, 59
Great Depression (1930s), 60
Greenberg, R.H., 96
Greenfield, H.I., 173
Gregory, B., 152
Grimen, H., 191
group development, 95, 120
Guidano, V.F., 148, 151
Gustavsson, B., 68

hagiography (of charismatic leader), 207
Hales, C., 172, 173
Hamilton, E.E., 95
Hamilton, R.T., 170
Hammer, M., 161
Hampden-Turner, C., 81, 90
Handy, Charles, 217
Hannan, M.T., 42, 189
Harman, W., 70
Harris, K., 136
Hass, N., 102
Hassard, J., 117, 118, 216
Hawthorne studies, 2
Hedberg, B., 114, 217
Heenan, D.A., 102, 103
Heidegger, M., 137
Heitman, E., 102
Heraclitus, 139
hermeneutics/hermeneutic circle, 84, 90, 91
Hernes, G., 191
heterogeneity, 166–7, 169–70, 171
hierarchies, 45–6, 58, 59, 64
   typologies, 6–9, 11
Hirsch, P.M., 96, 97, 99
Hirschorn, L., 149
Hobbes, Thomas, 204
Hock, D.W., 59, 65, 68
Hollander, J., 120
Holmstrom, B., 166, 168
Hols, E., 218
Holsti, O.R., 99, 219
homeostasis, 67
Höpfl, H., 202, 203
horticultural metaphors, 101, 103
Horton, T.R., 100, 102, 104, 105
Huber, G., 196

Huberman, A.M., 111, 119, 123
Huey, J., 100
Hughes, Ted, 113, 116, 119–20, 122–3
human action systems, 57
Human Relations movement, 58
human resource development, 95
human resource management, 114
hypertext structure, 64
hypothesis-testing, 233, 235

IBM, 44
identity dilemmas, 180
identity formation, 208–9
idiographic approach, 220, 221
idiosyncratic metaphors, 30–2, 236–8
illusions, 16, 206
image, 221, 227
    metaphors, 31–3, 130, 157
    in poetry, 112–16, 122–3
Images of Organization (Morgan), 10, 11,
    17, 21–35, 57, 132, 238–9
Imaginization (Morgan), 22, 27, 30–1, 111,
    116
imaginizing, 22, 27, 30–1, 111, 116, 235
impression management, 174
inappropriateness, errors of, 188
inchoate subjects, 202
individual (indivisibility), 136
individual–organization relationship,
    189–90, 192
individual action, 192–4
individualistic fallacy, 190
inductive metaphors, 10
industrial relations, 95
'inexpressibility' problem, 112–13
information, 193
    anxiety, 180, 181
    banks, 171
    overload, 70
    processing system, 62, 70, 115
    technology, 95
infrastructures, 59, 60
innovations, 34, 63–6, 68
    business fads, 53–6, 58
    embryonic metaphors, 12–13, 74–86
    metaphoric field and organizational
        change, 15, 147–62
Inns, D., 10
inside (actor-networks), 118
institutional approach, 43
institutional economics, 45, 46
institutionalized organizations, 43
insupportable meanings/roles, 210–11
intangibility (in service sector), 166, 169,
    172, 173–4

interaction (service sector), 172–4
intermediate metaphors, 217, 218
internal network organization, 67–8
internal programming, 152
internal realism, 135, 139
'Internet organization', 65
interventions, metaphors and, 155–62
ipsative questions, 221
irony, 8, 9, 17, 222–3
Irwin, A., 115
is/is not couplet, 139

Jackall, R., 177, 178
Jackson, B., 180, 181
'Jaguar, The' (Hughes), 119
Janov, J., 54, 57, 63
Jantsch, E., 57, 66, 67
Jayne, V., 100, 102, 103
Jeffcutt, P., 179
Jepperson, R.L., 193
Joerges, B., 96, 179
Johnson, L.W., 98
Johnson, M., 2–3, 9, 22–3, 25, 110, 117,
    119, 122, 125, 128, 150–2, 186, 213,
    215–16, 229, 237
journey metaphor, 25–9, 32–3, 237
    future directions, 16–17, 213–23
Jung, C.G., 68, 149, 150
juristic persons, 48
'justification', 187

Kanter, R.M., 64
Katz, J.H., 148–50, 156, 157
Kauffman, S.A., 56, 66, 69
Keeble, D., 170
Keidel, R.W., 156
Keizer, J., 218
Kelley, G.A., 221
Kelley, K., 53, 70, 240
Kendall, J.E., 95
Kendall, K.E., 95
Kennedy, A.A., 149, 222
Kermode, F., 120
Kets de Vries, M.F.R., 149–50
key skills, 177–8
Kilmann, R.H., 149
Knights, D., 132
knowledge, 26, 28, 90
    creation, 57, 65, 67, 141, 233, 235
    literal, 229–31
    of management consultants, 175–81
    organizational analysis, 129, 133–4, 137,
        141–2
    organizational competence, 192–6
    scientific, 5, 8, 214, 231
    tacit, 64, 67

Kogut, B., 185, 195
Kohler-Reissman, C., 219
Kraft, C., 68
Krantz, J., 221
Krippendorff, K., 188, 195
Kromer, G.H., 87
Kuhn, T.S., 76–7, 142, 148, 149
Kumra, S., 185, 217

labels, 178–9
Labich, K., 102, 104
Lakoff, G., 2–3, 9, 22–3, 25–32, 34,
    110–11, 117, 119, 122, 125, 128, 135,
    139–40, 150–2, 186, 213, 215–16, 229,
    237
language
    figurative, 4–5, 6, 22, 186–7
    games, 76, 78, 89, 91
    literal, 127, 131–6, 138–9, 141, 143, 186
    of movement (*rheomode*), 140
    in organization theory and poetry, 13–14,
        110–25
    popular management discourse, 10, 13,
        95–106
    thought and reality, 128, 130, 132,
        137–40
Language and Myth (Cassirer), 127
Latour, B., 118, 175, 180
Lau, C.M., 148
Lave, C.A., 193
Law, J., 118
Lawrence, A.T., 100, 102–4
Lawrence, D.H., 75
Lawrence, P.R., 2, 40, 62
Lazarsfeld, P.F., 192
leadership, 74–5, 81–5, 88–91
learning, 4
    organizational, 7, 16, 56, 148, 185–97
Lee, C., 100, 102, 104, 105
Legge, K., 112, 180, 181
Leibniz, G.W., 139
Lesly, E., 100, 104, 105
Lester, T., 100, 102
Lévi-Strauss, C., 81
Levin, S.R., 116, 122, 125
Levison, H., 149
Levitt, B., 185, 196
Lewin, R., 56, 57, 240
life-cycles, 24, 28–9, 31, 48, 154
life as journey metaphor, 25–30, 110
life as play metaphor, 27
Light, L., 100, 104, 105
Likert-scaled questionnaires, 221
limbic system, 67
Limerick, D., 63, 65

linguistic expressions, 27, 29, 30–3
Linstead, S., 97, 202, 203, 208
Liotti, G., 148
literal communications, 156–7, 162
literal identities, 231–3, 235
literal knowledge, 229–31
literal language, 127, 131–6, 138–9, 141,
    143, 186
literal meanings, 136, 156–7, 229
literal reference, 120, 121
literal similarities, 8
literary metaphor, 23
Little, I.M.D., 169
liturgical metaphors, 203–4
live metaphors, 9–10, 128–9
living organization, 12, 53–71
Locke, John, 134, 186
loosely coupled systems, 33–4, 63, 65–6,
    69, 132
Lorinc, J., 103, 105
Lorsch, J.W., 2, 40, 62
Luckmann, T., 3, 193
Lundberg, C.C., 95
Lyons, M., 104

machine metaphor, 9, 10, 31, 47, 50, 130,
    141, 153–4, 230
    mechanistic organizations, 2, 40
    mechanistic paradigms, 12, 57–62
McKinley, W., 101
MacLean, P.D., 53, 66
McLuhan, Marshall, 239
Maddrell, Julie, 200, 204–10
Mahoney, M.J., 148
management (organization development
    theory), 38–40
management consultancy, 10, 15–16,
    166–82
management discourse, 13, 95–106
management needs, 74–5, 81–5, 88–91
Management and Technology (Woodward),
    40
Mangham, I.L., 7, 22, 113, 117, 119,
    123–4, 177, 179, 217, 236–8
Mannheim, K., 76
Manning, P.K., 3, 4, 8–9, 219, 222
mappings, 25, 26, 27, 31
March, J.G., 39, 178, 185, 187, 193, 195,
    196
March, Jim, 79
Margulies, N., 172
market as organizational form, 45–6
Marks, M.L., 104
Markus, H., 148

Marshak, R.J., 4, 95–6, 148, 150–3, 156–7, 213, 218
Marshall, H., 219
Martin, J., 149
Marvell, Andrew, 120
Marx, R.D., 95
mass production/markets, 59–60
master-metaphor, 47, 239
mastery, 175–81
materialism, 70
Mazlish, B., 150
meaningful metaphors, 217–18, 219
meanings
    literal, 136, 156–7, 229
    of metaphors, 123, 124, 129
    symbolic meaning systems, 15, 147, 151–5
mechanical thematic coherence, 153–4
    see also machine metaphor
mechanistic organizations, 2, 40
mechanistic paradigm, 12, 57–62
medical metaphors, 99–101, 102–4
Meehl, P.E., 192
Meichenbaum, D.H., 148
mental chart (of managers), 81
mere appearances, 8
Merry, U., 150
meta-theory, 15, 147–62
metamorphosis, 154
metaphor and organization (issues)
    directions, 16–17, 213–23
    themes, 17, 227–40
metaphoric diagnosis/intervention, 155–62
metaphoric fields, 15, 147–62
metaphorical knowledge, 229–31
metaphorical language, 127, 131–3
metaphorical metamorphism, 83–5
metaphorization process, 128–31, 139–44, 238
metaphorizers, 135–7, 139, 140–1
metaphors
    anthropological, 11–12, 40–3, 45–9, 51
    anthropomorphic, 16, 185, 189–91, 192, 196–7
    appropriateness, 11, 21–35
    basic, 11, 21–9, 31–5, 216, 228, 236
    biological, 42, 47, 49, 51, 85, 189
    conceptual, 11, 23–4, 26–35, 216
    counter-metaphors, 13, 101, 103–6
    in downsizing, 98–106
    everyday, 25–9
    future value, 16–17, 213–23
    inevitability of, 1–2
    of metaphor, 129, 233–5
    as mode of thought, 21–2

ontological/epistemological status, 17, 130, 228–9
organizational research, 12–13, 74–92
organizations and, 10–17
parameters of, 29
postmodernism and, 117–21
problems with (and resolutions), 185–96
root, 7, 99–101, 103, 106, 217, 219
status of organization science and, 2–6
themes/issues (review), 17, 227–40
theories of, 133–7
types, 6–10
using for research, 220–2
metaphors-in-use, 16, 189, 217–19
'metaphors of organization' track, 216–18
Metaphors We Live By (Lakoff and Johnson), 23, 213
methodological individualism, 191
metonymy, 8, 9, 17, 222, 230–2, 235–6
Meyer, A., 96
Meyer, J.W., 176
middle management, 67, 159
Miles, M.A., 111, 119, 123
Miles, R.E., 57, 59–63 *passim*
military metaphors, 99–104 *passim*
Miller, D., 149
Milligan, Spike, 237
Mills, P.K., 172
mind of organization, 68–9
mission statement (as credo), 124
Mitchell, V.W., 166
Mitroff, I.I., 148, 150
Mittman, B.S., 100, 102, 103, 104
Moch, M.K., 148
mode metaphors, 44–5, 49, 50
modernism, 118
Molières, J.B.P., 84
Monot, J., 42
Morgan, Gareth, 1–4, 8–9, 12, 37, 46, 50–1, 59, 61, 69, 76–81, 85, 91, 95, 106, 111, 113, 115–17, 119, 122–3, 129–31, 148–50, 153, 156, 186, 188, 214, 217, 219–20, 222, 223, 230, 235
    Images of Organization, 10–11, 17, 21–35, 57, 132, 238–9
Morris, C.W., 96
Moskall, B., 103–5
motivation, 200–4, 210
movement, 200–5 *passim*
multidivisional organization, 60–1
Mumby, D., 22
'Myth of Objectivism', 117
'Myth of Subjectivism', 117
mythopoeic metaphors, 206–7

naming (role of metaphors), 96
narrative analysis, 219
natural persons, 48
Nayyar, P.R., 169
negative status, 4–6, 13–14
Nelson, P., 173
Nelson, R.R., 193, 195
neocortex, 67, 68
neomammalian formation, 67
network intelligence, 68
network organization, 12, 57, 60, 63–6, 69, 70
Nevis, E.C., 69
Newman, G., 100, 102, 104
Ng, S.H., 97
Nicolis, G., 57
Nielson, R.P., 148
Nietzsche, Friedrich, 137, 186
Nohria, N., 54, 96
nomothetic approaches, 220–1
non-constructivist view, 5
non-hierarchical typologies, 9–10
non-sociological theories, 43–5
Nonaka, I., 57, 62, 64, 65, 67, 71
Nordhaug, O., 192, 194, 195
North, Douglass, 45, 46
novel metaphors, 23, 30–2, 35
Nowottny, W., 129

Oberoi, U., 172, 173
obligatory action, 193
O'Farrell, P.N., 168
Olsen, J.P., 193
Olson, E.E., 150, 156
Oppenheim, A.N., 222
omission, errors of, 188
One-Minute Manager, 56
one-shot image, 31, 35
ontological metaphor, 17, 27, 78–9, 123, 130, 133, 135, 140, 213, 228
open systems, 33, 58, 61–2
operant learning, 67
oratorial styles/skills, 201–2, 204
order-giving hierarchies, 64
order-through-fit principle, 62
order-through-fluctuation, 69
Order out of Chaos (Prigogine and Stenger), 136
organic metaphors, 78–9
organic organizations, 2, 40
organism metaphor, 57–8
organismic paradigm, 57–8, 61–5
organismic realism, 139, 140
organisms, 2, 10, 12, 31, 47, 51
organization, mind of, 68–9

organization development, 4, 95
management consultancy, 10, 15–16, 166–82
metaphoric fields, 15, 147–62
'organization of metaphors' track, 16, 215–16
organization science (status of metaphor), 2–6
organization theory (development), 11–12, 37–51
organization theory and poetry (comparison), 13–14, 110–25, 186, 187–8, 231
organizational action, 7, 10, 16
problems (metaphor use), 185–92
solutions to problems, 192–6
organizational analysis, 14, 40, 77–8, 127–43
organizational change, meta-theory of, 15, 147–62
organizational culture, 95, 222
cognition in, 147–51
organizational evolution (stages), 12, 53–71
organizational forms, 45–6
organizational reality, 131, 151
organizational research, 12–13, 74–92
organizational sociologists, 40–3
organizations, metaphor and, 10–17
organizing mode, 44–5
Orton, J.P., 65
Ortony, A., 2–3, 5, 7, 97, 112, 122, 215, 219–21
Osterberg, D., 191, 195
Oswick, C., 4, 10, 213, 220
Ouchi, W.A., 222
outside (actor-networks), 118
Outhwaite, W., 132
Overington, M.A., 22, 113, 117, 119, 123, 124, 217

Packard, T., 218
Paetzold, R.L., 132
Pages, M., 124, 217
Paivio, A., 134
paleo-mammalian formation, 67
Palmer, I., 10, 81, 218
Panopticon, 78, 89
paradigm-shifting, 57
metaphorization and, 14, 130, 140–3
paradigms, 148, 219
of change, 57–66
organizational research, 12, 87–8
parameters of metaphor, 29
Parfum Hypnotique (case study), 200, 204–11 *passim*

Parsons, T., 2
'partial truths', 232–3
Pascale, R.T., 54, 69
passions, 203–4
Peet, J., 169
Pennsylvania Railroad Company, 59
performance, 193, 201, 202
perishability (in service sector), 169, 173
Perrow, Charles, 44, 45, 214
persuasion, 202–4, 205
Peters, T.J., 95, 149, 222
Petrie, H.G., 4, 141
Pfeffer, J., 41, 96, 103, 131, 132
phenomenology, 116–17, 121
Philips, D.L., 77, 79
phoric role (evangelical metaphors), 209–10
physical environment metaphors, 99–100
Pilarski, A.M., 102
Pinder, C.C., 4, 78–81, 91, 95, 131, 186–8,
    214–15, 217, 219, 230
platitudes, 178, 179
Plunkett, S., 100
poetry and organization theory
    (comparison), 13–14, 110–25, 186,
    187–8, 231
policy process, 95
political system metaphor, 47, 50, 51
Pondy, L.R., 96, 97, 149
Popper, K., 4, 142, 233
popular management discourse, 13, 95–106
population ecology, 42, 43, 187, 189
positive status, 3–4, 13–14
positivism, 121, 132, 133, 134
Post, G., 218
post hoc metaphors, 81–2
postmodernism, 112, 117–21, 133, 142,
    216, 222, 234, 236, 239
Powell, W.W., 43, 194
power, 6, 28, 112, 179
powerful people (in organizational
    research), 88–90
preference ordering, 193
Prelude, The (Wordsworth), 142
Prigogine, I., 57, 62, 65, 69, 136
'prism', 148
problem-solving approach, 141, 148
problematization, 175–6
product differentiation, 168
product diversification, 60
Psathas, G., 219
pseudo-gestalt, 121, 122–3
psychic prison, 10, 29–30, 32, 47, 51, 78,
    123, 130, 150, 186
psychoanalytic school (organizational
    culture), 147–8, 149–51

Pullinger, D., 102, 104
purposes (destinations), 26–30 *passim*
Putnam, H., 131, 135, 139, 140
puzzle-solving, 77–8
Pye, A.J., 22

questioning metaphors, 32–4

radical humanist paradigm, 78, 123
radical structuralist paradigm, 78
Ramirez, R., 3, 4, 10, 148, 214
Randall, R., 219
ranking metaphors, 221
rare skill metaphor, 11, 12, 38–40, 49, 50
rationality-surrogates, 176
Ray, M., 70
realism, 190
    organismic, 139, 140
    transcendental, 131–3, 139
reality, 112, 118, 131, 136, 150
    language and, 128, 137–40
    social, 3–4, 78, 79, 132, 134
    social construction of, 234–6, 239
    truth and, 119–20, 133, 135
rear-view mirror metaphor, 23, 27, 30, 237
Reason, P., 219
recipe metaphor, 44, 49
recognizing (intervention), 157–8
redundancy, errors of, 188–9
Reed, M., 95, 214, 234
'reference', 120
reflexivity, 127, 133
reframing (intervention), 157, 159–60
Reich, R.B., 100, 102, 103, 105
Reid, P.C., 100, 102, 104, 105
reintegrating (intervention), 157, 162
relational thematic coherence, 154, 155
releasing (intervention), 157, 161
religious metaphor, 124, 161, 202, 203, 207
repertory grid technique, 221–2
replacing (intervention), 157, 160–1
representationalism, 131–2, 137
reptilian brain, 66–7
repudiating (intervention), 157–9
research
    organizational, 12–13, 74–92
    process, 82–3
    strategy, 48–9
"resistance to change", 53
resource dependency theory, 41, 43
respondents (task force), 88–9
rethinking (intervention), 157
rheomode (language of movement), 140
rhetorical skill, 200, 201, 202
Richman, L.S., 98, 100, 102, 104
Ricoeur, P., 119, 120, 122

Riding the Waves of Change (Morgan),
    23–7, 30, 32–3
Rinzler, A., 70
ritual, 203, 230
Roach, J.R., 201, 202, 204
Robins, C., 148
Roethlisberger, F.J., 2
Romanelli, E., 62
root metaphors, 7, 99–101, 103, 106, 217,
    219
Rosenthal, S., 149
Rousseau, D.M., 190, 191
Rowan, B., 176
'rules of the game' metaphor, 46, 49, 50

Sackmann, S., 2, 3, 4, 22, 218
Salaman, G., 167, 175, 178
sand-castle metaphor, 214
sand-heap metaphor, 56
Sandelands, L., 37, 46, 50, 131, 217
Santa Fe Institute, 56, 59
Sapienza, A.M., 22, 96, 97
Saussure, Ferdinand de, 137
saying–seeing gap, 137–8
Schein, E.H., 149
Schelling, T.C., 191
schemata (governing beliefs), 148–51
Schneider, S.C., 96
Schön, D., 2, 6, 7, 11, 96, 148, 215, 216
Schultheiss, E., 95
Schwartz, H.S., 149
science, 14, 76–7, 79, 91, 111, 115
    traditional values, 4–6, 231–2
scientific knowledge, 5, 8, 214, 231
scientific management, 38, 54–5, 58
scientific revolution, 76–7, 149
Scott, W.R., 43, 48, 49
second-order change, 148–52, 157–8, 162
second-order cybernetics, 57, 70
second-order social constructionism, 133
self-consciousness, 70
self-organization, 57–8, 64, 66, 68, 234–5,
    238, 239
self-renewal, organizational, 63–4
Selfridge, R.J., 217
semi-anthropomorphism, 190
semi-durable business services, 173
semiotic analysis, 219
Senge, P.M., 87, 148
service characteristics, 166–7, 172–4
Siegelman, E., 150, 151
sign-images, 202, 203
'Silkworms, The' (Stewart), 75–6, 92
Silverman, D., 41, 193
similarity/difference tension, 121, 122

Simon, H., 39, 187, 193
single-loop learning, 87, 148
Skagen, A., 100, 102, 104
skills, 177–8, 192–5
    rare skill metaphor, 11, 12, 38–40, 49–50
    of rhetoric, 200, 201, 202
Skinner, W., 114
Skule, S., 195
Sloan, Alfred P., 60
Snow, C.C., 57, 59–63 *passim*
social constructionism, 111, 117, 123,
    132–3, 234–5, 239
Social Psychology of Organizing, The
    (Weick), 43–4
social realities, 3–4, 78, 79, 132, 134
socio-technical systems, 2, 61–2
sociologists, organizational, 40–3
Sokolik, S.L., 217
source domain, 2, 5, 7–8, 26–8, 185, 188,
    216
Southgate, J., 219
specialization, 58, 59
Spencer, Herbert, 2
Sperry, Roger, 70
spider plant metaphor, 30–2, 237
Srivastva, S., 3, 4, 7, 10, 22, 95–7, 106,
    120, 218
Stake, R.E., 219
Stalker, G.M., 2, 40, 217
Starbuck, W.H., 49, 175, 194
Steier, F., 132, 133
Stenger, I., 136
Sternberg, R.J., 6
Stewart, Douglas, 75, 76, 92
Stinchcombe, A.L., 40, 194
Stock, J.A., 168
story teller (management consultant role),
    10, 175–82
strategic alliances/partnerships, 162
strategy, 95
strong metaphors, 7
structural contingency theory, 40
structural functionalism, 2, 40
structure–conduct–performance paradigm,
    45
subject–verb–object structure, 138
'superficial metaphors', 216–17, 218
surface metaphors, 6–7, 215
Syedain, H., 103
symbolic communication, 156–7, 162
symbolic interactionism, 111, 117
symbolic meaning systems, 15, 147, 151–5
synecdoche, 8, 9, 17, 222
synergies, 63, 69
systems metaphor, 33–4

systems thinking, 57–8

tacit knowledge, 64, 67
Takeuchi, H., 57, 62, 64–5, 67, 71
Tao Te Ching, 138
target domain, 2, 5, 7–8, 26–8, 185, 188,
    216, 221
task force, 64, 67, 69, 159–60
    Australian study, 74, 81–5, 88–91
Tavistock Institute, 61–2
Taylor, F.W., 2, 38, 55, 58
Taylorism, 38, 54-5, 58
techno-economic paradigm, 87
'template', 148
temporary stability, 62–3
theatrical metaphors, 113, 123, 167, 201–2,
    238
thematic coherence, 153–5
theory-building, 37–40, 131–2
theory-in-use, 148, 150, 151
theory validation, 192
Theory Z, 56
third-order change, 150
Thomas, T., 102, 103
Thompson, J.D., 2
Thompson, P., 106
Thoreson, C.E., 148
thought, 142, 143
    reality and, 128, 130, 132, 137–40
'Thought-Fox, The' (Hughes), 113, 116
tightly coupled systems, 34, 65
"Time is Money" metaphor, 110
Tinker, T., 6, 12, 214, 219, 234
'To his Coy Mistress' (Marvell), 120
Toffler, A., 60
Tomasko, R.M., 98–100, 102, 104, 105
tool metaphors, 44–5, 49, 50
total quality management, 56
Tractacus-Logico Philosophicus
    (Wittgenstein), 137
Train, A.S., 102
training, 162, 206, 207–8
transaction costs, 168
transcendental realism, 131–3, 139
transformation, 140, 200–1
    liturgy and, 203–4
    metaphors, 47, 50–1, 211, 215
translation process (consultancy), 175–6
triple-loop learning, 148
Trist, E.L., 2, 62
triune-brain metaphor, 10, 12, 53–71, 150
tropes, 8–9, 129
    scope for, 17, 222–3
truth, 187, 232–3
    reality and, 119–20, 133, 135

Tsoukas, H., 2–5, 7–10, 95–6, 185, 187–8,
    214–15, 217, 219, 231, 234
turbulence, 167, 170, 171
Turner, M., 3, 23, 25–31 *passim*, 34
Tushman, M.L., 62
'Twelve Songs' (Auden), 114–15
Tylczak, L., 99, 102

unconscious school (organizational culture),
    147–8, 149–51
understanding (modes), 231–2
Underwood, L., 170
unit intelligence, 68
Useem, M., 98
'using metaphors' discourse, 128

Vaill, Peter, 22, 32, 33
Van Maanen, J., 133
Van Noppen, J.P., 218
Varela, F.J., 65, 66, 136
Vince, R., 10, 218, 219, 221
violence metaphors, 99–104 *passim*
virtues (of conformity), 208
virtuous circle, 90
visions (evangelical metaphors), 16, 201,
    204–8, 210–11
vividness (of metaphor), 220, 221
Vurdubakis, T., 180, 181

Waldrop, M.M., 56, 59
Walker, R.A., 172
Wallfesh, H.M., 102
Warner-Burke, W., 4
Warriner, C.K., 131
Waterman, R.H., 149, 222
weak metaphors, 7
Weber, Max, 2, 58, 193
Weick, K., 3–4, 22, 33–4, 43–4, 48, 50–1,
    65, 132–3, 148, 186–8, 193, 195, 217
Wheelwright, P.E., 204
White, H., 8, 9, 222, 230
Whitehead, A.N., 139–40, 142, 143
Wholeness and the Implicate Order (Bohm),
    138
Whorf, B.L., 186
Whyte, W.F., 219
Williamson, O.E., 45, 46
Wilson, D.C., 120, 123
Wilson, F., 96, 103
'Wind' (Hughes), 113–14
Winner, E., 222
Winter, S.G., 193, 195
Wittgenstein, L., 79, 137

Woodman, R.W., 148
Woodward, J., 40
Woodward, S., 172
Wordsworth, William, 142
World of Imagery, The (Brown), 127
world views, 123
Wright, Thomas, 204
Writing Degree Zero (Barthes), 138
Wrubel, R., 102

yogurt metaphor, 30–1, 32, 237

Zahra, S.A., 102
Zajonc, R.B., 148
Zand, D.E., 64
Zander, U., 185, 195
Zemke, R., 121
Zinszer, P.H., 168
Zucker, L.G., 43